State-building in Europe
The Revitalization of Western European Integration

Why and how was the process of Western European integration relaunched in the 1980s and 1990s? This volume suggests a new framework of analysis of the European state-building tradition. Based on qualitative research (including more than thirty interviews with protagonists) and detailed case studies and policy analyses (the genesis of the Single Market programme and the Single European Act, Esprit technology corporatism, biotechnology, EU regional and social policy), the authors show that new forms of cooperation between political and economic actors have developed, at both transnational and supranational level. The book shows how the European Commission, bureaucratic cabinets, national diplomats, transnational companies, pressure groups and representatives of the regions have set in motion a process that is changing statehood in Europe dramatically. This discussion of the origins of this process is a valuable contribution to the debate on the future of Europe in the world system.

VOLKER BORNSCHIER is Professor of Sociology at the University of Zurich. He is the author of fifteen books and numerous articles, most recently *Western Society in Transition* (1996).

State-building in Europe
The Revitalization of Western European Integration

Edited by Volker Bornschier

CAMBRIDGE
UNIVERSITY PRESS

University Printing House, Cambridge CB2 8BS, United Kingdom

Cambridge University Press is part of the University of Cambridge.

It furthers the University's mission by disseminating knowledge in the pursuit of education, learning and research at the highest international levels of excellence.

www.cambridge.org
Information on this title: www.cambridge.org/9780521781039

© Cambridge University Press 2000

This publication is in copyright. Subject to statutory exception
and to the provisions of relevant collective licensing agreements,
no reproduction of any part may take place without the written
permission of Cambridge University Press.

First published 2000

A catalogue record for this publication is available from the British Library

Library of Congress Cataloguing in Publication data

State-building in Europe: the revitalization of Western European integration / edited by Volker Bornschier.
    p.   cm.
Includes bibliographical references.
ISBN 0 521 78103 5 (hb)
1. European federation. I. Bornschier, Volker.
JN15.S74 2000   341.242'2–dc21   99-085966

ISBN 978-0-521-78103-9 Hardback
ISBN 978-0-521-78619-5 Paperback

Cambridge University Press has no responsibility for the persistence or accuracy of URLs for external or third-party internet websites referred to in this publication, and does not guarantee that any content on such websites is, or will remain, accurate or appropriate.

Contents

List of figures and tables	*page* vii
List of contributors	viii
Preface	xi
Acknowledgements	xv

Part I: State-building and Political Entrepreneurship 1

1 Western Europe's move toward political union 3
   Volker Bornschier

2 Tying up the Luxembourg package of 1985 38
   Patrick Ziltener

Part II: The Core Elements in Recasting the European Bargain 73

3 The origins of the Single Market 75
   Nicola Fielder

4 Esprit and technology corporatism 93
   Simon Parker

5 EC regional policy: monetary lubricant for economic integration? 122
   Patrick Ziltener

6 EC social policy: the defeat of the Delorist project 152
   Patrick Ziltener

Part III: Conclusions beyond the Single European Act of 1986 185

7 Lobbying for a Europe of big business: the European Roundtable of Industrialists 187
   Michael Nollert in collaboration with Nicola Fielder

8 Biotechnology in the European Union: a case study of
   political entrepreneurship   210
   Michael Nollert

9 European integration after the Single Act: changing and   244
   persisting patterns
   Patrick Ziltener

10 The state of the European Union   264
   Volker Bornschier

Appendix: List of interview partners   285
Bibliography   287
Index   308

Figures and tables

Figures

1.1	The genesis of the Single European Act	*page* 36
8.1	Dialogue committees of the Commission and interest organizations	239

Tables

1.1	Shares in world outward stock of foreign direct investment, selected countries, 1914, 1960, 1978 and 1992	22
1.2	World stock of foreign direct investment by headquarter region, 1980–1995	23
1.3	The distribution of the world's 100 largest transnational corporations according to home base and average global assets, 1992	25
2.1	The formation and development of political initiatives at European level and their expression in the Single European Act, 1981–1985	66
3.1	Steps towards the Single Market as the core element of the Single European Act	80
3.2	The role of industry: steps of the European Roundtable of Industrialists towards the Single European Act and beyond	89
6.1	Intergovernmental conference 1985: initiatives in the social policy area and their results in the Single European Act	158
6.2	Article 118 of the treaties establishing the European Communities as modified by the Single European Act	159
7.1	The centrality of Roundtable companies in 1994	205
7.2	Connectors between Roundtable companies, 1994	206
8.1	Expenditure on the biosciences in the EU, 1984–98	220

Contributors

Volker Bornschier was born in Witten, Germany, in 1944. After studying sociology, economics and psychology, he received his PhD in sociology in 1972. He has been a professor in the Faculty of Philosophy at the University of Zurich since 1981. He has published fifteen books and well over a hundred articles in leading social science journals and in edited volumes. His latest monograph is *Western Society in Transition* (New Brunswick and London, Transaction Publishers, 1996; with German and Chinese editions in 1998). He co-edited and contributed to the volume on *The Future of Global Conflict* (London, Sage, 1999). He is actively engaged in many professional associations (the International Sociological Association [ISA], the European Sociological Association [ESA], the Swiss Sociological Association, and the International Studies Association) and has organized parts of international or world conferences, for example, the panels on 'The Future of Globalization' at the 1998 ISA world conference in Montreal, and a series of sessions on the theme of 'Will Europe Work?' at the 1999 ESA conference in Amsterdam. Since 1997 he has been director of the Sociological Institute of the University of Zurich, and he is on the board of the World Society Foundation, which sponsors social science research world-wide (he served as president from 1983 to 1997). His areas of interest are social change and its various dimensions and manifestations, international competitiveness, economic sociology and questions of political economy and of world society.

Nicola Fielder was born in London in 1966 and moved to Switzerland at the age of 10, where she completed her education. She gained a Master's degree and a PhD in sociology from Zurich University. From 1992 to 1996 she collaborated on Bornschier's research team. Throughout her university studies she also worked part time in the area of employment and training and is at present directing a regional employment centre for the City of Zurich.

Michael Nollert, born in Zurich in 1960, received his PhD from the University of Zurich in 1991. He is senior member of Bornschier's team at the Sociological Institute in Zurich. From 1993 to 1995 he was a research fellow at the University of Trier (Germany). His research areas are political sociology, social conflicts (collective protest, crime), corporatism, European associations, and intercorporate relations. At the moment he is working at the University of Zurich, directing research on interlocking directorates in Switzerland and the Netherlands. He has published numerous articles and a book.

Simon Parker earned his BA Honours in political science from Concordia University in Montreal. He was awarded a Master's degree in international relations at Sussex University, where he submitted a thesis on the potential of a Gramscian theory of global hegemony entitled 'Theories of Hegemony: The Confusing and the Confusion of American Hegemony'. He has worked for the Open University, the City University and the University of Zurich in both teaching and research positions. Currently, he teaches history and geography at the Riverside School in Switzerland.

Patrick Ziltener was born in St. Gallen, Switzerland, in 1967. He studied sociology, history and economics at the University of Basel and at the Freie Universität in Berlin and received his MA in sociology at the University of Zurich in 1994. From 1995 to 1997 he was coordinator of the research project 'The Genesis of the Single European Act' at the Sociological Institute of the University of Zurich, where he currently works in both teaching and research positions. His PhD thesis on 'Strukturwandel der europäischen Integration' ('The Structural Transformation of European Integration') was accepted by the University of Zurich in autumn 1997. He is involved in exchange and cooperation in research on European integration within the European Sociological Association.

Preface

Western Europe's move toward political union entered widespread public debate only at the beginning of the 1990s. In fact, it had begun almost a decade earlier, culminating in 1985 in a bargain that recast the European Community: the Single European Act. At the time, these events hardly received the attention they deserved. However, they marked a historic step from a Community paralysed by lethargy and budgetary squabbling in the 'Eurosclerosis' era to one in which the Community proved its worth by creating political structures 'that will give it a prime role in helping define the post-Cold War world order', as the Community presented itself to the world at Seville's 1992 Universal Exposition. One key protagonist of the decisive events, in fact one of the architects of the Single Market project, commented as follows: 'There are turning points in history. Frequently only dimly perceived at the time but later clearly identified. The renaissance of the Community which was launched by the Internal Market Programme and, in its wake, the Single European Act is likely to prove such a turning point' (Cockfield 1994: 157).

The significant change within the Community during the mid-1980s became evident in two events that find their expression in two documents published by the Community: the Commission's White Paper (CEC 1985) for the European Council (heads of state and governments) regarding the completion of the internal market, and the Single European Act, adopted in December 1985 by the European Council and formally approved by the Council of Ministers (ministers of foreign affairs) on 28 February 1986. The White Paper was a political initiative of the Commission. As such it was not exceptional. Within the European Community the Commission is a supranational body, whose independence from the member states was set out in the treaties of 1958. The Commission is simultaneously a partner of and in opposition to the Council (Fusion Treaty, Article 15). Because of the multitude of its functions, the Commission plays a key role within the Community – it is its motor, has a right to make proposals in the legal process (which then are agreed upon by the Council) and has the exclusive right to propose initiatives. The plans, programmes and memoranda of the Commission are believed to advance the development of the Community. All this was agreed upon in the treaties of 1958, albeit the Commission's position vis-à-vis the Council was in fact weakened during the years of the so-called Luxembourg Compromise.

The White Paper had already been roughly prepared when Jacques Delors assumed the presidency in January 1985. As our research shows, the first initiatives of the Commission to complete the internal market can be traced as far back as 1981. The internal market project was a collaboration between the Commission and the European Roundtable of Industrialists (ERT). The ERT is an informal panel founded on the initiative of Commissioners Etienne Davignon and François-Xavier Ortoli in April 1983; it was composed of seventeen top European industrialists, and was later expanded to forty members. This informal panel linked the leading European transnational industrialists with the protagonists of the Commission. Wisse Dekker – head of Philips and a central figure in the Roundtable – created with his paper 'Agenda for Action: Europe 1990' (see Dekker 1984, 1985b) an important conceptual basis for the White Paper 'Europe 1992' by the Commission's vice-president Lord Cockfield (CEC 1985). European transnational business urged the Commission to act as a political entrepreneur.

Of course, formally and as foreseen by the constitution, the member states of the Community had to become active and renegotiate the original treaty for the Single European Act. According to our hypothesis, which has also been substantiated empirically, the initiative did not originate in the Council (representing the member states). The Council agreed on and transformed the new project compiled earlier by the Commission into applicable law. The renewed treaty brought about a marked broadening and overstepping of the original EC treaties. In our understanding, the Single European Act marks the transition to statehood (see also chapter 1). It regulates policy cooperation at European level by treaty and changes existing treaties of the Community at the same time, and it is for precisely this reason that it is called the *Single European Act*.

This volume – going to press a dozen years after the Single European Act became definitely effective – reports on our research of this significant and remarkable shift in European state-building. Obviously, the fully mature Western national state is not the final West European innovation. In the European Union following this qualitative change in integration, the European state is once again remodelled and forced out of its national boundaries. We focus on the forces and protagonists of the 1980s. This is in no way a classical historical analysis but a theoretically guided attempt to look for the social forces that produced this (in historical perspective) astonishing new beginning of European state-building.

The volume is divided into three parts, at the beginning of which the individual chapters are briefly introduced. In Part I we reflect on the world systemic forces, on the institutional and conjunctional preconditions that paved the way for the Commission's political entrepreneurship in the 1980s. Our theory suggests an elite pact that shapes our understanding of the decisive events beyond the current neofunctionalist and neorealist explanations of European integration. It focuses on a bargain between European transnational corporations and the Commission. Two groups of actors – transnationals and states – are considered to shape the world political economy via the theoretical mechanism of the world market for social order and protection. In this theoretical framework of competition among political entrepreneurs for mobile capital and of competition among economic entrepreneurs for state services and protection, we may assume similar competitive strategies for both classes of actors. Not only transnationals but also states may form strategic alliances or even merge. Such mergers of state services are, however, much easier if supranational institutional preconditions are present and available for political entrepreneurship. The mechanism of bargaining between political and economic undertakings and the implied economic competition between governments are part of a cyclical theory of social change, which refers to the rise and decline of societal models and of hegemons (Bornschier 1988, 1996). The pressure to rearrange the political economy is most urgent when cornerstones of a societal model (Keynesianism) and interstate coordination run into crisis and when the relative decline of the hegemon (United States) and emerging new competitors (Japan) jeopardize the stability of the world political economy. Since these events became apparent during the 1970s, the theory can suggest an explanation of why the initiative was taken in the early 1980s and not sooner or later. To date, the originally quite constrasting views on the role of the supranational and transnational intervention to push the Single European Act in the 1980s seem to converge in the recent debate (see Moravcsik 1998, 1999).

In Part II we put the hypotheses derived from our theory to the empirical test by analysing four relevant policy areas that formed the core in recasting the European bargain as manifested in the Single European Act: the Single Market; the imitation of Japanese technology corporatism; building up a supranational cohesion regime through the revised regional policy; and the attempt to tie the envisaged societal model to European postwar traditions by establishing – albeit less forceful – cohesion and social and economic convergence as goals at the Community level.

Part III contains chapters that offer conclusions beyond the Single European Act. The first focus is the evolution of the European Roundtable of Industrialists – the powerful ally of the Commission in pushing the internal market. The second topic is the European biotechnology policy up to the mid-1990s – the working of technology corporatism outside the integrated circuit sector where it originated at the beginning of the 1980s. These developments from a later period are used to reassess the relaunch of the mid-1980s, to evaluate the processes it triggered and to look at the evolution of the actors involved. The volume ends with a chapter reflecting the outcome: the state of the European Union. Rather than looking at it as an unfinished federal state, we interpret this European state of nations as a renewed compromise between old European processes – nationalism and liberalism.

The Bibliography includes the numerous documents we used in our research. The complete list of all our interview partners – from the Commission, the roundtables, participants in the policy-making process, and major political actors as well as experts – is in the Appendix.

Acknowledgements

The research reported in this volume was initiated by a guideline paper by the editor presented at the First European Conference of Sociology in August 1992 on 'The Rise of the European Community. Grasping toward Hegemony? Or Therapy against National Decline?' (see Bornschier 1994). However, the research would not have been possible without external funding, which considerably augmented the editor's own institutional resources and thus allowed the engagement of several junior researchers in the project and to pay for fieldwork expenses.

A first research phase from 1992 to 1993 on 'The Acceleration of Western European Integration as a Part of the Social Transition at the Core of World Society' was partially funded by the World Society Foundation (Zurich, Switzerland), whose contribution is gratefully acknowledged. At this stage, Nicola Fielder started her intensive fieldwork to investigate the origins of the Single European Act, but several others (Felix Keller, Michael Nollert, Irene Bloch and Doris Aebi) also contributed to certain research questions. Considerably larger funding for continued research on 'The Origins of the Single European Act' has been provided by a grant to the editor from the Swiss National Science Foundation (grant no. 12-41988.94), for which we are indeed very grateful. Nicola Fielder, Michael Nollert, Simon Parker, Felix Keller and Patrick Ziltener participated in this second research phase from 1995 to 1997; Patrick Ziltener was also in charge of coordinating the research team. In order not to exceed the normal book length and to guarantee coherence, not all our accumulated research results could be included in this volume. Furthermore, the present volume benefited a lot from the copyediting done by Richard Schauffler, who also translated a couple of chapters. We would like to thank him as well as Ann Stafford who translated one chapter, Heinz Gabathuler for his fine work on the index and Marianne Schindler for her careful proofreading and secretarial help. Finally, we would like to acknowledge the stimulating and helpful comments and suggestions we received from numerous colleagues, as well as at conferences where we presented results from our research, among them the First, Second and Third European Conference of Sociology (1992 in Vienna, 1995 in Budapest, and 1997 at the University of Essex in Colchester, England) and the Eighth International Conference on Socio-Economics (July 1996 in Geneva). Grateful mention should be made of Volker Rittberger's very early suggestion to include members of the Committee of Permanent Representatives of the member states in Brussels (COREPER) on our list of interviewees. Special thanks go to our numerous interviewees – protagonists, witnesses and experts (see the list in the Appendix) – who shared their memories, views and time with us, thus contributing enormously to the empirical base of this volume. Last but not least, mention should be made of the various helpful comments by anonymous reviewers for Cambridge University Press who stimulated the final revisions of the typescript.

I
State-building and Political Entrepreneurship

Western Europe's move toward political union in the middle of the 1980s took place after years of Eurosclerosis and its impact was only dimly perceived by most observers at the time. Chapter 1 by Volker Bornschier develops a novel explanation for this remarkable shift in Europe's political economy. In the context of the then fading lustre of the United States, the hegemon of the postwar era, and the seemingly limitless economic ascent of Japan, the path toward economic and political union represented Europe's attempt to remain a player in the post-hegemonic round of competition. The resurgence of economic globalization that started in the 1970s and a tighter closing of ranks by the European states are contradictory only at first glance. The first implies a shift in power between the state and the economy in favour of the transnational economy, to which regional integration is an answer, a new deployment of an old weapon by states. In the political world economy, first economic enterprises and then states compete with one another. On the other hand, economic enterprises and states are dependent on each other. The supply of state-based order and support as a locational condition and the demand for this by economic enterprises must be united in practice. Here, negotiations are the typical form of exchange. Chapter 1 suggests that the qualitative change of West European integration in the first half of the 1980s was the result of an alliance between European transnational corporations – represented by the European Roundtable of Industrialists – and the Commission. It is made very clear that this was the decisive impulse, the necessary condition to overcome Eurosclerosis.

However, neither the Commission nor such an informal group as the European Roundtable of Industrialists can change or amend the treaties between the member states. This can result only from a successful intergovernmental conference, which presupposes a number of prerequisites, especially the constitution of a 'balanced' package deal. Chapter 2 focuses not on the causal factors behind the single initiatives but on the 'tying up' process and the corresponding interest mediation among the actors involved, a process that was concluded after several months of negotiations at the Luxembourg summit of December 1985. Based on the theoretical considerations of chapter 1 and completing it, the reconstruction of this process furnishes the proof that even the final phase of the genesis of the Single Act cannot be explained in a purely intergovernmentalist matter. With respect to both the impulse that triggered the relaunch of European integration – the alliance between transnational corporations and the Commission – and the complicated constitution of the Luxembourg package that made the elite bargain palatable to the member states, the Commission as a supranational actor was of paramount importance. These two chapters together serve as a background for the sectional analyses in Part II, which survey the formation of the main political initiatives – the Single Market project, technology corporatism, social and regional policy – that were anchored in the Single Act and, in some areas, the further development of these policy areas.

1 Western Europe's move toward political union

Volker Bornschier

The revitalization of Western Europe

The 1980s witnessed dramatic changes in world society. Political orders that seemed to be rigidly fixed changed within only a few years. The sudden acceleration of West European integration is a case in point and the topic of this volume. To be sure, another historic event needs mentioning. In the short time between November 1989 – the fall of the Berlin Wall – and the end of 1991 – the official dissolution of the Soviet Union – the East–West conflict, which had marked the postwar era, became history.

In a booklet distributed at Seville's 1992 Universal Exposition, the European Community (EC) presents itself to the world as follows:[1]

Now an economic giant, the Community is striving to consolidate the Single Market into an economic and monetary union and to put in place political structures that will give it a prime role in helping define the post-Cold War world order. (CEC 1992: 2)

Since the post-Cold War world order is mentioned in the above quote, the coincidence in time of the Treaty on European Union – agreed by the heads of state and government of the European Community at their summit in Maastricht in December 1991 – along with the dissolution of the Soviet Union and German reunification could suggest that state-building in Europe and the end of the East–West divide are related. However, this is a mistaken perspective. Western Europe embarked on its path to a *new* and *additional* form of statehood as early as the first half of the 1980s, as manifested in the Single European Act signed in February 1986 by the then twelve member states.

After so many years during which the Community was paralysed by lethargy and squabbling over budgets, this relaunch of the Community

---

[1] The exhibition presented in the Community Pavilion was entitled: 'From Renaissance Europe to the Renaissance of Europe'. One main topic in the pavilion was 'The European Community: A Great 20th Century Discovery' – the theme of the 1992 Expo being 'The Age of Discoveries'.

in the mid-1980s was remarkable. The 1991 Maastricht Treaty on European Union continued this earlier move to a new European state level beyond the nation-states; it was not as exceptional when compared with the new beginning in the 1980s, although in terms of public attitudes it was more controversial.

What influenced the remarkable relaunch of integration in Europe, which culminated for the first time in the mid-1980s? The aforementioned publication of the European Community provides a clue that illuminates the framework within which the revitalization of the politico-economic development of Western Europe must be positioned – the so-called triad: 'The Community is one of the three pillars, along with the United States of America and Japan, on which the system of pluralist democracy and market economy is built' (ibid.). During the 1970s and early 1980s Western society found itself caught between the advent of a new technological style and the dissolution of its Keynesian era politico-economic regime. The dissolution of the societal model, which brought many years of economic crisis in its wake, went hand-in-hand with a relative economic decline of the United States – the Western hegemonic power of the postwar era – and the seemingly steady ascent of Japan. The new Far Eastern industrial giant set about pushing the European powers from second place behind the United States, into third place.

These challenges – the loss of hegemonic stability and the emergence of a strong new competitor – were clearly perceived by Europe's economic and political elites of that time, and their leading protagonists responded with a European answer advocating competition in a world of hegemonic transition. Yet, the European Community's claim to a 'prime' role could be misunderstood as a bid for mastery in global affairs. This was simply not the case, as the protagonists knew quite well.

The political Euro-entrepreneur Jacques Delors, who assumed the presidency of the EC Commission in Brussels on 7 January 1985, and brought fresh impetus to the Community by building on initiatives that dated back to the early 1980s, clearly stated in an interview the order of the day (Delors 1991: 20f.): 'Out of the dynamic economic and commercial power which we already are, a great political power must develop.' He explained this with reference to a 'historical responsibility' and felt it would be sad if 'the Europeans of the year 2010 . . . were to become mere spectators of history'. Anxiety about projecting European brilliance into the future appears in Jacques Delors' warning: 'We must move quickly; otherwise Europe will become an archaeological excavation site, where Americans and Japanese search for lost ideas and ways of life' (Delors 1991: 21). State-building needs political entrepreneurship; and in this context, one of the leading figures who met the challenge, Jacques Delors, has already been mentioned. But since the new project was taking form beyond the level of the nation-states, the institutional independence of the EC Commission, which was already stipulated in the original treaty of the Community of 1958, was surely a prerequisite for initiative and supranational entrepreneurship.

But for whom do state-builders venture such a project against the historical forces of the vested interests of nation-states? One motive was mentioned: projecting Europe's role into the future. To be sure, states that want to be successful in the long run need to seek legitimacy in the eyes of their citizens. Consequently, the concept of the 'European social area' presented by Delors to the European Parliament only two months after he assumed presidency of the Commission was designed to balance the Common Market project, whose leading architect was Lord Cockfield, then the Commission's vice-president.

In order to explain why, one has to consider that states and business in the capitalist world political economy are inextricably interrelated. States provide territorially bounded public goods which – if of good quality – help economic enterprises to prosper. This applies not only to the average firm that normally does business only within the framework of a single state, but more importantly – and this is a point neglected in the recent debate on globalization – to transnational corporations. In order to compete successfully, these corporations, although economically active around the world, need a strong home base allowing for economies of scale in large markets with common economic regulation. They prosper if backed by strong governments that protect their interests both at home and abroad. It was Etienne Davignon, vice-president of the Commission at the end of the 1970s and in the early 1980s, who recognized that global competition required a strategic view of science and technology and who became the architect of what later was termed the new technology policy of the Community. However, in the context of bargains between the demand for and supply of public goods and protection in the world, it is not only the interests of enlightened European statesmen that are involved, but also those of the transnational European economic elite. Among many others, Wisse Dekker, president of Philips Electronics, was an influential spokesman for this group in the early 1980s.

Europe met the challenge of the changing world political economy briefly outlined above by initiating a new European societal model, for which the Single European Act marks the beginning. This not only brought several new key elements to the political economy of Western

Europe, but also added a new and additional level to European statehood.

This chapter is aimed at generating explanations and providing a fresh perspective on what was happening in Europe during the 1980s and what is still under debate in the 1990s. The remaining chapters of this volume will investigate in detail whether such hypotheses hold when confronted with the facts. We begin this chapter by placing the revitalization of European integration in the 1980s in the context of European state-building. In the remainder of this chapter we elaborate our explanation of the integration thrust and the key actors involved in it.

State-building in Europe

Why do we stress the role of the Single European Act in the course of West European integration, given that the process had been proceeding for about twenty-five years prior to that treaty? The Act is the decisive point of departure for European economic integration toward a new, additional level of statehood in Europe. Under the banner bearing the magic inscription 'Europe 92', Western Europe was preparing to transform itself economically and politically. How can this be viewed within the framework of the European state-building process?

Looking back

Elsewhere, we have analysed the tortuous paths of capitalist and state evolution (see Bornschier 1988: ch. 11; 1996: ch. 10). The process of state-building is normally divided into phases. A frequently cited model was suggested by Stein Rokkan (1975, 1981), according to whom the fully mature nation-state can be recognized by four features: *central power, standardized culture, political mass participation* and *extensive redistributive policies*. In a developmental perspective, Rokkan identifies the following phases: penetration (the extension of central control over a territory and a population); standardization (the homogenization of administration through the creation of a bureaucracy and of the population through the creation of the nation); participation (increasing political participation of expanding groups leading to mass participation); and redistribution (the elaboration and coordination of redistributive policies by the welfare state).

In contrast to this developmental theoretical approach, we have advanced a different formulation. We see the modern state as the outcome of a multitude of conflicts, which it still reflects today. These are expressed, for example, by the tension between the state as a community striving for equality and as a power centre. Furthermore, in the course of its conflictive evolution the state was forced to assume a number of functions by a system that was always more extensive than any particular state, however powerful the latter may have been.

Economic and economically motivated competition in the European and later the expanding world system was the starting point and attendant circumstance of this conflictive process. Max Weber already saw states and capitalism as interrelated, and the condition of their conflictive dynamic, which promoted state-building as well as the unfolding of capitalism, is the decentralized state system, i.e. the absence of a world state. This conflict selects ever more efficient forms of the state and the capitalist economy. To this day, two opposing principles – nationalism and liberalism – have been the basis for and the permanent accompanying features of modern state-building, their interplay shaping the modern state. Nonetheless, the unfolding of the state project did not take place in only one location; rather, the opposition of these principles and the originally very differently shaped states adopted a zigzag course through Europe.

From a long historical perspective, we suggest that social arrangements that enjoyed high-quality protection had an edge over their competitors in the world system. This should be understood in comparative-historical terms, i.e. social formations as compared with their contemporary competitors. For this reason they were successful and, for a while, leaders in capitalist development. Freer arrangements of wage labour, greater opportunities for larger parts of the population, and more liberal institutions were typical of all the industrial leaders of the modern world system. This also holds when one goes back beyond Venice and North Holland, which pioneered the world economy project in European modernity. Since the nineteenth century, this option, typical of ascending social formations, became even more urgent owing to increasing levels of industrial complexity. Those who tried to 'buck this trend' never reached the peak of the world industrial pyramid.

The tortuous paths of state evolution and of the development of capitalism suggest that the modern state originated from diverse roots, but that competition between models enforced convergence. In the encompassing framework of the world political economy there is little use in trying to assign primacy to the *political* logic of economic action or the economic logic of political action. It seems obvious that the market and economic competition are politically motivated and based on political will. As collective goods of this kind cannot be produced by the market, the political logic of economic action naturally applies. At the same time, the economic logic of state policy also applies, because collective goods as prior conditions for markets – provided and regulated by the state – compete with each other. It is no surprise that such interrelationships resulted in the European welfare state, since claims to basic goods and equal opportunity cannot be adequately met by economic dynamics alone. Unless it meets such claims, capitalism may not last. However, solutions to the problem of creating legitimacy are not without their contradictions. Social welfare – according to Stein Rokkan the final stage of the fully mature West state – will be rearranged in the future. The welfare state cannot be considered the final West European innovation in this regard, and the emergence of a new supranational European level of statehood should be understood in this context.

Situating the recent move

West European integration represents in some respects a continuation of, while in other respects an overcoming of, previous features of the European state-building process. The continuation of the 500-year-old European state-building process refers to the concentration of politico-territorial rule (Elias [1969] 1977) – an implosion of originally 500 state-like structures to only two dozen (Tilly 1975: 15). On the other hand, the European Union exhibits features that point to an earlier successful yet atypical state project to be discussed at the end of this section.

West European integration is a social innovation in several respects:
(1) The process will mean the end of a multistate balance of power in Europe. The problem of the distribution of power at the core of the world system was posed anew after Western Europe lost its previous undisputed leadership earlier in the twentieth century. Thus, West European integration by no means creates a concentration of power for the whole of the capitalist core, which will remain at least trilateral.
(2) The unification project does not conform to two crucial characteristics of state-building according to the West European model (Rokkan 1975, 1981). As far as can be anticipated, the future Union will not have a prominent central authority or a standardized culture. Thus, the integration process will not continue the European nation-state-building tradition.
(3) During previous changes of the societal model, one constant was obvious: the articulation of the linkage between the political and economic realms, although it differed between societal models, always took place within the framework of nation-states. Through

the Single European Act and later the Treaty on European Union, for the first time a supra-state linkage of the two realms has been created that goes beyond loose international regimes. This is new, as is the extension of welfare state issues to the interstate determination of life chances.

(4) Finally, West European integration is developing in the direction of a new state level that exhibits certain similarities with an earlier European state project (see below). However, for the first time in European history, the state is relying not on military structures for the integration of such a huge and economically potent body, but rather on a legal and economic community, which does not aim to deprive its members of their cultural specificities.

Legal and economic issues are the point of departure for some remarks we would like to make on statehood. A community as a type of political body is characterized by the rule of shared laws based on treaties. According to the dominant doctrine, communities are not (federal) states in the true sense (Nicolaysen 1991). From a social science perspective, such an exclusive distinction does not make much sense, however. In any case, communities are characterized by supranationality according to legal principles (Nicolaysen 1991). In sectors specified by treaties, sovereignty is assigned to the community and thus supranationality is created.

To distinguish communities from states, constitutional law points to the fact that communities cover only limited goals, that is, communities are only a means of functional integration (Nicolaysen 1991). Here we must ask whether Europe's goals have really been as limited as this since the emergence of the Single European Act.

How communities can claim statehood could be determined on normative-theoretical grounds. Yet, for empirical sociology it is also useful to define statehood as a variable with threshold values in a descriptive, factual way. Whether statehood in this sense is reached depends not only on threshold values, however, but also on the societal type that circumscribes the role of the state. The characteristics of the societal type under discussion are the market economy and political democracy.

As economic actors, the people in the states of the European Community became fully integrated citizens of the Community with the adoption of the Single European Act. With respect to citizenship, the new Community is only indirectly endowed with legitimacy by these economic actors by way of democratic elections of the heads of state and government who negotiate and renew the treaties. This is true despite the fact that the European Parliament is directly elected and has been gradually upgraded by the Single European Act and the subsequent revisions. Its increased weight notwithstanding, the Parliament's jurisdiction does not match the jurisdiction of national parliaments. If we measure these developments with reference to the criteria of the societal type, we must therefore conclude that statehood is being developed in a different way.

Yet, in the important sphere of the market economy, statehood has already gone quite far. With reference to the market economy we can thus claim that a community assumes state character: (a) if important public goods are created by the community; (b) if the community has its own financial jurisdiction and its own fiscal resources; and (c) if remaining central areas of state functions (e.g. foreign policy, security, currency) are at least coordinated between the member states and if the community is at least party to such coordination. According to such a list of criteria, the European Community can be said to have added a level of proper statehood to the European political system since the adoption of the 1986 Single European Act (ratified 1987) – and thus prior to the 1991 Maastricht Treaty on European Union (ratified in 1993).

Some points of clarification must be added to these observations. The significant change within the Community during the mid-1980s becomes evident in two events that find expression in two documents published by the Community: the Commission's White Paper (CEC 1985) for the European Council (heads of state and government) regarding the completion of the internal market, and the Single European Act, adopted in December 1985 by the European Council and formally approved by the Council of Ministers (ministers of foreign affairs) on 28 February 1986. The White Paper was a political initiative of the Commission; as such it was not exceptional, because within the European Community the Commission is a supranational body, whose independence from the member states was already set out in the treaties of 1958. The Commission is at the same time a partner of and in opposition to the Council (Fusion Treaty, Article 15). Owing to the multitude of its functions, the Commission plays a key role within the Community – it is its motor, has a right to make proposals in the legal process (which then are formally agreed upon by the Council) and is mandated to take initiatives. The plans, programmes and memoranda of the Commission are believed to advance the development of the Community. All this was already agreed upon in the treaties in effect since 1958.

The White Paper had already been prepared when Jacques Delors assumed the presidency in early 1985. The first initiatives of the

Commission to establish the internal market can be traced back at least to 1981. The completion of the internal market project was worked out between the Commission and the European Roundtable of Industrialists (ERT). The ERT is an informal panel founded on the initiative of Commissioners Etienne Davignon and François-Xavier Ortoli in April 1983; it was composed of seventeen top European industrialists, and was later expanded to forty members. Wisse Dekker – head of Philips, already an influential figure in the ERT and later its president, who formulated the 'Agenda for Action: Europe 1990' (see Dekker 1984, 1985b) – and Lord Cockfield – then vice-president of the Commission, under whose auspices the White Paper 'Europe 1992' (CEC 1985) was drafted – were bound together by more than common intentions. At least since April 1983, the informal panel of the ERT (informal because it is not a body within the institutional framework of the Community) linked these two protagonists of the transnational European economy and the Commission.

Naturally, formally and as foreseen by the constitution, the member states of the Community had to become active and renegotiate the original treaty for the Single European Act. According to our hypothesis, the initiative did not originate in the Council (representing the member states). The Council only transformed the new project into applicable law. The renewed treaty brought about a marked extension and superseding of the original EC treaties. The Single European Act, with the single market as its core element (see chapter 3), marks the transition to a new supranational level of statehood.

The Single European Act is called *single* precisely because it regulates European policy cooperation by treaty and changes existing treaties of the Community at the same time. Since its adoption, the new superior body of the Community, the European Council (heads of state and government of the member states), coordinates political and economic policies with the president of the Commission, who is a member of the European Council with equal rights.

The intentions of the new formulation of the treaty are evident. The Single European Act is explicitly understood as a step towards European union (see its preamble). Part II of the Single European Act includes changes to the original European Economic Community treaty affected by the new one, and Part III regulates political cooperation in Europe. In the first instance, the provisions regarding the establishment of the internal market by the end of 1992 are worth mentioning. These conceptions of 'Europe 92' were the most prominent in the headlines at the time.

The Community had already operated as a common market.

However, despite the elimination of tariffs on intra-EC trade, the domestic markets of Community members had remained fairly fragmented owing to non-tariff barriers that proliferated and even intensified during the economic downturn of the 1970s. Only the completion of the internal market programme, which erased the variety of non-tariff barriers that sheltered domestic firms from competition, created, via deregulation or harmonization, a single market for merchandise, services, labour, and capital. This provides both greater opportunities for economies of scale as well as economies of common governance. In terms of protection and regulation, this means a restructuring: the locus at which the public good is provided is the Community and no longer the single member state.

The renewed treaty also involved substantial changes in the institutional frameworks. The procedure for enacting law changed as follows. The majority vote in the Council was extended. Now, for all decisions concerning the internal market, qualified majority votes are stipulated. In connection with the alignment of legal regulations, either a qualified majority vote or the mutual recognition of the equivalence of regulations in the member states is called for. Further, the participation of the European Parliament in formulating legislation and its budgetary authority are expanded. Finally, the treaty broadens the role of the European Court of Justice by way of coordination with the Court of First Instance.

In addition, the agreement concerning extensions of the earlier authority of the European Community as well as new authority is worth mentioning. The section regarding the progress of economic and social cohesion (Part V) represents a new jurisdiction. This area is supposed to shape the policies of cohesion and represents a collective good: solidarity.

What is more, the Community obtains the authority to support research and technological development to advance international competitiveness (Part VI). This section is designed to shape technological capital for international competition, which again is a collective good. Last but not least, environmental policy now partly falls under the jurisdiction of the Community (Part VII).

Earlier authority has also been significantly extended, for example in connection with social policy (improvement of working conditions, minimum standards, dialogue between social partners) and economic policy (the anchoring of the European Monetary System and its corresponding institutional changes).

These briefly described elements of the renewed treaty allow us to speak of the Community's statehood with respect to the sphere of the market economy insofar as it provides public goods on its own rather than simply coordinating member state activities. For the first time, a supranational provision of such goods common to the Community is detached from the nation-states of the members. It should be made very clear that this did not abolish the nation-states; quite the contrary. The member states, although they lost competencies to the Community, remain powerful because they have the sole legislative power in terms of the revision and extension of Community law.

Therefore, the European Union remains a somewhat strange hermaphrodite, between a state confederation and a federal state. Is it not too early to speak of state-building in Europe? In many respects, the new form is a novelty, but it has at least one European antecedent which made history for a century. Earlier in this section we already pointed to the very different roots of state-building in Europe. The theory of the social contract also distinguishes between these two poles: the 'contract of association' and the 'contract of domination' (Dahrendorf 1992: 47). In a philosophical perspective, Immanuel Kant can be linked to the former variant, whereas the latter can be traced back to Thomas Hobbes. During the aforementioned process of amalgamation, the modern core state was influenced more strongly by the 'trade and economic state' as a 'contract of association' than by the colossal rapacious states founded on domination and military power. The European Union supports this process towards a state characterized by a plurality of power centres at different levels bound to the principle of subsidiarity and numerous checks and balances. Similarities with the Republic of the United Netherlands cannot be overlooked despite the centuries that lie between the two.

In *The Perspective of the World*, Fernand Braudel ([1979] 1984) reports the boundless astonishment of contemporaries in the face of the vertiginous rise and unexpected power of such a small and in some respects entirely new country as North Holland. 'Can the United Netherlands be called a "state"?,' Braudel (1984, 3: 193) asks, and then goes on to explain:

the seven provinces considered themselves sovereign, and that they were moreover divided into tiny urban republics. It is also true that none of the central institutions – the Council of State or Raad van Staat . . . and the States-General which also sat in the Hague and was a permanent delegation of ambassadors from the provinces – had in theory any real power at all. Every important decision had to be referred to the provincial States and approved by them unanimously. Since the interests of the provinces diverged considerably – in particular those of the coastal from those of the inland provinces – this system was a perpetual source of conflict.

Apart from the 'vertiginous rise', it is possible today to detect many parallels with the European Union in this description by simply changing certain institutional designations.

Theoretical considerations

The decline of the Keynesian societal model

Elsewhere we have analysed Western society as a sequence of rising and decaying societal models (Bornschier 1988, 1996). Since the beginning of the nineteenth century three societal models can be discerned:
(1) The liberal societal model of the founding era, formed after the liberal uprisings of 1830–48 and dissolving in the late 1860s.
(2) The class-polarized model of the post-foundation era, originating following the widening of political participation and the extension of compulsory education in the 1880s and dissolving after the turn of the century.
(3) The societal model of the re-allocative market economy and welfare state era that integrated neocorporatist and Keynesian elements in varying degrees, originating among pioneers (Sweden, United States, Switzerland) in the early 1930s and spreading after the Second World War. Since the late 1960s, this model has begun to dissolve and, since the early 1980s, has actually entered a phase of decay in certain countries (most obviously the United Kingdom and the United States).

In order to further clarify the term societal model, it seems appropriate to discuss somewhat more precisely the three spheres – i.e. normative theories, politico-economic regime, and technological style – that were linked to each other in the last societal model.

Normative theories

The swing in doctrines related to economic policy was very important for the last societal model. The then emerging normative theory for solving economic and social problems may be summarized using the following formula. The state was regarded as the solution for pressing problems that were the result of both the world economic crisis and a new technological style. Yet, the state was not only the solution; normatively fixed state intervention also allowed the integration of reformist socialism into the new societal model. Solidarity and redistribution, two socialist demands, were no longer in fundamental contradiction with a liberal position. The new guiding principles of economic policy in the welfare state era legitimized solidarity and redistribution as virtues that would stimulate economic growth. Yet the neoliberal and monetarist uprisings of the 1970s undermined the basic consensus regarding normative theories that had lasted for decades and introduced a new motto: Less State Intervention – More Freedom.

Politico-economic regime
The dominant normative theory of the neocorporatist–Keynesian societal model, with its interventionist guiding principles, created the possibility for a class pact for economic stability, social pacification and growth, thus promising a 'democratization' of wealth. The past societal model was therefore characterized by two new linkages within the politico-economic regime: first, a new linkage between the economy and the state; second, a new linkage between capital and labour. However, from a comparative perspective, the extent of cooperation and linkage of interests has differed among core countries. Despite the similarities, one finds different degrees of neocorporatist policy-making, i.e. of intermediation of organized interests coordinated by the state.

Technological style
Procedural changes in the chemical industry were originally the key element of the technological style of that era. Using the new flow production, it became possible to produce the key factor – energy (oil) – at diminishing relative prices for a long time. In addition, there were significant innovations in the shaping of formal organization. Mention should be made of 'scientific management', the division of labour, and the reorganization of large corporations. The growth of the firm was conditional upon a far-reaching separation of ownership and control, which in turn led to changes in the composition of the economic elite. By redistributing income and positions in favour of the distinctly enlarged middle classes, the renewed organization created mass demand, which reinforced mass production and the diffusion of the technological style. Finally, the new style offered a new mix of goods.

The 1970s announced the advent of a new technological style integrating and linking new productive, distributive and administrative elements. This style was formed during the 1980s by successively substituting information intensity for the material and energy intensity of the former style. The advance in productivity was a result of increasingly inexpensive micro-electronics and digital telecommunications. Computers are the new key product and chips the new raw materials. By changing the shape of organizations, the structure of jobs and the patterns of consumption, the new style will alter the appearance of social life – the changes being possibly even more dramatic than those resulting from the former style.

The state meets technology

The notion of technological style was originally proposed by Carlota Perez (1983, 1985), and later developed by Bornschier (1988, 1996). The advantage of Perez's approach in comparison with earlier conceptualizations of technological change (e.g. Schumpeter) is that she models the socio-institutional sphere – governed by states – as an indispensable element of technological style. Today we are witnessing a shift toward a new technological style. 'Telematics' or 'digitalization' is the new key project that has replaced 'automobilization'.

In order to understand discontinuous technological change in a model of the sequence of technological styles that shape markets, the structure of firms and lifestyles, it is necessary to examine the links between two subsystems that embody important aspects of the concept of technological style. Carlota Perez points to two interrelated subsystems of the process of the succession of technological styles: (1) the techno-economic subsystem, which is characterized by faster adaptation due to the logic of more individualized choices, and (2) the socio-institutional subsystem based on the collective logic of political choices, in which change is more conjunctural.

Both the techno-economic and the socio-institutional subsystems adjust to each other during a long-term economic upswing. The adjustment of the socio-institutional system is a necessary part of the evolution and diffusion of the new technological style. The institutional infrastructure that is able to support a new technological style is subject to a political logic. This needs to be defined, and new institutions need to be created in political struggles, not only within nation-states but also in the world market and the world polity.

A new technological style starts to emerge only when the old style reaches the limits of further diffusion and profits based on it decline. Even if the advantages of the new style become obvious, it cannot take over immediately. A struggle between the two styles thus begins, which can be compared to Schumpeter's (1939) notion of 'creative destruction'.

The other important brake on the emergence of a new style is the mismatch between the two subsystems: 'The transition to a new techno-economic regime cannot proceed smoothly, not only because it implies massive transformation and much destruction of existing plant, but mainly because the prevailing patterns of social behavior in the existing institutional structure were shaped around the requirements and possibilities created by the previous paradigm' (Perez 1985: 445).

The contradictions between the new technology and the old institutions explain the kind of limited economic recovery that occurred in the 1980s, while institutions such as Keynesianism, welfare states and labour unions came under pressure or even deteriorated. The coherence of the technological style begins to dissolve as soon as the long-wave economic peak is reached, i.e. when the permeation of the style, with its specific range of products, reaches saturation point and induces a surge of investments aimed at rationalization. To reach an equilibrium of production and consumption, two kinds of invention are necessary. Innovations aimed at saving labour in the productive apparatus alone (i.e. innovations that increase output with the same work-time input) lead to disequilibria if they are not linked to inventions that fascinate people so that they want to spend their leisure consuming these goods and services, and are even prepared to work overtime to acquire them. In the Keynesian societal model, flow technology and Taylorism were examples of process innovations, whereas television sets and cars represented the second type of invention, leading to the supply of hitherto unknown goods and services.

During the alteration of the technological style these two types of inventions do not occur simultaneously. This is a built-in disequilibrating mechanism that increases disparities and delays the emergence of a new style. This disparity produces its effects slowly because initially induced industries continue to expand. To take the example of the automobile, the induced growth effects consisted of the army of mechanics and gas station employees, the new tourist industry and public investments in roads, bridges and tunnels. Still, the downswing triggered by the mismatch of production with consumption gains momentum and is reinforced by entrepreneurs who act defensively in the face of crisis. They rationalize their production through new methods that already incorporate elements of the coming technological style. The widening gap between process and product innovations during the transition from the 1960s to the 1970s has been demonstrated empirically by Alfred Kleinknecht (1987). Only the match between the technological possibilities and the institutional infrastructure brings about a fresh range of products and services, and thus a new match between productive opportunities and consumption that leads to the unfolding of a new technological style.

European proposals for technology corporatism and protection

The supranational political entrepreneurs in Europe were well aware of these transitions by the end of the 1970s and the beginning of the 1980s. Etienne Davignon, at that time vice-president of the Commission, is a case in point. In an essay 'Europe at the End or Before a New Upswing?' which he published in a volume edited by Ralf Dahrendorf (1981) – himself a former Commissioner – Davignon outlined the policy recommendations that later became part of the new Community legislation. Davignon looks at the competition as one between industrial nations, spurred by the emergence of new competitors, involving structural adjustments of old industrial branches and innovation with regard to new ones, among which he especially mentioned micro-electronics, space and biotechnology. He suggested that in the competitive restructuring the resulting future world division of labour should be left neither to accident nor to fate but should instead be the result of concerted policies to foster innovations embedded in 'reasonable' decisions about investment and research. He especially pointed to the route Japan had already chosen earlier in this field (Davignon 1981: 169). What he proposed was nothing less than an 'independent European answer'. Davignon's postulates were the following:

First of all, a market for the introduction of new products must be established, where the demand regarding the creation of European norms and standards as well as the expansion of public demand can be stimulated. Secondly, there must be real support to enable sufficient positioning in the world markets . . . Finally, Europe should make it possible to improve coordination of the respective national research and development activities.' (Davignon 1981: 183; our translation)

The point of reference is very obvious. Under the heading 'The Telematics Revolution: the Barriers Must Fall in Europe', Davignon points to the new technological revolution already going on, with the core area in telematics:

The question is whether the Europeans – and this really concerns the whole continent and not simply a country or several countries – want to gain one of the first places in the current competition or whether they will content themselves with passively observing the strategies that their American and Japanese competitors are following. The answer is simple. Europe can no longer allow itself to stand aside when modern technology is on the agenda, otherwise it must accustom itself now to the fact that it will soon be ranked among the also-rans. Our autonomy is at stake. (Davignon 1981: 184; our translation)

This project of technology corporatism and of protection was clearly linked to the other core areas of the renewal:

We want to create a truly European market, a common market, which offers businesses the same chances that their American and Japanese competitors have. (Davignon 1981: 185; our translation)

In order to legitimize his approach he continues:

Quite a few people ask themselves why the EC Commission does concern itself with telematics. Furthermore, they say that on the telematics market everything appears to be going well and that business 'copes very well without the technocrats from Brussels'. But that only serves to confirm our diagnosis; that is, that in Europe one just muddles through . . . Europe manufactures only 10 per cent of world production of highly developed electronic components, whereas the EC represents 25 per cent of the world market in this sector. That means that the distance from our competitors will become increasingly larger. European industry must set itself the goal of producing one-third of the world market in the area of telematics by the end of the 1980s. This is a difficult goal but it is attainable – and it is the unanimous opinion of all, that is, of governments, business and the EC Commission. (Davignon 1981: 186; our translation)

From this early statement (published in 1981!) it becomes obvious that protagonists in the Commission coded the transition towards a new European societal model in terms of competition with 'Japan' and the 'USA' and that early on they proposed a European answer in the form of a proposal by the EC Commission (Davignon 1981: 187).

This approach not only shaped the later Single European Act (see above) but became part of the official normative theory of the Commission. Karl-Heinz Narjes (1988: 396), then vice-president of the Commission stated:

It was not until 1980 that the Community was able to take a strategic view of science and technology. It was then that the Commission first stated its belief that it was not possible to devise a new model for society, to secure Europe's political and economic autonomy, or to guarantee commercial competitiveness without a complete mastery of the most sophisticated technologies.

By the early 1990s the approach of technology corporatism and protection had become a standard core element of EC policy. The Commission justified its common procedure by pointing to competitive pressure and insufficient R&D funds in information technologies (CEC, 1991a: 8). 'The Community therefore developed a global strategy in the first half of the 1980s in close collaboration with industry and with research institutions' (CEC, 1991a: 10; our translation). This is followed by a list of different elements, the support of business as well as measures against side-effects and a vision: 'preparation of the transition to a society, in which information is seen as a raw material, which is used in agreement with the social partners and on the basis of the corresponding offers for education and training' (CEC 1991a: 10).

20   State-building and political entrepreneurship

It was not only protection inside the EC that was envisioned in these tasks. In the words of the Commission: 'Considering the growing challenges in the area of Information and Communication Technologies the Community must prove its joint action towards third party states. This applies to the bilateral relationship of the EC to the US and to Japan, as well as in international institutions like the General Agreement on Tariffs and Trade, International Standards Organization or International Telecommunications Union' (CEC 1991a: 71).

Key structures and shifts of globalization

During the late 1980s a new term entered popular discourse: globalization. At least five different dimensions of globalization need to be distinguished: common ecological constraints, values and institutions, globalization of communication, political globalization, and economic globalization. Here we briefly consider only the last.

Economic globalization means globe-spanning economic relationships. The interrelationships of markets – finance, goods and services – and the networks created by transnational corporations (TNCs) are the most important manifestations of this. Transnational corporations are companies owning business assets in more than one country. TNCs thus own stock of foreign direct investment (FDI). Foreign trade and foreign direct investment can be considered mutual substitutes only to a limited degree. Normally there is considerable overlap between foreign trade and foreign direct investment patterns; about half of world trade is channelled by TNCs. Before we come to structures of foreign trade and stocks of foreign direct investment let us briefly look at shifts in the relative importance of foreign trade and stocks of foreign direct investment in the world economy.

The relative importance of both foreign trade and stock of foreign direct investment increased in the postwar era, although not continuously. Exports as a percentage of GDP of Western developed countries (Bairoch 1996: 175) fluctuated around 9 per cent between 1950 and 1968 and, after a 'dramatic' surge, fluctuated between 14 and 15 per cent from the middle of the 1980s to 1993.

World stock of foreign direct investment in relation to world product (Bornschier and Chase-Dunn 1999: 295, table 14.2) was around 4.5 per cent between 1960 and 1980 (rising slightly from 4.4 to 4.8) but had doubled by 1991 to 8.5 percent. This obviously large increase of the relative weight of foreign trade and foreign production is also referred to as evidence of a 'recent' economic globalization. But this assumption of a recent increase is a myth not backed by historical figures. As early as

1890 and 1913 we can observe figures of the relative importance of foreign trade and foreign direct investment that were reached again only in the 1980s (Bairoch 1996; Bornschier and Chase-Dunn 1999), and the growth rate of world trade between 1870 and 1913 was even a bit higher than that between 1980 and 1990 (UNCTAD 1994: 127). Obviously there are tides of globalization in the world economy. The Keynesian societal model of the hegemonic West, which started with democratic pioneers in the early 1930s following the world economic crisis, was a long period of limited globalization when compared with earlier and later periods. When the Keynesian societal model started to dissolve around the end of the 1960s, foreign trade and foreign direct investment began to surge. This has led to increased competition in the world political economy since the late 1960s – one of the decisive elements, we suggest, for an explanation of the integrational thrust in Europe.

Structures in the global economy

As can be seen from table 1.1, during the British hegemony about half of the total stock of foreign direct investment (FDI) was owned by transnational corporations headquartered in the United Kingdom. In 1914, US companies already owned 18.5 per cent, almost the same as companies headquartered in France and Germany together. During the heyday of American hegemony, about half of the world stock was owned by companies headquartered in the USA. This position has been rapidly deteriorating since the end of the 1960s, one indication of a relative industrial decline of US hegemony since that time.

Other indications of considerable shifts in the postwar era relate to shares in world production: the US and West European shares have been declining since 1967 whereas Japan's share has been increasing until the advent of the 1990s (UNCTAD 1994: 157). The same applies to shares in world trade (see Bornschier 1988: 410). Western Europe's share rose from 1950 until 1972 but declined in the 1970s and 1980s, whereas the share of the United States has been declining since the late 1950s. Japan's share in world trade has continuously increased since 1950, and continued to do so even during the 1970s and the 1980s.

What we can learn from these facts, and especially from the longer view that the 1914 figures in table 1.1 make possible, is that hegemonies rise and decline, and these are rather long-term processes. Moreover, we observe the often forgotten fact that hegemonic states in the world political economy, i.e. those that can set the rules of the game, not only have comparatively large internal markets (in Britain's case) or even a

Table 1.1. *Shares in world outward stock of foreign direct investment, selected countries, 1914, 1960, 1978 and 1992*

	Percentage of world total			
	1914	1960	1978	1992
United States	18.5	49.2	41.4	25.3
United Kingdom	45.5	16.2	12.9	11.4
France	12.2	6.1	3.8	8.3
Germany	10.5	1.2	7.3	9.2
Japan	0.1	0.7	6.8	13.0

Source: UNCTAD 1994: 131 (based on John H. Dunning).

huge one (in the case of the USA), but also have the strongest position in the world with respect to transnational corporations. Therefore, for economic transnationals to be allied with a strong state, or even better with a hegemon, seems to have provided a competitive edge. Thus, transnational business and strong states (in terms of internal market and external stature) are competitive advantages – something that advocates of the thesis that economic globalization will result in a 'withering away of the state' completely ignore.

Let us briefly look at Japan, a strong nation-state with a considerable internal mass market after the war. Compared with Britain early in the twentieth century and with the USA in mid-century, Japan's position is still moderate in terms of the share that Japanese transnational corporations control. But, compared with the big European players (Britain, France and Germany), Japan has not only threatened to push them from second place behind the United States into third place, but has actually succeeded in doing so (see table 1.1). Europe reacted, as we already know from earlier statements in this chapter. Let us therefore look now at the aggregated figures for the European Community given in table 1.2.

Table 1.2 shows a remarkable share of the stock of foreign direct investment owned by European economic transnationals headquartered in the European Union. This share increased after the relaunch, but this was mainly due to new members. Compared with the Japanese and even the US share, this aggregated European Union share looks quite impressive and does not invite fears about the EU's future world position.

But the figures in table 1.2 tell only half the story. Two arguments are relevant here. First, part of the 'foreign' direct investment of European transnational corporations is actually located within the European

Table 1.2. *World stock of foreign direct investment by headquarter region, 1980–1995*

	Percentage of world total			
	1980	1985	1990	1995
North America:				
USA and Canada	47.3	42.6	30.5	29.8
Western Europe	46.1	45.6	50.7	48.8
EU share	39.8	39.1	42.3	44.3
Developed Asia:				
Japan and 'Four Tigers'	3.9	7.1	14.2	16.1
Other	2.7	4.7	4.6	5.3
TOTAL	100	100	100	100
US$ billion	514	686	1,684	2,730

Source: computed from UNCTAD 1996: 245–8.
Notes: The shares for the European Community and later European Union (EU) cover only the member states at the time. The new members Spain and Portugal added 0.9 per cent to the 1990 figures, and the new members Sweden, Finland and Austria added 3.25 per cent. The 'Four Tigers' are Hong Kong, Singapore, South Korea and Taiwan.

Union. The share figures for the European Union are thus not exactly comparable to the ones for Japan and the United States, since owning stocks in France in the case of a Dutch transnational corporation does not mean overcoming the same obstacles as owning similar stock there for a Japanese or US company. Figures for intra-EU 'foreign' direct investment by European transnational corporations are very difficult to obtain (see United Nations 1993), but rough estimates for the years between 1975 and 1985 suggest that 21 per cent of the total foreign direct investment flows to the European Community originated from transnational corporations headquartered in the European Community itself (United Nations 1993: 48f). If these figures are correct, they reveal the astonishing fact that intra-EC foreign direct investment has been much lower than intra-EC trade, which according to easily available standard sources was slightly higher than 50 per cent around 1980. This would suggest that until the completion of the internal market in 1992, which was legislated by the Single European Act, the barriers to investment were more substantial than the barriers to trade. And, looking at it from the perspective of the early 1980s, only after eliminating the many non-tariff barriers and the creation of common governance for doing business in the European Community would European transnational corporations achieve stronger economies of scale, which would trigger many cross-border acquisitions and foreign direct investment. This is what the Single Market, which came into effect in 1993, made possible. One important implication of this is that, in terms of building up a stronger home base beyond the nation-state, i.e. by taking advantage of economies of scale and common economically relevant governance in a truly integrated market, deregulation within the European Community must have been among the prime interests of the European transnational business.

Big shots and small fry among the transnational corporations

The second argument for why the aggregated EU figures of its share in the world stock of foreign direct investment do not tell the whole story relates to the size of transnational corporations. In the mid-1990s, almost 40,000 transnational corporations were doing business around the world through their almost 270,000 foreign subsidiaries. Compared with the figures for 1968 this is a big increase (Bornschier and Chase-Dunn 1999: 295, table 14.1). Yet, most of these TNCs are comparatively small fry. Let us therefore consider the big shots – the group of the world's 100 largest transnational corporations.

In 1992, these 100 largest transnationals held about US$3.4 trillion in global assets. We need to stress here that even these big shots of the world economy have a strong home base, since on the average 'only' about 40 per cent of their global assets are outside their home countries (figures from UNCTAD 1994: xxi). From the figures in this source we can estimate that the largest 100 transnationals had average global assets of US$34 billion and an average foreign asset – i.e. outside their home country – of US$13.6 billion. Compared with average foreign assets of only US$57 million in the whole universe of the transnational corporations, this is one indication of the enormous concentration and huge differences in size.

Let us now, in table 1.3, turn to the distribution of the largest 100 transnationals according to home base and average assets. Among the largest 100, the numerical shares of economic transnationals headquartered in the United States, Japan and the European Union correspond well with the respective shares in the total world stock of foreign direct investment. What is striking in table 1.3 are the differences in average size according to global assets – both in the home country and abroad. Among the 100 largest transnationals, those headquartered in the United States and Japan are huge on the average, and the average assets of Japanese transnationals equal those of the US transnationals. The TNCs from the European Union, however, are on the average only half

Table 1.3. *The distribution of the world's 100 largest transnational corporations (TNCs) according to home base and average global assets, 1992*

Home base	Number of TNCs	Average assets at home and abroad (US$ billion)
European Union	43	25.4
United States	29	46.6
Japan	16	46.4
Switzerland	6	19.7
Canada	3	9.9
Other	3	14.1

Source: Computed from UNCTAD 1994: 6–8.
Notes: The top 100 are selected from the universe of 39,000 TNCs according to the absolute size of their foreign assets. Membership in the EU as of 1 January 1995. 'Other': one each headquartered in Norway, Australia, and New Zealand.

the size of their counterparts in the triad. We can conclude that, among the big shots of the world economy at the beginning of the 1990s, the Europeans were comparatively weak, at least on average and in terms of assets. This evidences a big motive at the beginning of intensified world economic competition: to look for a change by aspiring to economies of scale and protection in a greater European area.

Processes in the world political economy

The political and economic spheres are necessarily linked in the world. This is why political and economic entrepreneurs have to bargain to come to terms. States in the market economy cannot prosper without enterprises, which for their part need state services and protection. Elsewhere, we have explained and analysed the underlying theoretical ideas in more detail (see Bornschier 1988: ch. 14; 1996: ch. 3).

The world market for protection argument is inspired by the work of Max Weber, Otto Hintze and Frederic C. Lane, and emphasizes that social order, also termed protection, is a territorially bounded public utility. Production, trade and financial transactions are conditional upon social prerequisites; they require protection. Property rights must be respected and people have to be motivated or forced to engage in exchange relationships. Protection is by no means a secondary factor of production, but is at least as important as labour, knowledge, organizational resources, financial means and credit. In our perspective, protection is a neglected element of national economic production functions; it represents social capital provided and maintained by states. Governments, which can be understood as political undertakings, produce 'order' and sell this public utility to capitalist enterprises as well as to the citizens under their rule. By means of supplying this utility, governments affect the locational quality of their territory in the framework of the world economy.

One important implication of this is that states engage not only in politico-military competition, but also in genuinely economic competition within this world market for social order. This is the case not only because capital and labour are to a certain extent mobile among states, but also because different social orders imply varying degrees of long-term economic success. Governments normally react quite sensitively to this world market for social order. In an attempt to keep their political and military equilibrium they are forced to produce the political preconditions for economic success. If they fail or perform only unsatisfactorily, they can neither attain nor preserve core status in the world economy.

In order to understand the basic argument better let us emphasize that protection, although politically created, shares certain characteristics with land, insofar as it is also territorially bounded. The implications of this theory can be stated from the point of view of states or capitalist firms: first, those states will be the strongest that provide effective protection conducive to innovation and investment at a cost that is worth the services; secondly, those capitalist firms will prosper the most that can choose or are fortunately placed in a network of economic transactions effectively protected, again at a price worth the services. Advantages thus accrue to both sides: higher returns due to effective protection provide competitive edge for capitalists and enhance their accumulation, while higher returns due to more taxable income when enterprises prosper also provide a larger resource base for the state. We stress that in our theory it is not the capitalist state per se that is most favourable to economic success, but any state that reconciles capitalist profit logic with claims to legitimacy among citizens, based on demands for security, equality and efficiency. Although legitimacy is attached to a social order, we suggest that its enduring effect rests not on ideology but on features of the social structure that reflect the meeting of such demands.

Having at least briefly presented all the elements we wish to use for the generation of hypotheses, we move now to an explication of the latter.

Explanations for the integrational thrust

The accelerated integration of Europe has spurred an intense scholarly debate (Sandholtz and Zysman 1989; Moravcsik 1991; Cameron 1992; George 1993; Bornschier 1994; Green Cowles 1995; Robinson 1995; Fielder 1997; Ziltener 1999); and Moravcsik's (1998, 1999) most recent, respectable contributions are aimed not at closing but at renewing the debate over the fundamental causes of European integration. Here, we propose to mention only very briefly the controversy between neofunctionalists and neorealists in the political science debates to clarify the particularities of our own approach.

Neofunctionalism and neorealism

The analysis of West European integration has revived the old controversy between neofunctionalists and neorealists (George 1991: 20–4), while some contributions represent a combination of perspectives (George 1992, 1993; Cameron 1992).

The central idea behind neofunctionalism is that of a 'spillover', and here a distinction is made between 'political spillover' and 'functional spillover'. Functional spillover pertains to the dynamics that occur when states decide to integrate certain economic sectors, forcing them to integrate further sectors in order for the integration of the first to succeed. These dynamics are seen as resulting from the interdependence of economic sectors. Political spillover is the result of a new political reality in connection with the shift of political decisions from the national to the supranational level. As decisions are now made at the supranational level, relevant interest groups and other political actors shift their lobbying to the supranational level to influence the decision-making process. Those interest groups that benefit from integration then start pressuring their national governments into shifting ever more political functions to the supranational level. According to neofunctionalist theory, both spillover processes should be spontaneous and incremental because they result from the internal logic of integration. They not only occur in the lower realms of politics, but move from these technical areas to higher political fields of state sovereignty such as defence, security and currency.

Neorealists, on the other hand, believe that because governments have been elected by the people, and therefore have legitimized power, they remain the truly significant actors in the integration process and defend national interests. Neorealists do not believe that a spillover from low to high politics will occur. Defence, security and currency, which represent the essence of state sovereignty, will remain excluded from the integration process. Yet, the neorealists see the power structure in the overarching and global context as an important element reactively influencing states' decisions.

Neorealist explanations of this kind have various weaknesses, which stem from the fact that these perspectives regard nation-states as the only relevant actors and take too narrow a view of government motives. Neofunctionalism, on the other side, has too limited an understanding of transnational actors, and neglects the possibly far-reaching initiatives stemming from them.

Transnational corporations in search of a political entrepreneur

The theoretical perspective advanced earlier may overcome some of the theoretical limitations resulting from an approach centred on policy. As already mentioned, two kinds of 'enterprises' are relevant for the processes in the world economy: states and firms. Thus, a framework is suggested that integrates supply of, and demand for, order. Together with the rise and decay of societal models, this approach seems promising, especially when we focus on questions of timing and of the protagonists behind the relaunch of European integration in the 1980s.

According to our argument, states compete with each other not only in a politico-military sense – the classical form of their competition – but also in the framework of the world economy, essentially mediated by the production factor of social order guaranteed by the state. Thus, states also compete in a genuinely economic way and, in addition, they are forced to re-create, improve, or qualitatively reorganize interstate regulatory mechanisms in case they should break down or prove insufficient.

The idea of competition for protection on the world market enriches the theoretical apparatus in one important respect. The economic motives of political undertakings – even more, the view thus implied that states are producers of economically valuable goods – become important. Such motives are added to the classic ones of security and power politics. In this our perspective differs from the neorealist approach. It also differs from neofunctionalism because the economic motives of state actors become predominant when the world economy is central to status distribution and when transnational corporations increasingly force states to compete with each other as sites of economic activity.

If we start from the competition of political entities supplying order and economic enterprises demanding order, it is easy to assume similar strategies for states and economic enterprises. While competing they may cooperate, build strategic alliances or even merge. Contrary to the neofunctionalist argument, such processes are not automatic results of internal spillovers; rather, they are primarily generated by the competitive conditions of the world political economy. Such strategic alliances or even mergers are much more likely to happen – or may only be possible – if supranational institutional preconditions are met and available for political entrepreneurship. This was the case with the European Commission, whose independent role was stipulated at its inception in 1958.

Our theoretical perspective thus differs in important respects from the functionalist and realist theories of international relations. The argument from the theory of protection rent is as follows. European transnational corporations asked the political entrepreneurs in Europe to provide them with the locational advantages their rivals were enjoying in the United States and Japan. This demand stimulated the negotiation of a new state project along the lines of a wide homogeneous market combined with strategic planning, particularly with regard to the ever more important production factor of technology.

This project was forged in the informal European Roundtable of Industrialists (ERT). With his paper 'Agenda for Action: Europe 1990', Wisse Dekker, a central figure in the ERT, created an important conceptual basis for the White Paper authored by the Commission's Lord Cockfield. The EC Commission acted as a political entrepreneur, launched and popularized the project, overcame the resistance of governments, and submitted it to the Council for decision. The Commission's own motives and interests are discussed briefly below.

It should be made clear that it was not European businesses as such that pushed the project, since most of them took advantage of national protection within the early phase of the European Community, when non-tariff barriers to trade and many restrictions on investment and national monopolies still prevailed. Thus it was also not the European business associations, which already existed at the Community level and represented numerous enterprises, but rather the transnational European business elite, with their considerable business stakes outside their headquarter countries, who were pushing to have the same opportunities as their global competitors by broadening their home base (allowing for greater economies of scale) and by getting support from strategic technology policy. This is not to suggest a conspiracy theory of European integration, since the position of European big business as represented in the European Roundtable was overtly clear and publicly stated. This becomes evident from the first Policy Memorandum of the

European Roundtable of Industrialists, which was officially transmitted to the Commission in 1983:

> Despite the efforts of the European Community to liberalize trade, Europe remains divided into national markets with different industrial structures. This prevents many enterprises from reaching the size necessary to withstand the pressure of competition from non-European concerns. But the European market must serve as a single 'home base' so that European firms can develop into powerful competitors on world markets. (Niggli 1989: 167)

This is not to say that all other business was against the project, but the others were fragmented in terms of interest and on average rather neutral; some would gain, some would lose. This divided position contrasts with that of the European transnational corporations, all of which were on the winning side and had the resources to take advantage of the new possibilities.

Furthermore, our explanation does not completely neglect the political entrepreneurs of the existing nation-states in the Community. On the average, however, they needed to be pushed hard – a process that actually took many years (see also chapter 3), since their national constituencies were diverse in terms of winners and losers created by deregulation. Thus with respect to political entrepreneurs in Europe, our hypothesis is very clear: in the end it was the transnational level that was decisive.

Discussion

Our hypotheses were truly ex ante ones that needed to be tested empirically, and the remaining chapters in this volume explain what we have gathered in terms of detailed evidence, from which readers may draw their own conclusions. Yet, we must admit that we were aware of the fine and inspiring work of Sandholtz and Zysman (1989) when we started studying the qualitative change of European integration in 1991. They had already pointed to changes in the world economy as necessary factors for the revitalization of the European integration project. Drawing on our own previous research in other fields, we extended and refined this approach to European integration.

What happened in the world political economy during the decisive years we mentioned? For decades Europe had ceased to be the centre of the world political economy. After the 'civil war' of 1914–18, the European powers had to relinquish this role to the United States, which actually assumed it only after the Second World War. The European powers took their place behind the United States after the Second World War and were startled when, owing to the hegemonic decline of the United States since the end of the 1960s, the previous stability of the world economic structure was no longer guaranteed and the impressive rise of Japan thrust Europe into third place in the world.

This perspective has been linked to the interests of the European transnational corporations. The competitive disadvantages of Europe as an industrial site were first directly felt and articulated by the European transnational corporations. After the economic crisis of the 1970s, the United States and particularly Japan recovered much more easily than a Europe immobilized by 'Eurosclerosis' – a term coined by American observers. The United States, despite its loss of competitiveness, was able to take advantage of its own huge and rather homogeneous internal market; and Japan enjoyed the advantage of its elaborate strategic planning, which had been essential for Japan's extraordinary rise for decades. It was the (certainly mild and flexible) 'planned economy', tied indeed to capitalistically inspired business and oriented to long-term strategic goals that made Japan big, without being laissez-faire.

The other pressure for Europe's revival concerns the cyclical dynamics of societal models. The Western societal model disintegrated towards the end of the 1970s. Former hegemonic normative theories such as Keynesianism were replaced by monetarist and supply-side oriented ones after the world summit in Bonn in 1978. In 1982 the new doctrine was anchored in the Organization for Economic Cooperation and Development (OECD) paradigm for a new economic policy of the Western world. The technological style, characterized by Fordist mass production, reached its limits, and the political shifts at the turn of the 1980s destroyed the unquestioned position of former politico-economic regimes in the postwar era. In terms of this approach, recasting the European Community can be explained as a move towards a renewed European societal model, a remarkable innovation in terms of European history. Many statements by Commissioners support such a view, for example: 'Truly '1992' will mean a transformation of society. Mentalities and habits will change. Everywhere the key players in the economy realize that the future lies in the fullest sense in Europe' (Karel van Miert, Member of the European Commission, quoted in CEC 1992: 8). Recently, key EC publications can even be found using one of our central terms (Bornschier 1988, 1996). The White Paper of December 1993 declares: 'The *new model of European society* calls for less passive and more active solidarity' (CEU 1993: 15, emphasis added).

The relative decline of the hegemon

We have mentioned the relative losses of the economic position of the United States in the 1970s and 1980s. But hegemony also has an important institutional dimension. In this view, the relaunch of the European Community must also be seen as an answer to contradictions inherent in the interventionist role of the state – a cornerstone of the neocorporatist-Keynesian societal model. Economic interventions are free of major interstate conflicts only if they are embedded in, and curbed by, international regimes.

One important pillar of this coordination was the US dollar–gold exchange regime of Bretton Woods. In 1971, the United States, which had established this system, was no longer in a position to defend the dollar. From an institutional viewpoint, the hegemonic power of the USA was abdicated at the moment when it gave up the exchange system that it had created by 'suspending' its obligation to maintain the US dollar–gold parity. By 1973, as the European countries were forced to switch to floating rates, the system of fixed exchange rates completely broke apart, and the discipline of coordinating economic policies no longer existed. The important, even irreplaceable linkage had broken, because – as hegemonic stability theory would argue – no country was in a position or willing to guarantee the international exchange system. The hegemonic crisis of the United States and the disintegration of the societal model, which depended on interstate coordination of economic policy, are mutually linked. Both factors work together to explain the integrational momentum of the European Community in the 1980s.

We consider as a sufficient explanation, however, the alliance of European transnational economic and political entrepreneurs at the supranational level to ensure Europe's economic position in the world by strengthening the home base and thus to guarantee Europe's future prosperity. Both interests were easy to put together since in this respect they were indeed congruent. Our explanation proposes to answer the question: who were the actors, who gave the impulse for the relaunch? By pointing to an elite bargain between the two classes of European elite – transnational and supranational – we do not imply that these two were decisive for other aspects of European integration. The formal role of the Commission, as spelled out in the treaties, may vary in its effectiveness. Before the 1980s the Commission was not always a strong actor in European politics, and in the 1990s this situation is again similar. Once the project was successful, the European transnational elite turned instead to normal interest-group politics, albeit within a new institutional setting. The Roundtable is still active and has even expanded its membership over time, but it does not seem to be influencing further European state-building – although it has a big stake in moulding concrete policies within the framework achieved.

The interests of the Commission itself and the significance of citizens

So much for the origins of the elite pact. Apart from 'more market and strategic planning of technology', shaping solidarity and cohesion was a cornerstone of the Single European Act from the beginning. Indeed, it was Delors' project to supplement 'more market in the community' – the European approach to a socially embedded deregulation – with, in his words, an 'espace européen organisé'. The welfare state, which offered a base of equal life chances for its citizens, has been a specifically West European strength during the postwar era. Delors explicitly used this as a building block of the renewed European societal model. It is clearly embedded in the normative theories (see chapters 5 and 6). To be sure, the emphasis on this in the Single European Act and even in the later Treaty on European Union remained limited. This may be explained as a tactical choice. But the substantial increase in financial endowments of the regional funds in 1988 and the cohesion fund created by the Maastricht Treaty are evidence of a novel, supranational approach towards equalizing life chances within Western Europe.

Although we have argued that the Commission took up the demand by transnationals for a larger market and greater strategic planning, we do not wish to promote the false impression that the Commission was acting only as an overall agent for the European transnationals – as the agent for the transnational European capitalist class – and had no interest itself in the launching of a project that included more than mere national deregulation and quasi-corporatist steps to advance technology. Enlightened state-builders most probably know from European history that successful state projects always take better care of the interests of citizens, compared with their less successful competitors. Delors knew that too, and it coincided with the interests of the supranational political entrepreneur.

Political entities and their representatives must legitimize themselves. In this respect, the situation of the EC Commission is very precarious. Even if the European Parliament was somewhat strengthened by the Single European Act, normal democratic legitimization is still achieved only indirectly through the democratically appointed and controlled representatives of the member states in the Council. This situation, even before the Single European Act, weakened the Commission as it simultaneously strengthened the Council. As a result, the political ambitions of the Commission were blocked. However, at an earlier point the Commission began, through opinion polls, to make direct contact with the citizens of the European Community to find out their views on political questions. Under the auspices of the Commission, a biannual survey of the opinions of EU citizens has been conducted since the early 1970s – the so-called Eurobarometer studies.

As an improvised substitute for the weak representation of the European population, this polling of opinions by way of the Eurobarometer has a considerable political function for the Commission insofar as it endeavours to legitimize its policies by reference to popular acceptance of the Community project. However, at the end of the 1970s and beginning of the 1980s, support for the European Community sank to a long-term low and remained there until 1984 (see Bornschier 1996: 366). At the end of this period in which 'Eurosclerosis' was reflected in the mood of the public, the new Delors Commission began to make the project to rebuild Europe more palatable to citizens. Since then, Delors has made 'Europe '92: The Social Community' his political platform: 'More social equality in Europe – a lively and humane society, is what the EC is seeking for its 340 million members' (CEC 1992: 2).

After launching the political package, which included not only the interests of the European transnationals but also the Commission's quest for legitimacy – i.e. a larger market, strategic planning and social cohesion and convergence – and which was then formalized in the Single European Act, public support among the citizens of the Community increased sharply after 1985 until the early 1990s, as the poll results show (see Bornschier 1996: 366; Sandholtz 1993: 22). Without a doubt, the social dimension is the weakest part in the new political package of the 1980s – partially owing to the resistance of some member countries, particularly the United Kingdom.

Final remarks on competing explanations

The emphasis in our explanation is on the timing of events and the protagonists relevant for Europe's move toward political union in the mid-1980s. As the 1980s dawned, certain constellations became apparent. The Western societal model had decayed during the 1970s, and the hegemon was no longer able to guarantee stability. Europe was confronted with Japan's success in mastering the world economic crisis on the one hand, and challenged by America's experiment under President Reagan to defend its world economic position on the other. At this juncture, the 'demand' of transnational European business and the 'supply' of the supranational EC Commission met and provided the impetus for a relaunch of integration, by renewing the European societal model to create the conditions for post-hegemonic competition in the world economy.

Our explanation for the rebuilding of Western Europe is somewhat similar to the explanation advanced by Sandholtz and Zysman (1989) and can also be brought into line with Stephen George's (1993) idea of the linkage of supranational and national levels. Of course, the European transnationals not only exerted influence on the Commission but were also mediated by national governments, which were thus forced to take up the case of the Commission. But we maintain that the supranational link was clearly more influential.

Our perspective is, however, in clear contradiction to Andrew Moravcsik's (1991) purely neorealist explanation. He claims that the Single European Act can be explained as the playing out of the national interests of the three big member states: Germany, France and Britain. In what amounts to a sort of game theory explanation, the three big states are seen to have converged on the lowest common denominator of their national preferences. This view stresses that the heads of government and their direct representatives took the lead in the negotiations and produced the breakthrough that is represented by the Single European Act (SEA). The substantial difference between his and our theoretical positions has become evident from this chapter. On an issue-specific level, one of the core empirical questions is thus whether the governments of the big countries took the lead via the EC Council of Ministers (intergovernmental institutionalism) as Moravcsik originally maintained, or whether this role was played by the transnationals together with the EC Commission (transnational and supranational institutionalism), as we maintain. Figure 1.1 not only schematically summarizes our arguments but also lists the competing hypothesis. Recently, however, Moravcsik (1998, 1999) has changed his position, at least with regard to the supranational and transnational intervention that pushed the Single European Act of 1985. He concedes the supranational and transnational influence and acknowledges that the 'highly technical "package deal" [of the SEA was] backed by a new, transnational constituency of multinational firms' and 'supranational entrepreneurs had a significant, if still decidedly secondary, influence on the SEA' (Moravcsik 1999: 285, 292).

Not at all in dispute, however, is the extraordinary significance of the thrust toward a new beginning in the mid-1980s, which continued with the Maastricht Treaty on European Union, by which time European integration had become more controversial among the European public. Some thoughts about why this is so will follow at the end of this volume (see also Anderson 1995a: 451). In any case, Europe is on the move; although struggling with the problem of unemployment, it looks toward the future and articulates nothing less than 'the new model of European society'.

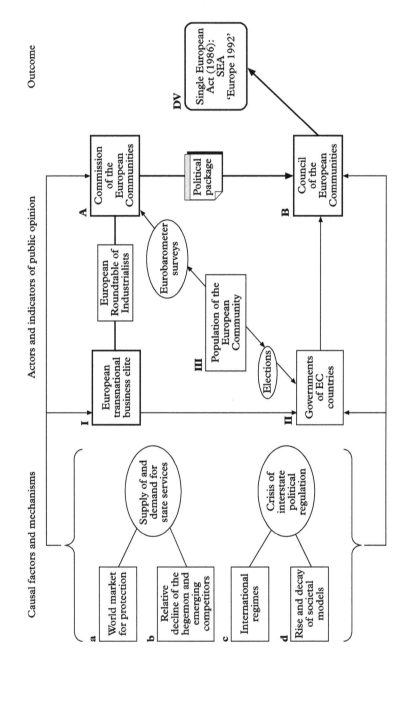

Figure 1.1 The genesis of the Single European Act

Legend:

a,b,c,d	Causal factors and mechanisms
I, II, III	Social actors
A,B	Central institutions of the European Community along with the European Parliament and the European Court of Justice, as defined by the Treaties of 1957 and 1965.
DV	Dependent variable: the Single European Act (1986), a restructuring, deepening and widening of the European Community.

Comments:

1. According to EC law the final resolution on the Single European Act can only be passed by the Council. This is not a point of debate. It is the path to the final agreement on which the various authors differ.

 - *Elite Bargain*   (a,b,c,d) -> I -> A -> B -> DV (Single European Act)
 'transnational networks & supranational institutionalism'
 - *Alternative Elite Bargain*   II (mainly the 'big three': F, GB, FRG) -> B -> DV (Single European Act)
 'intergovernmental institutionalism'

2. The population of the European Community (III) influences the process indirectly via the elections of the respective governments and through the Eurobarometer surveys.

2 Tying up the Luxembourg package of 1985: prerequisites and problems of its constitution

Patrick Ziltener

> 'L'initiative vient toujours d'en haut!'
> Frédéric Moreau in Flaubert's *Education sentimentale*

A considerable part of the debate on the reasons for the integration thrust in the 1980s is based on the not always precise differentiation between statements on the origins of political initiatives, the corresponding agenda setting, the mediation of interests and thus the transformation of the initiative and its adoption. This is shown with the often undifferentiated use of the terms '1992 Initiative', 'EC reform', 'Single European Act' (SEA), etc. Furthermore, the origins of political initiatives and the prerequisites for their success (or failure) are often imprecisely distinguished from each other. This chapter chronologically and logically follows chapter 1 in that it reconstructs the process of the construction of a successful package deal, the Luxembourg package, by making reference to the analysis of the causal factors of the integration relaunch. The *Luxembourg package*[1] is hereby defined as the entirety of the agreements on the insertion or amendment of articles in the EC treaties, as they were formulated during the intergovernmental conference in 1985, which together form the *Single Act* and which were adopted by the Council of Ministers in 1986.

The first section presents some theoretical considerations on the conditions for success of a package deal. The following section describes important integration projects and processes for forming alliances. The first six months in 1984 are seen as the 'take-off' phase for the SEA.

---

[1] The Luxembourg package must not be confused with the so-called Luxembourg Compromise, the informal regulation enforced by De Gaulle during the integration crisis in 1965/6. According to this regulation, each government has a right to veto in the case of 'vital national interests'. This agreement enforced the principle of unanimous decision in the Council of Ministers and was therefore of major importance for the institutional blockades of the EEC in the following years. An actual *veto culture* emerged (Teasdale 1993). The Commission and the European Court of Justice never accepted this regulation. On the connection between the Luxembourg Compromise and the SEA, see chapter 9.

The Commission's changing role, its actual 'rebirth' as a result of an altered situation and as a precondition for the creation of a negotiation package, is then discussed. The SEA being such a heterogeneous treaty, the question of 'authorship' can hardly be answered *in globo* in a sensible way. To answer the question, the Luxembourg package has to be deconstructed into its different elements. I therefore present an overview of the origins of the different elements of the SEA and the logic of the entire Luxembourg package.

On integration projects and the prerequisites for their success

The strongest arguments for an intergovernmentalist explanation can inevitably be found in the analysis of the negotiations at an intergovernmental conference, which is the prerequisite for a change in the EU treaties. In such a process it becomes very clear that the national governments are still the strongest actors in the political system at the European level. It is hardly contestable that they view the EU through the lens of their own policy preferences and that they try to ensure that negotiation outcomes are as close as possible to what they perceive to be their respective national interests.[2] However, it can also be argued that an intergovernmental approach cannot adequately explain the result of an intergovernmental conference. Below, in marked contrast to neorealism and other theoretical approaches, we conceptualize some theoretical constructs that can be used as the theoretical framework proposed here for the analysis of the process that we refer to as 'tying up the Luxembourg package'.

National, transnational and supranational actors have different normative ideas on the desired aims of the European integration process and the necessary, appropriate and possible means for their realization. In the following, the entirety of these normative ideas of a collective actor on aims and means is defined as the actor's *integration project*. An integration project need not be coherent and without contradictions, and in most cases it is not. It can be changed not only, as in the case of the member states, as a result of change of government, but also as a result of a change of policy preferences, shifts in the underlying interest structure, experiences from strategic policy, altered external pressure and/or altered reception of this pressure, etc. Therefore, integration projects are always concrete and historically determined. They result from compromises

---

[2] To Moravcsik (1991: 25), 'EC politics is the continuation of domestic policies by other means'. For the following, see also Sandholtz (1993: 3), Pierson and Leibfried (1995), H. Wallace (1996a,b), W. Wallace (1996).

between different interests. Several parties can agree on a joint integration project. In this chapter, several integration projects will be described: the federalist projects, the change in French European policy, and the project of the Delors Commission and its influence on the Luxembourg package.

In studying the development of the European integration process in its different stages, analytical essays and statements by the parties concerned very soon reveal the decisive importance of so-called *package deals*. Typical conditions for the development of package solutions are negotiation systems with a pluralist structure of interests, with several parties that are more or less equal with respect to organizational resources. On the EU level, such negotiation packages gain a specific relevance, mainly owing to institutional particularities, especially the dominant position of the member states' governments. The unanimity principle in the Council of Ministers – which was the normal case up to the SEA and still dominates in many policy areas – makes political barter (*logrolling*) inevitable. This especially applies to changing the treaties at intergovernmental conferences.

The following conditions must be fulfilled so that a negotiation package ready for adoption can be constituted:

(1) As a prerequisite, the integration projects of the actors involved must contain common elements that could form the core of such a package. This requires *relatively convergent political orientations*.
(2) A party is necessary that not only suggests initiatives, but also carries out the strategic focusing and mediation of interests and elaborates compromise wordings that the majority can accept (*political entrepreneurship*). A successful package needs to be supported by an alliance of several parties (*non-hegemonic cooperation*).
(3) *Dynamizing factors*: first, there need to be institutional and/or informal procedures at several levels that prevent blockade strategies or at least impede them, secondly, a package solution is a temporary compromise, a balance of powers in flux, which is agreed to only in consideration of expected developments.

These points are elaborated below.

Relative convergence

Relative convergence in the perception of the actual challenges and problems and of basic policy orientations, especially of national economic policies, is a necessary, but not a sufficient, condition for an integration thrust.[3] Relative convergence does not at all mean an

---

[3] The importance of relative convergence as a prerequisite for an integration process is commonly accepted. For Moravcsik (1991: 21; 1998: ch. 5), an 'essential precondition

'identity of interests'; rather it means an increasing overlapping of the concepts of content, means and range of state regulation. This is the precondition for the definition of one or more core projects of common interest. These have to be so important within the framework of the entire political and economic concept of the parties involved that they are prepared to accept the elements of the compromise that are undesirable from their point of view – the costs of reaching the aim.

In his evaluation of the possibilities for a *relance européenne* (European relaunch) at the beginning of the 1980s, Hrbek (1982: 16) noted that the deepening of the Community requires 'a certain amount of homogeneity or at least visible convergence of basic positions, of conceptions of aims and means including the priorities which need to be considered'. This was definitely not the case in 1982 and it did not seem to be likely in the near future. Several developments changed this in the two following years. Of central importance was the series of changes of government in the EC states toward conservative governments or government coalitions dominated by conservatives (see Cameron 1992: 56ff; Jones 1993). The end of the socialist/communist government in France in 1983, in which Jacques Delors[4] was minister for economic affairs, was also the end of the last attempt in Europe to revive the Keynesian societal model.[5] From 1983 onwards, economic policy orientations were relatively convergent in Western Europe, heading

for reform was the convergence of economic policy prescriptions of ruling party coalitions'. For Cameron (1992: 58f), the general 'rightward shift in the ideological center of gravity' greatly facilitated the development of 'an initiative that, above all, sought to create a market free of the intrusions and obstacles erected by interventionist governments'. See also Sandholtz and Zysman (1989: 108ff).

[4] Delors' role in this change is illuminated by the fact that the adopted austerity and stabilization plan carried his name. There are good arguments for Moravcsik's (1998: 373) claim that 'it may well be that Delors' action as finance minister of France contributed as much to the SEA as did his actions as president of the Commission'.

[5] All political actors estimate that the political changes in France had a large influence on the integration process. Etienne Davignon (EC Commissioner until 1984) replies to the question of why the integration thrust started in 1985/6: 'a number of things had appeared. One was the total failure of national measures to deal with the economic crisis. The clearest example of that was the failure of the reflation policy of the Mauroy government after the change of majority in France, after Monsieur Mitterrand won the election; basically it was all to the advantage of the neighbours of France, who exported more into France, and in no way to the advantage of French producers. Measures of a national nature taken to try to improve employment, did not work, sectoral measures did not work, it appeared that what was needed was something at a European level' (interview on 6 April 1993). According to Karl-Heinz Narjes (EC Commissioner 1981–88), too, the big thrust for the Single Market became possible only after the French government under Mitterrand 'left its course of national, socialist economic policy' in 1982/3 (in an interview with *Der Spiegel*, No. 1, January 1989). To Védrine (1996: 286), Mitterrand's European policy from 1984 to 1992 was inconceivable without the austerity measures (*rigueur*), without which the French–German tandem would not have functioned.

toward austerity (see Uterwedde 1988: 189). This does not mean that there were no more policy differences between national strategies in Western Europe. The political spectrum from Thatcherist policy to socialist modernization policy in France remained broad and this caused the majority of the disputes during the integration relaunch of the 1980s.

As a further prerequisite, a positive reference to the 'European level', to the institutions of the Community, is needed within the framework of convergent strategies. For a long time, this was missing in the case of the French socialists and the British Labour Party, since the EC was perceived more as part of the problem than as part of the solution. Even after the re-orientation of the French socialists in their European policy, a certain caution towards the Community institutions remained for some time. The EUREKA project, an initiative by the French government that was more multilateral than supranational, proves this.

Political entrepreneurship

Given the definition of one or several core projects, the 'fine tuning' starts: the package has to be tied. Institutional questions and procedural modalities have to be solved. On the basis of its power in steering the political process at European level, the Commission was successfully able to use its role as political entrepreneur to promote its integration project again and again.

The initiative function of the Commission as a 'constitutional assignment' has already been pointed out in chapter 1. Another important point when defining political entrepreneurship is the 'ambition' of the half-yearly changing Council presidencies. These have important functions for pushing or delaying certain *dossiers*, as is especially evident in social policy (chapter 6). This definitely applies to intergovernmental conferences, where the country with the presidency fulfils a strategically important function concerning the formulation of mediatory compromises.

The main question is the implementation of majority decisions in the Council of Ministers, since this implies that the 'reinsurance' of the national governments is either given up or preserved, i.e. the possibility of blockading further integration dynamics. Resistance to integration has to be cleared, with side payments and/or exemption regulations (safeguard clauses, opting out, etc). Package solutions are based on political logrolling. Hubert Védrine, Mitterrand's adviser, describes how each political initiative is linked to consideration of which exchanges could be tied to it. These can even reach beyond the EU framework.⁶

In contrast to the neorealist approach, we hold that package solutions are complicated negotiation results that do not have to be based on the *lowest common denominator*. Acceptance depends much more on the perception of a 'well-balanced outcome' by all parties. At the least, the costs must not exceed the expected advantages in consideration of the further development of integration. In comparison with international regimes, owing to the level of integration already achieved, withdrawing participation in the integration process is tied to much higher costs. Therefore, parties whose interests have not been considered 'adequately' tend to demand far-reaching exemption regulations that allow an opting out with regard to further integration steps rather than leave the EU.

Non-hegemonic cooperation

The European integration process is based on non-hegemonic cooperation, because no state can enforce further progress as a result of its power resources and/or institutional position (see Moravcsik 1991: 25). Therefore, each integration step requires *an alliance of several states*. History has shown several times, however, that it has never been possible to carry out such an integration project without or against the countries that are politically at the centre of European integration, especially Germany and France.⁷ This is an unwritten European 'constitutional reality' which is strongly embedded in the consciousness and strategic calculations of the actors, as many interviews have shown.

Nevertheless, the smaller states are by no means a *quantité négligeable*, i.e. politically negligible factors. The EU's decision-making system partially compensates for real inequality with formal equality. Several smaller states can 'pool' their political weight and, combined with their aggregated authority in the decision-making process, they can maximize their influence. The Benelux countries have often done this and continue to do so. However, the relative smallness of member states seldom leads to a common interest or even an integration project; this is only

---

⁶ Védrine (1996: 283): 'Ces échanges ne se limitent pas, en effet, au seul champ communautaire: la France est presque toujours engagée ailleurs au même moment – au Conseil de Sécurité, dans la préparation du prochain sommet des Sept, par exemple –, dans d'autres négociations où elle peut avoir besoin de tel ou tel de ses partenaires européens.'

⁷ The same applied to questions concerning the budget: nothing could be adopted against the will of the two net payers (until 1985), Germany and the United Kingdom.

likely to happen when discussing rules of procedure. Alliances between states with similar structural conditions, as well as similar political and economic interests, independent of their relative size, are much more frequent. In the case of monetary policy at the intergovernmental conference in 1985, Belgium joined France in demanding an expansion of EC competences, whereas the Netherlands, being a country with a strong currency, tended to favour Germany's position.

Dynamizing factors

The most neglected factor in explaining the integration thrust of the 1980s is the one that Delors called 'dynamics'. This means not the spillover effects that the neofunctionalist integration theory refers to (Haas 1958; Lindberg and Scheingold 1970), but the fact that the planning horizon of actors usually surpasses the current political agenda. Some parts of the integration project can strategically be postponed and addressed later, after the adoption of the package, when the constellation of actors has changed or after the revision of the project. Again, the changing Council presidency is very important among the member states, as it is linked to a considerable amount of power to set the agenda.

Dynamics result from integration projects, not from functional spillover effects. It is a question of political and economic interests whether or not, for example, tax harmonization, social policy regulations, a monetary union or, as a general alternative, regulatory competition of systems are seen as 'logical' consequences of an integrated market.

Projects and alliances

The period of the formation of relative convergence between member states was characterized by a number of mostly unsuccessful integration projects. In studying two federalist[8] or institutionalist initiatives, some prerequisites for failure can be determined. In addition, beneath this history, some factors can also be identified that in mid-term assumed large importance.

---

[8] In this section and in the following, the term federalism/federalist is used in the sense of a project to establish common institutions at European level ('centralization'). In the German language, the term means the exact opposite, namely the maintenance or creation of a decentralized institutional structure. The term 'federalist integration projects' refers to the generalized wish to establish or extend European institutions.

The Genscher–Colombo initiative, 1981[9]

Named after the German and the Italian foreign ministers, this initiative for a 'European Act' as a 'step towards union', towards 'Europe's political unity', aimed at the completion of the Common Market, a common foreign policy and an increase in majority decisions in the Council of Ministers. The integration project included the development of a number of areas such as research and technology policy and social and regional policy.

The German–Italian integration project had a strong federalist orientation. In both countries, there was consensus among the different political parties on the desirability and feasibility of a West European federal state, with control and legal authority increasing with the expansion of economic competences. Accordingly, the European Parliament, in particular, would have to be developed into an actual analogue to national parliaments. This was clearly rejected by the British, Danish and French governments.[10] Even increased cooperation in foreign affairs, which was the area most likely to achieve consent, there was resistance from Ireland as well as reservations by the United Kingdom and France in view of an expansion into security policy.

During the German Council presidency,[11] this initiative led to the adoption of the Stuttgart Solemn Declaration (1983), which avoided the term 'Act'. Concerning institutional development, the most important points it contained were the confirmation of an active and expandable role for the Commission as well as the statement that the implementation of decision-making procedures as provided in the Rome treaty (i.e. majority voting in the Council) is of decisive importance for improving the EC's capacity to act. However, the Stuttgart Declaration did not represent fundamental agreement to a common integration project. An effective limitation of the Luxembourg Compromise was not made (Teasdale 1993: 572). Moreover, five of the ten member states (France, the United Kingdom, Denmark, Ireland and Greece) confirmed their adherence to the national power of veto on principle after the conference. Along with the results of the following Greek Council presidency, especially the failure of the summit in Athens, this refutes the thesis that Stuttgart represented the launch of the rocket's first

---

[9] In *Europa-Archiv* 2–1982; cf. Genscher (1981), Hrbek (1982: 12ff). On German EC policy in this period in general, see Bulmer and Paterson (1987), Wessels and Regelsberger (1988).

[10] For the French position see Secrétariat d'Etat auprès du Premier Ministre and Commissariat Général du Plan (1983: 85). This report emphasizes that an 'Act', if it were to be adopted, would have to be far removed from its original ambitions.

[11] See Ungerer (1983a,b), Mertes (1983).

stage, as the German foreign minister Genscher stated in retrospect (1995: 368).[12]

In addition to the non-binding Solemn Declaration, 'special negotiations' were also adopted in Stuttgart. Monthly special conferences of the Council were to prepare a package solution for the Community's most important problems (budget, financing, agricultural policy, enlargement). All governments agreed that the problems should be solved as a package. According to the Greek prime minister, Papandreou, the Stuttgart 'compromise between diverging concepts' did not prove to be sustainable, as it was based on 'contradictory and ambiguous formulations' (*Europa-Archiv* 3-1984, D65). The existing possibilities for dealing with a question or postponing regulations on other questions had been practically non-existent. 'A solution in one area required a compensating solution in another. That was the sense of the "package", or, if you prefer this term, of the overall solution.' (ibid., D64). The Athens summit in December 1983, at which a package solution was supposed to be adopted, failed entirely, so that even the usual common conclusions were renounced.

Even if the first attempt towards a solution for the EC's structural problems failed, fields had been outlined in these special negotiations, confidence had been built up and the directions of possible compromises explored. However, the Commission criticized the procedure chosen in Stuttgart as a 'distortion of the community's procedures', which fortified the 'tendency to progressive hypertrophy of the role assigned to the European Council' (ibid., D69). The Commission had reached a very low point in its influence.

The European Parliament draft treaty on European Union

A second source of initiatives for a federal Europe, in addition to the German–Italian cooperation but not separate from it, is the European Parliament. In 1979 it was directly elected for the first time and it has been looking for a new, more adequate role ever since. Following an initiative by MPs around Altiero Spinelli (the so-called Crocodile Group), the European Parliament established a committee on institutional problems in 1981, 'convinced that the fact that it has been elected by direct universal suffrage gives it both increased authority and

---

[12] The second step had been the SEA, the third had been the Maastricht treaty. Doutriaux (1992: 94) also advocates the thesis of 'relaunch of the European construction in Stuttgart in 1983'. Grosser (1989: 384f), however, states that the failure of the European summits in Athens in December 1983 and in Brussels in 1984 showed how unproductive the pompous Solemn Declaration had been.

additional duties in the performance of its democratic tasks'.[13] A draft treaty establishing the European Union[14] was presented early in 1984. This draft proposed a transition from the method of intergovernmental cooperation to 'common action' in an institutional equilibrium between Parliament, Commission and Council in many policy areas. In the Council, general majority voting was planned, except in areas where it was explicitly stated otherwise in the treaties. The recourse to 'vital national interests' (Luxembourg Compromise) was given a transitional period of ten years to its complete abolition.

The Italian and German Members of Parliament had already dominated the committee; the plenary vote also showed that the draft was mainly supported by MPs of the original core Europe – except France. Hopes that the draft could become a crystallization point for a more thorough debate soon disappeared. The draft was never discussed by the national governments, but became a topic of academic debates. It was given a symbolic reference in Council decisions, and a Commission spokesman called it the 'decisive impulse' towards EC reform (Ehlermann 1988: 57). Nevertheless, it remains unclear what led to the SEA being mentioned in close connection with the European Parliament draft treaty.[15] The sole fact that the draft was never discussed in the Council, but also a comparison of the contents, reveals the fundamental difference between the approaches of these initiatives.

The most important reason for the failure of the federalist integration projects between 1981 and 1984 was their institutionalist orientation. This approach of creating a supranational state could and can rely only on the consent of mainly the political elite of some member countries, and partly also their populations. Without the other two big member states, or with their only partial inclusion, especially France, the German–Italian project did not stand a chance of initiating real change. As a supranational actor, the European Parliament is too weak to develop sufficient pressure towards this aim. Until mid-1984, the Commission was greatly slowed down by the EC's overhang of internal problems in its function as a political entrepreneur. Apart from the

---

[13] Resolution of 9 July 1981; in Gazzo (1985: 18).
[14] In *Europa-Archiv* 8–1984, D209ff. See the most comprehensive Bieber, Jacqué and Weiler (1985) and Wessels (1984).
[15] As, for example, Schnorpfeil (1993: 25f); similarily, Sidjanski (1992: 155). Lodge (1985: 204) characterizes the debate on EC institutions at the Milan summit as being 'the direct result and culmination of the European Parliament's pressure to reform EC decisionmaking in line with its draft Treaty establishing the European Union'. Biehl (1988: 64), however, speaks of a failure of the European Parliament's constitutional initiative; he states that the SEA has a different, namely intergovernmental, character.

preparations for the southern enlargement, it was primarily the demands for special clauses by Greece and the United Kingdom that burdened the EC political system. PASOK, winner of the 1981 elections in Greece, had promised a referendum on EC membership during its election campaign and demanded a special status for Greece in the EC, justified with reference to its comparatively lower level of economic development. During the preparation of the EC budget for 1980, the prospect of the United Kingdom having to pay about 20 per cent of the member states' financial contributions and only receiving about 10 per cent of the community's expenditure appeared. This was mainly due to the fact that the agricultural sector in the United Kingdom is much smaller and thus receives comparatively much less 'profit' from the common agricultural policy, which at that time was still about three-quarters of the EC budget. The conservative Thatcher government made this a central issue, which dominated all European Council meetings up until Fontainebleau (June 1984). The government's pertinacity and political inconsiderateness on this question led to one of the worst paralysations of the EC apparatus for five years. Whether justified or not, the battle-cry 'I want my money back!' was traumatically imprinted on the memories of many people who were active in the EC political system at that time, as we gathered from practically all the interviews.

Two developments in 1983 were of great importance for the preparation of the integration thrust. First, in April 1983 the European Roundtable of Industrialists (ERT) was founded, and thus for the first time a transnational coalition of large-scale entrepreneurs that could directly influence further EC development was under way (see chapter 7). Secondly, the French government definitively abandoned 'Keynesianism in one country' and reoriented its European policy.

The French project of a European relaunch

By the second year of the French left government, the necessity for medium- to long-term alternative strategic concepts had emerged. In June 1982 – the month of the first austerity measures – a working group of officials from the Commissariat du Plan and the foreign ministry, of scientists and of industrial and trade union representatives was established. This working group had to evaluate 'the areas where and the states with which it would be desirable to start negotiations to establish agreements or programmes of cooperation by taking into account the action of the EC' (our translation), with reference to the preparation of the ninth plan (1984–8).

The final report, *Quelle stratégie européenne pour la France dans les années 80?*,[16] was presented in April 1983. The reason for its suggestions is its analysis that no West European country is capable of mastering the large challenges on its own, namely Europe's decreasing competitiveness in the triad competition, the micro-electronic revolution, the employment problem and the crisis of social systems. Only European initiatives could prevent the decline into an 'economic balkanization' (p. 29). The suggested measures included the creation of a large market (by eliminating non-tariff trade barriers), which, however, must be defended against the outside. They also focused on the promotion of technological research and development as well as industrial cooperation. This was closely linked to the proposed creation of a 'social Europe', since this would be the only way to overcome workers' resistance to technological innovation (p. 35).

The report acknowledged the widespread scepticism concerning a new launch of the project for a 'social Europe', due in no small part to the history of the French memorandum for a European social area in 1981. That memorandum advocated EC-wide cooperation in employment policy; it was practically ignored – with the exception of support from the socialist European parliamentary group and Danish interest in some of the social policy suggestions – and was never discussed in the Council. The report made the point that an *'ambiguïté fondamentale'* existed toward the precise role of the European level (p. 177). At the institutional level, a return to majority decisions in the Council of Ministers was suggested in certain cases, 'tout en respectant l'esprit du compromis de Luxembourg' ('respecting the spirit of the Luxembourg Compromise'; p. 86). A revision of the treaty, the report said, would not necessarily be required for this. The report also suggested a Europe with different integration speeds (*Europe différenciée*) if there was resistance to further integration steps. Additionally, the Commission presidency should be strengthened.

Jacques Moreau, president of the working group,[17] emphasized that the present construction of Europe had been developed along the German–French axis and that it was to be expected that Germany

[16] Secrétariat d'Etat auprès du Premier Ministre and Commissariat Général du Plan (1983). On the background of French European policy, see especially Uterwedde (1988), Wurm (1993), Lequesne (1993) and Gerbet (1995).

[17] It can be said of Jacques Moreau that he embodied the French integration project. A socialist and trade unionist (CFDT) like Delors, he was elected Delors' successor in 1981 as chairman of the European Parliament's Economic and Monetary Affairs Committee (1981–84); at the same time he was a member of the European Parliament's institutional committee that elaborated the draft of the treaty, then adviser to the Delors Commission and later president of the Economic and Social Committee (1988–92). He complains that the institutional dimension of European integration was neglected in this report (interview on 18 September 1996).

would continue to be available for a '*projet commun*'. This question should be the main focus of France's European strategy, according to Moreau (p. 17f). The report played an important role in preparing the French presidency of the Council in the first six months of 1984.

Mitterrand had already made a 'basic decision for Europe' (Grosser 1989: 386) – the franc was to remain within the European Monetary System – without consulting the minister for European affairs (Lequesne 1993: 62). In the course of 1983, French European policy increasingly became an 'inner-circle topic' which was discussed among a very small number of top politicians. The huge power of the French president, due to his constitutional position, enables such processes. According to Haywood (1993: 281), 'all Mitterrand's major Euro-initiatives have been kept secret until the last minute'. Shortly before the beginning of the French Council presidency, Mitterrand nominated a close confidant, Roland Dumas, as the new minister for European affairs. This was linked to a distinct up-grading of the European affairs ministry (Lequesne 1993: 64).

Especially in Bonn, these changes were carefully observed – and understood. According to Genscher, the German embassy in Paris considered Dumas' nomination to be a decision of great importance for European policy. They knew of the close friendship between Dumas and Mitterrand (Genscher 1995: 367). Another directive decision by Mitterrand was also of great importance for the re-establishment of German–French confidence. A high-level German diplomat told us in an interview that 'the unspoken, atmospheric reservations' against Mitterrand – that he might be a 'windiger Geselle' ('dubious fellow') – began to melt away as the break with the communists became predictable.

The take-off, 1984

With the economic policy convergence, a Single Market started to emerge as the main project of a new integration thrust. However, it was still a long way to a comprehensive package solution to revitalize European integration. The projects differed tremendously as regards the necessity and the scope of an institutional reform of the Community. Additionally, there were varying concepts of the Community's role in industrial policy and the harmonization of regulations as a necessary follow-up to the realization of the Single Market.

First of all, the problems that were paralysing any further progress had to be solved: (a) the British desires for budgetary correctives; (b) the necessary increase in financial resources; and (c) control of agricultural expenses. Mitterrand took an important, active role in this process, a role that can only partially be explained by the French Council presidency. He actually assumed the political entrepreneurship owing to the lack of confidence that the Commission enjoyed at that time. It is generally noted that in 1984 Mitterrand preferred to discuss his projects in bilateral talks with other heads of government.[18] In Brussels, it was often commented that the Commission had become the secretariat of the Council of Ministers. The series of special negotiations that had already been started in 1983 was thus continued. According to De Ruyt (1989), who claims that the genesis of the SEA began with the French Council presidency, the numerous bilateral contacts (instead of Council meetings) emerged as a new way of dealing with problems.

The British perceived increasing chances of an answer to their demands. Thatcher (1993: 537) writes that she hoped for a shift in Mitterrand's position, the French president being 'someone who relished a diplomatic success and would probably be prepared to sacrifice French national interests – at least marginally – in order to secure one'. As a reason for the French efforts to solve the budget question, Foreign Secretary Howe (1994: 399) reveals the fact that France was facing the transition to becoming a net contributor to the Community budget.

It took another failed summit to aggravate the situation (Brussels, March 1984). Then the United Kingdom, facing increasing pressure from other member countries, realized that a compromise had to be found to stay in the game. According to Taylor (1989: 8; see Moravcsik 1998: 351), the British took the French threats of a *Europe différenciée* seriously.

Mitterrand used a series of occasions to advertise the French initiative. His speech to the European Parliament in May 1984 was especially important, where he said: 'A new situation calls for a new treaty ... which must not, of course, be a substitute for existing treaties, but an extension of them to fields they do not currently cover. ... France, ladies and gentlemen, is available for such an entreprise.'[19] For Mitterrand, this included a restriction of the national power of veto to 'specific' cases, not its general abolition. Once again he emphasized the necessity of a 'Europe of different speeds or variable geometry'.

[18] E.g. Stadlmann (1984: 451); see Kohl in *Europa-Archiv* 10–1984, D287.
[19] In Gazzo (1985: 85). According to De Ruyt (1989: 49), this speech was understood as a 'coup d'envoi de la nouvelle initiative institutionelle'. Again, a few interpretations see this speech as replying to the European Parliament's draft treaty. In my opinion, because of the coincidence in time, Mitterrand appears to be referring to it purely rhetorically. This is revealed by the fact that the French initiative had a strong intergovernmental orientation; in particular, it did not consider an extension of the European Parliament's role.

At the European Council in Fontainebleau in June 1984, the budget problem was solved.[20] The British agreed to a compromise suggestion elaborated through close German–French cooperation (see Genscher 1995: 370). This compromise solution did not indicate a fundamental agreement on the future development of the EC, but it did mean that the way to further reform was no longer obstructed. The heads of state and government followed Mitterrand's suggestion (Lequesne 1993: 148) and established an Ad Hoc Committee for Institutional Affairs (the so-called Dooge Committee) to discuss institutional issues of the future reform. Members of this committee were personal representatives of the heads of state and government as well as representatives of the Commission. Therefore, as Mitterrand explained after Fontainebleau, the committee stood 'outside traditional structures', even though still linked to the Commission.[21] The 'special path' was thus continued. The work in the Dooge Committee soon showed that the European Parliament's draft treaty, despite Parliament's demands, would not be used as a basis for negotiations between member states.

Therefore, the beginning of the constitution of the Luxembourg package can be dated to mid-1984 (see Moravcsik 1991: 39; 1998: 352, 360f). But that goal was still a long way ahead. Another development during the French Council presidency was also of great importance: the course for a new Commission was set.

The rebirth of the Commission

The Commission under Gaston Thorn, like all Commissions since the Luxembourg Compromise, was suffering strongly restricted capacities to act. Emil Noël, secretary-general of the Commission, describes this as follows:

From being the moving spirit or arbitrator when the Council could decide by qualified majority only upon a Commission proposal, it found itself relegated to the role of a mere technical adviser when unanimity became the rule. The result was, irrespective of the calibre of the Commissioners and the Commission's President, the Commission's influence dwindled and the supreme power of the Council was confirmed, although the Council was unable to make full use of this power. (1987: 5)[22]

---

[20] The agreement to the complex package cannot be reported here, though it can be reconstructed quite easily; see especially *Europa-Archiv* 15-1984, Ungerer (1984), Butler (1986).
[21] In his press conference on 26 June, 1984 (*Europa-Archiv* 15-1984, D445).
[22] However, George (1991: 15) states that a re-strengthening of the EC Commission that already started with the assignment of Commission president Roy Jenkins, who carried out a fundamental reform of the internal structure of the Commission. Thorn completed it and established a basis for Delors' policy.

Several times, Thorn tried to start institutional reform initiatives, in vain. With the *Cassis de Dijon* decision which the European Court of Justice ruled in 1979, the Commission had actually been given a strong weapon for achieving a Single Market. Its importance was realized only after a second judgment in 1980. During the recession, the Commission was very cautious about applying it, and it was not until 1984 that it increasingly made references to the judgment.[23] The most important achievements of the Commission were in research and development policy, with the Esprit project, an initiative of Commissioner Etienne Davignon (chapter 4).

The previous history of the Delors Commission begins with Mitterrand's diplomatic offensive in spring 1984. The political diary of Mitterrand's adviser, Jacques Attali, allows a precise reconstruction of how the president achieved Germany's approval of a French president of the Commission, even though it should have been a German according to implicit rules (see Howe 1994: 404). In bilateral talks, Mitterrand ruled out the most promising candidate, Etienne Davignon, who had been the most prominent member of the previous Commission. According to Attali (1993: 617), Mitterrand spoke to Belgian Prime Minister Martens mentioning his scepticism about Davignon; he said Davignon was accused of being too America-friendly and was also from the European aristocracy. Be that as it may, towards the end of the French Council presidency, the list of candidates for the Commission presidency consisted of two important French politicians, both of whom had been ministers in the Mauroy government until the middle of 1984: ex-Foreign Minister Claude Cheysson and Jacques Delors.

Delors appeared more likely to embody an imaginary centre of the different political landscapes in the EC than Cheysson. Furthermore, Delors' central role in the implementation of the French austerity policy had received high marks from other national governments as well as from political adversaries. Delors had been 'credited with reining back the initial left-wing socialist policies of President Mitterrand's Government and with putting French finances on a sounder footing' (Thatcher 1993: 547, see also Howe 1994: 404). Thus Delors' candidacy also found support in London.[24]

It became clear to Delors on his 'inaugural journey' through the

---

[23] This was indicated to me by Jacques Pelkmans, who also made me realize that the application of this judgment presupposed enormous mutual confidence among the member states.

[24] See also Attali (1993: 651). Thatcher initially supported the candidacy of Davignon (Attali 1993: 659).

capitals of the EC member states[25] that the completion of the EC internal market by means of deregulation, as proposed by European business representatives, must become the sole undisputed core of the new thrust toward integration.

The politics of Jacques Delors

Referring to Delors' role, it is often pointed out that 'the initiative' had already been prepared before the new Commission's assumption of office. Here again, a distinction must be made: the Single Market project was indeed practically elaborated (see chapter 3); but the question of how far and which institutional reforms it should be linked to was by no means solved. Additionally, and Delors knew this, the Single Market project could only be enforced in a package together with integration steps in other policy areas, especially 'flanking measures'. Personally he had already consistently endorsed the Common Market as the only basis for a project opposed to the decline of Europe. In contrast to the views of some national governments and interest groups, however, for Delors as well as for the French government, the creation of an internal market was not an end in itself. As the Commission president often repeated: 'on ne tombe pas amoureux d'un grand marché!' ('One does not fall in love with a big market!') An increased comprehension of Delors' policy and its motives is necessary, since he strongly determined the Commission's integration project from 1985 until the Maastricht Summit and beyond.

As a minister in the Mauroy government, Delors explained his basic orientation in economic policy in an article in 1981 as a careful dose of different instruments: cautious stimulation of the national budget; a socially fairer tax system, which encourages saving and entrepreneurial initiative; an active employment policy (training, mobility, job placement); an anti-inflationary monetary policy; a more differentiated credit policy, connected with structural reforms with the goal of effective decentralization and market competition; and flexible planning aimed at structural recovery, which would make it possible to take advantage of the achievements of the new industrial revolution. The goal is a largely decentralized economy, in which a functioning market and planning based on incentives are mutually reinforcing, which in turn concentrates power on the most important national goals (Delors 1981: 107f).

A central aspect of his concept was *concertation*, the involvement of 'social partners' in the formulation and implementation of political

[25] He met with heads of state and government and with national parliamentarians, as well as with trade union leaders and employers; see Delors (1992); Ross (1995a).

programmes. As minister of finance he invited entrepreneurs and union representatives to talks, and in the interest of the trade unions advanced a law based on the Swedish model concerning the arrangement of wage-earner funds (*fonds salariaux*).

In contrast to many other French politicians, including those in his own party, the EC and in particular the Common Market had always played an important, positive role in Delors' politics. In his 1981 article on the situation in France he wrote that, in order to withstand the external challenge, France not only must get on with the tasks of the 1980s, it must also be able to count on the fact that European cooperation will develop positively, whereby the domains of industry, energy and research receive priority and do so on the basis of a genuine common market. Likewise, according to Delors (1981: 107), the EC must absolutely pursue a common external policy if it is to strengthen its autonomy and to secure its future.

Because of the unusual position of the political current in the so-called *Deuxième Gauche* to which Delors belongs, it is useful to examine its roots, looking at Delors' political biography.[26] Delors' view of the world was stamped by *personalisme*, a progressive form of Catholic social doctrine, which demarcates itself from liberal, utilitarian individualism and from the communist collectivism. Its emphasis on agreement, balancing competing interests, and cooperation between different societal groups was surely a root of Delors' project. Delors became involved in a union, the Confédération Française et Démocratique du Travail (CFDT) and became a director in its research department. In 1961 he published an article entitled 'A Trade Union Approach to the Commissariat au Plan', the central French planning apparatus. In this article he proposed an annual meeting of the government, the employers and the unions, which would fix a minimum wage and an average level of wage increases. In return for being fully associated with the planning process – what he called 'democratic planning' – the unions would accept binding agreements. This was Delors' stepping stone to the French Commissariat du Plan.

In France at this time there was still no such *politique contractuelle*, the analogue to the Swedish and German neocorporatist model. In February 1968, on the basis of a report by Delors and François-Xavier Ortoli (later to become EC Commission president), tripartite talks were held under Pompidou, where for the first time employers and the communist trade union, CGT, sat together at the same table. Chaban-Delmas, the reform-minded prime minister under Pompidou, summoned Delors as a

[26] Biographical details from Grant (1994) and Ross (1995a).

consultant on social affairs. From this position Delors strongly advocated the development of a *politique contractuelle*. The talks resulted in approximately sixty so-called *Contrats de Progrès*, company agreements between employers and unions over wage increases, working hours and other issues.

'*Social-delorisme*' (a term coined by the French magazine *L'Express*), understood as a political current within the *Deuxième Gauche*, was characterized from the beginning by its basic reformist attitude and its affirmation of the market mechanism in combination with social responsibility. Another basic tenet was a belief in the superiority of *concertation* as opposed to administrative management. A certain proximity to German or Swedish social democratic models cannot be overlooked.

After joining the Socialist Party under Mitterrand, Delors entered its circle of experts, where he took over the area concerned with international economics. Beginning in 1976 Delors served for three years as a representative in the French National Assembly. In 1979 he was elected to the European Parliament, where he was chairman of the economic and monetary affairs committee. He belonged to the so-called Amigo Group of social democratic parliament members, which included among others Ripa Di Meana of Italy (later a member of the Dooge Committee and the Delors Commission); Piet Dankert of the Netherlands (later president of the European Parliament); and Jacques Moreau.

Although the new integration launch had to start with the economic sphere, it was always Delors' aim to bring the project back into 'balance' ('*rééquilibrer*') to achieve the primacy of politics (Delors 1992: 17). For Delors, European cooperation is the fight not only against economic decline but also against social regression (Delors 1992: 70). The 'European societal model' (*le modèle européen de société*) has a central orientation function for Delors; it is characterized by values such as solidarity, a high level of social protection, and *concertation* of all partners in production. It is no surprise that one of Delors' first measures as Commission president was to revive the social dialogue at the European level (see chapter 6).

As the only supranational political entrepreneur, a 'corporate actor' (Coleman 1990) with established political independence, fully developed rights of initiative and thereby great possibilities in agenda-setting, the Commission was well suited for implementing Delors' project. 'Intelligent maximalism' is the institutional duty of the Commission.[27] Delors conceived the Commission in its central role as '*ingénieur de la*

[27] A term used by Ross (1995a: 95). For further evidence regarding the role of the Commission, see Louis and Waelbroeck (1989), Ludlow (1991), Hrbek (1996) and

construction européenne' (engineer of European construction) and made it clear from the time he took office that the Commission's right of initiative would be fully utilized (Delors 1992: 46). It must develop the capacity to exhaust its restricted possibilities as far as they are given by the treaties and allowed by the intergovernmental context.

Ross (1995a: 158ff) speaks of a 'Delorist leadership system'. There was a gradual, but wholesale, change of administrative leadership at Directorate General level. Nearly all newly appointed people enjoyed the confidence of Delors and his cabinet. Delors' cabinet was the backbone of the system. Larger than that of other Commissioners, it included about ten people, three-quarters of whom were French, many coming from the French Socialist Party and/or the CFDT. The head of cabinet, Pascal Lamy, whose view of the world was also derived from a left-Catholic standpoint, had worked with Delors in the French ministry of finance and had participated there in the preparation of the economic change of course in 1982–3. The non-French members were recruited predominantly from EC Directorates General. When necessary, his cabinet bypassed those of other Commissioners and established parallel networks to achieve the desired results. Delors' hierarchical, centralized managerial system also attracted, hardly surprisingly, internal and external criticism ('Bonapartism').

The question of which integration steps in which policy areas and of which institutional reforms could be linked to the Single Market project was decisive for the Delors Commission right from the beginning. According to Cameron (1992: 51), 'by broadening the range of issues to be discussed', Delors created 'the possibility for bargains, trade-offs, and alliances to be struck across the issues of market reform and institutional reform'.[28] On the basis of the considerations in this chapter, this means no less than creating the possibility of a package solution and thus the adoption of the entire Luxembourg package, *including* the Single Market project.

The Commission not only had the confidence of the national governments, but also planned its work with an exact knowledge of what was possible by exhausting all available means. It had a new strong

Cini (1996); for the institutional prerequisites of the Commission's capacity to act, see Schmidt (1998: 49ff).

[28] Cameron (1992: 51) goes even further: 'Moreover, in proposing an intergovernmental conference on the two subjects of reform, Delors and his Commission succeeded in giving the internal market initiative the aura of progressive, democratizing reform. The conflation of market enlargement and institutional reform may have further promoted the internal market initiative by attracting it to some segments of the political elite and the public who would otherwise have been opposed to it or, at best, indifferent.' I do not think that it was the institutional progress achieved by the SEA that was attractive to the 'federalists'; rather it was the inherent possibilities of an extended dynamics.

leadership, which indeed actually enabled the Commission's important role in the constitution of the Luxembourg package in the first place.

Tying up the Luxembourg package

The previous sections have shown how the prerequisites for the adoption of the Luxembourg package were each fulfilled step by step in the years preceding 1985: relative political convergence, the overcoming of the paralysing obstructions and blockades, and the rebirth of the Commission as political entrepreneur. In this section, the dynamics of the SEA negotiations will be reviewed. Since only a survey of a much broader research project can be given in the following, I have chosen to present this synopsis in a table. First of all, however, I shall make a few preliminary methodological remarks.

As mentioned at the outset, a heterogeneous treaty such as the Single Act must be broken down into its individual parts. But even if the individual elements are analysed, it is not easy to determine the 'authorship'. How can this question be 'operationalized'? Surely, the most important indicator for doing this is the extent to which one or several actors are interested in a *dossier*, in the advances and initiatives as well as the 'ambition' of the project. The content of a political initiative has to be compared with the outcome, in this case Council decisions and the SEA's final version. Then it can be decided which has been enforced in principle, partially, and/or modified within the entire compromise.

With such an evaluation, for example, the extraordinary importance of the cooperation between the Commission and the European Roundtable of Industrialists regarding the Single Market project can be proved. Or it can be shown that the two French initiatives of 1981 (*espace social européen*, or European social area) and 1983 (*espace industriel européen*, or European industrial area) were relevant for the content of the SEA to extremely different extents'.

Of course, not all elements of the SEA can be traced back to a particular, concrete initiative, especially on questions of the further institutional development of the EC (e.g. majority voting in the Council, European Parliament rights). These have often been on the agenda permanently or repeatedly since the foundation of the EC, and are part of a general reform debate. However, the integration projects of the different governments and of the transnational and supranational actors can be reconstructed relatively well on the basis of their bargaining position and suggestions before and during negotiations.

Furthermore, the EC's institutional characteristics, especially rules of procedure, have to be considered when determining the 'authorship'.

For example, as mentioned above, the country holding the Council presidency has a decisive organizational initiative function (first half-year of 1985 Italy, second half-year Luxembourg). Then there is the extraordinary role of the EC Commission: Even though an intergovernmental conference strengthens the role of the national governments and their Permanent Representatives compared with the normal EC decision-making process, the Commission, if it has the political and organizational capability, can play a strategically important role. In the case of the Luxembourg conference, the Commission anticipated proposals from member states in some areas. The member states forwent submitting proposals or made only amendments. Naturally, this renders the evaluation of 'authorship' more complicated.

'Deconstructing' the Single Act, it must never be forgotten that the package could be adopted only as a whole.

The decision for an intergovernmental conference: Pandora's box is opened

In March 1985, the Dooge Committee presented its final report.[29] The committee had evaluated the possible content of a project for the 'establishment of a political unity' (preface). The following aims were given priority:

- creating a genuine internal market by the end of the decade on the basis of a precise timetable, the immediate mutual recognition of national standards, the free movement of capital and the creation of a European financial market, hand in hand with the strengthening of the European monetary system, the promotion of economic convergence and the creation of a technological Community;
- promoting the common values of civilization: measures to protect the environment, the gradual achievement of a European social area (dialogue between employers and employees, regulatory harmonization, promotion of common cultural values);
- searching for an external identity by strengthening political and security cooperation.

On the basis of the submitted reservations and added remarks by individual representatives of heads of state and government, the controversial points can easily be identified. Apart from very frequent reservations by the Danish and Greek representatives, there are also German reservations about a further development of the monetary policy and about economic policy convergence, and Irish reservations about cooperation in foreign policy (security policy). However, the most

[29] Ad Hoc Committee for Institutional Affairs, Report to the European Council, Brussels, 29–30 March 1985, Luxembourg 1985.

important disagreements occurred concerning institutional reform. On the question of the voting procedure in the Council, the Danish, Greek and British representatives were against the establishment of a new general principle that decisions should be made by qualified or simple majority. British and Greek reservations were also submitted against the extension of the European Parliament's functions. The report ends with the suggestion of an intergovernmental conference to negotiate the draft treaty on European Union.

The following months were characterized by a Franco-German-Italian accord on taking a qualitative step forward (possibly via a new treaty) at Milan (Lodge 1985) on the one hand and by a strong diplomatic offensive by the United Kingdom to prevent an intergovernmental conference on the other hand.

The British integration project[30] focused on two elements: the internal market and increased cooperation in external policy. In the memorandum *The British Government's Approach*, the following was outlined:

The United Kingdom wants to see greater European unity. Within the European Community this means Europe united as a single market. We also want unity in dealing with the outside world: a Europe united in its approach to external policy, which not only consults together but acts together and is seen by others as a cohesive political entity.[31]

To reach these aims, an intergovernmental conference was not considered necessary. It was even considered dangerous, since it would, as Foreign Secretary Howe put it, open a 'Pandora's box' full of federalist-oriented suggestions for changing the treaty. To establish a Single Market, the British suggested a legally non-binding gentlemen's agreement on the inclusion of national vetoes on these questions, which hardly found an audience.[32]

The Italian government wanted to enforce a decision for an intergovernmental conference within its Council presidency.[33] Article 236 of

[30] On the background and history of British European policy, see especially Volle (1989a, b), George (1990) and Wurm (1993).
[31] Memorandum for the House of Lords Select Committee on the European Communities: *European Union*, prepared by the Foreign and Commonwealth Office; in Select Committee on European Legislation, *21st Report, Session 1984–85*, Appendix; citation on p. 21.
[32] 'Many times I explained this informal 'British' approach to groups of bewildered continental parliamentarians, for whom charters, declarations, solemn acts, single acts, constitutions even, were their real *raison d'être*' (Howe 1994: 408).
[33] The strategy of the Italian government was known and the Milan decision was predictable. In May, Foreign Minister Andreotti, after informal consultations in the various capitals, presented a 'draft mandate for the Intergovernmental Conference' to his colleagues. He also explained his intentions in an article in *Corriere della Sera* on 25 June 1985 (both documents in Gazzo 1985). See, in contrast, Howe (1994: 409).

the Treaty of Rome enables the convening of an intergovernmental conference by majority decision in the Council.[34] The 'federalist bloc' strongly supported this procedure. They knew that the decision of the French government, which was ambivalent concerning the question of institutional reform, would be decisive. From the point of view of the Danish diplomat Møller, who had been a representative on the Dooge Committee: 'They rightly targeted France as the key to the whole issue. If they could swing France to support a conference to amend the Treaty, they reckoned they would rally the original six member states (plus Ireland) against the sceptical and reticent British, Danes and Greeks' (Møller 1988: 195).

In close German–French cooperation, the positions in the different policy areas were coordinated, and extended by talks with the Italian government. A series of ambitious suggestions by the federalists were victims of this procedure. The governments of the three Benelux countries also met to formulate a common position. They focused on institutional reform, especially the generalization of majority voting in the Council, and the extension of the competences of the Commission and of the European Parliament. They demanded decisions concerning a single market and a common technology policy in order to mobilize the whole European technological potential and to strengthen the European Monetary System and its further development.

Meanwhile, the Commission was very busily elaborating its proposals. At the Milan Summit (28/29 June 1985), it presented the White Paper on Completing the Internal Market and a memorandum for a technological community, and both met acceptance. As foreseen, the Italian president, Craxi, demanded a vote on convening an intergovernmental conference, which was actually adopted against votes from the United Kingdom, Denmark and Greece. This led to a dramatic situation (see Genscher 1995: 373; Thatcher 1993: 548ff). France and Ireland had changed sides, which was decisive. From Møller's point of view:

> There is no reason to underestimate the significance of this event. It meant a fundamental swing in France's European policy and tilted the balance between member states. France had hitherto pursued a sceptical or negative line towards an institutional reform. Now France was ready to negotiate such a reform, albeit without specifying how far it was prepared to go. (Møller 1988: 196)

Milan was the stage for the decision to link the realization of the Single Market project to institutional reform. Pandora's box was opened. This extension of the reform process was a prerequisite for the

---

[34] Definitely an important institutional prerequisite for the integration thrust of the 1980s. It is a speculation, but an interesting one, to imagine the development if unanimity had been prescribed – the *Europe differenciée*?

acceptance of the Single Market and put it into a broader context (see Cameron 1992: 56). This may have brought the definitive support of all those who had favoured the Genscher–Colombo initiative, the Stuttgart Declaration and the draft treaty of the European Parliament.

The intergovernmental conference: the 'chainsaw massacre'[35]

As early as July 1985, the Luxembourg Council presidency presented a first draft treaty. In September, the two working groups in charge of preparing the conference were constituted: the Dondelinger Group for the revision of the treaties, and the Political Committee for 'political cooperation' (common foreign policy). Without much effect, the European Parliament recollected its own draft treaty in its statement at the inauguration of the intergovernmental conference (IGC) and demanded to be included in the elaboration of the treaty.

At the first meeting of the intergovernmental conference, on 9 October 1985 in Luxembourg, Commission president Delors recalled the meaning of this act with dramatic words and presented the integration project of the Commission. He announced proposals in the following areas: the internal market, technological research and development, the environment, economic and social cohesion, the powers of the Commission and the European Parliament, monetary aspects and culture. Concerning the areas of energy, industry and health policy, the Commission forwent presenting proposals as it assumed that progress could also be made in these areas without amendments to the treaty (*EC Bulletin* 9–1985, 1.1.1).

In principle, the bulk of these proposals was already in the Commission's programme for 1985. Yet, the Commission's active role and the extent of its proposals was still a surprise for many. In this way, the Commission helped to define the agenda and dissuaded many governments from putting forward ideas of their own.

According to Delors, the conference table would have remained empty during the first six to eight weeks if the Commission had not presented any proposals. He defined four areas in which the Commission wanted to concentrate on the extension of the EC's competences: the Single Market, research and technological development, economic and social cohesion, and a 'certain monetary capacity' ('*capacité*

---

[35] The reconstruction of the intergovernmental conference is based mainly on interviews with political actors, periodical EC bulletins, the documents in Gazzo (1985, 1986), newspaper articles, Kramer (1985), Gulman (1987), De Zwaan (1986), De Ruyt (1989), Grant (1994), Attali (1993), Ross (1995a), and Middlemas (1995).

monétaire'). The last area was Delors' careful term for the *dossier* with the least chance of being adopted.

The most remarkable element of the Commission proposals is 'economic and social cohesion'. This area had not appeared in the negotiations before the intergovernmental conference. In the Commission programme for 1985, the project for a 'European social area' and regional aid were separate. The Commission also did not present any proposals on social policy as such. On the one hand, this is surely connected to the role that the Commission allotted to the social dialogue. On the other hand, I also interpret this as an expression of Delors' strategy of bundling up these politically sensitive areas into an additional package of 'flanking measures' with a new title. The aim was to tie these areas as closely as possible to the core project, the Single Market, not least as a result of the experience of the 1981 French initiative for a social area. Delors also argued in this way in presenting the Commission's project. The Commission assumed that realizing the Single Market would have negative effects if there were no supporting measures. From his point of view, supporting measures were: the development of less privileged regions, the improvement of employment possibilities and of living and working conditions, the promotion of social innovation and the transformation of declining sectors. As well as transferring finances, he wanted a coordination of national economic policies. The embodiment of the Commission project would have entrusted the Community institutions with a relatively comprehensive welfare state mandate.

The strategy of creating a 'supporting package' did not work. Ireland, Italy and Greece rejected the 'overloaded' cohesion package, and demanded concentration on the interstate transfer of resources. It was not just the wealthier member states – for fear of massive expansions of the redistribution of resources – that rejected the transfer of competences in economic policy; Greece rejected this as well. Additionally, the strategy was foiled, especially as regards the harmonization of social policy, when the British enforced the explicit non-application of majority voting concerning workers' rights and interests (Art. 100a).[36]

Owing to the initiative of the Danish government, social policy was actually discussed after all during the conference, with the effect that

---

[36] This suggested interpretation takes into account the position of the peripheral states, thus explaining what Moravcsik (1991: 46, 1998: 372) describes as follows: 'in late September and early October 1985, Delors dropped strong advocacy of monetary and social reform and chose to stress instead the links between internal market reform, majority voting, and the increases in structural funds needed to gain support from Ireland and the Southern countries.'

occupational health and safety were linked to the core project (see chapter 6).

In addition to the Commission's political entrepreneurship, German–French cooperation also played an important role during the intergovernmental conference. Thatcher (1993: 552) writes that 'the Franco-German axis was again as strong as it had been under President Giscard and Chancellor Schmidt'. This was the case on all levels, not just at the higher level of the European Council, where – at joint working breakfasts – Mitterrand and Kohl 'prestructured' the following meetings.

During the intergovernmental conference the fact was reconfirmed that nothing could be enforced against the will of Germany and/or France. The political power of Italy and the Benelux states was insufficient to balance, together with the Commission, German or French doubts and reservations. Furthermore, as soon as the German–French cooperation weakened, the intergovernmental conference lacked a driving force to turn the Commission's far-reaching proposals into generally acceptable treaty texts. A political observer explained that the reason success can be achieved only in the event of German–French agreement is because all measures either cost Bonn money or restrict Parisian sovereignty.

In October, a European Parliament delegation took the floor at the intergovernmental conference. The European Parliament had actually been regularly informed about the state of affairs. However, the delegation criticized the non-observance of the Parliament's draft treaty and called for stronger participation in the final work of the conference. In particular, the planned improvements in the European Parliament's competences were considered to be absolutely insufficient.

The Council presidency stated in its interim results that most delegations considered it vital to preserve the present institutional balance and thus not to alter the distribution of powers between the different Community institutions. Other delegations pointed out that it would be difficult to avoid making some adjustment to the present institutional balance if the envisaged reform was to have any real substance.

In some areas an agreement was achieved quickly, especially concerning the extension of foreign policy cooperation, which had been planned as a separate treaty for some time. The environmental regulations, where majority decisions were not proposed, also caused no difficulties.

Within the internal market *dossier*, a lot of harmonization proposals were left out. The British, who advocated the principle of fiscal competition, fought successfully against the planned tax harmonization. The safeguard clauses referring to the Single Market threatened to multiply during the conference. The fact that these were again reduced is attributable to Delors' efforts and his German–French support. The Danish and the German governments in particular, anxious to avoid any lowering of their high national standards for health, safety and environmental protection, enforced the possibility of maintaining higher national protection standards in these areas.

On the question of financing the Community research and technology policy, Delors complained about an 'unusual coalition of those who do not want to do much and those who fear that money will go into this area instead of into structural funds' (press conference on 27 November 1985, in Gazzo 1986: 83ff). The most disputed issues were the question of European Parliament rights and the monetary policy *dossier*.

Delors described the way the concept of an *'espace organisé'*, an 'organized area' (as it was understood by the Commission), was dealt with – its increasing reduction to deregulation – as a 'chainsaw massacre' (ibid.).

During the final phase of the intergovernmental conference, unified pressure from the German–French duo was again desperately needed, as well as several rings of the alarm bell from the Commission, for the completion of the package. This was not achieved until the 28-hour meeting of the European Council in Luxembourg itself (2/3 December 1985). Even after intensive negotiations by the foreign ministers at the weekends preceding the summit, some points had remained unclear.

Not until a follow-up meeting in the middle of December did Delors manage to unite the two areas (a common foreign policy and the other *dossiers*), which had been planned as two separate treaties for a long time, into an *Acte Unique*, or single document. The name of the package, which emphasizes the unity of the elements, was proposed by the Commission president. Table 2.1 presents an overview of the formation and development of political initiatives at the European level and, if relevant, how they are reflected in the Single European Act (SEA).

The SEA: 'Constitutional reform serving the Common Market'?

The Commission spokesman defined the SEA as a 'constitutional reform serving the Common Market' (Ehlermann 1988). This touches the core of the Luxembourg package, especially if qualified majority voting is used as an indicator of the transition to supranationality. The principle of qualified majority voting – the abolition of the 'veto culture'

Table 2.1. *The formation and development of political initiatives at European level and their expression in the Single European Act (SEA), 1981–1985*

Policy area:	Initiative(s)	Supporters[a]	Opponents[a]	Mode of agreement	Outcome
Single Market	Roundtable of Industrialists/Commission, White Paper adopted at Milan; submission to the IGC by the Commission			Consent; in dispute: range and scope of necessary harmonization; some reservations and temporary exemption clauses	Art. 13–19 SEA, Declaration nos. 3, 4, 6 (Annex SEA); Art. 8 a–c, 99, 100a, mod. Art. 57, 59, 70, 84 of the Treaties
Research and technology policy	Commission/Information Technology Roundtable (Esprit); F with German support (EUREKA); Commission submission adopted at Milan ('new technological dimension')[b]; submissions to IGC by Commission, G and DK	Benelux		Consent in principle; controversy over decision-making process (G, F, UK gave up rejection of majority voting; unanimity maintained for framework programmes; protection of net contributors)	Art. 24 SEA; Art. 130 f–q of the Treaties
Cohesion policy	Greek demands for more transfer payments; submissions F to IGC by Commission, IRL, F and GR	I (P, SP)	G, UK act as brake	Agreement by postponing question of amount of finances	Art. 23 SEA; Art. 130 a–e of the Treaties
Monetary policy (anchoring the European monetary system, monetary union as goal)	F, Commission; submissions to IGC by Commission, B, NL	I, LUX	G, UK, NL	Germany yielded; G and UK elaborated compromise suggestion as a last offer	Art. 20 SEA; Art. 102a of the Treaties
Social policy[c]	French initiative for a European social area (1981); submissions to IGC by DK, B, F and Commission		UK, G	Partial agreement with restrictions	Art. 21, 22 SEA; Art. 118a, b of the Treaties
Environment policy	Submissions to IGC by G, Commission and DK			Consent (unanimity rule maintained)	Art. 25 SEA, Declaration no. 9 (Annex SEA); Art. 130r–t of the Treaties

Issue	Initiative	Supporters	Outcome	Reference
Cultural policy	Submissions to IGC by Commission, NL and I		Could not be discussed any further owing to lack of time	–
Foreign policy cooperation	Genscher–Colombo initiative; British and German–French submission at Milan; submissions to IGC by I and NL		Consent; dispute over institutional organization	Art. 30 SEA
Institutional development:				
Change of treaty through IGC (according to Art. 236 of the Treaties)	European Parliament demand, Dooge Report; I, G	Benelux, IRL, F, Commission	UK, GR, DK	IGC 1985
Expansion of the executive competences of the Commission	Submission at Milan by Commission; submissions to IGC by Commission, NL	Benelux	Majority decision at Milan; opponents outnumbered	Art. 10 SEA, Declaration no. 1 (Annex SEA); Extension Art. 145 of the Treaties
Foreign policy cooperation: creation of a (separate) political secretariat	French proposal, part of German–French submission at Milan		Consent in principle, but necessity for change of treaty disputed; agreement by postponing fixing of implementation regulations	
Extension of European Parliament's competences	Genscher–Colombo initiative; German submission at Milan; submissions to IGC by G and B	Commission,[d] Benelux	Refused	–
Creation of the possibility of 'institutional differentiation'	French initiative; French submission to IGC	Commission, UK, F	Agreement to compromise suggestion: small extension of competences (so-called cooperation procedure)	Arts. 6–12 SEA
		Commission UK	Refused	–

[a] 'The table can be read only 'positively'; i.e. a blank under 'Supporters' or 'Opponents' does not mean that the initiative was not supported or opposed but that the data do not allow a secure and/or unequivocal identification.
[b] The Commission and the French government worked together in close cooperation after Milan to elaborate the initiative.
[c] See the detailed table 6.1 (p. 158).
[d] The Commission rejected the establishment of a separate secretariat, and demanded the 'uniformity of the institutions'.

Source: based on the analysis of primary sources, interviews with actors and secondary literature (see note 35).

– was not generally prescribed and was closely restricted to a few areas. The institutional reform thus remained closely circumscribed. The role of the supranational actors – the Commission and the European Parliament (see Bieber, Pantalis and Schoo 1986) – had been strengthened only to a very small extent.

The SEA is a package solution based on logrolling. The Single Market project had to include the interests of the countries with comparatively higher standards of protection (health, environment, etc.) as well as those of the economically less developed countries. As regards cohesion policy regulations, it was a question of setting up – under the Commission's clear leadership – the supporting measures of regional policy for the Single Market, i.e. compensatory payments for opening up markets in the Southern countries.

There was consent on embodying of research and technology policy in the treaties. The controversial question was the extent to which the interests of the three big contributors (Germany, France and the United Kingdom) were to be protected by maintaining the principle of unanimity voting. The smaller member countries and the Commission managed to enforce the introduction of majority voting on individual research projects (Art. 130q), while unanimity remains necessary for the adoption of framework programmes.[37]

The package character is also visible in respect to the inclusion of monetary policy regulations. Opposing this inclusion, Germany and the United Kingdom were confronted with a strong pressure group (France, Belgium and the Commission being the core). In the course of the conference, the German government realized that the entire package was in danger if such regulations were not included. Annoying the British, the German government gave up its principled resistance; through close cooperation between Germany and the United Kingdom, a compromise formula was elaborated beyond which both countries were not prepared to go. Even if this primarily stipulated the status quo, it did mean the explicit 'embodiment' of a *dossier*, an important prerequisite for further dynamics in this field.

Also, from the perspective of the individual countries it is evident that the SEA was a package solution based on logrolling. In exchange for the realization of the Single Market, the United Kingdom had to accept institutional reforms, the inclusion of new competences in the treaties as well as a predictable extension of regional compensation (cohesion policy). The British government did not consider the price too high and

---

[37] This outcome contradicts Moravcsiks' (1991) thesis that the SEA can be explained solely by an agreement among the three big member states, which had a policy focusing on the principle of the maintenance of sovereignty.

was therefore quite satisfied with what was achieved.[38] The bartering character is especially noticeable in a summarizing statement by the British foreign secretary, Howe (1994: 457), on the first stage of the integration thrust in the 1980s:

The Cockfield single-market programme was all put through pretty well on time and we were enabled to carry the free-market case into other fields – further than many of our partners had expected. On the other hand we found ourselves facing on some social and environmental matters a more extensive use of Community powers than we had regarded as foreseeable or legitimate. Both trends can probably be attributed to the impact of the Single European Act upon what might be called the 'culture' of the Community and its institutions. The habit of working together, of sharing sovereignty, of give and take, which we had so strongly urged for the Single Market was not something that could be ruthlessly confined.

However, it would be wrong to reduce the SEA to a barter between the United Kingdom and the other EC member states. The German government put aside political doubts concerning the regulatory orientation of the planned common technology policy and agreed to a future large financial burden, reluctantly accepted monetary policy provisions and had to accept distinct restrictions regarding the (desired) institutional reform. The original French integration project had a much stronger emphasis on intergovernmental cooperation. Although the initiative in technology policy can be considered partially a French success, their integration project was only weakly embodied in other areas. This includes social policy, and an extremely weak formulation emphasizing the goal of monetary union was adopted only after a huge effort.

The federalists, who were given some federalist rhetoric in the Preamble, criticized the outcome. The SEA was far from being the federalists' hoped-for 'quantum leap'. In particular the improvement of the position of the European Parliament was considered completely inadequate. The European Parliament stated that the SEA, 'in spite of the few improvements it contains, is far from establishing the European Union to which the Heads of State and of Government of the Member

[38] Thatcher wrote that she had been pleased with what had been achieved in terms of the content of the SEA and indicated that she had no regrets about having signed it. Majority voting for the enforcement of its core element, the creation of the Single Market, was accepted by all. In this manner the 'interests of Great Britain' were preserved: 'I had surrendered no important British interest . . . The first fruits of what would be called the Single European Act were good for Britain. At last, I felt, we were going to get the Community back on course, concentrating on its role as a huge market, with all the opportunities that would bring to our industries.' (Thatcher 1993: 555f). For Taylor (1989: 14) 'the SEA can be judged a considerable British achievement. In its details it reflected UK interests in a nuanced and comprehensive way.' See Wurm (1993: 347) and Middlemas (1995: 148).

States have repeatedly made formal commitments'[39]. For the Commission, the SEA was 'a compromise showing progress', even if on the whole it did not fulfil the Commission's hopes.[40] Delors announced the continuation of the Commission's strategy.

Those who advocated more ambitious integration projects felt that the negotiation process was disappointing on the whole; some even thought it had been a 'chainsaw massacre'. For these actors, however, it was more important that after several years of total stagnation there had been negotiations at all that offered the prospect of further integration steps. The price had been high, since the nation-state lost its regulating capacities as a result of the complete opening of the market, and their substitution at supranational level was (and is) rather insecure. It is precisely this dynamic perspective of certain actors that is decisive for understanding the beginning of the integration thrust in the 1980s; without it, the integration thrust of the 1980s, and especially the debate about the 'social dimension' and the project of economic and monetary union, cannot be understood.

On 16 January 1986, despite its harsh criticism, the European Parliament approved the SEA by 209 to 62 votes with 14 abstentions. The Italian government had made the European Parliament's approval a condition of its consent. The foreign ministers signed the SEA on 17 February 1986 in Luxembourg, with the exception of the Italian, Greek and Danish foreign ministers. These had to await the outcome of the Danish referendum on 27 February. The SEA was approved by 56.2 per cent of the Danish population, so that the last three foreign ministers signed the SEA.

Conclusion

In the first section, I suggested a list of conditions for the successfull constitution of a negotiation package:
(1) prerequisite: common elements in the integration projects due to relative convergence;
(2) political entrepreneurship and the formation of alliances;
(3) dynamizing factors: institutional procedures, projects to extend integration, strategic postponement.

The process that led to the conquest of previous obstacles to integration and to the constitution of a political package that could be adopted can be reconstructed as follows:

The implementation of a Single Market and technological coopera-

---

[39] European Parliament statement on 17 April 1986, in Gazzo (1986: 147f).
[40] *EC Bulletin* 12–1985, 1.1.1; see Gazzo (1986: 108f).

tion were the decisive common elements of the integration projects of the political and economic actors starting in 1983, after the collapse of the final attempt to revitalize the Keynesian societal model (point (1) above). Whether and to what extent these were to be linked to institutional reform was controversial. The decision in favour of an intergovernmental conference was enabled:

- because its opponents could not present a plausible alternative process for reaching the objective of a Single Market;
- because of the pressure from the 'federalist bloc' and the Commission, to whom the Single Market and institutional reform were part of a project for further integration and who received support from the French government for the extension of supranationality (point (2)),
- because of institutional mechanisms (majority decision for convening an intergovernmental conference) (point (3)).

With the opening of 'Pandora's box', a series of interested actors was able to elaborate initiatives in various policy areas, which were embodied in the Single European Act with varying success. In this process, the role of the Commission was important because its skillful policy management contributed a lot to opening *dossiers* and leaving them open, as well as finding compromise solutions (point (2)).

Studying the integration thrust in the 1980s shows that the Commission's treaty-based monopoly on initiatives does not apply in reality, especially in specific historical phases such as the years from 1983. Before the Commission's 'rebirth', political entrepreneurship was repeatedly taken up by individual national governments or certain 'blocks', sometimes even bypassing the Commission. This definitely changed during the preparatory phase of the 1985 intergovernmental conference. At an intergovernmental conference itself, the Commission's power is inevitably diminished, even if it exploits its role to the full, as it did in 1985.

Part of the Commission's newly won strength can surely be explained by the support from the German–French tandem; the entire reform dynamics is unthinkable without its pace-making function (point (2)). Additionally, the European economic elite supported the Commission in the two core areas, which gave the Commission special possibilities of influence. The Commission successfully established a campaign around the adopted Single Market programme to rehabilitate the EC as a whole.

The initiative was started from above, based on bargains between political and economic elites. This continued the tradition of European integration. Jacques Delors (1993: 3) defined it as the 'Jean Monnet method'. Accordingly, the method of the Community's founders amounted to a 'kind of enlightened despotic government':

Competence and freedom of the mind were seen as a sufficient legitimization for action; the subsequent consent of the population was considered adequate. The secret of success consisted of creating an inward dynamics, of clearing resistance to integration by bundling different economic interests together and enabling decisions on comprehensive negotiation packages. (Our translation)

This statement contains some of the aforementioned conditions for an integration thrust: the creation of dynamics, the bundling of interests and the creation of package solutions.

The interests behind the relaunch of European integration varied. Some wanted to create a more adequate basis for economic competitiveness in the world market through the liberation from barriers to economic rationality; others wanted to regain national sovereignty in the sense of capacities for regulatory action and intervention with the objective of elevating the social achievements of the postwar model to a higher level. The fact that the outcome, the Single Act, corresponded much more to the former interests only superficially confirms an interpretation of the process as lowest-common-denominator bargaining. Rather, the many minor treaty amendments in the Act – though neglected in most analyses – eventually turned out to be important for subsequent integration dynamics.

II

The core elements in recasting the European bargain

Without doubt, the internal market programme was the core element in recasting the European bargain with the Single European Act of 1986. Chapter 3 by Nicola Fielder reports the findings from analysing the relevant documents and from interviewing protagonists, witnesses and experts (see list of interview partners in the appendix to this volume). How energetically the Commission pushed the internal market and how vigorously the European Roundtable of Industrialists demanded it is clearly revealed by the empirical evidence. Chapter 3 points not only to the mutually reinforcing constellation at this transnational and supranational level, but also to the linkages between national and supranational levels in explaining the decisive events of the mid-1980s. The evidence for the latter – which has already been suggested in the literature – thus slightly modifies our original hypothesis.

The European proposals for technology corporatism are researched in more detail in chapter 4 by Simon Parker. From this it becomes evident that these initiatives go back to the late 1970s and also that the resulting new procedures clearly pre-date the Single European Act, which, however, included the by then established new praxis into Community law. The finding of a certain post-SEA disintegration of the alliance between the Commission and the Information Technology Roundtable is worth mentioning. We will come back to this when we deal with developments in a later period (see Part III).

The internal market as well as European technology corporatism were obvious manifestations of elite bargains between the Commission and the various Roundtables. How do we explain the other elements of the integrational thrust of the 1980s? Chapter 5 by Patrick Ziltener analyses why the cohesion target was anchored in the Luxembourg package and suggests that the extension of EC regional policy was in principle a side payment in order to gather enough support among the member states for the core element of the revised treaty: the internal market. This chapter shows that the alliance between the European Roundtable of Industrialists and the Commission to push that core element would have been ineffective if the Commission had not been successful in offering a balanced package deal. In the end this initiated an important step in the direction of a supranational structural policy and the beginning of a new cohesion regime.

Was the politicization of social policy following the Single Act an after-effect of intensified economic integration or was weak social policy regulation together with the abundance of social rhetoric merely an expression of selling the elite pact to the European public? Neither was the case, concludes Patrick Ziltener in chapter 6. He suggests that the Europeanization of the social dimension was a cornerstone in the Commission's integration project – it was not of special interest to the Roundtable and it was backed only by few governments. This suggests clear evidence for the Commission's own interests in this area, independent from both the Roundtable and most governments. Why, then, was the social dimension ranked relatively low in the Luxembourg package? The design of this policy area in the Act agreed upon in early 1986 remained narrow for merely tactical reasons so as not to endanger the strategic goal of the renewal of the societal model in a European framework. The tactical procedure of anchoring this policy area moderately in the Single Act was risky. In the long run, the entire strategy, as measured by the original intentions of the supranational political entrepreneur, failed – as evidenced by the defeat of the Delorist project.

3 The origins of the Single Market

Nicola Fielder

Introduction

The Single European Act was formally approved by the European Council in February 1986. When Maastricht hit the headlines in the early 1990s, the Single European Act instantly became history. However, it was the Single Market programme – the main content of the Single European Act – and the years of preparation leading up to it that really gave new momentum to European integration after the 'Eurosclerosis' of the 1970s.

The process that led to the Single European Act was never publicly discussed. The architects and initiators of the Single Market have not become household names; however, it is these protagonists and their efforts that are the subject of this chapter.

The thesis guiding our empirical research on the new momentum in European integration suggests a collaboration between the Commission of the European Communities and European transnational business represented by the European Roundtable of Industrialists, as stated in more detail in chapter 1. This explanation contrasts with other theories, which have placed the governments of the three main European Community member states – Germany, France and the United Kingdom – in the foreground. The empirical evidence to support our explanation was gathered by analysing various articles and papers and the official documents of the European Communities and from interviews with witnesses and protagonists of the integration process.

Three main points from the contents of the Single European Act must be emphasized. First, Article 13, which provides an amendment to Article 8a of the EEC Treaty, requests the institutions of the Community 'to adopt measures with the aim of progressively establishing the internal market over a period expiring on 31 December 1992. The internal market shall comprise an area without internal frontiers in which the free movement of goods, persons, services and capital is ensured in accordance with the provisions of this Treaty.' Secondly, the Single European Act states that unanimity of decisions is no longer required for regulations and directives pertaining to the establishment of the internal market, but that 'the Council shall issue directives, acting by a qualified majority'. Thirdly, the Single European Act moves away from the objective of a harmonization of national laws and regulations, which had proven time consuming and fruitless, and calls for the mutual recognition of laws and regulations between member states, setting only minimal standards.

The Single European Act was the decisive step towards the completion of the internal market, installing the relevant proposals of the White Paper of 1985 as Community law. The White Paper from the Commission to the European Council contains 300 proposals necessary for the completion of the common market and includes a timetable for the realization of the proposals made.

But what were the reasons for this sudden acceleration of European integration? Why did it happen in the early to mid-1980s? Who were the main actors behind this relaunching of the Single European Market? Theoretical explanations have been suggested in chapter 1. Here we look at the empirical evidence. At the level of the formal legislative process, it is impossible to decide between the competing hypotheses (see chapter 1). Of course, the Council formally approved the Single European Act with its core new element of the Single Market. For constitutional reasons, this could not be otherwise. However, in order to glimpse behind the scenes – to detect and clarify the social forces at work and to see who were the important protagonists – we analysed documents published before the decision. This is described in the next section of this chapter. In order to substantiate our explanation, we had to verify the documents and supplement them with interviews with protagonists and witnesses. This was necessary because our thesis stresses the informal relationships and negotiations between the representatives of different social forces which, precisely because of their informal character, are not clearly reflected in documents. In the following section we therefore present in detail the evidence from our interviews. In order to demonstrate the parallel development of initiatives from the Commission and from the Roundtable of European Industrialists, we then present the sequence of initiatives taken by the European Roundtable to push the Single Market. Finally, we evaluate this evidence against the claim that the Council, and especially the three big member states, pushed the initiative. Here, we draw on valuable evidence from interviews with members of the Committee of Permanent Representatives (COREPER).

What the official documents reveal

The first document to be looked at is the White Paper of June 1985 from the Commission to the European Council (CEC 1985). The White Paper consists of 300 proposals and was compiled by the Commission; the full title is *Completing the Internal Market. White Paper from the Commission to the European Council*. Various authors attribute a lot of the writing of the White Paper to Lord Cockfield, the Internal Market Commissioner in the first Delors Commission, but not all of it.

The most relevant part of the White Paper, as far as the question of the actors in the acceleration of the integration process is concerned, is the introduction, which includes quotes from declarations by the European Council and states:

> The Heads of State and Governments at the European Council meeting in Copenhagen in 1982 pledged themselves to the completion of the internal market as a high priority. The pledge was repeated at Fontainebleau in June 1984; at Dublin in December of that year; and, most recently, in March 1985. The time for talk has now passed. The time for action has come. That is what this White Paper is about. (CEC 1985: 5)

As Lord Cockfield said in an interview (9 March 1993), these declarations were quoted deliberately not to pay tribute to the heads of government but to nail them, to demonstrate to them that what was proposed in the White Paper, was what they had asked for and, in doing so, to force them to take positive action – a point also emphasized by Maria Green Cowles (1995). A further important fact is that the necessity for mutual recognition of laws and regulations and a return to majority voting are already included in the White Paper and do not first appear in the Single European Act (see also chapter 2).

In the White Paper various references are made to previous documents pertaining to the internal market, for instance the 'Programme of the Commission for 1985', which was presented to the European Parliament on 6 March, in which the Commission states that: 'The Commission will be asking the European Council to pledge itself to completion of a fully unified internal market by 1992' (CEC 1985: 4). The document on *Consolidating the Internal Market* (CEC 1984b) includes the following central statements, which we quote here in full:

> 4. If the beneficial effects of the internal market have been only partly realised, this is because, in spite of the spectacular progress made in the 1960s, the integration process slowed noticeably in the second half of the 1970s as the periods of economic recession were accompanied by a foot-dragging decline in the decision-making capacity of the Community lawgivers and by a decline in the observance of rules laid down by law. But in the early 1980s the European

78   The core elements in recasting the European bargain

Council imparted a fresh political impetus and significantly revived the process of establishing the internal market. (pp. 1f)

8. This decisive breakthrough [realization of the internal market] will require neither new policies nor new budgetary resources. But what is needed is the adoption of a limited number of proposals that are already before the Council, the beneficial effects of which will far outweigh the adjustment efforts intrinsically associated with this dynamic venture. (p. 3)

44. The Council's inaction cannot relieve the Commission of its obligation to take whatever measures are necessary to ensure the free movement of goods within the Community under conditions which are consistent with the aims of the Treaty. (p. 14)

The 'fresh political impetus' mentioned under point 4 of the document came at least in part from the Commission itself, as the documents *Communication from the Commission to the Council on the State of the Internal Market* (COM (81) 313) of 17 June 1981 and *Commission Communication to the Council on Re-activating the European Internal Market* (COM (82) 735) of 15 November 1982 show. Here again are some of the central comments in full detail:

III. However, the continental dimension of the European internal market is an indispensable condition for the success of the historic process of structural change which European industry must carry out in the eighties, to ensure the consolidation of the international competitiveness of European industry and to reaffirm the European Community as the most important partner in world trade. (CEC 1981a: 2)

V. The decline in confidence which threatens the internal market must immediately be halted by convincing political action. (ibid: 2)

VII. The European Council is therefore requested
– to confirm the basic importance of the internal market for the Community and emphasize the need for its rapid achievement;
– to instruct the Council of Ministers to achieve tangible progress in the second half of 1981. (ibid: 3)

Another interesting paragraph on the very first page of COM (82) 735 demonstrates the strong belief of the Commission that European businesses must be assured that their activities will be able to develop in an economic unit comparable in size to those of Japan and America. The Commission states that such assurance has not been achieved because the necessary decisions have not been taken by the Council, despite the fact that the problem issues have been clearly identified and fully discussed (CEC 1982a: 1).

These statements show that the Commission realized the importance, in fact the necessity, of a Single Market for European business, even if they do not specifically state that European business was at that time pushing for such a programme.

The origins of the Single Market 79

The documents show clearly the energetic support of the Single Market programme from the Commission. The answers given by the European Council, on the other hand, appear as automatic responses without any real content. As early as 1982 the European Council declared: 'The European Council . . . instructs the Council: – to decide, before the end of March 1983, on the priority measures proposed by the Commission to reinforce the internal market.'[1] Very little was forthcoming, however. One year later the same applied to the 'Solemn Declaration on European Union' (pp. 1f):

The Heads of State or Government of the member states of the European Communities, meeting within the European Council, are convinced that, in order to resolve the serious economic problems facing the member states, the Community must strengthen its cohesion, regain its dynamism and intensify its action in areas hitherto insufficiently explored.

And, in the same document:

The Heads of State or Government underline the particular importance of the Commission as guardian of the Treaties of Paris and Rome and as a driving force in the process of European integration. They confirm the value of making more frequent use of the possibility of delegating powers to the Commission within the framework of the Treaties. (ibid.: 11)

However, the heads of state or government allowed themselves plenty of time, stating that they would 'subject this Declaration to a general review as soon as the progress achieved towards European unification justifies such action, but not later than five years from signature of the Declaration' (ibid.: 20).

The main results of the analysis of Community documents are presented chronologically in table 3.1.

The analysis of documents provided a first indication of the importance of the Commission in pushing the Single Market programme into being; similar evidence cannot be found in the documents adopted by the European Council.

European business is also mentioned in the European Communities' documents as a chief supporter of the internal market programme. Further evidence for the importance of these actors was then gathered from interviews with witnesses and further documentation, including an article by the president of FIAT, Giovanni Agnelli (1989), which states that '1992 was born for sound economic reasons and those forces continue to be its engine. Ironically, it was politicians who in 1957 first

---

[1] 'Declarations by the European Council Relating to the Internal Market', in *Completing the Internal Market. White Paper from the Commission to the European Council.* June 1985, p. 3. These declarations were included in the White Paper in order to nail the heads of governments to comments they had made, according to Lord Cockfield in the interview I did with him.

Table 3.1. *Steps towards the Single Market as the core element of the Single European Act*

- *Communication from the Commission to the Council on the State of the Internal Market* (17 June 1981, COM (81) 313 final):

    The decline in confidence which threatens the internal market must immediately be halted by convincing political action. (p. 2)

    This initiative was on the agenda of the Meeting of the Council, 29–30 July 1981. Although the European Council (heads of governments and states), meeting on 29 and 30 June, 'echoed the alarm sounded by the Commission', there was no effective action (quoted from the *Communication from the Commission to the Council: Consolidating the Internal Market*, June 1984, p. 8).

- *Commission Communication to the Council on Re-Activating the European Internal Market* (15 November 1982, COM (82) 735 final):

    As the Commission has never ceased to affirm . . . European undertakings must be assured that their activities will be able to develop in an economic unit similar in size to the American market and distinctly bigger than the Japanese market (. . .) To date, this has not been achieved. Although the problem issues have been clearly identified and fully discussed, the decisions have not yet been taken. (p. 1)

    Following this the European Council convened in Copenhagen, 3–4 December 1982: 'The Heads of State and Governments at the European Council meeting in Copenhagen in 1982 pledged themselves to the completion of the internal market as a high priority' (quoted from the White Paper, CEC 1985: 5). The outcome of the meeting was highly influential on the Solemn Declaration on European Union in Stuttgart, 19 June 1983.

- (*Communication from the Commission to the Council: Consolidating the Internal Market* (13 June 1984, COM (84) 305 final):

    The Council's inaction cannot relieve the Commission of its obligation to take whatever measures are necessary to ensure the free movement of goods within the Community under conditions which are consistent with the aims of the treaty. (p. 14)

    The renewed drive will produce results only if the business community is again convinced that the European market is attractive. (p. 3)

    This initiative was highly influential on the following events:
    The Meeting of the European Council in Fontainebleau, 25–26 June 1984:

    It [the European Council] asks the Council and the Member States to put in hand without delay a study of the measures which could be taken to bring about in the near future the abolition of all police and customs formalities for people crossing intra-Community frontiers. (Quoted from the White Paper, 'Declarations by the European Council Relating to the Internal Market', CEC 1985: 3)

    The Meeting of the Council in Dublin, 3–4 December 1984:

    The European Council . . . agreed that the Council, in its appropriate formations, should take steps to complete the Internal Market, including implementation of European standards. (Quoted from the White Paper, 'Declarations by the European Council Relating to the Internal Market', CEC 1985: 3)

    The 'Programme of the Commission for 1985', presented to the European Parliament on 6 March 1985:

    The Commission will be asking the European Council to pledge itself to completion of a fully unified internal market by 1992.

The Meeting of the Council in Brussels, 29–30 March 1985:

> [T]he European Council laid particular emphasis on the following . . . fields of action:
>
> (a) action to achieve a single large market by 1992 thereby creating a more favourable environment for stimulating enterprise, competition and trade; it called upon the Commission to draw up a detailed programme with a specific timetable before its next meeting. (Quoted from the White Paper, 'Declarations by the European Council Relating to the Internal Market' CEC 1985: 3)

- *Completing the Internal Market: White Paper from the Commission to the European Council* (June 1985):

> The Heads of State and Governments at the European Council meeting in Copenhagen in 1982 pledged themselves to the completion of the internal market as a high priority. The pledge was repeated at Fontainebleau in June 1984; at Dublin in December of that year; and, most recently, in March 1985. The time for talk has now passed. The time for action has come. That is what this White Paper is about. (p. 5)
>
> Europe stands at the crossroads. We either go ahead – with resolution and determination – or we drop back into mediocrity. We can now either resolve to complete the integration of the economies of Europe; or, through a lack of political will to face the immense problems involved, we can simply allow Europe to develop into no more than a free trade area. (p. 55)

The White Paper was approved at the Meeting of the European Council, Milan, June 1985.

- *Single European Act* (1987)

> The Single European Act . . . is an expression of the political resolve voiced by the Heads of State or Government, notably at Fontainebleau in June 1984, then at Brussels in March 1985 and at Milan in June 1985, to transform the whole complex of relations between their States into a European Union, in line with the Stuttgart Solemn Declaration of June 1983. (p. 27)

---

conceived the idea of a common market – often over objections from the business community. Now the situation has been reversed; it is the entrepreneurs and corporations who are keeping the pressure on politicians to transcend considerations of local and national interest.'

What our interviews revealed

The interview partners consisted of two former Commissioners, both repeatedly named by various authors as important protagonists in launching the completion of the Single Market, one member of the internal market Directorate General in one of the aforementioned Commissioners' team, four representatives of national governments and as such members of the Committee of Permanent Representatives, two founder members of the European Roundtable of Industrialists, the head of the European representative office of a major European corporation, and a top official of the Union of Industries of the European

Community (UNICE), all of whom had been in Brussels since the early 1980s or longer; and other informants (see list of interviewees in the appendix to this volume).

Only a few interviewees expressed the need to remain anonymous; most seemed used to being interviewed for articles and their names being mentioned. However, in respect for the wishes of some of the interviewees, only three witnesses will be named here as they are extremely important protagonists and did not express the wish to remain anonymous.[2]

Lord Cockfield served as Minister of State for the UK Treasury from May 1979 to April 1982, as Secretary of State for Trade from April 1982 until June 1983, and as Chancellor of the Duchy of Lancaster from 1983 until his nomination by Margaret Thatcher as British Commissioner in September 1984. During his term as Secretary of State for Trade he served as the British representative on the Internal Market Council, which was founded by the European Council in Copenhagen in December 1982. He was a vice-president of the Commission and was Commissioner responsible for the Directorates General Internal Market (DG III), Customs Union and Taxation (DG XXI) and Financial Institutions (DG XV).

Vicomte Davignon was Commissioner for Belgium in two EC Commission terms of office. From 1977 until 1981 he was head of the internal market Directorate General (DG III) and from 1981 until the end of 1984 he was the Commissioner responsible for industry, energy and research. Since 1987 he has headed the Société Générale de Belgique and become a member of the European Roundtable of Industrialists, the body he himself established in 1983.

Professor Dr. W. Dekker was President of Philips Electronics N.V. for many years. He has recently become chairman of the Supervisory Board of Philips. From 1988 until 1992 he was chairman of the European Roundtable of Industrialists and has been a member of the Roundtable since the very beginning.

The Philips company actively supported the European market integration process. In 1985, for instance, the company submitted a report to the Commission entitled 'Europe 1990. An Action Plan for Europe'. The report was prepared under Wisse Dekker's instruction and was seen by most observers as the basis for the White Paper (see Dekker 1984, 1985b).

---

[2] I will, however, refrain from putting names to any of the quotations taken from the interviews, as some of the interviewees asked not to be quoted. This was mainly due to the fact that not all the interviews were held in the interviewee's mother tongue, which inhibited two of the candidates.

One of the first points to be evaluated was the names mentioned by the interviewees. Generally, Jacques Delors and Lord Cockfield were spoken of as the most important people at the time in pushing the integration process forward. Etienne Davignon is seen as the initiator and promoter of discussions between the European Community and the European industrialists regarding what was necessary to keep European industry in competition with the United States and Japan. These dicussions led to Esprit and various other invaluable programmes. Another name that was mentioned frequently was that of Karl-Heinz Narjes, the Commissioner responsible for the Internal Market General Directorate before Lord Cockfield:[3]

Davignon of course after a while left the Commission, because he had been there for two terms and then he went to the Société Générale de Belgique and he also became a member of the European Roundtable of Industrialists and he has been absolutely one of the driving forces, he has been very active and very useful.

Well, in fact less spectacular progress had already been made by the previous Commission under the leadership of Mr. Narjes, who was then responsible for industry, but that was more a process of *petits pas* . . . and then the company Philips of Eindhoven, they presented here a sort of agenda for European enterprises towards integration and it was all about the internal market, so that when President Delors came and when Lord Cockfield was nominated to be responsible for these matters, they put the threads together and made a formal proposal, a comprehensive proposal of all that had to be done to achieve a true Single Market and they attached to it a timetable, and those two elements – comprehensiveness and a timetable, a fixed calendar – were the main causes of success and these two aspects facilitated the progress towards the internal market.

Various interviewees said that the success of Delors and Cockfield was based on work done by Narjes, but that they were the ones who succeeded in putting the work into a simple political programme that could be easily implemented and that included an end date.

It is interesting to see that the names mentioned first were names of members of the Commission. The importance of the Commission as a whole was also emphasized by all the interviewees, for example in the following quotations:

Underlying this is what has always been my view and also Jacques Delors' view

---

[3] Karl-Heinz Narjes was *chef de cabinet* of Walter Hallstein during Hallstein's presidency of the Commission (1958–1967). He then headed the Directorate General for press and information until 1972, when he returned to German politics. From 1981 he again headed a Directorate General, this time taking responsibility for the internal market and customs union in the Thorn Commission. He continued to play an important role in the first Delors Commission, taking over new responsibilities such as information technology.

and that is that the Commission is the driving force of the Community, it always has been. If you look at the times when the Community makes great progress, it's because you had a strong Commission. The Community made great progress when you had a strong Commission under Hallstein at the beginning, the Community made great progress when you had a strong president in Jacques Delors in the first of the Delors Commissions, when you get a weaker Commission, in the second Commission, progress is slower and when you get a much weaker Commission, as you have under the third Delors Commission, you wonder really where you're looking to for the progress at all. The Commission is the driving force of the Community and this is why it's so important that it's right of initiative should neither be taken away nor watered down and it is of necessity that the Commission is the driving force, because if you have twelve member states where else can the driving force come from, because the tendency of member states is to start by looking after their own interests. I've always said that the Community is a little bit like a stage-coach drawn by twelve horses some of which have got harnessed in the wrong way round; it's only the chap with the whip who makes them run at all and the chap with the whip is the Commission.

The Commission itself, President Delors, his Commissioner for the Internal Market and Industry, and the ministers of industry at that time [were the main actors in the Single Market project]. Also important is the fact that the social partners in the Community first have been invited to discuss together at Community level with President Delors about all consequences of the internal market, this has been the beginning of the social dialogue, and, secondly, they have rapidly agreed on supporting the Commission in [its] efforts to pushing the governments ahead and I think the Commission has played a very effective and well-organized role.

Because of the fact that the local governments are so reluctant very often to act and to give away a little bit of their authority, they have created a vacuum, in that vacuum Brussels, the Commission has worked, they have taken initiatives, Cockfield, the White Paper, and other things, they take initiatives.

Two interviewees mentioned that, as the Council does not have any right of initiative, the initiatives must come from the Commission. All interviewees confirmed the active and creative role of the Commission among the European Community institutions. However, all the interviewees voiced the opinion that the support the Commission received from European industrialists for the Single Market programme was absolutely vital.

I think [the influence of the European Roundtable of Industrialists on the Commission and the White Paper was] very strong, but not to such an extent that the industry could more or less dictate what they have to do; that of course was impossible, but there has been a very, very fruitful cooperation between the Roundtable and the Commission.

Once a majority of industrialists, not only industrialists, I mean, services and so on and so forth, started playing an important role, once the reaction that the governments began getting from what I call in a vague term economic operators became: 'No, this is not nonsense, you must look at this carefully, because we are interested in this also,' there was a change in the atmosphere, so what came about was a certain consistency, in between what the people were saying everywhere, people who didn't like it were saying it in Brussels and were saying it at home, people who liked it were saying it in Brussels and were also saying it at home, and so this created a sense that something might happen and created this sense of delegation and enterprise, which I think was very important. I think, if the Commission comes up with the best proposals in the world, which nobody supports, they will die; it needs somebody who says, it's not only intellectually interesting or stimulating, it's also something – and I can permanently come back to my point – that we need (. . .).

In addition to showing the connections between the Commission and industry, these quotes also suggest support for Stephen George's (1993) network theory, which stresses the importance of looking at the links between the national and the supranational levels.

Other EC institutions are not reported in the interviews to have had close contact with the industrialists and are not mentioned as important actors in the process of completing the internal market. Contact with the Council was and is mostly indirect through the Commission or via the national governments.

The European Parliament was said to have supported the work of the Commission, but its role was not actually emphasized by any of the interviewees. The most important national politicians appear to have been Kohl, Thatcher and Mitterrand, but in their roles as final decision-makers not as initiators.

The interviews with former Permanent Representatives showed that the work of the Committee of Permanent Representatives has increased over the years, but again they are not initiators; they build more permanent links between the Commission and the national governments and prepare decisions, trying to come to a general agreement before a proposal is put before the Council. The UNICE official was the only interviewee who mentioned working with the Permanent Representatives. Members of the European Roundtable go directly to their government leaders with what they have to say. One member did not even know what the Committee of Permanent Representatives is.

All the interview partners emphasized the fact that the Single European Act was the result of a new impetus and not the reason for it. The Single European Act did at the time produce other innovations, but the Euro-pessimism of the seventies was broken by new initiatives as early as 1981 and 1982.

The belief that global structural changes and the failure of national strategies were an important prerequisite for the acceleration of the integration process, which all the authors on European integration voiced, is echoed in the remarks of the interviewees:

It became clear that there was an important concern about the increased competition out of Japan and out of the United States and so it became clear that the instrument which was lacking to improve the competitivity of the European industry was to enjoy the advantages of one single market, and it slowly filtered through that this was a real need.

[I]f we want to survive in the world of competition, especially vis-à-vis the Japanese, that we have to have an economy of scale, as an industry we must have an economy of scale, and the economy of scale was not available at that time, because we were operating in all kinds of different countries. (. . .) So then the idea . . . gradually became very clear that we must have a united Europe, and of course there was the EC, there was the Treaty of Rome, but there was not much substance in it yet, it was all political talk and there was not much done really for industry, so then we thought we should give it a little push.

[A]bove all there was the industrial syndrome, and this is terribly important, that during the last ten years, the lost ten years, the United States and Japan had continued to surge ahead and Europe had fallen behind and there is one statistic I always used to quote, because you only need one, and that was that in the field of information technology the European Community accounted for 30 per cent of the demand and 10 per cent of the production. You only need that one statistic to show what had happened.

In summary, the interviews show a general consensus for the hypothesis of Commission leadership with invaluable support from European industry. This support was made very clear at both national and supranational level, and was perhaps voiced most comprehensively by the members of the European Roundtable of Industrialists, although they were certainly not alone. In various statements made during the interviews it became apparent that the Commission was the European Community institution to which industry and other organizations made their needs known. Very little direct contact was kept up with the Council and even less with members of the Committee of Permanent Representatives, although such contacts did exist. However, contacts were made via governments.

There also seems to be general agreement on the main protagonists: Delors, Cockfield, Davignon and, in the preliminary stages, Narjes. There is a slight question mark over who gave the European Single Market programme its end date of 1992. Some claim it was Delors; others say it was Lord Cockfield. What is clear is that the actual achievement of putting the proposals for the creation of a Single Market into a simple yet complete political programme with a clear time-frame was one of the most important steps towards the completion of the internal market.

One comment frequently made about Delors was that after his election as president of the Commission he travelled to all the national governments and discovered that there was agreement in one policy area and that was the Single Market, which was why he made this his goal. I propose that this agreement had been reached as a result of preparatory work by the previous Commission, but also of the influence of industrialists on their national governments.

Lord Cockfield undeniably played a leading role in the integration process over a long period of time, as he himself is quick to recall. However, he could not have succeeded on his own. He received great support from Delors, as he remarks in a speech he made in December 1992 (Cockfield 1992: 3):

In these more troubled days when reputations can so often be clouded by unjustified criticism may I say that the complete trust invested in me by Jacques Delors, his clarity of vision and unfailing support were a major factor in the success of my own endeavours.

For quite some time he also enjoyed the support of Margaret Thatcher. Furthermore, one must not forget that he was also supported by all the other Directors General and their staff, not to mention his own staff, as he states in the same speech mentioned above and as mentioned by one of the interviewees. There were very few people in the Commission who did not support the Single Market programme wholeheartedly.

If Cockfield was the main executor of the completion of the internal market, Davignon – whose support for the integration process continued long after he left the Commission – was certainly the far-sighted political entrepreneur who paved the way. His visions (see chapter 1) and efforts to set up contacts with industry and his initiative to establish the European Roundtable of Industrialists – thus creating important channels through which the demands and proposals of industry could be communicated – were vital elements on the road to a Single Market.

The initiatives of the European Roundtable of Industrialists

Founded in 1983, the European Roundtable of Industrialists was the strongest and most visible supporter of the Commission's Single Market programme, though not the only one. Its efforts to influence national governments were invaluable, (see also chapter 9). The members are charismatic personalities who have something to say and are used to making themselves heard.

It is not a coincidence that a Commissioner – Etienne Davignon – was one of the main instigators of the Roundtable. The cooperation between

Commission and Roundtable has continued, although it is perhaps less intense now than it was at the time of the build-up to and the implementation of the Single Market programme as the core element of the Single European Act.

The similarity of the views of the protagonists from both the Commission and the European Roundtable of Industrialists was obviously already evident at the beginning of the 1980s. The Commission argued in one of its 1982 communications to the Council that European firms must be assured that their activities would be able to develop in an economic unit similar in size to the American market and distinctly bigger than the Japanese market (see table 3.1). The Roundtable expressed the very same view in its first Policy Memorandum, officially handed over to the Commission in June 1983. This stated that, despite the efforts of the European Community to liberalize trade, Europe remained fragmented into national markets, which prevented enterprises from reaching the size necessary to compete with non-European corporations. It demanded that the European market must develop into a single 'home' base in order for European companies to become better competitors (see table 3.2).

In analogy to table 3.1, the development of the initiatives taken by the Roundtable is presented in table 3.2. The table shows the chronological initiatives taken by the European Roundtable of Industrialists to promote and accelerate the Single Market programme. What is striking is the parallel development of the initiatives from the Commission and from the Roundtable. This substantiates the evidence from our interviews, which stress the close cooperation between both groups of protagonists to push the project of an effective Single Market.

We can thus conclude that our research has produced a variety of evidence that clearly contradicts the contention by Moravcsik (1991) that the initiative was taken by the big three prevailing in the Council. Rather, our theoretical explanation of an elite pact between the European transnationals and the EC Commission is empirically substantiated by the documents as well as by our interviews with witnesses, who confirm the tight cooperation between the Roundtable and the Commission in preparing the Single Market.

Discussion

One could object that, in relying on official documents and on interviews with members of the Commission and of the European business elite, one naturally dismisses the role the Council and the big three member states played (as suggested by the competing hypothesis).

Table 3.2. *The role of industry: steps of the European Roundtable of Industrialists towards the Single European Act and beyond*

1982/1983: P. Gyllenhammar promotes a 'Marshall Plan for Europe' to increase growth and to build industry and infrastructure in Europe.

Autumn 1982: Meeting between Gyllenhammar and Davignon. List of possible candidates for a European Roundtable of Industrialists.

6–7 April 1983: first meeting of the European Roundtable. First point of discussion: the lack of a homogeneous Euro-market.

1 June 1983: second meeting: 'European Roundtable Charter'.

10 June 1983: Memorandum to Commissioner Davignon: 'Foundations for the Future of European Industry':

> The European market must serve as the unified 'home' base necessary to allow European firms to develop as powerful competitors in world markets.'

January 1984: third meeting of the European Roundtable: European Venture Capital Association (EVCA) formally announced, designed to encourage transnational investments in Europe and forge close relations between new technologically innovative firms and large industrial companies.

December 1984: 'Missing Links: Upgrading Europe's Transborder Infrastructure': first official report published by the European Roundtable:

> It has been evident since six nations signed the Treaty of Rome in 1957 that Europe's political and economic destiny lay in closer co-operation and fewer trade barriers. Yet progress towards the creation of a European Common Market continues to be frustratingly slow. (p. 7)

11 January 1985: 'Europe 1990: An Agenda for Action' (Philips/Wisse Dekker).

June 1985: 'Changing Scales'.

14 June 1985: European Roundtable–EC Commission meeting. (Since June 1985 European Roundtable–Commission meetings have taken place every six months.)

28 November 1985: telexes from CEOs of major European multinational companies to their national governments:

> As leading industrialists based in the European Communities . . . we urge you to exercise your full influence so that the forthcoming topmeeting will produce concrete results. Stop. Not only is the credibility of European political leaders at stake, but European industry badly needs a clear signal that the major objectives of the Treaty of Rome will be realised within the next five years. Stop. Even a clear statement that this would not be the case, would – although not hoped for – be helpful as this would end the prolonged period of uncertainty with which industry has to cope under the present situation and which forms a significant obstacle on the way to expanding our activities and intensifying our efforts to build a strong and competitive European position.' (Telex from Wisse Dekker to J. C. Ramaer, 28 November 1985)

June 1986: 'Europe is Urgent' symposium. Watchdog group: Internal Market Support Committee (IMSC).

September 1986: 'Making Europe Work'.

June 1987: statement by IMSC on indirect taxes and message to government leaders at the Luxembourg summit: 'show political will, or European industry will invest elsewhere'.

December 1987: letter from Sir Patrick Sheehy (IMSC) to Lord Cockfield:

> The IMSC. . .remains in full support of your proposals as the only means of removing the barriers at the frontiers and we have taken every opportunity to say so to national governments. It will be no surprise to you to learn that we have had a very negative response. We have therefore decided to redouble our efforts to find ways of presenting our arguments in a persuasive way.' (Quoted in Maria Green Cowles 1995: 519f)

First of all, it has never been a question of debate that the Council is *de jure* the decision-maker in the European Community and it is not a matter of debate here. It is a given fact. The question remains, however, of how these decisions are made and how much *initiative* comes from the Council.

Looking at the evidence presented above and by Green Cowles (1995) in full detail, it is revealed that in the case of the Single Market the Council was not left with much room to decide. The governments of the member states knew exactly what was at stake. They had been lobbied by industrialists in their own countries and urged by the Commission which path of action should be taken.

What was the role of the members of the Committee of Permanent Representatives, the mediators between the Council and the Commission? They prepare all the decisions of the various Councils and thereby render the workload of the ministers and heads of state and government more manageable. If the permanent representatives in their preparatory meetings have found that an issue is uncontested among the member states, then the Council simply gives the final stamp of approval. In other cases there may be some details left for debate. On the other hand, the permanent representatives also inform the Commission about the views of the Council. In some cases the Commission may modify its proposals if they meet with strong resistance in the preparatory discussions of the Committee of Permanent Representatives.

Our interviews with members of the Committee of Permanent Representatives, however, did not reveal any indication of the Committee of Permanent Representatives being involved in any sort of initiative regarding the Single Market. This adds to the evidence that the Council or heads of governments were not the initiators. In fact the Single Market project was so well prepared that it went through Council fairly smoothly in the end.

How energetically the internal market project was pushed by the Commission is clearly revealed by our empirical work. This political initiative of the Commission was not exceptional, because within the European Community the Commission is a supranational body, whose independence from the member states was already set out in the treaties of 1958. The Commission is at the same time a partner of and in opposition to the Council (Fusion Treaty, Article 15). Because of the multitude of its functions the Commission plays a key role within the Community – it is its motor, has a right to make proposals in the legal process (which then are agreed upon or rejected by the Council) and holds the mandate to take initiatives. The plans, programmes and memoranda of the Commission advance the development of the

Community. All this was agreed upon in the treaties in effect since 1958. The Commission did not always use its power to launch initiatives, as was mentioned in chapter 2. One must be careful, however, to avoid simply seeing the Commission as a homogeneous entity. As one interviewee pointed out, even in a weak Commission, such as the Thorn Commission, there were what he termed 'barons', strong Commissioners, in this case Davignon and Ortoli.

A further important fact is the openness of the Commission towards industry and organizations such as UNICE. As one interviewee put it, 'in some ways the Commission welcomes the influence of pressure groups'. When we review the role of the European Roundtable of Industrialists, we must not forget that industry is represented by other organizations as well. In the case of the Single Market, however, the European Roundtable was the predominant representative. But it would be false to conclude that European big business could dictate; rather 'there has been very, very fruitful cooperation between the Roundtable and the Commission', as one of the protagonists stated in his interview. This is what our hypotheses spelled out in chapter 1 suggest, and it is modelled in figure 1.1 on page 36 as a bold line – without arrows – between the two actors. It was a close cooperation of the two actors. They both needed each other and neither could have succeeded without the support of the other.

This, however, was not only a mutually reinforcing constellation at the supranational level, but also a multi-level phenomenon. Linkages between national and supranational levels in explaining European integration processes are also emphasized by Stephen George (1993). Indeed, we found that the influence of the European transnational corporations was exerted not only directly on the Commission, but also through their national governments, which were thus compelled to fall into line with the Commission. In addition, the Commission not only could count on European big business lobbying their governments but strengthened its impact by assigning to the European Roundtable a quasi-official status in Brussels. In turn, the weight of the Roundtable gave decisive support to the Commission's project. It was this kind of collaboration that paved the way for the Single Market project.

This finding of a multi-level process suggests a slight modification of the hypothetical scheme in figure 1.1 on page 36. In contrast to the graphical presentation there, the influence of the European transnational business elite on their national governments should better be symbolized by a *bold* arrow, as between the Commission and the Council, because our investigations suggest that this influence was just as vital for the completion of the Single Market.

While pointing to the importance of the alliance between the Roundtable and the Commission, it is important to remember that this chapter deals only with the Single Market policy area and the conclusions derived from the empirical evidence related to this cannot simply be transferred to other policy areas. This is probably particularly true in the case of the European Roundtable of Industrialists. For obvious reasons the Single Market was a project that was extremely close to their hearts. On the other hand, over the years the European Roundtable has expressed interest in other areas with various publications. However, there are invariably certain areas that would not be of interest to the members of the Roundtable. As one interviewee mentioned, other associations such as UNICE are forced to take a stance on every issue. The European Roundtable in contrast picks out subjects that it sees as being of economic, strategic and political core interest and importance.

The initiative role of the Commission is easier to generalize and also supported by our findings on other policy areas in this volume. In the 1980s it effectively provided political entrepreneurship and assumed responsibility at the European level. This is evidenced in one of the most important documents that the Commission of the European Communities has ever completed – the White Paper of 1985 launching the Single Market.

In 1985, elites in Europe decided to go ahead. How the European integration will evolve only the future will show. In any event, it will have been built on foundations that were laid by the initiative and collaboration of the Commission of the European Communities and the European Roundtable of Industrialists.

4 Esprit and technology corporatism

Simon Parker

Framing the question

The Single European Act of 1986 incorporated a new Article enshrining the Commission's power to enact technology policy. This chapter examines the roots of this change in the European political economy. We have focused on the creation of the European Strategic Programme of Research and Development (Esprit) in the early 1980s because we believe that it was through the creation of this programme that the Commission won the right to be active in the field of technology policy. The later inclusion of a specific article in the revised treaties can be seen as a case of formalizing an existing practice.

Furthermore, we will analyse this policy initiative in order to determine whether or not, in both its design and execution, Esprit may be said to constitute an incidence of technology corporatism, a concept that has already been briefly introduced in chapter 1. The issue that concerns us here is from where or from whom the new initiative in the realm of technology policy came and which interests were behind it. In this way it addresses the notion that political entrepreneurs heard the call of European transnational firms to improve the offer 'Europe' as a condition for their remaining in Europe – which was phrased more along the lines of 'this is what needs to happen in our economic, social and political system if we are to be able to succeed in the international economy'. The thesis is that political actors heard this plea from capital and went about trying to achieve changes in the economic and social system that suited capital, all the while keeping in mind that these changes had to be sold to the public, and in this sense fulfilling one of the basic roles of the state, which is to legitimize the social, economic and political order. For this reason, chapter 1 refers to the Single European Act as an elite pact constructed between transnational capital and political entrepreneurs in the European Commission. Chapter 3 has suggested evidence that this view is adequate for explaining the genesis of the Single Market programme. Here we analyse whether analogous forms of cooperation between European transnational corporations and the Commission were the basis of the institutionalization of technology policy at the European level, the second remarkable element of the Luxembourg package to change the political economy of Europe. This is why we review the history of Esprit in more detail, identify the main protagonists and assess their roles. We then investigate whether the decision-making process in the 1980s in the field of technology policy can be characterized as 'technology corporatism'.

The notion of technology corporatism

Technology corporatism is employed in the above-mentioned theoretical context to denote a state of affairs in which industry, the state and 'science' (alternatively, politics, economics and science) cooperate in order to achieve a more competitive 'societal model' (Bornschier 1996: 377). This concept is based on Bornschier's understanding of the Japanese experience and it clearly differs from traditional notions of corporatism, which denote a particular relationship between the state, capital and labour.

Several problems exist with this definition, particularly in relation to one pillar of the so-called corporatist structure, namely that of science. At times, science, in this theory, is constructed as an actor or participant in a political process termed corporatist owing to the institutionalized roles of three actors, thus making a link with the traditional state–capital–labour corporatist model (Bornschier 1996: 387). At the same time however, science, or technology as it is frequently called, is also referred to as the field in which this corporatist structure is said to exist, as in the term 'technology corporatism'. Clearly, it would present difficulties for the theory if science is taken to be both a participant and also a context. It also leaves unanswered the question of who, if we are referring here to actors, is science? In the case of Esprit, it is not strictly true that there were no representatives other than those of the Commission and the leading European information technology (IT) companies present. However, the participants who came from universities or research institutes were few in number and apparently of limited influence. In EC Commissioner Davignon's testimony before the House of Lords Select Committee on the European Communities, these participants are mentioned in the general description of the Esprit decision-making process, but then never again referred to once Davignon has turned to explaining to the Lords how things really work.

However, the idea of technology corporatism may still be usefully employed if we do not insist on making corporatism a triangular affair. Thus, relationships between actors within the policy-making process and in the consequent execution of that policy may be termed corporatist if a central actor (in this case capital), which normally exists outside the state structure, is given an institutionalized role in the state policy-making process. We do not employ the concept of corporatism simply to describe a situation in which the influence of a particular actor or actors in public policy-making is significant. Such situations are far from uncommon and may have much to do with the individuals concerned and therefore do not represent any kind of a change in the principles that may be said to lie behind state action. To be clear, what we find interesting and novel in the case of Esprit is not the fact that capital exerted significant influence on a public policy-making process but that this influence was institutionalized at the European level.

To summarize the argument: we will use the term 'technology corporatism' to refer to a particular form of relationship between actors in the policy-making process in the field of technology, in particular information technology and the Esprit programme which dominated the Commission's activities in this field. We will not attempt to create a 'third force' (science) as a participant simply to make the label corporatist appear more immediately relevant. Rather, we will consider this relationship to be corporatist to the extent that it is institutionalized.

However, our research has suggested that the influence of the European Information Technology Industry Roundtable appears to have declined since Esprit was established, although its formal, institutionalized role in the decision-making apparatus of Esprit remains unchanged.[1] Therefore, we caution that, although formal corporatist relations may continue to exist, it may be wrong to conclude from this that the relationship between the Commission and industry has remained unchanged.

Coinciding interests

We argue in this chapter that industry, in the form of the European Information Technology Industry Roundtable, played a vital role in the design of Esprit and that this role became institutionalized when the Council accepted the Commission's proposals to establish the Esprit programme. Furthermore, because this role was institutionalized, we may speak of technology corporatism as being present.

---

[1] This raises the question of whether it is sufficient to examine relationships on the basis of institutionalized links alone or if there must be some way of assessing influence and integrating this into our analysis.

It is interesting to note that the role of the information technology (IT) industry was one of the strongest cards the Commission had in its hand when it sought approval for its IT plans. The Commission was at great pains to show member states how closely it was working with industry in designing Esprit, that the programme was industry designed rather than coming from bureaucrats in Brussels.

The interests between the European leaders of IT industry and the Commission coincided around a particular project, not on all issues, and not permanently. In the case of the Commission's technology policy there was such a coincidence of interests over a specific problem in the first half of the 1980s (Europe's performance in the new high technology industries). This alliance resulted in concrete policies, but the interests of both parties later diverged, and thus their relationship today looks quite different from the way it did a decade ago.

According to Bornschier's theory, European integration was largely a result of political entrepreneurs responding to the demands of European capital. The findings of Fielder in regards to the internal market project and the importance of corporate interests represented by the European Roundtable of Industrialists suggest support for this theory (see chapters 1 and 3). In the case of technology policy, in particular IT policy, the picture is slightly different.

The Esprit initiative

The initiative that became Esprit, which we suggest was the foundation for the enlargement of the Commission's responsibilities in the realm of technology policy later confirmed in the Single European Act, originated in late 1979 with the Commission and not industry, and thus with political entrepreneurs rather than capital.

However, there is no question that an informal alliance was constructed between representatives of the largest IT firms and the Commission similar to the alliance around the issue of the internal market policy. Out of this alliance emerged concrete policy initiatives that the Commission then advanced to the Council. Furthermore, this alliance was in turn crucial to the success of these proposals. Specifically, this alliance resulted in the creation of a proposal that would see the Commission overseeing a research programme designed to 'provide the basic technologies which European industry needs to be competitive with that of Japan and the USA' (CEC 1982b).

The European Strategic Programme for Research and Development in Information Technologies (Esprit) was the final name given to the project. The intention of the programme was not simply to channel public resources into industry to provide the means to achieve a 'catch-up'. Instead, the goal was to create incentives in order to encourage inter-firm and academic-industry collaboration based on the realization that such collaboration was necessary in order to (a) pool resources and (b) end duplication of research (CEC 1982b). As much as generating new products, the programme would be seen to be successful insofar as the links established between firms became ongoing and independent of Esprit itself. Thus Esprit was intended to foster a change in the way European firms related to one another. The leitmotiv for the programme was the apparent Japanese success in involving private firms in setting public policy objectives in specific industrial areas, and the evident close collaboration between American industry and academic research institutes and universities (see Mytelka and Delapiere 1987; CEC 1982c: 10, 24–5; House of Lords Select Committee on the European Communities 1984: 169–70).

In order to achieve this goal of encouraging inter-firm collaboration, specific projects within the programme had to include firms from at least two different Community countries. To discourage the idea that the programme was a new way of offering public subsidies to private activities, all funding commitments were on a 50/50 basis between the Community and participating firms. As this programme was envisioned as a way of responding to the threat of American and Japanese IT dominance, foreign firms were banned from participating. For reasons that we will discuss in more detail below, the projects were limited to collaboration in pre-competitive research and development (R&D). Five main areas were selected upon which Esprit would first concentrate: advanced micro-electronics, advanced information processing, software technology, systems for office automation, and computer integrated flexible manufacturing (CEC 1982c: 8–10).

The Council agreed to the Commission's request to begin a pilot phase of Esprit at the Versailles European Summit in June 1982. This phase was launched when the initial call for proposals was made in February 1983 with the Commission in possession of a budget of 11.5 million ECU. In November 1983 the Commission took a request to the Council for funding of Esprit proper, following the generally acknowledged success of this pilot phase. This request was for a ten-year programme, broken into two five-year phases. The Council eventually agreed to the Commission's request in February 1984. By 1984 then, Esprit I was up and running. Understanding the climate from which it arose, and accounting for its relatively speedy victory over Euro-scepticism, however, requires going back to developments of the previous decade.

The technology-gap scare of the 1970s

According to many observers at the time, Europe was not responding successfully to the technological revolution under way since the 1970s. Furthermore, it was increasingly argued that failure to respond successfully now would mean that Europe would not be in possession of the key to the economies of tomorrow. Even worse, Europe would in all likelihood then become an economically dependent region and its very existence as a unique culture would be threatened.

At the end of the 1970s there was a general feeling that the IT revolution posed a double threat to Europe. On the one hand lay the importance of IT to the economies of tomorrow – master these technologies now or the race for economic survival will be lost. In this view, if the race were lost and Europe became dependent on foreign sources for this key raw material, the consequences would be nothing short of catastrophic. Ultimately, according to a report drawn up within the Science, Research and Development Directorate General of the Commission (DG XII), nothing less than the distinct quality of European society stood to be lost in the struggle.

> The basis for Europe to participate in the international division of labour is highly exposed if not already in imminent danger. If Europe does not master the new information technology, the survival of European industry in a free trade world economy is at risk. This is equivalent to putting the existence of our open economies, and of our open societies, into question. Unfortunately the questions of industrial survival and societal design are often treated as if they were separate or even conflicting objectives. (FAST 1984: 70)

> The autonomy of Europe's economy (and the diversity of sociocultural identities in Europe) will, to a great extent, depend upon the capacity for scientific and technological innovation in the space/electronic technology sector (FAST 1984: 165).

This view was held not just in Brussels. The head of planning staff in the German foreign ministry, Konrad Seitz, author of *Die japanisch-amerikanische Herausforderung: Deutschlands Hochtechnologie-Industrien kämpfen ums Überleben* (Seitz 1991), expressed the same sentiment when referring to the debate unleashed by the American announcement of the Strategic Defense Initiative (SDI) a few years later: 'the research effort undertaken here [SDI] could make a decisive contribution to bringing about the technological advance which would drive the American economy forward into the twenty-first century and at the same time make Europe definitively dependent' (Seitz 1985: 154).

Although it is important to note that the discussions that culminated in Esprit pre-dated the announcement of SDI, the Commission began to argue that intervention was necessary in order to reverse a trend already seen to be menacing. In making this argument, the Commission adopted two approaches. The first concerned itself with the issue of why the IT sector required government intervention if it was to grow as it should (and the normative undertones here are indeed very strong). The other addressed the question of why this intervention would be better made at the European level, i.e. if overseen by the Commission.

The Commission had begun to argue, in the late 1970s, that high-tech industries, in particular the IT industry, have special characteristics that warrant, if not require, government action in the form of various kinds of support. According to this analysis, there is a chronic tendency for under-investment by industry. The existence of limited incentives for companies to undertake investment is due to the fact that much of the R&D carried out is long term and high risk. Also, owing to the considerable costs involved in R&D in this industry, there are very high barriers to entry (for a review of the market failure arguments justifying government intervention in the IT sector, see Müller 1990).

This is frequently considered to be a problem that justifies state intervention when the social benefits of investment, in terms of the developments that result (for example the protection or creation of a country's competitive advantages), may be shown to outweigh the private, corporate gains. The Commission in this case took the view that the social gains did indeed outweigh the private:

Concurrently, with the present economic crisis, Europe is suffering from declining competitiveness in its industry. This has resulted in an increasing loss of markets and in a consequent rise in unemployment. Increasing competition from Europe's major industrial competitors is being experienced even more in the high technology industries which are the key to Europe's future growth . . . [because] . . . [i]nformation technologies affect the entire fabric of the economy. Their rapid application offers the key to increased competitiveness in virtually all main sectors in manufacturing industry and in the service sector . . . [and] . . . it is also a major growth sector. (CEC 1982c: 1).

This technical-barriers-to-investment argument is often countered with the claim that, if business is not willing to invest in something, then there is usually good reason for this. The Commission's response to this criticism, which forms the basis of the second prong of its two-pronged argument, is the construction of the 'European logic' view (called the 'Costs of Non-Europe' by the Commission). This same argument underpins the internal market project.

In this view, the commercial weaknesses of European companies, not just in the IT industry, are due to the absence of a market large enough to make the attainment of economies of scale possible. Only the presence of such economies of scale would permit R&D costs, which are particularly high in the IT industry, to be recouped, and thus provide the necessary incentives to investment. This was the prime advantage enjoyed by Europe's American and Japanese competitors, according to the Commission. 'We want to create a truly European market, a common market, which offers business the same chances that their American and Japanese competitors have' (House of Lords Select Committee 1984: 185).

Compounding the problem of fragmented markets in the European IT industry is the presence of nationalistic habits, national procurement policies and lack of harmonization of regulatory policies and of technical standards (see Sharp and Pavitt 1993; Müller 1990). The lack of common standards is particularly damaging because it means that not even in basic components can economies of scale be reached. It had been estimated in the early 1980s that critical mass in sales could be reached with the capture of about 5 per cent of world market share. At the time the European market represented 25 per cent of the world IT market, thus giving European firms a potentially sufficient home market in which to achieve economies of scale. It was reasoned that a large part of Europe's failure to achieve this level could be accounted for by the fragmentation of their 'home' market. Japanese and American success was taken as proof of this proposition. It was argued that the Americans and Japanese were able to operate profitably in the various European national markets only because they can subsidize the production of non-standardized products for smaller markets from their high-volume sales of standardized products in their home markets, where they have long achieved economies of scale.

Although it is beyond the scope of this chapter to go into detail on this point, it is worth noting that the Commission's arguments about the potential benefits of economies of scale, and therefore of the internal market, have come in for criticism for a number of reasons. Criticism has included a critique of the methodologies used to calculate the figures presented as supporting the 'costs of non-Europe' scenario (Tsoukalis 1993: 90–2; see also Cutler 1989). There are also those who point out that economists are prone to speak increasingly of diseconomies of scale in today's post-Fordist economy.[2]

[2] When the multi-plant, multi-product firm is now commonplace, in 'those practical discourses on management which are not burdened with an obsolete model of the firm, the concept of economies of scale has been increasingly marginalised' Cutler (1989: 63); Sharp and Pavitt (1993) have pointed out that, 'the fixation with scale has meant that governments failed to recognise that size could not compensate for poor management; indeed often, as Britain learned to its cost, it often compounded the problem.' An interesting research paper could be to analyse the discourse relating to the Single Market

Nevertheless, the Commission was largely successful in making the case that the creation of a European market and home base for European companies was necessary, as the eventual success of the Single Market initiative indicates. What it still had to prove was that a European effort to rescue the IT industry was called for, rather than the 'national champions' strategies of the past. It did so by convincing enough people that,

> as regards technology development projects of international size, the Community alone is able to provide the strategy, market and potential framework which can give to these projects their full weight, and impact on the European innovation potential . . . [sic] . . . The Community can play a more direct part where the European dimension allows more efficient new ways to stimulate, such as the promotion of more European cooperation groupings and joint ventures at enterprise level in key sector technologies, or the promotion of new technology-based firms with a European market perspective. (CEC 1981b: 8).

These 'new ways to stimulate' firms active in the IT industry centred around encouraging inter-firm cooperation, particularly at the R&D stage, in an attempt to emulate what was seen to be the basis for the success of Japan and the USA (Japan through the Ministry of International Trade and Industry (MITI) and the USA through the constant movement of employees from one company to another) (see CEC 1981b: 14–15).

In 1977 Etienne Davignon became Commissioner for Industry (DGIII) with the intention of changing the Community's image of being concerned only with propping up sunset industries such as steel to a more positive one of encouraging growth in the industries of tomorrow. In testimony before the House of Lords Select Committee on the European Communities, Davignon reported that when he came to look closely at the IT industry he had been dismayed by the lack of incentives for firms to collaborate with other European firms. 'There was no incentive for cross-border co-operation. Every state had programmes, and very often they were good, but because they were of a national nature there was no incentive for cross-border co-operation.' (Davignon, House of Lords Select Committee 1984: 169).

Davignon looked to the USA and Japan in particular as offering models that Europe needed to adopt. Specifically, he credited the close collaboration between firms and acknowledged the part played by the state in directing or focusing research effort in Japan as playing a

project because most of it is shaped around the metaphor of 'purifying' the member state economies by removing barriers to (natural) trade that exist as a result of policies (i.e. man-made).

significant role in the economic and technological success of Japan. Davignon was not alone in seeking new models that would provide answers to Europe's problems, and across Europe changes were under way in policies that affected IT.

Poor national responses

Sandholtz (1992) has argued that national politicians were also seeking new ways to promote their high-tech industries in the early 1980s, and were thus in what he terms a 'policy adaptive mood' at the time when Esprit was first proposed. Although it is true that the national champion strategies of the past were increasingly being openly criticized, Sandholtz may be overestimating the extent to which they were in fact discredited. Although Davignon's call to seek European solutions to industrial problems was publicly accepted by almost everyone at the time, it would be too much to deduce from this that national champion strategies were no longer accepted. If it were the case that national champion strategies were no longer a popular policy instrument, it would be surprising to find that as late as 1994 the Commission was still publishing studies in which it claimed that national champion strategies cannot be sustained any longer (Delapierre and Zimmermann 1994: 159). Rather, it seems reasonable to conclude that there was an awareness that European initiatives could help, but they were never really intended to replace national champion strategies.

Nevertheless, there was a change under way in most member states in science and technology policies. This shift was on the whole towards a policy direction that saw the state playing an important role in encouraging industry-industry and industry-academia collaboration, i.e. the cornerstone of technology corporatism. In a survey of science and technology (S&T) policy from 1980 to 1984 in France, Germany, the Netherlands, Sweden and the United Kingdom, Lederman noted that in each of these countries important changes in emphasis and approach had recently occurred (Lederman 1985: 131–2). Although Lederman pointed out that there are differences between the countries in the exact priorities set and means selected, all undertook public policy changes that were aimed at: increasing funding levels for academic research; strengthening efforts to focus S&T resources on economic and social objectives; building activities to encourage academic–industry–government research and training cooperation; enacting special programmes and creating incentives to increase industrial R&D and international technological competitiveness. Furthermore, these countries had all selected the same core areas on which to concentrate these efforts, namely information technology,[3] biotechnology, production technology and materials science.

United Kingdom
For example, the Alvey Programme in Great Britain has almost exactly the same objectives and employs essentially the same means as Esprit in achieving those objectives. Indeed, the very same people running the Alvey Directorate were responsible for overseeing Britain's work within Esprit, and the similarities between the programmes were so great as to become an issue within Britain.

France
In 1981 the French government under Mitterrand began its famed policy of national economic revival, and here as well the IT sector occupied an important plank in the government's plans to remake France into a strong and independent economic power (see Moynot 1987). The IT industry figured importantly in this plan to rejuvenate French industry, and measures included the nationalization of leading firms such as Thomson and Bull. As well, there was a concentration of public resources into particular IT areas in the Filière Electronique, although management of the new state firms was encouraged to collaborate with European firms. These goals, as well as those intended to raise the purchasing power of French consumers, required massive increases in state funding.

By 1983, however, it had become clear that the spending levels involved in these plans were not sustainable over a longer period of time by one country alone. The result was a marked shift away from a go-it-alone policy towards a strong pro-European policy, and France became a champion of European efforts. As one indication of this shift, the minister for research and industry, who had headed the drive to make France an independent power in the IT industry, Jean-Pierre Chevènement, was replaced by the pro-European Laurent Fabius in 1983. Interestingly, Fabius was chairman of the Council of Research Ministers of the EC when the Commission's Esprit programme eventually came up for approval (the reaction from the Research Council was highly supportive). It had taken the French government less than three years to evolve from a vigorous promoter of national champions and independence into an enthusiastic advocate of European collaboration.

The reasoning behind the new attitude towards Europe within the French government is spelt out in an analysis prepared by a top-level

---

[3] In Britain, 1982 was declared the 'Year of Information Technology'.

think tank of the French government in 1982/3 (Secretariat d'Etat auprès du Premier Ministre et Commissariat Général du Plan 1983; Mytelka 1995; Sandholtz 1992: 146–51). In a wide-ranging consideration of what France's strategy towards Europe should be for the 1980s, the IT industry is singled out for its importance and a detailed case built for expanding incentives for inter-firm collaboration at the European level.

Germany

The situation in the Federal Republic of Germany has never been so clearly pro-European in the field of IT as it was to become in France (Sandholtz 1992: 152–4). Nevertheless, when Hans-Dietrich Genscher appointed Konrad Seitz as head of his planning staff, a shift towards a more pro-European stance became evident. During the years Esprit was being developed, the German government was essentially split between those who favoured the principle of state intervention to support key industries (and there was little disagreement that IT was one of these), and those who thought the market should be left to provide the solutions to the industry's acknowledged problems. The former could be found in the ministry of research and technology, and were therefore open to the underlying philosophy of Esprit, although they had reservations about the extent of it, and the latter were dominant in the ministry of finance and economics.

For these reasons, Germany was one of only two states (the other being Britain, although for reasons that had little to do with Esprit itself) to raise significant opposition to the approval of the first phase of Esprit. Germany's concern however was with the expansion of the Commission's budget that Esprit entailed, rather than with any fundamental opposition to the programme (Ward and Edwards 1990: 114).

In general, Davignon's intentions and later the goals embodied in Esprit, and indeed the approach taken with regard to improving the competitiveness of high-tech industry in Europe later confirmed in the Single European Act, did not run against the grain insofar as the emerging consensus on public policy for advanced technology was concerned. Rather, when the Commission took its approach to the matter to the member states it was more or less pushing against an open door. To this extent, it is accurate to conclude, with Sandholtz, that member states were in a 'policy adaptive mood'.

Indeed, the arguments in favour of focusing attention on and adopting measures to improve the Community's competitive position in the new technologies were so successful that they paved the way for Article 130 of the Single European Act. The various paragraphs of this Article reiterate the conclusions already reached in the debate surrounding the launch of Esprit, such as the primary need to strengthen the scientific and technological base of European industry and to encourage international competition. The consensus that the Community should involve itself only in programmes or activities that support pre-competitive research is found in Article 130f. The paragraph immediately following describes the necessity of encouraging collaboration among European firms (see De Ruyt 1989: 202–7). Esprit had broken new ground, was at the time considered a success and therefore was used as a model for setting out the Community's rights in the field of research and technology.

The failure of earlier European IT initiatives

Although member states were in a relatively receptive mood at the time, the Commission faced a hurdle in convincing industry itself that it had the competence and the vision to offer industry the kind of support it felt it required. In particular, the Commission had to overcome a certain amount of mistrust of intra-European collaboration on the part of industry owing to the failure of the UNIDATA initiative. This initiative had been one of the most important such collaborative attempts to date.

UNIDATA was a collaborative project, begun in 1971 in the form of a consortium between Philips, Siemens and CII in order to start producing mainframe computers. Their goal was to compete with IBM, which dominated the market at the time in Europe and around the world. The project, which had been moving at a snail's pace, was undermined in 1975 when the French government, which owned CII, decided to merge it with Honeywell-Bull. This would have the effect of bringing an American firm into the consortium, which had been created as a response to the American dominance of the market. Both Siemens and Philips made it clear during the pre-merger discussions that Honeywell-Bull would no longer be welcome in the consortium. Both also made it clear that without the participation of CII there was not much point in continuing the joint effort. The French government decided to press ahead with the merger and consequently the consortium and the attempt it represented (to find a European response to foreign domination) came to an unhappy end (Sandholtz 1992: 96–7).

The Commission had secured agreement from the Council in 1974 for a medium-term project on the application, development and production of data-processing systems by linking it to the UNIDATA project. The collapse of UNIDATA left this project in the field of data-processing without a leg (or mainframe?) to stand on, with the result that there was no longer a coordinated response in Europe to the American and growing Japanese dominance of this market (Sharp 1989: 204–5).

This unsuccessful attempt at intra-European collaboration also poisoned the waters of European collaboration for the rest of the decade, and hung over the discussions with industry that had begun on an informal basis in the Directorate General of the Commission for Industry (DG III) towards the end of the 1970s. This was one of the reasons there was no great enthusiasm for intra-European collaboration in the IT sector, even though there was, as was pointed out earlier, a growing feeling that such collaboration was necessary.

To compound this scepticism towards collaboration between European firms, industry's view was that the Commission was not technically competent to carry out significant policies in the IT sector. Furthermore, they reasoned, even if they were able to overcome this problem of competency, industry saw the Commission as handicapped by the fact that the Council usually took so long to come to a decision that even those policies that might have an effect came so late that they were doomed to be ineffective (Sandholtz 1992: 98–9).

Designing the programme

In 1978, determined to take action in the field of IT, the Commission created a secretariat within the Science, Research and Development Directorate General (DG XII) in order 'to contribute to the definition of long-term Community research and development objectives and priorities and thus to the development of a coherent science and technology policy in the long term' (FAST 1984: 187).

The group was officially named Forecasting and Assessment in the Field of Science and Technology (FAST) and was charged with studying the effect of structural change within the Community.[4] Davignon, who was Commissioner for Industry (DG III) at the time, began working with members of the FAST team looking into long lead-time R&D which is characteristic of many IT products (source: interview 1, see appendix to chapter). Eventually, Davignon was to take over this specialist group by moving it into his Directorate General and having it report directly to him, thus by-passing the regular bureaucratic channels within the Commission. Davignon gave the group the new title of Information Technology Task Force (ITTF) (Ringrose 1994: 74).

[4] The report of the FAST group was submitted to the Commission in December 1982, and later published under the title *Eurofutures: The Challenge of Innovation* Commission of the European Communities in association with the journal *Futures* (FAST, 1984).

As part of its work, the ITTF proposed a draft 'European Strategic Programme for R&D in Information Technology' for discussion with industry in late 1979 (interview 1). According to the FAST report, the final Esprit proposal was the result of a 'preparatory research project of about 18 months duration which was conceived within FAST' (FAST 1984: 165). In the literature on the subject, the shape of the programme that was to become Esprit is generally agreed to have emerged out of the roundtable discussions held between Davignon and the largest IT firms. There is evidence that suggests that the draft proposal came from the Information Technology Task Force first, but then was significantly revised with industry (interviews 1 and 2). Nevertheless, there is little disagreement over the conclusion that the initiative came first from Davignon and his team and was developed further with industry. For the purposes of this chapter, it is sufficient then to note that the initiative did not come from industry in the first place.

The draft proposal, which already stressed the promotion of intra-European collaborative research, was presented to an informal meeting of the largest twelve firms in the IT industry, namely Siemens, Nixdorf, Olivetti, Thomson CSF, GEC, ICL, AEG, Plessey, Philips, CGE, CII-Honeywell Bull, STET. The Information Technology Task Force had wanted to ascertain industry's reaction to its proposals before taking them to Davignon. According to the GEC representative, such roundtable discussions were originally 'part of a rather wider industrial discussion organised by the Commission in terms of how European industry should respond, particularly to the Japanese threat in the total scheme of information technology, computers, telecommunications and all of the industrial implications of information technology' (House of Lords Select Committee 1984: 35). This industry group became known as the Big 12, and not long after, in 1980, they established themselves as the European Information Technology Industry Roundtable (EITIRT) in order to advise the Commission on the development of European R&D programmes in the Information and Communication Technologies (ICT) domain (EITIRT 1995) and to coordinate their work with the Commission.

Initially, industry was sceptical about the benefits and workability of collaborative research, being still bruised after the UNIDATA failure and continuing to doubt the Commission's competence (Sharp 1989: 209). Also, the idea of collaborative research with European firms, which was what the ITTF proposal contained, was not immediately welcomed by the group. An English participant in the first roundtable discussions recalled:

In this country and throughout the EEC, we were very slow to recognise [that collaborative research could benefit all parties]. We started with the assumption that companies were going to compete with one another and therefore they could not possibly share research results. (House of Lords Select Committee 1984: 35–6)

Nevertheless, the discussions continued and the participants in the roundtable studied the proposal, and considered the arguments, as well as going over the figures, until they were more convinced that what was being proposed was reasonable. At this point the Information Technology Task Force, under Roland Hüber, felt confident enough to take the draft proposal to Davignon, who was the one with the power to make it actually happen (interview 1).

However, Davignon was not prepared to accept the proposal until he had heard for himself industry's opinion of it, so in 1980 he called together the heads of the Big 12 (comprising 70 per cent of the industry at the time) and officially tabled the proposal for discussion (Sharp 1989).[5] This meeting is usually considered to be the moment when the European Information Technology Industry Roundtable was formally founded, although it must be remembered that this group had in fact been meeting regularly before this date.

At Davignon's roundtable meeting he heard that the Big 12 were in general agreement with the outlines of the proposal. The addition of Davignon's charisma and political skills then made the difference in terms of winning industry's full commitment (interviews 1, 2 and 3). Despite their initial scepticism, the participants eventually agreed that collaboration was possible in the form put forward and should focus on pre-competitive research in order to avoid two potential problems. First, the participants were competitors and this way they would not have to share secrets with each other about products that were close to the market (interview 4).[6] Secondly, such collaborative agreements would not run foul of Community competition legislation (Walsum-Stachowicz 1994: 110–11).

Moreover, one can see in Esprit's focus on pre-competitive research an incomplete resolution of the struggle between what Cox (1993) calls state-capitalist and hyper-liberal societal models. Mytelka argues that:

Underlying the design of ESPRIT was also the strong antipathy to state

---

[5] The members of the original discussions were representatives from the Big 12, and from DG III, DG XII and Narjes' cabinet.
[6] This problem proved to be real when in the Fourth Framework Programme, as a result of public pressure to move the projects closer to the market in order to show tangible results of the time and money being spent on Community R&D programmes, the IT companies found themselves unable to put together the same number of agreements precisely because they were competing with each other in the fields covered (interview 4).

intervention in the economy that constituted the reigning ideology of the day. Administrative guidance of the sort that MITI has made famous, industrial policy and even the type of indicative planning practised in France were spurned and market forces enshrined. This was also the period in which governments in Europe and North America equated partnerships with collusion and anticompetitive behaviour. Combined, these two ideological predilections led to an initial emphasis on pre-competitive R&D projects within ESPRIT. (Mytelka 1993: 57)[7]

However, the fact is that Esprit did entail granting a significant role for the Commission in the IT industry, particularly in bringing firms together (the broker-state). As will be discussed below in more detail, the framework created to manage the programme called for close cooperation between industry and the Commission, suggesting that a clear separation of state and capital was not achieved. For this reason we believe that the outcome had more in common with the state-capitalist model than with the hyper-liberal one.

As mentioned, it is significant that it was the Information Technology Task Force that made the initial proposal, in contrast to the Single Market project, where the initiative came from the European Roundtable of Industrialists (ERT, not to be mixed up with the IT Roundtable). In terms of Bornschier's thesis (that Esprit was the result of an elite pact between industry and political entrepreneurs in Brussels), however, the fact that the initiative came from the latter and not from industry is not so significant. There is no disagreement among observers that both industry and the Commission worked out the details of the programme and went on to form an alliance of sorts (of which more below) to get the programme accepted in the Council. Therefore, we may still speak of an elite pact.

Once Davignon had heard that industry stood behind the programme he then felt he needed to know that they would take the programme seriously and actually do something with the money. For this reason he made funding for projects available on a 50/50 basis; that is, the Commission would put up 50 per cent of the costs of a project and the project members themselves would bring the other 50 per cent. According to Davignon, this funding arrangement was not popular among the firms present because they were 'accustomed that in the old systems, who paid was the national government, so you had a shared programme, the Community paid x per cent and the budget of the state paid x per cent', and the company put up little, if anything. Davignon's strategy was to ensure that the Commission's money would be well spent:

---

[7] See also Kennedy (1989), who suggests that the concern with 'competitiveness' has replaced a concern with industrial policy.

I said: 'How will I know that this scheme is really something, which is for you of the essence, not something that you are ready to do to get a subsidy, but something, which is so important in your strategy that you are ready to put your money on the table, because you feel it's that important'.(Interview 5)

This tactic also meant that the programme would be twice as large as whatever figure the Council agreed to. Since this figure was unlikely to be large at first, this mechanism allowed the programme to be large enough still to make an impact. Indeed, the fact that Davignon approached the Council with a modest spending request, made even more attractive by being presented in the form of a pilot project requiring no long-term commitment of funds, is regarded as important to the success of his proposal (Sharp 1989: 209).

We agree fully with Peterson when he concludes:

In political terms, Davignon and the Commission, and later the French proponents of Eureka required support from Europe's Big 12 firms to place collaborative R&D on the agenda of European governments, and ultimately to channel the political momentum for new schemes to support of wider political agendas. The Commission's agenda included overcoming the EC's history of failure in collaborative programmes, new collaborative programmes, and ultimately linking support for collaborative R&D to the [Single European Market] initiative. (Peterson 1991: 280–1)

When the backing of industry had been won, the next step was to go about convincing the member states that the Commission should have a role to play in trying to improve the state of Europe's IT industry, and then that this programme, which by now officially carried the name Esprit, was the right way to do it.

Selling the programme

In May of 1982 the Commission presented the Council with a communication entitled *Towards a European Strategic Programme for Research and Development in Information Technologies* in which it clearly spelt out its analysis and intentions in the IT sector (CEC 1982c). In proposing a European Strategic Programme of Research and Development in Information Technology, the Commission was basing its competence to act in this field on Article 235 of the EEC Treaty, which permits the Commission to take the appropriate measures in areas where the treaty has not provided the necessary powers.

In June of the same year the Council of Research Ministers concluded that the Community indeed required such a programme in order to increase the competitiveness of the IT industry. It recommended that the Council of Ministers make available funds for the pilot phase, details of which were soon to be presented by the Commission. In August the Commission presented its proposals for this pilot phase, with a budget of 11.5 million ECU. In the meantime, IT Roundtable companies discussed with their respective home governments their enthusiasm for the programme, and in December 1992 the Council gave its approval (interviews 4 and 6).

The thirty-eight projects undertaken in the pilot phase of Esprit were generally deemed to be a success, and when in June 1983 the Commission presented the ten-year Esprit Phase 1 to the Council for approval there was little opposition to the plan itself. There was, however, difficulty in getting approval for the budget of the programme because of the opposition of Germany and Britain. Both countries had made their approval of Esprit contingent on an acceptable solution to the question of budgetary reform. It must be stressed that these reservations were not due to any real disagreement with Esprit, or because the two wished to see an alternative plan enacted (Ward and Edwards 1990: 113–14). Rather, at the time Britain was pushing for a change in the way its financial contributions were calculated, and Germany was trying to limit the Commission's expenditures, and to achieve this, insisted that funds for Esprit be found within the Community's Framework Programme (i.e. funds already allocated).

In the end, the Commission responded with a compromise proposal and an agreement was reached in February 1984 on a budget of 750 million ECU over five years and 1,500 million ECU over ten years, and staggered so that no new money would be required for the first two years. After the agreement had been reached, Thatcher publicly stated on several occasions her and her government's support for Esprit, singling it out as precisely the kind of programme the Community should be mounting. Nevertheless, her strategy of holding Esprit hostage had been very unpopular both at home and with her partners on the Council.

To review, the agreement finally reached was for the first five-year phase of a ten-year programme of funding for collaborative research in the field of IT, with the aim of strengthening Europe's competitiveness in this industry. Consortia involving two or more companies, universities or private research institutes from at least two countries within the Community (and exceptionally from outside it) could bid for money to support pre-competitive R&D projects in one of the five fields selected. These fields were: advanced micro-electronics, with a special emphasis on the design and production of very large-scale integrated chips; the design of software technology; advanced information processing; office systems; and computer-aided manufacturing, or robotics.

In all the interviews we conducted, the importance of industry lobbying of national governments in getting Esprit accepted by the Council was repeatedly stressed.[8] Therefore, we may conclude that industry, through the European Information Technology Industry Roundtable, had become the ally of the Commission in putting forward a proposal that increased the scope of the latter's competences, and in transferring authority over technology policy to a significant degree to the Commission. Industry, again through the Roundtable, had played an integral role in drawing up the Esprit programme. As mentioned above, the fact that the Commission had been captured by industry in this field was the Commission's trump card in securing agreement to Esprit in the Council (see Davignon's comments, House of Lords Select Committee 1984: 170).

Corporatist technology policy in practice

Thus, there is evidence of technology corporatism in the way in which Esprit was drafted, i.e. in the policy-making process. As the following discussion will illustrate, there is also evidence of technology corporatism in the execution of this policy, where the institutionalized influence of the European Information Technology Industry Roundtable in particular, but also of industry in general, is noteworthy.

Esprit is a ten-year programme although its budget is allocated in five-year instalments. A workplan is devised on a yearly basis which specifies the exact areas for which funding will be made available and for which project proposals may be submitted. The Information Technology Task Force (ITTF) – which was later converted into the Directorate General of the Commission for Telecommunications, Information Industries and Innovation DG XIII – adopts the annual workplans once they have been agreed with two other bodies, the Esprit Management Committee and the Esprit Advisory Board (Sandholtz 1992; Ringrose 1994; Walsum-Stachowicz 1994; and various Commission documents). The ITTF also organizes the evaluation of projects submitted by independent experts, and passes these recommendations on to the EMC.

Membership of the Esprit Management Committee (EMC) consists of two representatives from each member state, usually from government but occasionally from industry or academia. Voting is by qualified majority. The EMC, as well as being consulted on the draft of the yearly workplans, also has an important say in the selection of projects,

---

[8] For a study that reaches a similar conclusion, see Peterson (1991: 276).

ensuring through its input that the policy of *juste retour* (fair return) is adhered to (Ringrose 1994: 130–1).

The Esprit Advisory Board (EAB) plays a similar role to that of the EMC in that it gives advice on the workplans and in the selection of projects. It is made up of experts selected by the Commission from industry and academia, officially working in a private capacity. During the first years of Esprit, up to half of the membership of the EAB was from Roundtable firms; the rest were from universities, small and medium-sized enterprises and research institutes. Only later were information technology users included in the EAB. This remains one of the important places in the policy execution process where the interests of industry are represented.

Still, the influence of the Roundtable companies is felt strongest in the aptly named Esprit Steering Committee (ESC) even though it has no official standing. Membership is essentially the Roundtable firms, plus academics and small and medium-sized enterprises to give it added legitimacy. The ESC's role is to give advice to the ITTF/Commission and it was set up originally to advise Davignon on the creation of Esprit. It was through the ESC in particular, but also through the Roundtable's informal contacts with ITTF/Commission members, that industry controlled the shape of Esprit during the early years. On the basis of her interviews, Ringrose concludes that, 'in the closed forum of the ESC, Esprit's largest projects were designed and because those projects received the majority of Esprit funds, Esprit's budget was effectively dispersed according to gentlemen's agreements in the ESC' (Ringrose 1994: 128).

It would seem possible then to conclude that not only was the relationship between the Commission and the European Information Technology Industry Roundtable very close, but, because it was institutionalized, we may speak of an instance of technological corporatism. The Commission depended heavily on the technical input of the Roundtable in designing and executing Esprit. It also depended on the lobbying influence of the Roundtable firms with the governments of their member states in the quest to secure agreement to the expansion of the Commission's competences.

Clearly, such a relationship of dependence of political actors upon organized industrial actors is not without its parallels in many political systems, nor is it something novel for industrial interests to have influence on policy-making within a democracy. But, to summarize the argument so far, what is novel and noteworthy here is the extent to which organized interests, the European Information Technology Industry Roundtable in particular, played an institutionalized role in the policy-making process and in the execution of this policy at the European level.

Technology corporatism ten years on

Although we have concluded that the relationship between the Commission and the European Information Technology Industry Roundtable is an incidence of technological corporatism, the influence of the EITIRT, in the view of both the Roundtable and Directorate General officials (DG XIII), has declined considerably since the 1990s (interviews 1, 3, 4, 6). We are thus faced with the question of what this means for their corporatist relationship.

On the one hand, the formal integration of the Roundtable of European information technology firms into the policy-making process involved in Esprit (setting the objectives and focus of the programme and project selection, as well as taking part as project participants) has not changed significantly, although there has been a marked decrease in the percentage of projects in which members of the Roundtable are involved. Thus, the institutionalized role has not changed much as such. On the other hand however, the openness of the Commission to the input and influence of the European Information Technology Industry Roundtable has declined to a significant extent, to the point where both recognize that the relationship has undergone a major change.

If the key point, as we have argued in this chapter, is the institutionalized aspect of the Roundtable's influence in the field of information technology, then this influence has been only slightly reduced by the developments just described. The decline in influence occurred as a result of other interests being represented in the policy-making process, thereby breaking the Roundtable's monopoly on industrial policy input. These interests are for the most part also industrial ones, including enhanced visibility of small and medium-sized enterprises and increasingly software producers, as well as organized representations from foreign firms (for example, American producers' associations, the American Chamber of Commerce, etc.) (interview 4). These developments reflect a recent change in focus of the Commission towards support for user interests in the Community.

In terms of the more informal side of the Roundtable's influence however, there is general agreement that it is no longer as popular among policy-makers in the Commission as it once was (interviews 1, 4, 6; Walsum-Stachowicz 1994). Nevertheless the decline of the influence of the Roundtable in policy-making in Brussels is not easily measured. It may be illustrated by the views of those involved that the Commission is no longer so eager to listen to the Roundtable's views. Alternatively, we may see it in the decline of the share of Esprit projects going to its members.

We may also find evidence in the failure of proposals made by the European Information Technology Industry Roundtable in 1989 to further institutionalize their role in technology policy-making in the Community. One proposal, contained in a White Paper issued by the Roundtable, recommended that regular meetings between its working groups and officials from the Directorates General who were concerned with these technical areas be held on a regular basis (interview 3; Roundtable, internal paper). Such meetings had been taking place but were not bound to do so on the basis of any formal agreement.

More ambitiously, the European Information Technology Industry Roundtable called in this paper for meetings between the chief executives of the Big 12 and the president of the Commission and his/her Commissioners, also to be held on a fixed, regular basis. The Commission declined to accept these proposals. We are thus left with the question of whether the fact that the proposals were not accepted should be taken as a symbol of the Roundtable's declining influence. Or, equally, we could ask whether the fact that the Roundtable felt it necessary to formalize a relationship that had existed for many years might be evidence that it too perceived a weakening of its influence which it hoped to arrest. At the minimum, it would seem safe to conclude that there has been a decline in the Roundtable's influence with the Commission relative to its influence when Esprit was launched.

Concrete answers to the question of why the Roundtable's influence is decreasing are difficult to find. The Commission's inability to live up to its promises regarding funding for the Joint European Submicron Silicon Initiative (JESSI) is cited as one reason for the Commission 'losing the industry lobby'. Another may be found in the public criticism by Brussels of an apparent lack of European 'engagement' by industry. Members of DG XIII and the European Information Technology Industry Roundtable also had a serious falling out over the issue of billing for hours worked on Esprit, with DG officials accusing the industry of over-billing (interview 1).

In her study of corporate influence on the policy-making process in the information technology sector in Brussels, Walsum-Stachowicz concludes that, from a position of almost total monopoly of corporate policy input into Esprit, the Roundtable's influence has significantly weakened (Walsum-Stachowicz 1994: 279–80). Several reasons are offered for this development. One view is that it is a result of the increasing ineffectiveness of the Roundtable itself in putting forward a coherent strategy or view as it sought to expand its mandate. From focusing on purely technical matters associated with information technology, the Roundtable has begun to put forward positions relating to wider issues of the shape of the Community's economic and political system (see recent EITIRT position papers, including EITIRT (1995) *Europe and the Global Information Society* in which the Roundtable describes its mission as contributing 'to a dialogue with the European Commission on all aspects of EU policies and programmes in the information and communication domain').

This move has accentuated the divergence of interests held by members of the European Information Technology Industry Roundtable. When, for example, the Roundtable turns to address the question of state intervention in or regulation of industry, the fact that Thomson is still owned by the French state means agreement will necessarily be difficult to reach. Such differences remained hidden when the group was addressing only technical matters (interviews 2 and 3). The result has been positions or statements that are often so watered-down and non-committal in terms of a specific policy direction (in other words, they comprise lowest common denominator preferences) that they have been of little substance and carried little weight (interviews 4 and 6; see also Walsum-Stachowicz 1994: 291–2).

Although there is some recognition of this as a factor explaining their declining influence in Brussels, Roundtable members themselves point to another factor. They claim that their voice, rather than having grown less sure, has simply been drowned out by the proliferation of voices in Brussels, both as Community membership has expanded and as other groups have organized and taken their case to Brussels (interviews 3, 4, 6). Interest group representation in Brussels is certainly exploding and the Commission is becoming the lobbying target of more and more interest groups, so this explanation may hold some truth.

The Roundtable of IT industrialists also argues that it has become less and less interested in attracting the Commission's attention. It has become a general complaint among the largest in the IT industry that the Commission's technology policy has become too 'politicized' by the addition of objectives that are no longer strictly technology or industry driven. As a result, the Commission's policies have become less effective as they have increasingly been linked to Community goals in the fields of social cohesion or regional policy (interviews 2, 4, 6). In their review of Community technology policy, Starbatty and Vetterlein have suggested that it is indeed no coincidence that Article 130f–q of the SEA, which lays down the Community's brief in Research and Technology, is preceded directly by articles referring to its responsibilities in the realm of economic and social cohesion (Starbatty and Vetterlein 1989: 147). One of industry's complaints is indeed that the Commission has begun using the former to meet its needs in the latter.

With this politicization of technology policy, the resulting policy is of less and less relevance to the larger IT companies that make up the European Information Technology Industry Roundtable. As one industry official put it, what is the point of Siemens bringing a less technologically advanced company from, say, Greece into a consortium simply to supply a component when the same is available down the street from a well-experienced provider (interview 2)? Clearly, the only difference for Siemens may be that it no longer qualifies for EU money in supporting this venture. According to industry, the potential of strengthening the international competitiveness of Europe's IT industry has been sacrificed to 'politics'.

Walsum-Stachowicz also suggests that member state governments are more inclined to be open to Roundtable lobbying when they have a national champion on it. We have suggested that having the backing of these national champions was one reason Esprit received such a warm reception by member state governments when it was originally tabled. However, as the Community has expanded southward, more countries without an IT national champion are represented in the Council. As such, it is hardly surprising that the focus on supporting Europe's larger IT firms, most of which come from larger states, has shifted towards a focus on small and medium-sized enterprises, sometimes the only firms a country may have in the IT industry. The relative weight of the pro-IT intervention has been reduced as a consequence (Walsum-Stachowicz 1994: 318). Furthermore, many of these newer members are precisely those countries to which the bulk of social and regional policies are directed. This may also account for the apparent 'politicization' of technology policy.

Yet another factor warrants consideration in analysing the decline of the Roundtable's influence in Brussels, namely, the role that structural change in the economies of Europe and in the IT industry itself has played in changing the terms of the game. In the first place, the question needs to be posed: how relevant are programmes that portray the world in terms of competing blocs when the major players within the international economy are becoming globalized? Equally, is it possible that the Roundtable's influence has declined because 'Europe' is no longer so important to its members, which are increasingly global in their operations and strategy and thus paying less attention to their relationship with policy-makers in Brussels?

Although there is no doubt something in this argument, it must not be forgotten that, for all their presence in global markets, European IT firms are still European based insofar as the largest proportion of their sales and their strongest market position continue to be found in Europe. Siemens, for example, conducts nearly 60 per cent of its business with customers outside of Germany, but still around two-thirds of all value-added work takes place in that country, suggesting that even the label 'European' may be exaggerated. As a result it cannot be the case that Europe is no longer important to these companies, although it may be possible to argue that a European strategy alone can no longer be sufficient.

It is beyond the scope of this chapter to offer more than a few passing thoughts on this question. Those remaining large IT firms of European origin are increasingly global companies (as many argue they must be to survive) and thus the criticism that they exhibit a lack of engagement in things European would seem misplaced – it is their strategy to be global and not simply European. Indeed, the goal of Esprit was to make them global players, even though a good deal of the rhetoric was about enhancing Europe's place in the international economy.

Furthermore, some criticism has been levelled at the Commission's policies in the technology sector, in particular that of Esprit, as representing a strategy of catch-up (Mytelka 1993), where too little emphasis is placed on the conditions that generate innovation and technological development. On the one hand, as suggested above, the link made between Esprit and the internal market strategy, and thus the importance of economies of scale, is arguably relevant only when an established market is being challenged. In the case of integrated circuits, to take one example, economies of scale had been attained by Japanese and American firms long before the Europeans mounted their defence. This meant that American and Japanese firms enjoyed first-mover advantage, and any company seeking to challenge their market position would have to capture similar economies of scale to do so.

But this might only be the case in technological catching-up, which involves challenging established market positions in the context of an open, liberal economy where simply barring access to markets is no longer a widely acceptable policy option. In the case of technological innovation, it may be far more important to pay attention to the factors that contribute to the innovative dynamic, and here small and medium-sized enterprises may play a central role.

Furthermore, there has been a shift away from supporting the growth of an indigenous IT industry as an end in itself towards placing questions of national or 'bloc' origin in the background and concentrating on matters of how technology is used and integrated into the economy and society. This focus apparently gives more weight to market-push rather than technology-push objectives. For example, in a recent official description of Esprit placed on the Internet, we are told that the Fourth Framework programme is focused on the emerging information society and the construction of its infrastructure. In the 1980s and early 1990s, the Esprit programme followed a technology-push policy in which emphasis was 'placed on encouraging cooperation between IT enterprises and strengthening the Union's information technology industry. Now the focus is on helping to develop the services and technologies that underpin the emerging information technology. To do this effectively means paying greater attention to the needs of users and the market' (Esprit electronic home page at http://www.cordis.lu/esprit/home/html).

How much of this change is a result of the realization that large IT firms are not European but global, and therefore that there is little to be gained in transferring public money to them? It is certainly possible to claim that small and medium-sized enterprises are more bound to a particular geographical location than are the large IT firms of the European Information Technology Industry Roundtable. And clearly, the information society in Europe, if it is created, will not then get up and move off-shore. As a result, it may be easier to create a consensus on spending money on something anchored and 'European' rather than 'global' and footloose.

As we can see, explanations of the declining influence of the EITIRT tend to fall into one of two categories. First, there are arguments that maintain that the Roundtable became increasingly unhappy with the Commission and its policies both because those policies were less effective and because they were increasingly less relevant to members of the Roundtable as their business strategies evolved. A second line of explanation focuses on the Commission and its perceived move away from dependency on and happiness with the Roundtable and its members. Also within this category are arguments that suggest that the goals of the Commission changed following expansion of the Community, in particular the increasing use of technology policy to satisfy other goals such as regional cohesion. Clearly, there is significant overlap in both sets of explanations and many are mutually reinforcing rather than being mutually exclusive.

What does this mean for our theory of technology corporatism? We began with the thesis that, when the participation of a private (non-state) actor is institutionalized in a public policy-making process, then we may speak of corporatism. We have shown that such a relationship existed in the field of IT policy between the Commission and the

European Information Technology Industry Roundtable and we have therefore referred to this as a case of technology corporatism. However, we have also suggested that this relationship had changed in significant respects a decade later.

In the case of the EITIRT and the Commission, various changes occurred, internal and external to the process, that altered the place of the relationship we have described as corporatist in the general policy-making process (as well as in the business strategies of the firms involved). In addition, the goals of both industry and the Commission changed. As we suggested at the beginning of this chapter, the interests of industry and those of the Commission coincided around a particular project and formal structures were created that were appropriate to implementing that project. However, although a corporatist structure in the realm of European technology policy was created which remains, the interests of both the Commission and industry have changed, putting into question the relevance of such formal structures for analysis.

In a very formal sense, as long as decision-making within the Esprit programme remains unchanged, i.e. the Roundtable's influence remains institutionalized, then we may continue to speak of technology corporatism as being present. Clearly, though, this would not be helpful because it overlooks the fact that the relationship has changed in a fundamental way. Therefore, our theory must be made to take account of the fact that merely being party to an institutionalized relationship is not enough to guarantee significant influence over that process. Similarly, that process itself may become less important to the actors concerned, as we suggest has occurred in the case of European technology policy.

We may therefore conclude from this that analysis must focus on the interests of actors involved in policy-making processes and not simply the institutional structures within which these relationships exist. As the interests of actors change over time, formal structures may no longer be the defining influence over their actions or of policy outcomes, as the case of European technology policy illustrates.

Conclusion

This chapter has presented support for the view that the common European technology policy – first embodied in the Esprit project – was a core element of the integration relaunch and was initiated by the Commission, albeit in close collaboration with the largest European information technology companies. Our research, consisting of a review of primary and secondary sources and interviews, leads us to the conclusion that member states played only a minor role in this process, contrary to the view prevalent in many studies of this subject.

It is clear that during the late 1970s and early 1980s there was a general shift within European states towards a policy of supporting high-technology industries, which foreshadowed the guiding principles of Esprit. However, the Commission at this time was able to seize the initiative at the European level and secure member state agreement to a programme that had the private and public support of the largest information technology companies acting through the European Information Technology Industry Roundtable, and thereby succeeded in significantly expanding its own powers.

Insofar as the shape of technology policy is concerned, this chapter draws attention to the fact that the Commission acted as an agent in encouraging increased collaboration between large firms, universities and private research institutes in the information technology industry, rather than leaving this solely to the market. The Commission accomplished this primarily through its command of funding resources with which it was able to instigate the formation of an influential information technology industry lobby. For this reason, we may speak of this new constellation of interests and role of the state as of a form of technology corporatism, boldly exemplified in both the design and the execution of Esprit.

Looking at the practice of this collaboration ten years on, we find, however, that the influence of the European Information Technology Industry Roundtable in the policy process has declined. Therefore, we end by cautioning that the degree of influence exerted by actors may not be directly deduced from the fact that they can be said to be party to a corporatist relationship.

Appendix: interview partners used as sources in this chapter

1 Mr R. Hüber, Director of the Information Technology Task Force of DG III under Commissioner Davignon.
2 Mr J. Moritz, Deputy Director of Corporate Research and Development, Siemens.
3 Mr W. Wagner, Director, Industrial Office European Information Technology Industry Roundtable.
4 Mr J. Vanhumbeeck, Siemens, Liaison Office to the European Union.
5 Vicomte E. Davignon, Commissioner, DG III (transcript from Nicola Fielder's interview).
6 Dr N. Hazewindus, Corporate Product Development Coordination, Philips International.

5 EC regional policy: monetary lubricant for economic integration?

Patrick Ziltener

The cohesion target – introductory remarks to chapters 5 and 6

Along with the internal market project and technology policy, regional and social policy elements are additional important political dimensions of the integration thrust of the 1980s. The consistency with which the *cohesion target* is reinforced in its various formulations in the conclusions of European summit meetings and annual Commission programmes is impressive. This no doubt reflects the societal consensus in all member states of the EC regarding the necessity and desirability, in accordance with Marshall's famous definition of social policy, 'to use political power to supersede, supplement or modify operations of the economic system in order to achieve results which the economic system would not achieve on its own' (Marshall 1975: 15). The principle of state-organized balancing between classes and regions was and is a central element of the Western postwar model (Bornschier 1996), even when there were and are different forms and levels of development among the member states (see Esping-Andersen 1990; Schmid 1995). This societal consensus continues to exist in Western Europe, as surveys show (Ferrera 1993), even during the present tumultuous times of fiscal crisis and system rebuilding.

In this context, the definition of the functions that the European Community, as one level of statehood in Europe, is supposed to take on remains controversial. In fact, in the 1980s the *cohesion target* was anchored in the treaties, which represented a marked expansion of the 'welfare state mission' of the Community. For the proponents of a European federal state, the existing EC functions in this domain are stages on the way to a supranational system of social policy regulation with financial equalization. Others characterize the regional and social policy elements as 'bargaining chips required to soothe members that feared the rigour of the open market that was promised' (Colchester and Buchan 1990: 22), as the price for the deepening of economic integration, whose realization promised to create 'benefits for all' (see Cockfield 1994: 44f).

Chapters 5 and 6 aim to explain the status of the social policy and regional policy elements in the integration thrust of the 1980s. In both cases, the question arises as to which protagonists seized the initiative(s) that became part of package deals. The concept of the integration project is taken up again (see chapter 2). The determination of the role of the various protagonists involved in this process is explained in these chapters by examining the degrees of 'success' in the two policy areas and their present state of development.

The main focus of this chapter is the reconstruction of the development of EC regional policy between 1984, the 'take-off' phase of the integration thrust, and 1988, when the 'promise was redeemed' through the adoption of the Delors Package, that is, when the regional policy regulations of the Single European Act were realized. This is preceded by a section on the origins of regional policy in the Community in the 1970s. The last section contains a comparative look at the regional policy component of the Maastricht intergovernmental conference along with some theoretical conclusions, and shows that the process that took place between 1985 and 1988 had a paradigmatic character.

Framing the question

From the obvious close connection between the extension of EC regional policy and important advances of European integration, the thesis that this policy is in principle a *side payment* can be derived. On the one hand, it is said that regional policy is not a core aspect of the process (despite the fact that a package deal might not have come into existence without these elements). On the other hand, in the context of the 'logrolling' that is part of the process, such side payments buy approval and eliminate the possibility of blocking the integration project.

The side-payment thesis is widely debated among scholars, especially in the neorealist literature, with its emphasis on the dominance of the intergovernmental principle in EC regional policy. The counter-position disputes the reduction of the dynamic in this policy arena to interstate negotiations, emphasizes the role of supranational protagonists, and uses the neofunctionalist spillover mechanism as part of its argument. According to this argument, integration in one policy area should result in pressure for integration in other policy areas; in this case, market integration should create increasing pressure for the construction of a supranational regional balance.

The side-payment thesis abbreviates the development of EC regional policy to certain moments, as a rule to the European summit meetings. That equalization and compensation payments serve as a lubricant in the context of package deals is undisputed. What is not taken into account, however, is that in the case of regional policy we are dealing not only with an *ongoing system* of financial transfers without foreseeable end, but with a system that was increasingly organized according to supranationally formulated criteria.[1] Thus: if a policy package can be approved only with side payments, then the allocation of functions with respect to the distribution of resources, i.e. the division of authority between the different levels, is not necessarily fixed yet. For Schmitter (1971: 237), this was the second fact that had to be explained, in addition to the *scope* of issues to be resolved through integration; namely, the question of the *level* of authority that was delegated to regional institutions.

The range of possible designs for compensation is defined by two ideal-typical variations: (a) an interstate financial transfer, whereby resources are determined according to criteria worked out through the national political systems, and in which the Commission's only function would be that of a 'clearing house', or (b) a supranational polity, which uses the grant and support funds according to criteria and objectives defined through the political system at European level.

The actual policy represents a mixture of elements of both types; the ratio has clearly changed in the course of development. The question of the reasons for anchoring regional policy in the treaties must therefore be expanded into a question about the reasons for the respective design of its praxis. This leads to surprising results with respect to assessing the role of certain protagonists.

A brief look at the beginning: regional policy for the *juste retour*

In the EEC treaty of 1957, the regional policy dimension appears in various contexts. In the preamble, the formulation of a regional policy goal was accepted: the member states are 'anxious to strengthen the unity of their economies and to ensure their harmonious development by reducing the differences existing between the various regions and the backwardness of the less favoured regions'. (EC treaties, Article 235).

---

[1] The formulation of Allen (1996: 209) follows a similar line, according to which the debate revolved around whether or not the growth of the structural funds 'has promoted a new pattern of "multi-level governance" or reflects side payments to facilitate package deals'.

However, nothing was said about EC functions as a means for achieving this goal; the utmost confidence was placed in the equalizing effects of the Common Market.

The funds established through the Treaty of Rome had a regional policy dimension to their activities from the beginning. The European Agricultural Guidance and Guarantee Fund (EAGGF) provided means for the modernization of agriculture. The Treaty of Paris (1951), which established the European Coal and Steel Community (ECSC), intended to use financial methods for regions with problems that emerged as a result of structural economic changes (conversion assistance).[2] The European Investment Bank (EIB) granted loans and secured funding for various activities including investments that contributed to the attainment of the Community's aforementioned goal of harmonious development, and above all infrastructural projects. As a bank, the EIB followed the normal economic principles for granting credit.

It should be noted that the legitimacy of regional policy at the level of the nation-state is expressly acknowledged in the EC treaty in that such state intervention does not fall under the general prohibition against measures distorting competition (see Article 92, Treaty of Rome).

On the one hand, this absence of a comprehensive common regional policy is attributable to the relative homogeneity of the then Community of six; only Italy encompassed a large problem area (Mezzogiorno). On the other hand, welfare state balancing functions were indisputably the domain of individual nation-states in the early phase of European integration, and regional policy was primarily perceived in terms of its social components, and to a lesser extent as an instrument of economic guidance (Tömmel 1994: 38).

In this early phase, regional policy initiatives and demands emanated from the supranational bodies. The European Assembly (which later became the European Parliament) demanded consideration of regional policy concerns with the implementation of EC policies as well as the coordination of regional development efforts at the level of the nation-state. The Commission formulated its first regional policy goals in the early 1960s. In 1965 it published a *Report on Regional Policy* (*EC Bulletin* 8–1965) in which it emphasized the necessity for Community-wide measures. This was justified with the argument that the Common Market had intensified regional disparities. As instruments for addres-

---

[2] The European Social Fund (ESF) awarded funds for labour market policy measures for vocational training and resettlement of unemployed people. More than any other country, West Germany profited from this arrangement, which very quickly led to the demand for a stronger regionalization of the disbursements. In the reform of 1983 it was decided that 40 per cent of the ESF funds should go toward the prioritized crisis regions.

sing this problem, the report recommended the coordinated expenditure of existing funds and interstate policy coordination. The efforts to stimulate the creation of a special regional policy fund came from the Economic and Social Committee. The integration crisis of 1965–6 terminated this first debate. The Commission undertook a new venture in 1969, but this did not resonate in the Council.

The establishment of the original regional fund was part of a package deal that included the first round of enlargement of the EC in 1973 (Denmark, the United Kingdom and Ireland) as well as the economic and monetary union (EMU) project. Comparatively speaking, the two island nations were less prosperous countries with clear regional problems. What might have been decisive was that the United Kingdom with its small agricultural sector, was to become a net contributor to the Community budget, whose primary expenditures were agricultural subsidies. What the British wanted was an institutionalized subsidy from the EC for British expenditure in those regions, not a Community regional policy with a supranational steering centre.

In 1969, the agreed upon monetary union project was approved only through the use of compensatory payments. Italy, in particular, which had frequently used changes in the exchange rate of the lira as an instrument to strengthen the competitiveness of its export-oriented industry, raised demands in this regard. Along with new members the United Kingdom and Ireland, Italy formed a pressure group allied with supranational actors, each of which had clearly different motives for the demand for a financial redistribution within the Community.

At the Paris summit in 1972, the European Regional Development Fund (ERDF) was established. Its goal was the elimination of structural and regional imbalances within the Community. The determination of the financial scope of the fund was postponed, principally because West Germany and the Netherlands made their approval contingent on the final realization of the EMU. Shortly afterwards, the EC was severely shaken by the oil crisis and the recession that followed. The EMU project vanished without a sound in the eddy of the anti-crisis strategies of the individual states (see Busch 1978).

The planned regional fund did not fall victim to the crisis. In 1974 the Labour Party came to power in the United Kingdom, 'a party not enthusiastic about Community membership' (George 1991: 194) and one determined to renegotiate the conditions for British membership. This demand was confronted by a strong French–German alliance. The problem of the British contribution became intensified through the increasingly pressing Italian–Irish demand for a common regional policy. The governments of these two countries threatened to boycott the European Council at the end of 1974 if the realization of the agreed-upon fund did not occur. As a result, a positive decision was taken at the meeting: the fund would be instituted on 1 January 1975, and the granting of funds[3] would be carried out according to a fixed ratio. Although another supranational institution was erected in the process, we cannot speak of a true supranationalization of regional policy in light of how the fund worked. With the fixed distribution ratio, the principle of the *juste retour* (fair return) was adhered to, that is, the claim of the member states to a balanced relationship between payments and receipts, and not a regional policy based on superordinate criteria. A coordination of national regional policies was not intended, nor was there any anchoring of Community regional policy in the treaties. The European Regional Development Fund was based on Article 235,[4] whereby each decision falls explicitly under the unanimity rule of the Council. According to the terms of the so-called Luxembourg Compromise, this was the generally accepted rule; however, being based on this part of the treaty constrained future possibilities in this domain. Thus, the national governments were in the driver's seat and the functions of the Commission in this regard were accordingly minimal.

In the context of the first reform of the Regional Fund in 1979, the Commission managed to set up a 'quota-free sector', whose funds could be allocated according to the Commission's own criteria and also outside of the domain defined by the national governments. The argument for a common policy in this area was that compensation for the negative effects of European integration was also supposed to be made through Community policy. However, the Council restricted this sector to 5 per cent of the fund's resources. Nevertheless, this should not be underestimated in terms of its importance for the further development of regional policy at the European level. With it, the principle of regional policy as a *juste retour* measure was undermined, and the supranational institutions were on their way to supranational policy-making.

In the context of the establishment of the European Monetary System (EMS), Ireland and Italy again raised the demand for an increase in

---

[3] This amounted to 1.3 billion ECU for three years; in 1975 the expenditures for regional policy comprised 4.8 per cent of the Community budget. The total amount was far lower than that regarded by the poorer countries as a minimum; this amount was only about half of the sum contained in the Commission's proposal. The European Parliament criticized the inadequate allocation. Thus, the fund was 'too small to have any significant impact on regional disparities and thus cannot be seen either as the basis for a serious common regional policy or as a significant contribution towards the sort of convergence that would have aided the EMU process' (Allen 1996: 213).

[4] According to Article 235, the so-called general clause, the Community can become active anywhere it believes necessary 'in the course of the operation of the common market'.

compensation payments. However, this time they did so without the support of the British, who were sceptical about the EMS. But the United Kingdom too would have profited from the extension of the Regional Fund. A new form of compensation was agreed upon, namely subsidies on the interest rates of multi-annual credits for the two countries (George 1991: 197f).

Some important elements for the further development of Community regional policy can be derived from this short presentation on its origins. Among these is surely a confirmation of the interpretation of EC development as a sequence of package deals, within which financial transfers represent an important component. The postponement of the decision regarding the level of funding is something that we will return to in our discussion of the summits in Luxembourg (1985) and Maastricht (1991).

The connection between the admission of new member states and the questions of financial compensation is evident. The result of this phase of EC enlargement would certainly have turned out to be more significant if it really had been about cushioning the blow of EMU, and not predominantly about a *juste retour* measure. Equally important to note is the advancing role of the supranational institutions,[5] in particular the Commission, even if they only succeeded to a limited degree in this phase. Here one must always keep in mind the way the Community functioned in the era of the Luxembourg Compromise.

Southern enlargement and reforms

During the stagnation phase of European integration, which lasted until 1984, the possibilities for the Commission were largely constrained (see chapter 2); thus the initial dynamic in the area of regional policy remained as yet undeveloped. With the EC's second big round of enlargement, encompassing the Mediterranean countries of Greece (1981) and Spain and Portugal (1986), another extension of regional policy was foreseeable. The Commission's interest was in linking the necessary expansion of the fund through the southern enlargement to a supranationalization of authority over regional policy.

At first this did not succeed. The admission of Greece in 1981 made the Council increase the means of the Regional Fund. But these covered only the additional costs of support for Greece, while for the remaining

---

[5] With respect to demands for a European regional policy beyond an interstate logic, the Economic and Social Committee went the furthest. It also introduced – to my knowledge for the first time in the history of EC regional policy – the proposal for including subnational state bodies in the policy-making process.

states (whose percentage in the allocation ratio declined) the funds de facto remained the same.

With its proposal for a new fund regulation in 1981,[6] the Commission strove to rebuild the previous system. Instead of approving only single projects, broad programmes were to be developed that were designed to lend greater coherence to regional policy. With these programmes the possibility of indirect influence over the policies of the member states would have been created. Moreover, the Commission demanded an increase in the quota-free sector to 20 per cent of the fund. In addition, the content of support was supposed to be modernized in the direction of a more strongly innovative structural policy. The European Council accepted the programme approach in 1983 but did not follow the remainder of the Commission's proposal. Instead, it revised the previous system of fixed allocation ratios into a system of indicative ranges (upper and lower boundaries for a particular country rather than a fixed quota). Simultaneously, to the sorrow of the Commission, it decided to abolish the quota-free sector.

The new fund regulation[7] adopted during the French Council presidency in 1984 nevertheless represented a crucial step in the direction of a supranational structural policy. According to Article 5, 'Community programmes' were to be promoted and 'national programmes of Community interest' were to be supported as a matter of priority. This meant de facto a total realignment of the fund with respect to Community goals. According to the regulation, the determination of these goals takes place through the political system at the European level. Through the introduction of indicative ranges, pressure is exerted on member states' policies, because only with an alignment of these policies with Community goals can contributions from Brussels be maximized. Varfis, the Commissioner then responsible for regional policy, wrote that, although the proposals of the Commission with respect to the new Regional Fund ordinance were not fully incorporated, its concerns were largely addressed in the improved content of the new ordinance.[8] Tömmel (1994: 54) comes to the conclusion that the ground that the Commission lost through the abolition of the quota-free sector could be recovered many times over in the long run through this reform.

Greece's earlier date of admission, relative to Spain and Portugal,

---

[6] In *EC Bulletin* 4–1981. The Commission counted on the reform proposals of the Economic and Social Committee. The demand for reform was also emphasized by the European Parliament and external expert committees.

[7] *Official Journal* L 169/1984; for an overview see Franzmeyer, Seidel and Weise 1993: 17ff. The decision on the Commission's demand for a doubling of funds for the ERDF was postponed; the reform came into effect on 1 January 1985.

[8] In his foreword to COM (85) 516 final.

created political friction that demanded 'lubricants'. Although not following the British demand for a renegotiation of contributions, Greece's socialist government pleaded in a 1982 memorandum for special status within the EC for its country, including exemption from certain regulations and financial assistance. Prime Minister Papandreou justified his demand for additional financial resources with reference to the need to solve the structural problems created by underdevelopment in the Mediterranean region, and simultaneously to address the negative effects of the (desirable) enlargement of the Community to the Iberian countries.[9] He thus sent a message that Greece's approval of southern enlargement was going to be obtained only through the granting of side payments.[10] With the Integrated Mediterranean Programmes, adopted at the end of March 1985, the 'Greek problem' was solved. This involved a special measure with a seven-year term, from which areas in France and Italy also profited. It did not fall directly under the Regional Fund, although it was partially financed through it. The only conflicts that arose were over the level of financial assistance.[11] According to McDonald (1985: 134f), fund payments in the years following Greece's admission to the EC played an important role in PASOK's renewed electoral victory in June 1985, because they made public works projects and income increases for farmers possible. Surely this development contributed to the increasingly more pragmatic European policy of the Greek socialists. Their actual 'pro-European turn' took place later, however (see Kasakos 1991).

The side-payment character of the Integrated Mediterranean Programmes was made particularly clear by the fact that these were one-time measures and not ongoing programmes. Nevertheless, these measures had consequences for the further construction of the system, because the Commission advanced its regional policy project through this framework. This was done by the Commission building elements of its project into these measures, for example the extension of its control functions and cooperation with implementing authorities at regional and local levels. Tömmel (1994: 84) argues that, through the creation of new, informal structures for negotiating policy concepts and their implementation and ad hoc programming, a fundamentally new mode

---

[9] In his speech of 13 December 1983 before the European Parliament (*Europa-Archiv* 3/1984, D67).

[10] The Integrated Mediterranean Programmes were quite correctly described as side payments or even more bluntly as the buying of Greece's vote. Out of many similar statements, we make reference here only to the customarily direct remarks of the British prime minister in her memoirs: 'the Greek Danegeld had to be paid . . . Greece could expect a bonanza' (Thatcher 1993: 546).

[11] 4.1 billion ECU, of which Greece was assured 2 billion, were authorized.

of operation was created, a new 'style', which constituted direct cooperation between the Commission and member states and simultaneously guaranteed the Commission 'gentle' dominance over the whole event. In this way the Commission based its role on the disbursement of funds; it took the initiative for a programme and exercised influence over its content through the criteria for granting funds.

Thus, each extension of EC regional policy is connected with a conflict over authority between the intergovernmental and the supranational level. On the basis of the growth of authority in the relevant area – better put, the progressive conquest of authority by the Commission – and with the support of the European Parliament and the Economic and Social Committee, by this time the regional policy of the EC had clearly become more than an interstate *juste retour* system. The admission of Spain and Portugal would not by itself necessarily have resulted in a change in the system, but could have signified a simple *enlargement* of the system, as in the case of Greece. However, since 1984 the enlargement had been overlaid with a powerful new integration dynamic, whose roots were described in chapters 1 and 2.

Anchoring the cohesion target: regional policy in the Luxembourg package

From the beginning it was clear that the creation of an internal market would have regional policy implications. In this context and under the heading 'completion of the Treaty', the Dooge Committee report emphasized the goal of the 'promotion of economic convergence', within which it included 'the promotion of solidarity amongst the Member States aimed at reducing structural imbalances ... through the strengthening of specific Community instruments and a judicious definition of Community policies'.[12] The argument of Greece in the comments added to the final report by the Greek representative to the committee, Iannis Papantoniou, are noteworthy in this regard:

The overall gains from economic integration are not only unevenly distributed, but may also disguise losses for the less prosperous regions. The creation, therefore, of an integrated market and a technological community needs to be supplemented by a very substantial effort to strengthen the Community's cohesion by promoting regional development and the convergence of living standards.[13]

On the one hand, the basic concept behind the Greek integration

---

[12] Ad Hoc Committee for Institutional Affairs, Report to the European Council, Brussels, 29–30 March 1985, Luxembourg, 1985.
[13] Ibid., comments by Mr Papantoniou, Annex B.

project was that the convergence of economies is a prerequisite for further integration. However, the Greek government was against the strengthening or expansion of supranational procedures. On the other hand, the demand for greater compensation payments, which were supposed to make convergence possible, was linked to every subsequent step toward further integration.

The starting point for the negotiations taking place at the intergovernmental conference, which led to the adoption of the Single European Act in December 1985, was unfavourable for the Greek position of scepticism toward the deepening of integration. Spain and Portugal, allies in the fight for compensation payments in exchange for the total liberalization of trade, did not yet participate in the conference as full members. Moreover, they were generally much more favourable toward further integration. This was also true of Ireland, which was an ally in regional policy too; the Irish, given their traditional neutrality, were primarily concerned with the issue of foreign policy cooperation. Blocking the intergovernmental conference was only a theoretical possibility, considering the strong alliance among France, Germany, Italy and the Benelux countries, especially since the foreseeable core issue of those negotiations, the internal market project, was also a central concern of the United Kingdom. Therefore the only possibility for Greece was to seek to maximize both exemptions and compensatory payments.

On the question of regional equalization payments, the economically weaker countries had found a strong advocate in the Delors Commission. As shown in the previous section, the Commission had succeeded in clearly developing its own role in Community regional policy in conjunction with fund reforms. As a result of its 'rebirth' in the context of the revitalization of the integration process after 1984, the political weight of the Commission in the decision-making process generally increased (see chapter 2, p. 52). The Commission moved decisively to use the new dynamic to extend and strengthen the supranationalization of regional policy.[14] The strategy of the Commission at the inter-

[14] See Delors' report to the European Parliament on the Commission's working programme for 1985 in *Europa-Archiv* 7/1985, D195. Delors had already sharply criticized the mode of operation of EC regional policy in 1983 when he was still a minister in the French government: 'The regional fund is no more than the clandestine operation of "*juste retour*" or "fair return". The administration which gains is the one which has the best contacts and which best known [sic] how to use the formulae. As to the social fund, no-one really knows where they are anymore . . . This structural fund must be reformed just as the agricultural structure funds.' Nevertheless, he defended the fundamental necessity of European 'financial and social solidarity'. For this purpose, Delors continued, real Community instruments and truly encompassing programmes needed to be developed, 'instead of this itsy-bitsy practice of a fair return'.

governmental conference was to bundle the relevant measures together into a 'flanking package' designed to co-opt the opposition and to link this as closely as possible to the internal market project. Delors said in his speech at the opening of the conference that the creation of a large market can have positive effects for all only if it is supported by such measures (*EC Bulletin* 9–1985, 1.1.1).

Using the term 'economic and social cohesion', the Commission advanced various social and structural policy proposals.[15] According to these proposals, the goals of Community cohesion policy would have been very broad (Article 1 – Objectives): 'Community action will aim at strengthening its economic and social cohesion in particular by improving the living standards, working and employment conditions of the peoples of the Member States, and by reducing the disparities between its different regions and the disadvantages of the poorer regions.' According to the proposed Article 2, these objectives would have been taken into account in all measures associated with the creation of the internal market and Community policies. In light of the relatively scarce resources of the Community, the Commission also envisioned a central role for itself in coordinating the policies of the member states.

Delors' strategy did not meet with approval, even by those countries interested in the extension of regional policy. These countries criticized the overloading of the regional policy portfolio. As a result, the proposed 'flanking package' was disassembled, but the concept of cohesion remained a label on the dossier.

The Commission's project included proposals for anchoring and defining the objectives of the structural funds in the treaty. The role of the Commission in the organization of credit was to be strengthened, i.e. it was to be allowed to enter into contracts for borrowing, to grant loans, and to act as a guarantor for loans. In the treaty as proposed, a regulation was to be approved that envisioned a reform of the structural funds with the goal of improving coordination and increasing their economic and social efficiency. Although this reform required the unanimous approval of the Council, qualified majority voting would generally apply to future decisions. Delors justified the necessity of a reform of the structural funds by noting that over the course of time these had lost their corrective function and served only to redistribute appropriations. The goal, as he saw it, must be a real coordination of all

Speech by Delors at a colloquium in Paris, October 1983, published in Vandamme (1985: ix–xx); quotation from p. xvf.

[15] 'Commission's Proposals of 30.9.1985 on Cohesion, the Powers of the Commission, and Culture' (in Gazzo 1986: 38f). The Venturini Report (1988: 41) describes the Commission's view of the logic of the SEA as 'building a balanced area without frontiers'.

financial instruments, a diversification of their resources and a concentration of their interventions on more clearly defined tasks (*EC Bulletin* 9-1985, 1.1.1).

During the conference, Greece and Ireland submitted a paper with proposals regarding regional policy, but these had no great impact in light of the extensive and highly polished (through multiple revisions) proposal by the Commission (see Grant 1994: 75). The French government's 'Amendment on Differentiation and Cohesion' (in Gazzo 1986: 53.), largely supported the Commission's proposal, including the extension of its role in the capital market. Regarding the question of qualified majority voting in the Council, however, the French adopted a more reserved posture.

No one disputed the principle of anchoring the regulations on 'economic and social cohesion' in the treaty, especially with respect to references therein to the regional fund. The economically weaker countries emphasized that appropriate practical provisions in this sector were a condition for acceptance of the proposals on the internal market and also wanted concretely to define the financial level of these measures.[16] Other member states emphasized the opportunities and the generally positive effects of an internal market and believed that in principle 'cohesion' was independent of the internal market, and was above all a political problem that could be managed in the first instance by the will of individual states to adopt an economic policy approach to the problem (*EC Bulletin* 9-1985, 1.1.2). Again and again, Delors clarified to this tendency that the policy package had to be taken as a whole, including the compensatory policies. At the same time, he played a moderating role with respect to the regional policy demands and here made reference to the intended reform of the European Regional Development Fund. In a provisional appraisal, he noted: 'Although there is an unusual coalition of those who would like more and those who do not want much in the area, it seems to me we could reach a solution.' He simultaneously warned of a 'clumsy compromise on budgetary transfers. We have greater ambitions for the Community.'[17] The package-deal character of the emerging compromise solution is revealed by Delors' complaint that, in the area of technological development policy, there was a negative constellation of forces composed of those who remained basically sceptical of these measures and those who were afraid that too much Community money would flow into this area instead of into the structural funds.

[16] Report by the Council Presidency of the Preparatory Group, 21 October 1985 (in Gazzo 1986: 58).
[17] In his press conference of 27 November 1985 (Gazzo 1986: 86).

At the December 1985 session of the European Council there were no longer any basic differences regarding the regulations on economic and social cohesion. Italy still demanded the inclusion of a regulation regarding the financial provision of the structural funds, which required the funds be disbursed 'in an adequate manner'. In response, other governments wanted to safeguard themselves against continuing demands by introducing a requirement that this be done 'in the context of the available budget'. Both were initially taken up at the meeting only to be dropped in response to the immediate reservations of several member states.[18]

The result of the intergovernmental conference with respect to regional policy was Article 23 of the Single European Act, which became Article 130a–e of the EC Treaty. For the first time, this explicitly anchored the Community's regional policy in the treaty and thus made it an accepted and integrated part of EC politics.

Article 130a contains a general formulation of the EC's goal of strengthening its economic and social cohesion in order to promote the harmonious development of the Community as a whole. This is concretized by the provision that the gap between the various regions and the underdevelopment of the least-favoured areas should be reduced. As mentioned above, this did not correspond to the original project of the Commission to bring together social and regional policy concerns. The approved formulation does, however, provide a clear basis for a Community regional policy. The question of when the 'harmonious development of the Community as a whole' can be said to have been achieved and what constitutes the economic and social dimensions of 'cohesion' remains open (see Vogel-Polsky 1991: 56). More concrete and more readily operationalized is the goal of reducing the gap between the regions. It is also important that in this Article the regions are mentioned without any reference to their national affiliation, that is, the nation-state's mediation of their interests.

The second paragraph, however, emphasizes the level of the member states in a manner that was not foreseen in the Commission's project. Both the Commission and the countries interested in promoting regional policy regarded as a success the formulation that the goals named in the first paragraph would be taken into consideration in all Community policies and in the realization of the internal market. The position of the economically liberal countries is reflected in the formulation that the realization of the internal market as such contributes to the realization of the regional policy goals.

[18] Instead, reference was made in one of the SEA declarations (No. 8) to previous decisions in this context (*EC Bulletin* 12–1985, 1.1.3). See Toth (1986).

In comparison with the original proposal by the Commission, the definition of the instruments to be applied turned out to be relatively restrictive. The expansion of the Commission's possibilities through granting it a role in the capital market was not accepted, and the enumeration of the existing structural funds was designed to preclude a mandate for the creation of new ones. The definition of the tasks of the Regional Fund (Article 130c) corresponds with the formulation of the 1984 rules governing the fund: the intention is to contribute to the 'development and structural adjustment of regions whose development is lagging behind' as well as to 'the conversion of declining industrial areas'. The last two paragraphs define the procedure for reforming the structural funds. Any proposal by the Commission must be approved unanimously by the Council; the implementing decisions must be taken with a qualified majority vote. As we have already mentioned, regulations regarding the provision of funding were avoided; it was clear to all participants that this had to take place in the context of a package deal that would include the other important financial questions (the increase of the Community's own resources, the reduction of agricultural subsidies).

Commission President Delors characterized the regional policy aspect of the SEA as a 'balance', which offered the Community an opportunity to overcome its present existence as a free trade zone (*EC Bulletin* 11–1985, 1.1.2). He stated: 'We followed a path that is somewhat removed from the idea of "*juste retour*". One of our fundamental ideas is to ensure that the structural funds are not conceived of in a narrow budget perspective of "*juste retour*", but instead constitute a contributory factor towards the Community's economic and social cohesion.'[19]

The then prime minister of Luxembourg and president of the European Council, Jacques Santer, described the formulation of the paragraph on structural policy as the result of a 'difficult equilibrium', one that in the eyes of many failed to live up to their bold vision of what could have been done. The Single Act, however, pointed out which way to go (*EC Bulletin* 12–1985, 1.1.1).

Despite its formally restricted power, the Commission was able to play an important role in the area of regional policy at the intergovernmental conference. Not only did it put the first proposal on the table, around which further negotiations were held; in a manner of speaking the Commission became the 'spokesperson' for the economically weaker countries. As a supranational political entrepreneur, the Commission supported the expansion of the system in accordance with

---

[19] In his press conference of 8 January 1986 (Gazzo 1986: 109).

the basic goals of the European integration process, in conjunction with its own interest in strengthening its role in policy formulation and enlarging the pool of available resources. With the established unanimity principle regarding the regulation of the funds, the governments of the net-payer countries were in the driver's seat. Although it was hardly practical to hold back or reverse the development toward supranational policy-making, they still possessed crucial leverage through postponing the determination of the financial resources of the fund. With the demand for rationalization and increased efficiency (Article 130d), requests for the further development of regional policy increased, even though the previous reform, adopted in January 1985, had just come into effect and had hardly made an impact. In this way, the internal reform dynamic of EC regional policy, which resulted primarily from the difficulties of policy implementation, was overlaid and reinforced by an innovation thrust 'from outside', which itself was the result of the difficulties of economic integration (Tömmel 1994: 57). Simultaneously, it was emphasized on a regular basis that the EC must not go down the path toward becoming a 'redistribution machine'.[20] The secretary-general of the Commission, Emil Noël (1987: 9), defined the heart of the matter in that debate over funding resources: 'The main beneficiaries are loudly demanding that they be increased, while other Member States are unconvinced that the money is put to good use, and suspect that it is more a matter of straight budget transfers than of real aid for economic development.'

The difficult redemption of the promise: the first Delors Package

Establishing the funding for regional policy promised by the Single Act was only possible in the context of rearranging the revenues and expenses of the Community and a more equitable distribution of contributions.[21] Very quickly it became clear that the individual dimensions could not be compartmentalized as they had been by the Council of Ministers.

In the first half of 1986, the Commission did not want to rush the sought-after development by prematurely raising budget problems. The majority of Commission members agreed that this would provoke a crisis, since at this time each discussion would escalate into sterile

---

[20] See, for example, the remarks by Peter M. Schmidbauer, then Bavarian state minister, in *EG Magazin* 9–10/1985: 3.
[21] Along with the well-known British demands, the main problem raised in this regard was the regressive effect of the VAT-dependent contributions to the EC budget; this was criticized because of its discriminatory effect on economically weaker countries.

confrontations. Delors in particular pleaded for deferring discussion of financial problems for the time being. The counter-position was articulated by Commissioner Ripa di Meana, who believed that 'eluding the financial crisis, prevaricating and postponing, is to bury one's head in the sand, which is not new in the Community history, and which led to the current impasse' (*Agence Europe*, 26 June 1986: 7). The June 1986 summit did not result in any conclusions regarding regional policy. Delors made it clear to the press that the southern member states had emphasized that the establishment of the internal market must be accompanied by parallel advances in structural policy.

A Commission study group led by T. Padoa-Schioppa was assigned to clarify the regional effects of the planned internal market and to elaborate policy recommendations. The 1987 report of this group, which took its name from its Italian chairperson, came to the conclusion that, in order to improve the efficiency of the allocation of resources, the internal market must be accompanied by the expansion of both the structural funds and the European Monetary System, which would ensure economic and monetary stability and equity. This legitimated initiatives by the Commission in the area of regional policy; however, the report itself, making reference to the subsidiarity principle, advocated a wide-ranging relinquishment of regulatory measures at the European level and the 'competition of rules', which was later invoked against other Commission projects, including those in the social policy area (Padoa-Schioppa 1987; see Venturini 1988: 73; Vogel 1991: 36).

Preparing the Delors Package

In autumn 1986, proposals were prepared in internal Commission seminars that in their subsequent modified form became known as the Delors Package.[22] No formal agenda was established; the first deadline dealt with the elaboration of the Commission's overall strategy for the remainder of its mandate as well as for the budgetary and financial problems of the Community. A second deadline was set for agricultural and structural policy and the reform of the funds.[23]

---

[22] This descriptive label was given at a press conference of the Belgian government at the beginning of its Council presidency (the first half-year in 1987). The name was taken up by the press and its use quickly spread, according to Falkner (1994: 146), whose research is primarily based on an analysis of the press releases of the press agency *Agence Europe*, and on whom I relied in this section.

[23] The first product of work in the area of structural policy was the document COM (86) 401 final of September 1986 on the contents and procedures for the application of an integrated concept, in which the goal of coordination of the different structural policy activities was elaborated.

Regional policy 139

There are indications that the British government sought to prevent debates on economic and social policy as well as the future funding of the EC during its Council presidency (second half of 1986). Although the Commission had already sought an initial discussion of these problems at the London summit in 1986, they were not put on the agenda. Nor were the structural funds mentioned in any of the Council documents presented by the Council presidency. Delors was granted only ten minutes to speak on the future funding of the EC. The European Parliament referred to this situation as a 'growing lack of a connection between Council decisions under the British presidency and both the economic and social reality of the Community and economic and social proposals backed by the Commission and the Parliament' (*Agence Europe*, 12 December 1986).

At the conclusion of the summit, Delors announced that he would make a tour of the capitals at the beginning of 1987 'to explain the Commission's proposals for future finance for the Community, and again to revise them if necessary' (*Agence Europe*, 4 December 1986: 5). This decision appears to have come about under pressure from the national governments, which wanted to register their views before the Commission's proposals were made public. The national governments might have been motivated by their experiences with the dynamic new Commission at the intergovernmental conference. At that time, the Commission had advanced its projects on the basis of three papers submitted by three Commissioners responsible for these areas: *New Own Resources for the Community* (Commissioner Christopherson), *The CAP and the Development of the Community* (Commissioner Andriessen), and *The Reform of the Structural Funds with a View to the Economic Cohesion of the Community* (Commissioner Varfis). In Varfis's paper he proposed that the mechanisms of the structural funds (with the exception of the regional fund) should henceforth not follow any strict regionalization but should be guided by 'goals' established on the basis of previously agreed upon priorities; this was done to ensure that the proposals would at least have a chance of being accepted by the governments. Within the Commission, there were controversies over the most promising strategy for carrying out its project. Delors thought 'that taking too firm a position should be avoided, as this would risk causing reactions in the opposite sense and accentuate the differences between the various national governments' (*Agence Europe*, 9 January 1987: 5). Other Commission members wanted to formulate some points more sharply. Commissioner Ripa di Meana proposed an offensive strategy in cooperation with the European Parliament against the action demanded by the governments. The tour of the capitals demanded by the governments and their predictable *ex ante* voting was criticized (especially by members of the European Parliament) as an inadmissible restriction of the Commission's right to take the initiative. The European Parliament itself felt excluded from this informal negotiation process in any case. Delors declared that his trip 'will make no change in the Commission's institutional role and . . . in no way modify the Parliament's powers' (*Agence Europe*, 8 January 1987: 1). One gets the impression that Delors hoped to improve the odds for the Commission's ambitious project by coordinating the Commission's plans with and obtaining informal pre-approval of them from the individual governments rather than following the regular Community decision-making process.

Searching for a compromise on a tour of the capitals

In addition to the sixteen-page document on the reforms prepared by Delors, the heads of state and government were also presented with the aforementioned three papers on specific topics. The positions of the governments probably did not surprise Delors. Greece, Spain, Portugal and Ireland emphasized the urgency of the structural funds reform and wanted the agricultural subsidies lowered in favour of cohesion payments. An increase in the Community's own resources was supposed to make the latter possible, independent of the complicated and lengthy reform of the agricultural policy that was anticipated. France and Germany did not want fundamentally to change the mechanism of Community agricultural policy, a central component of the 'basic business structure' of the EC since its inception. In addition, Delors had to wrestle again with the new right-wing French government over support for regional policy. Prime Minister Jacques Chirac criticized the structural funds as 'une pompe à finances pour les pays en voie de développement de l'Europe' ('a financial pump for the underdeveloped countries in Europe') and announced an alliance with Germany and the United Kingdom to block the whole package. The Netherlands and the United Kingdom pressed for a lowering of the agricultural subsidies and an improvement in budget discipline; the British government renewed its demand for an equitable distribution of contributions.

The final version of the Commission's project was presented in February 1987 along with its slogan, *Making a Success of the Single Act*.[24]

[24] Communication of the EC Commission of 15 February 1987 regarding a new perspective for Europe (COM (87) 100 final; see *EC Bulletin*, Supplement, 1–1987). Later expanded in COM (87) 101 final on financing the budget and COM (87) 64 final on the agro-monetary system. See Jacques Delors' speech 'Réussir l'Acte Unique' before the European Parliament on 18 February 1987 (Delors 1992: 50ff; *EC Bulletin* 2–1987).

It contained a proposal to increase the Community's own resources to 1.4 per cent of the GNP of the EC, doubling the assets of the structural funds as part of a macroeconomic growth strategy; this was linked to the completion of the internal market. By means of an alignment and concentration of regional policy support into five goals, the Commission planned to reach the necessary efficiency threshold for Community policy. The reform of the Regional Fund continued that of 1984 and reflected the experience gained with the Integrated Mediterranean Programmes. In particular, the close involvement of regional and local bodies in all stages of the programme implementation process from planning through monitoring to assessment was to be strengthened and formalized.

The Commission's project found support in the European Parliament and the Economic and Social Committee (*EC Bulletin* 11–1987); both bodies demanded an even greater increase in the assets of the structural funds. The Economic and Social Committee called the doubling of assets completely insufficient and also wanted economic and social forces incorporated into the policy-making process in addition to government agencies. The Union of Industrial and Employers' Confederations of Europe (UNICE) described the Commission's proposal as the 'correct approach [and one that] constitutes the minimum required for achieving the economic objectives of the SEA'.[25] The European Trade Union Confederation (ETUC) also supported the Commission's proposal in principle, but criticized the lack of coherence of its strategy. The ETUC believed that structural policy was one of three elements necessary in a package of supplementary measures aimed at the completion of the internal market, the other two being the social dimension and a macroeconomic policy for growth and employment.[26]

In the Council of Ministers, the alignment with respect to priority goals and the concentration of funds was not controversial. However, conflicts arose as expected with respect to the division of funds between the so-called horizontal goals (which all countries could claim) and those that were reserved for interventions in specific regions. Blocs were formed along the usual lines when it came to the most controversial topic of the provision in funds. For the Mediterranean countries and Ireland, a doubling of funds was the minimum demand. The core countries pleaded for a system improvement instead of a system expansion, i.e. for an increase in the efficiency of intervention activities instead of a significant increase of funding. The countries interested in the

---

[25] UNICE position paper of 26 June 1987 on the 'Delors Package' and the reform of the structural funds.
[26] Position paper of April 1987 (ETUC 1988, Appendix to the *Activity Report 85/87*: 9f).

extension of the system linked their demands not only to support for other elements of the budget reform, but also to the realization of the internal market, and thus the realization of the SEA.[27] The United Kingdom stood alone in declining to support the whole concept.

The summit meetings throughout 1987 showed that the negotiations were still far from reaching agreement. In view of this situation and on the basis of the fact that they all supported the Commission project, UNICE, the ETUC and European Centre of Public Enterprises (CEEP) formulated a joint opinion in December, in which they demanded – in vain – a quick decision. Coordinated German–French efforts also failed to break the impasse. Delors revised the Commission's proposal numerous times, including one variant with a sharply reduced increase in the Community's own resources, according to which only the funds for interventions in less developed areas would be doubled. Even this could not produce a consensus.

Agreement on the Delors Package

In response to the failure of the special summit of February 1988 in Brussels, the Commission took up its original proposal again. The possibility of restricting the doubling of assets to funds for the economically weaker countries remained actively discussed. This would have meant a doubling of 56.6 per cent of the assets of the structural funds, since this was the proportion that went to the peripheral countries in 1987. In light of the looming failure of a third summit, the pressure on all the actors involved grew. Delors prepared his colleagues for additional emergency sessions and began to threaten the resignation of the entire Commission if the package was not approved. In a speech to the Economic and Social Committee, he denounced four or five member states for wanting to transform the internal market into 'a plain trade market' without supporting common structural and social policy measures (*Agence Europe*, 29 January 1988: 6).

At the critical summit itself, from the beginning everything revolved around the question of the realization of Article 23 of the Act – the issue of whether the principal support should be directed to less developed regions or to entire countries deserving support. The country-based solution, for which France was the principal advocate, was excluded by Italy. From the Italian point of view, a preferable solution was (as was proposed by the German Council presidency) that all regions with less than 75 per cent of the average economic output of

---

[27] Falkner (1994: 151) confirms the seriousness of these threats on the basis of her research.

the EC would be supported, since this would have included the Mezzogiorno region. Such a regulation would have excluded parts of Spain from structural fund intervention, however, which is why Spain's preference was the country-based model. An agreement was nowhere in sight, so the discussion moved on to other issues (e.g. the definition of the Community's own resources and agricultural policy reform). Since this resulted in more impasses, following the traditional joint breakfast Kohl and Mitterrand proposed that the negotiations be continued in the unorthodox form of bilateral meetings. These took place between the German presidency and the individual delegations, on the one hand, and the Commission and governmental representatives, on the other. In the end, the German Chancellor presented a compromise proposal that approximated the complete package adopted the following night.

The Delors Package cannot be described and evaluated in detail here (see *EC Bulletin* 2–1988; Lowe 1988; Franzmeyer, Seidel and Weise 1993). As indicated by its name, it represents a package deal, which essentially incorporates the following points:

(1) an increase in the Community's financial resources (an upper limit of 1.2 per cent of total annual GNP);
(2) a contribution rebate for the United Kingdom;
(3) reform of the agricultural policy (in particular, a lowering of the subsidies); and
(4) a generally intensified control of budget expenditures and regulation of the financing of the structural funds.

A doubling of all funds until 1993 was approved; in the meantime, the doubling of funds for the less developed regions (the primary objective) was approved until 1992. The region-based approach became generally accepted instead of the model based on focused support for entire countries.

The rough outline of the reform of the structural funds was provided by the Delors Package. On the basis of a proposal by the Commission the details were to be unanimously approved by the Council, with the implementation regulations approved through qualified majority voting.[28] Problems arose primarily over how to establish the exact list of regions to be supported. The British prime minister again attacked the principle of additionality, according to which EC monies must be used not in place of national funding, but only as a supplement to it. She was opposed to linking national spending to EC decisions, which would be an insult to the principle of national sovereignty (*Agence Europe*, 5

---

[28] See *Official Journal*, of 15 July 1988, No. L 185/9.

November 1988: 13). The Council reached final agreement on all issues at the end of the year (*EC Bulletin* 12–1988).

The structural policy of the Community was guided by the approved reform, which came into effect on 1 January 1989, and was oriented toward five priority goals:

- *Objective 1*: For regions where development is lagging behind (an action goal of the European Regional Development Fund, the European Social Fund, and the European Agricultural Guidance and Guarantee Fund). Such a designation is given to a region if the GDP per capita of the region falls below 75 per cent of the Community average. The goal of intervention is to open up the potential for regional development through investment, the creation and particularly the modernization of infrastructure, etc. Four-fifths of the resources of the ERDF are designated for these regions. In pursuit of this goal, the ERDF had secured funding for many such regions until 1993; according to the agreed upon formula for distributing these monies, approximately 16 per cent goes to regions in Greece, 33 per cent to Spanish regions, 25 per cent to Italian ones, 18 per cent to Portuguese ones, and 6 per cent to Irish ones.
- *Objective 2*: For the adjustment of regions most negatively affected by industrial decline (action goal of the ERDF and ESF). This designation is given if industrial employment is clearly in decline and unemployment exceeds the EC average. In 1988 two programmes were developed in this regard: RESIDER (conversion of iron and steel districts) and RENAVAL (conversion of shipbuilding areas). In pursuit of this goal, by 1993 the ERDF had secured funding for many such regions; approximately 39 per cent goes to regions located in the United Kingdom, 21 per cent to Spanish regions, 18 per cent to French ones, 9 per cent to German ones, 6 per cent to Italian ones, and 4 per cent to Belgian ones.
- *Objective 3*: Focus on long-term unemployment and the unemployment of youth (action goal of the ESF).
- *Objective 4*: Assistance for the adaptation of workers to industrial change (action goal of the ESF).
- *Objective 5*: Promotion of adjustment in the agricultural and fisheries sectors and in rural areas (action goal of the EAGGF). Prerequisites for qualification under this provision include a high proportion of employment in agriculture as a share of total employment in the region, a low level of income in agriculture, and below-average total regional economic output.

Two bodies with advisory functions were established. One of these had already existed in similar form as a committee of representatives of member states and the EIB; the other was a completely new advisory body, the Consultative Council of Regional and Local Authorities (CCLRA, an advisory board within Directorate General XVI). The CCLRA is composed of representatives of regional and local state authorities, who are nominated either on the basis of their expert knowledge or on the basis of their particular knowledge of the situation in their region of origin; the board's agenda is determined by proposals from the Commission.

The conditions for success

The eventual breakthrough with respect to the determination of financial resources and the reform of the structural funds can be attributed to several factors. The first of these is surely the well-reasoned, active and efficient strategy of the Delors Commission, for whom the Brussels decisions represented the 'third stage of the rocket' following the White Paper on the internal market and the Single European Act (see Ehlermann 1988; Biehl 1988: 67; Hort 1988: 424). A comparison of the final result with the original Commission project shows a surprisingly extensive congruence (see Sutcliffe 1995: 294; Allen 1996: 225f). At no time during the lengthy negotiations did their concept run up against a comprehensive counter-proposal. For Helen Wallace (1996b: 60), the Commission was able 'to make its own preferred proposals "yesable" to a surprising extent'.

Another factor that is difficult to weigh is the fact that the other supranational actors,[29] along with the large interest groups, stood behind the Commission's proposal from the beginning. However, that proposal was implementable only because it represented the redemption of the promise of extending balance through regional policy embedded in the Act and as such was supported by all national governments. The obstructionism of the United Kingdom, and partially also of France, can be explained in one sense as defence against what they viewed as excessive demands. In another sense, the delays in the approval of the Delors Package were central to the strategy of the net-payer countries to reach decisions on compensatory payments only once the implementation of the internal market had become irreversible. This was increasingly the case in the course of 1987, and probably finally determined

---

[29] Falkner (1994: 172) speaks justifiably of the 'secondary role' of the European Parliament and the Economic and Social Committee. The Commission informed them about its proposals only shortly before each of the crucial summit meetings, and the European Parliament president could expound the position of the European Parliament only in the context of a short audience prior to the beginning of the summit meetings.

with the decision of the Council of Ministers to liberalize the movement of capital completely. Internal Market Commissioner Lord Cockfield praises that as the crucial element for the breakthrough: 'because the Heads of Government knew that they were going to declare the Single Market irreversible when they came to the great meeting, the February meeting was concluding the Delors package no.1, it was because they knew that the Single Market was in the bag . . . that's the way the nexus goes round!'[30]

In addition it must also be noted that the approval of the ambitious package would probably not have been possible without the German willingness to pay for a remarkable share of the funding. This is no doubt based on the wealth of opportunities for the German economy in a single market and, further, on the specific integration project of the German government (see below).

An important step in the direction of a supranational structural policy

As indicated, the Delors Package and the reform of the structural funds meant much more than simply the determination of financial resources. The apparently 'technical' changes actually signified a clearly strengthened role for planning and implementation of European regional policy at the supranational level. This was not expressed in a formal expansion of the authority of the Commission, but resulted from the type and manner of the improvement and the increased efficiency of policy formulation and implementation. Through its definition of the criteria for receiving assistance and the regions to be assisted, and being charged with the control of the implementation of the programmes, the Commission expanded its authority.[31]

The balance of power between the Commission and the member states was shifted as a result of the enforcement of the additionality principle and the creation of an additional advisory body at the European level that was favourable to the Commission. Through the CCLRA, the Commission can coordinate its intentions with regional and local government authorities in advance of a decision. For Anderson (1995b: 131), 1988 marks not only 'the end of the second major accession wave in the Community' but also 'the beginning of the new cohesion regime'.

---

[30] Interview of 9 March 1993; see also Cockfield (1994: 46).
[31] Allen (1996: 227) comes to the conclusion that, 'whilst the overall level of funding is determined intergovernmentally, the Commission has gained a high degree of control over the designation of both structural-fund objectives and the 'designated areas' (note not regions) that they will apply to'.

Conclusion

In the total context of the integration thrust in the 1980s, regional policy is a relevant policy area. This can be demonstrated in quantitative terms: expenditure in the structural funds climbed from 4.8 per cent of the EC budget to 9.1 per cent in 1987 and to 28 per cent in 1992. In accordance with the decisions of Maastricht, 35 per cent of Community expenditure (33 billion ECU) was projected for regional policy in 1999. For the period 1994–9, around 170 billion ECU is available from the Community's budget for structural policies. Over the decade 1989–99, spending amounted cumulatively to 6.5 per cent of annual Community GDP.[32] This is far more than mere 'bargaining chips'.[33]

In addition, in the course of the 1980s and 1990s a series of qualitatively important shifts within the institutional order of the EC took place. This resulted in the anchoring of regional policy in the treaty via the SEA, and a number of important reforms of the regulations and concrete practices of regional policy. As we have shown, all this led to the development and transformation of the 1970s system of transfers among nation-states (*juste retour*) in the direction of a European structural policy instrument that follows extensive and supranationally defined criteria and objectives. Still, Community regional policy continues to display a 'hybrid' character.

'Maastricht' followed for the most part the same logic as the process between 1984 and 1988, with the monetary union project taking the place of the internal market. The peripheral countries tied the demand for an increase in compensation to the realization of both projects. An important difference between the intergovernmental conference of 1985 and Maastricht was the fact that Spain and Portugal were full members at the time of the latter, and that Spain made use of this status (and its comparatively greater weight). The Commission again took on a function that could be called that of an 'advocate', although in the interest of the approval of the total package it was forced to moderate the demands of these countries again and again. Spain wanted a form of side payments as more or less pure financial transfers and with it more

---

[32] Data from European Commission (1996a: 9). In order to emphasize the weightiness of this commitment, the Commission compares it to the Marshall Plan aid to Europe, which was equivalent to 1 per cent of US GDP per year and amounted cumulatively (1948–51) to 4 per cent of US GDP (ibid.).

[33] Here there is no mention made of *attaining* the goals (in particular with reference to the question of the social and environmental compatibility of both initiated and proposed projects). Tsoukalis (1993) evaluates the level of redistributed financial resources as significant for the budgets of the peripheral countries, but still far from what was necessary effectively to fight regional disparities or even decisively to promote convergence. See also the assessment by Tömmel (1994).

independence regarding the use of funds; this was defeated by the condition of efficiency controls imposed by the net-payer countries. In turn, this led to an expansion of the system at the European level as an obvious way out. A new fund was approved, the Cohesion Fund. This fund will contribute up to 90 per cent of the funding of investments.

In the union treaty, regional policy was ever more strongly oriented toward a modernization policy aimed at improving competitiveness. With the establishment of the Committee of the Regions, the participation of the subnational governmental authorities was enhanced and formalized further.[34] To the indignation of the peripheral countries, the budget decisions necessary for the Maastricht agreements were postponed and later approved in December 1992 as the Delors II Package.

At present the dynamic in this area seems to have reached a certain immanent boundary. The willingness of the net-payer states to pay has diminished owing to declining revenues and, in the case of the largest contributor, to the costs of German reunification. In addition, the capacity of the recipient countries to absorb funds (in the sense of using monies for projects meeting the criteria) is not unlimited. Moreover, there was a backlash against the previous mode of integration as such. In Maastricht, governments reacted against what they perceived as an all-too-dynamic Commission. The post-Maastricht crisis (Deppe and Felder 1993) revealed a general crisis of legitimation of the previous type of integration.

Our reconstruction of the development of EC regional policy in the context of the integration thrust of the 1980s revealed that a reduction of the logic of this policy area to any variant of intergovernmentalism is inadequate; this is true not only in the sense of the result of the changes since the Single European Act but also in the genesis of those changes. Not even an exclusive focus on intergovernmental conferences can ignore the important role of the Commission as political entrepreneur. Allen (1996: 225f), who – like Moravcsik (1998: 367) – clearly credits the Commission with the design of the reform of 1988, reduces its role in elaborating the essential framework for structural fund activity to the 'assistance' provided in a 'process of high-level interstate bargaining'. We think that the function of the Commission in several respects goes far beyond 'assisting'.[35] First, with the enhancement of its own role

---

[34] On this point see Engel (1991), Tömmel (1994: 59ff) and Timmermann (1995).

[35] Sutcliffe's (1995: 294) assessment of the reform of 1988 proceeds in a similar direction. Anderson (1995b: 133) emphasizes 'the Commission's capacity to turn the member governments' general recommendations for action into specific administrative arrangements that conferred on it an important role', and its ability 'to position itself as the actor best able to meet the demands of the member states for enhanced efficacy of the fund'.

Regional policy 149

(self-interest in the expansion of the system), the Commission was able to link the organization and implementation of agreements principally reached between governments. Secondly, in the aforementioned manner and with the incorporation of subnational governmental authorities, it was able to modify the basic structure of the policy arena, insofar as the monopoly of the national governments over the interplay between domestic and foreign policy was broken. This was a decisive step in the direction of multi-level governance.[36] Thirdly, it took on the role of supporter and advocate for the peripheral countries, especially for the new members. This was consistent with its quasi-federalist views, but also with the relative weakness of the state apparatuses of these countries.

The strategy of the Delors Commission was successful, even in terms of its temporal course. The embedding of the goal of 'economic and social cohesion' was the basis for a continuing dynamic in the area of regional policy (although the same cannot be said for social policy; see chapter 6). The method of postponing the establishment of the financial resources was in fact (from the point of view of the peripheral countries and the Commission) a risk. Their strategy succeeded because the net-payer countries were ready to fulfil the promise contained in the Single Act – as soon as the creation of the internal market was irreversible. The logic of this chain of events is often disregarded, which leads to deficient explanations of what took place.

The structural coupling of the extension of regional policy with processes of further integration is also emphasized in neofunctionalist theory. The concept of spillover is increasingly used in a 'less functionalist' way in the recent literature.[37] Here we return to the same old problem: we are not talking about processes that are set in motion at once, which lead to measures in other areas. Rather, we are speaking

---

[36] See Marks (1992: 214), Bullmann (1994) and Hooghe (1996); for evidence of the subsequently successful development of the influence of the regions in Brussels, see the analysis by McAleavey and Mitchell (1994).

[37] Marks (1992: 198) discusses the 'shift in Community resources to the structural funds' as '*forced spillover*, in which the prospect of a breakthrough in one arena created intense pressure for innovation in others'. For Swann (1996: ch 5), spillover also signifies the 'expansive logic' that led to the dynamic after the SEA. George (1991) revises and expands the concept, but in the case of regional policy comes to the conclusion that 'there seemed to be a clear functional spillover from the commitment to free the internal market to the expansion of the regional fund . . . although the Thatcher governments argued that it was not so' (George 1991: 227).

There are some formulations in older integration theory that are in line with what is presented here. Nye (1971: 202) speaks of 'deliberate linkages': 'In contrast to pure spillover . . . problems are deliberately linked together into package deals not on the basis of technological necessity but on a basis of political and ideological projections and political possibilities.'

about developments in several areas that are often simultaneous and interconnected. In the context of package deals, policies are introduced or expanded often as *anticipated* reactions against consequences perceived as undesirable.[38] Thus we are not dealing with mechanisms that become effective over the course of time, but rather with the political discourses of the involved actors, that is with their integration projects. Whether or not corrective measures accompany the creation of the Single Market and the level of government on which these will be established depends on their regulatory orientation.

The anchoring of regional policy in the treaty and the structural funds reform of 1988 can be explained only with reference to the fact that the peripheral countries, which understood that they potentially had less to gain from the internal market had at their disposal the possibility of blocking its implementation. As we have explained, buying them off through side payments could have been accomplished through a purely interstate financial transfer. However, the development of regional policy in the 1980s and 1990s was much more than this; it reflected two additional elements that are fundamental to the integration thrust of the 1980s: (a) a consensus that tends toward the notion that the costs and benefits of EC measures should be immediately distributed,[39] and that the creation of a Single Market alone ('negative integration') does not guarantee this; and (b) the general desirability of further supranationalization (among the representatives of federalist integration projects; see chapter 2, pp. 44ff).

One can say that this was the consensus among the large bloc of social democratic and Christian democratic governments on the European continent. For these countries, a European regional equalization system was an inevitable and desirable cornerstone of the integration thrust of the 1980s.[40] Exceptions to this rule include the United Kingdom, and

---

[38] For Anderson (1995b: 142), 'the anticipated spatial effects of the single-market initiative' were 'the main impetus for the sweeping reform of the structural funds in 1988'. For more on the anticipation of the consequences of the internal market see, especially the detailed discussion of the argument in Marks (1992). He proposes an argument that is based on the assumption of 'differential costs of economic risks', thereby incorporating 'unpredictability'.

[39] Similarly, Begg and Mayes (1993: 149) write: 'The reality of the EC is that the division of costs and benefits is central to the political agreements needed to proceed with integration.'

[40] The reference to the normative content of integration projects does not mean that a thesis of 'altruistic bargaining' in the context of European integration is being put forward here. The temporal sequence of the extension of regional policy makes its 'dependent', subordinate status quite clear. And the meaning of economic liberalization for peripheral countries is reflected in developments in the balance of trade between Spain, Portugal and Greece and the rest of the Community after they became members. One cannot present the regional policy of the EC as 'social policy'. There are

in a certain sense France, especially from 1986 to 1988. For the conservative British government, regional policy actually represented an undesirable, but inevitable, side payment. The reasons for the ultimate approval by both countries lie in the fact that both countries clearly profit from the resources distributed to achieve the second goal of structural funds intervention, namely the transformation of old industrial structures; in addition, the United Kingdom was able to push through a reduction in its contribution.

The decisive thing for the Commission as political entrepreneur was that its project of setting up and expanding a supranational structural policy was largely in unison with that of the large bloc of social democratic and Christian democratic governments. That was the basis on which it was possible to acquire authority in a step-by-step fashion. In addition, the Commission was closely allied with the governments of the peripheral countries. Moreover, it benefited from the experiences of several previous experimental and reform phases in this policy area, which gave it additional credibility. A comparison with the development of social policy shows how important these factors are for success in policy-making at European level.

no 'claims' to payments (entitlements) on the part of individuals or regions. Rather, regional policy is about the promotion of infrastructural investments, about an opening of regions, from which the entire European economic area potentially profits. The start-up or restructuring assistance for businesses in peripheral regions incorporates these into a new European division of labour.

6 EC social policy: the defeat of the Delorist project

Patrick Ziltener

Introduction

The relatively low rank of the 'social dimension' in the renewed push for European integration in the 1980s provides the starting point for three competing theses on the integration process.[1] First, the *cornerstone thesis* holds that, from the beginning, the Europeanization of social policy was a cornerstone of the integration project as conceived by the supranational political entrepreneur, the EC Commission, and certain governments. The conception of the social policy domain in the Single Act (most importantly, Articles 21 and 22 of the Single European Act, i.e. Articles 118a and 118b in the EC treaties) remained narrow for purely tactical reasons so as not to endanger the strategic goal of relaunching European integration. Second, the *supplement thesis* states that the core of the project, which was legally established by the Single Act, was the internal market. When it became apparent that this effort might not be successful (particularly owing to the public debate about its social consequences in the years 1987–8), it became necessary to provide, albeit belatedly, a social policy cushion for the impact of the internal market. According to neofunctionalist reasoning, the politicization of social policy following the Single Act was an aftereffect of intensified economic integration. The *packaging thesis* argues that the weak social policy regulations together with the abundance of social rhetoric were merely an expression of the selling of an elite pact to the European public; it was simply a matter of 'packaging the package'.

---

[1] The theses of this chapter were developed jointly with Volker Bornschier. A preliminary analysis of our research in this area, entitled 'The Politics of the "Social Dimension" in the Commission's Project to Revitalize Western European Integration', was presented to the Second Conference of the European Sociological Association (ESA), Budapest, Hungary, 1995 (part of which was published in Bornschier and Ziltener 1999). The first full version was presented to the 8th Conference on Socio-Economics/Communitarian Summit, Session on 'The Social Economy of European Integration' (Organizer: Professor Stefan Immerfall), Geneva, Switzerland, 1996.

According to this thesis, social policy regulations at the European level were not really sought after by the main actors.

The packaging thesis and the cornerstone thesis contradict each other. The explanatory power of the packaging thesis is undermined by the fact that the social policy content in the integration projects of important actors was far greater prior to the Single Act than it was during the intergovernmental conference and in the final agreement. On the other hand, the cornerstone thesis can thoroughly explain this fact as an expression of the tactical hindsight of the Commission and the national governments that were progressive on matters of social policy; the low social policy content of the Single Act was a result of 'postponing' rather than 'packaging'.

The fact that social policy first moved to centre stage some time after the passage of the Single Act can be explained by both the cornerstone thesis and the supplement thesis. The supplement thesis argues that it was the successful adoption of the White Paper *Completing the Internal Market* and ratification of the Single Act that awoke from their slumber those actors (in particular, the European trade unions) interested in social policy as part of the movement toward integration. By contrast, the cornerstone thesis assumes that social policy was an essential element of a renewed integration process from the beginning, and not a post facto supplement. The supplement thesis and the packaging thesis do not really contradict each other, but rather could be incorporated in an expanded explanation. After the adoption of the Single Act, those actors that stood behind a mere 'packaging' of the elite pact could not prevent other actors from pushing for the rhetoric to be turned into concrete policy measures, that is, the Europeanization of social policy.

Thus, the real difference among these explanations of the social policy debate lies between the cornerstone thesis, on the one hand, and the two other theses (the supplement thesis and the packaging thesis) on the other.

The focal point of the next section is the detailed social policy information from the intergovernmental conference in 1985 and the question of the roots of the different initiatives in this area. I then discuss the reasons for the incorporation of some minimal social policy elements into the Single Act and draw first conclusions regarding the assessments of the cornerstone and packaging theses. In the following section, the social policy elements of the Act are understood as 'vestiges' of a more expansive integration project, one that can be associated for good reason with the name Jacques Delors. I then examine the starting point for the subsequent creation of a social dimension, and the allies and opponents of this ambitious project. The supplement thesis is evaluated in conjunction with a discussion about the context for the new political dynamic with respect to social policy questions that developed after 1987. The subsequent history of the EC Social Charter and the Maastricht Treaty must be regarded as signs of the failure of the Delorist project, and I present the basis for this controversial assessment.

The chapter closes with a final evaluation of the three theses regarding the status of the social policy dimension of the integration thrust of the 1980s. From the analysis of the development of this policy area, some conclusions are also drawn with respect to the theoretical discussion of integration. From a comparison with the more successfully developed regional policies of the EC, some conclusions can be drawn regarding the domain of social policy.

Social policy in the integration relaunch

From the beginning, it was foreseeable that the domain of social policy would become the most controversial element of the integration thrust of the 1980s. In fact, the Ad Hoc Committee for Institutional Affairs (Dooge Committee) demanded in its final report, submitted to the European Council in Brussels in March 1985, a gradual realization of a European social area as the 'logical follow-on from an economically integrated, dynamic, and competitive Community'.[2]

The concept of a European social area goes back to a 1981 memorandum by the French government in which Jacques Delors was a cabinet member. In October 1981, Prime Minister Mauroy arranged for Deputy Minister for European Affairs A. Chandernagor to prepare a memorandum on the future of the EC in which, among other things, the creation of an *'espace social européen'* (European social area) was proposed.[3] This programme included three objectives:

(1) placing employment at the centre of Community social policy by developing cooperation and reorganizing Community policy;
(2) stepping up the social dialogue at the Community and national level, both within the company and elsewhere;
(3) improving cooperation and consultation on matters of social protection.

With the exception of Danish interest in some social policy recommendations, this initiative provoked no response from the other

---

[2] Ad Hoc Committee for Institutional Affairs, Report to the European Council, Brussels, 29–30 March 1985, Luxembourg. Point 2, 'Gradual achievement of a European Social Area' as part of Chapter B, 'Promotion of the common values of civilization'. See Thatcher (1993: 550).
[3] In *EC Bulletin* 11–1981; see Venturini (1988: 26), Lequesne (1989: 153f) and Falkner (1994: 188).

European partners and was never discussed in the Council. Nevertheless, this memorandum is the birth certificate of the concept of a European social area, which was taken up again some three years later by the French government during its Council presidency. In his speech on 7 February 1984 in The Hague, Mitterrand outlined the content of the concept, whose thrust was the fight against unemployment in Europe (*Europa-Archiv* 7/1984). As means toward this end he named, among others, a pan-European fixed reduction of working hours, the acceleration and universalization of occupational training and the expansion of social protection.[4]

At the same time, there were attempts at stimulating discussions between employer organizations and trade unions at the European level. At the inspiration of the French presidency (during the first half of 1984), and subsequently also the Irish presidency, meetings were held between the Council, the Commission, the Union of Industrial and Employers' Confederations (UNICE) and the European Trade Union Confederation (ETUC).[5]

Initially, these attempts at placing a social policy dimension on the agenda of the Community, which were made within the overall push toward integration, seemed successful. The Council of the Ministers of Social Affairs concluded with promising statements in June 1984 (*Social Europe* 2/1984): the creation of a European social area was characterized as inseparably connected with increasing Europe's competitiveness. Institutional differences between the social systems of the member states would not exclude the development of European social policy. The notion of a European social area was also contained in the Commission's programme for 1985, presented by Delors in his introductory speech before the European Parliament in March 1985. The realization of a large market must, according to Delors, go hand in hand with the creation and formation of a European social area. The positive effects of this large market would be lost if some member states should try to create for themselves a competitive advantage vis-à-vis other states at the expense of social policy. A European social area should prevent

---

[4] According to Haywood, the concept of an '*espace social européen*' fulfilled a dual function for Mitterrand domestically: (a) as a bridge between the pro- and anti-integration factions; and (b) as a means 'to distinguish PS [Socialist Party] Euro-policy from Giscardian policy, at the same time as socialist rhetoric was being stripped from PS texts. Insistence on a social dimension to the internal market softened the blow of accepting a neo-liberal structure, allowing the PS to retain a degree of socialist credibility' (Haywood 1993: 274f).

[5] See Savoini (1984) and Kohler-Koch and Platzer (1986). In the course of 1984 there was a series of informal contacts between the UNICE and the ETUC which were subsequently resumed.

social dumping practices, which have an adverse effect on overall employment (*EC Bulletin*, Supplement 4-1985).

These are but a few examples of how the 'European social area' project was repeatedly highlighted in official EC documents. However, until the intergovernmental conference, the social policy agenda was repeatedly set aside. At the important summit of the European Council in Milan, which adopted the White Paper on the completion of the internal market, maintaining radio silence on social policy was the order of the day.[6] A French memorandum, addressed to the Council, could do nothing to alter the situation. A section on 'The European Social Area' stated that the standardization of the internal market presupposed 'maximum homogeneity' in the social policy area.[7]

At the intergovernmental conference[8] in the second half of 1985, the attempt by the Commission closely to link a supplemental package of social and regional policy measures designed to mitigate the anticipated negative effects of the realization of the internal market failed (see chapter 2, p. 63). Delors argued that the realization of the internal market 'raises some extremely tricky problems, particularly with regard to safety and health. Harmonization of the rules is necessary because there can be no market allowing reasonable competition unless there is some measure of harmonization of the rules, and hence to some extent of enterprises' costs'.[9]

The strategy of the Commission failed and, through the subsequent separation of regional policy from social policy, no further concrete suggestions were made in this regard once negotiations began. Once the British pushed through the explicit invalidation of majority rule for the rights and interests of workers (Article 100a), it became clear that there was hardly any possibility for progress in this area. In the course of the

[6] In the integration literature this abstinence from social policy at the Milan summit was a 'negative decisive moment', a phrase that captures the fact that social policy would not become part of the project (Berié 1992: 57). Schlecht's (1990) thesis that the Commission did not see the development of the European social system as a logical prerequisite for the creation of a Single Market contrasts with our explanation of 'postponing' (see below).
[7] In *Europa-Archiv* 16/1985, D446. Recommendations included measures for the convergence of social security systems, for improvement of the systematic consultation of the 'social partners', and for the preparation of the concertation of elements influencing wage agreements in branches, particularly those in sectors regulated by EC rules (steel industry, textile industry, etc.).
[8] The reconstruction of the social policy debate at the intergovernmental conference in 1985 is based on interviews with protagonists who were directly or indirectly involved, an evaluation of the *EC Bulletin*, and the documents in Gazzo (1985 and 1986), as well as on De Ruyt (1989), Venturini (1988), Lequesne (1989), Attali (1993) and Howe (1994).
[9] Speech by Delors at the first session of the intergovernmental conference in Luxembourg (in Gazzo 1986: p. 25).

conference, Delors submitted a proposal according to which Article 117 would have been supplemented through the incorporation of the concept of a 'European social area'. Although the concept was firmly anchored in many Community documents and was not elaborated beyond that, it was nonetheless rejected.

The Commission had become repeatedly frustrated to such an extent that some national delegations then had to take up the effort to reopen the issue. A Belgian proposal for securing fundamental rights was incorporated into the Preamble of the Act. A French proposal wanted to create the possibility that, if the 'social partners' concluded a collective agreement covering at least three countries, this (upon recommendation by the Commission and with a qualified majority vote in the Council of Ministers) could be declared binding on the whole Community. This proposal had no chance, especially since the countries that did not want to touch the principle of *Tarifautonomie* (autonomy of the 'social partners' in collective bargaining) united in opposition with the opponents of every EC function in this area. This coalition almost overturned Article 22 of the Act (non-binding social dialogue at the European level; Article 118b of the treaties). The final formulation was taken from the Dooge Report.

An initiative of the Danish government for an article regarding the improvement of the work environment with respect to the health and safety of workers was successful and became incorporated as a modification to Article 21 of the Single Act (Article 118a of the treaties). The remarkable thing here is that the minimum requirements in this area are to be determined by a qualified majority of the Council. This is the only social policy area in the Act in which qualified majority votes of the Council are possible. In consideration of the southern member states, a regulation that provided a step-by-step application according to levels of development was incorporated. An accord regarding Article 21 first became possible after the end of the conference and after the British had pushed through additional restrictive formulations (paragraph 2 on protection of small and medium-sized businesses; paragraph 3 on the possibility of maintaining more stringent regulations). According to an interview with a high-ranking British diplomat, if these 'reassurances' had not been adopted, the article would have been overturned.

The various initiatives and their results are summarized in table 6.1, and the modified Article 118 of the treaties is presented in table 6.2.

Even prior to the conclusion of the intergovernmental conference, the Commission president announced with strategic optimism: 'That is the basis for a fresh start.' He thanked the 'happy initiative' of the Danish government, which promoted the social dimension 'in political

Table 6.1. *Intergovernmental conference (IGC) 1985: initiatives in the social policy area and their results in the Single European Act (SEA)*

Initiative	By	Mode of agreement	Results
'European social area'	France 1981; Dooge Report; Commission proposal at IGC: Incorporation in Art. 17 of the treaties	Rejected	None
Anchoring fundamental rights	Belgium	Agreed as general reference in Preamble	Preamble SEA (Section 3)
Improvement of the working environment	Denmark	Agreed after incorporation of various restrictions, e.g. small and medium-sized undertakings clause (United Kingdom)	Art. 21 SEA, Declaration No. 7 (Annex SEA); Art. 118a of the treaties
Fighting unemployment by means of coordination of the economic policies of the member states	Denmark	Rejected	None
Creation of the possibility of collective bargaining at European level	France	Agreed as non-binding 'social dialogue'; compromise proposal of the Commission	Art. 22 SEA; Art. 118b of the treaties

conditions which were not easy for it' while at the same time meeting the expectations of several delegations.[10] This statement only partially reflects the fact that a dramatic 'chainsaw massacre' (the term is Delors') of the social policy proposals had just taken place, one surpassed perhaps only by the one in the monetary policy area.

At a press conference on the last day of the Luxembourg Council, at about midnight, Delors was of the opinion that the social policy content of the Act must open a breach, if it was to be taken seriously (*EC Bulletin* 11–1985, 1.1.2). The choice of the word 'breach' might well have expressed the hope of a breakthrough by means of the established 'social dialogue'. The Italian Prime Minister Craxi criticized the open refusal of every attempt to shape European cooperation in the social area more concretely and more efficiently (ibid.). The national publics were only dimly aware of the social policy content of the Single Act, and for that reason it hardly played a role in the ratification debates.

In the integration literature, the social policy content of the Single Act

---

[10] In his press conference of 27 November 1985 (Gazzo 1986: 85).

Table 6.2. *Article 118 of the treaties establishing the European Communities as modified by the Single European Act*

Article 118
Without prejudice to other provisions of this Treaty and in conformity with its general objectives, the Commission shall have the task of promoting close cooperation between Member States in the social field, particularly in matters relating to:
– employment;
– labour law and working conditions;
– basic and advanced vocational training;
– social security;
– prevention of occupational accidents and diseases;
– occupational hygiene;
– the right of association, and collective bargaining between employers and workers.
To this end, the Commission shall act in close contact with Member States by making studies, delivering opinions and arranging consultations both on problems arising at national level and on those of concern to international organizations.
  Before delivering the opinions provided for in this Article, the Commission shall consult the Economic and Social Committee.

Article 118a (SEA Article 21)
1. Member States shall pay particular attention to encouraging improvements, especially in the working environment, as regards to health and safety of workers, and shall set as their objectives the harmonization of conditions in this area, while maintaining the improvements made.
2. In order to help achieve the objective laid down in the first paragraph, the Council, acting by a qualified majority on a proposal from the Commission, in cooperation with the European Parliament and after consulting the Economic and Social Committee, shall adopt, by means of directives, minimum requirements for gradual implementation, having regard to the conditions and technical rules obtaining in each of the Member States.
    Such directives shall avoid imposing administrative, financial and legal constraints in a way which would hold back the creation and development of small and medium-sized undertakings.
3. The provisions adopted pursuant to this Article shall not prevent any Member State from maintaining or introducing more stringent measures for the protection of working conditions compatible with this Treaty.

Article 118b (SEA Article 22)
The Commission shall endeavour to develop the dialogue between management and labour at European level which could, if the two sides consider it desirable, lead to relations based on agreement.

---

is predominantly seen as minimal, as representing little more than a codification of current practice (Moravcsik 1991: 43; 1998: 365), signifying a mere quantitative improvement in the available social policy instruments but hardly a qualitative leap (Schulte 1993a: 273), to be understood 'more as a "by-product" than a realization of the "social dimension" that had been planned from the start' (Berié 1992: 58, fn. 115).[11] The two following sections discuss the explanation of the social policy results of the intergovernmental conference of 1985 with reference to the three theses mentioned earlier and assess their meaning for the further development of EC social policy.

Explaining the content and the lack of content of the Single Act

The fact that the anchoring of the concept of a 'European social area' was rejected by the majority can certainly be interpreted through the packaging thesis; this is the direction of the analysis by Vogel-Polsky (1991). As long as it was only inconsequential rhetoric, there was no decisive resistance to the concept, but, as soon as it became an issue of including it in the treaty, it was no longer acceptable. The concept itself has never been defined concretely in any Community document; it was therefore associated in the first instance with the French proposals. That these were not capable of being approved had been foreseeable for a long time, based on the low level of resonance to the concept. However, the explanation of the lack of receptivity to the concept must be expanded. Another reason for it, as many interviewees from other national delegations as well as those in the Brussels apparat explained, was the 'specifically French' character of the concept and the strategy pursued. Whereas interviewees who were stamped by a Francophone political culture resonated to visionary concepts for the elaboration of policy, in other political cultures a tremendous scepticism prevailed toward such proposals, whose content is only vaguely outlined and whose legal consequences are therefore difficult to assess.

The adoption of Article 118a on occupational health and safety proved of far-reaching significance for the development of EC social policy. Two aspects were of particular importance: (1) the explicit establishment of majority voting in the Council (see Schnorpfeil 1994: 40): and (2) the lack of definition of the concept of the working environment. The competence of the Community was not actually broadened through Article 118a (see Pescatore 1986; Vogel-Polsky 1991); health and safety in the workplace were already explicitly mentioned in Article 118. The previously undefined concept of the working environment, however, can be traced back to the specifics of Danish labour and social policy legislation regarding the term *arbejdsmiljø*, which subsumes areas such as working hours and the protection of

---

[11] In this light, it is difficult to comprehend Sidjanski's (1992: 160f) assessment that social policy at the 1985 intergovernmental conference was an example of an *'engrenage dynamique'*.

youth. These two elements together enabled the Commission – which is responsible, on the basis of Article 100a, to strive for a high level of protection[12] – in conjunction with the European Court of Justice, to turn occupational health and safety legislation into the most important and successful area of social policy legislation in the Community (see Berié 1988; Eichener and Voelzkow 1994).

How can the adoption of Article 118a be explained? The Danish interest in the generalization of its legislation is not only sociopolitically but also economically motivated. A state that can generalize its 'regulatory style' and level of regulation to the European level dismantles its own 'locational disadvantages'. The costs of adopting such measures fall exclusively on other states. No doubt, one reason for the consent of the other governments to the Danish proposal was that most understood it relatively narrowly as a supplement to the technical occupational protections (safety of machinery, facilities, vehicles, tools, etc.) that belong to the core areas of the harmonization policy, in the sense of the reduction of import restrictions in the Single Market. In this respect there is a trade policy background to all this.[13] No one, not even the British government, wanted intra-European competition with respect to occupational health and safety.[14] Great Britain had legal regulations in this area that were comparable in scope and depth to those in other West European countries. Moreover, the European employers' association (UNICE) had also expressed its support for establishing baseline EC rules in the area of occupational safety.[15]

However, the question is not yet clarified as to how the British government accepted *majority voting* in the Council of Ministers in this area and thereby gave up its veto right. Thatcher was prepared to accept a larger number of majority decisions in the Council as the price for the internal market (Thatcher 1993: 553). Can one therefore say that Article 118a was a social policy element of a package deal? From our interviews with members of the British delegation at the Luxembourg intergovernmental conference, we know that majority decisions in the occupational and social policy areas were not acceptable, even as part of a package deal. Moreover, Article 118a was decided *after* the Luxembourg summit, at a session of the Council of Ministers, that is, at a time

---

[12] Article 100a, para. 3: 'The Commission, in its proposals envisaged in paragraph 1 concerning health, safety, environmental protection and consumer protection, will take as a base a high level of protection.'
[13] See Eichener and Voelzkow (1994: 388), Ross (1995b: 363) and Leibfried/Pierson (1996: 190).
[14] Everyone we interviewed made reference to this point.
[15] UNICE position paper, *The Social Dimension of the Internal Market*, 30 November 1988; see Tyszkiewicz (1989b: 49).

when the central issues of the internal market, research and development and cohesion were already signed, sealed and delivered. Obviously the British government believed, on the basis of an (implicitly) narrow understanding of the 'working environment' and through the adoption of restrictive clauses, that it was adequately safeguarded.

The further history of Article 118a is a definitive fight to the finish over how far the concept of the working environment would reach. By November 1986 the European Parliament had already demanded from the Commission a broad interpretation of Article 118a; the Economic and Social Committee followed suit (Beretta Report, in Venturini 1988). Every social policy action programme was accompanied by confrontations about the scope of the article. Everywhere that the Commission succeeded in making reference to Article 118a, prominent steps toward harmonization at high level occurred.[16] In 1991, for example, a directive on improving occupational health and safety for temporary workers was decided by majority vote, whereas both of the other regulatory proposals regarding the protection of temporary workers remained blocked. Thus, occupational health and safety have developed far beyond a set of minimum regulations enacted for the sake of the internal market into the most important area of EC social policy legislation with far-reaching regulations – most recently the 1996 European Court of Justice directive on working hours. In addition to the British government, UNICE President Tyszkiewicz (1989b) also severely criticized the Commission for its attempts to extend the validity of Article 118a and with it the use of qualified majority voting to areas that are expressly excluded by Article 100a. In his view, the politics of the Commission were not compatible with the spirit and letter of the Single Act (ibid.: 48).

The history of Article 118a reveals that, for some, it was clearly the nucleus of EC social policy legislation, whose development, in the sense of a 'balanced approach', had to be forced, particularly since no social policy demands could be pushed through at the intergovernmental conference in 1985. For others, the internal market was sufficiently enhanced in its social dimension by the narrowly confined European legislation on occupational health and safety as it applied to products and production.

[16] See Leibfried and Pierson (1996: 191). For the most part, one can attribute maximum use of the potentialities of Article 118a to the Commission, but not – Ross (1995b: 373) gives this impression – to the article as such. Another factor is the special function of the European standardization associations: Eichener and Voelzkow (1994) cover the important function of the technical committees of the European standardization organizations (CEN/CENELEC) and the clear overrepresentation of the high-regulation countries in them. See Konstanty and Zwingmann (1989).

Social policy 163

As we have mentioned, Article 118b only partially satisfied the projects of some actors regarding future collective bargaining at European level. Delors called it 'purely symbolic text', which was nonetheless important for the Commission because it was conducive to and legitimated the continuation of dialogue at the European level.[17] The article contained nothing more than the current practice, which had not been called into question by anyone (see Berié 1988). The decisive thing for UNICE was the aspect of voluntariness; again and again, it emphasized the difference between dialogue and collective bargaining.[18] Interviews with British diplomats yielded the same basis for the adoption of the article; in addition, reference was made (with ironic undertones) to the symbolic meaning of such texts for (continental) Europeans.

Our analysis of this phase of the revitalization of the European integration process showed that important actors were also pursuing inseparable social policy goals. These were relatively abstract, however (something that actors in favour of them also admitted); and at the Luxembourg intergovernmental conference they were unequivocally subordinated. Here the cornerstone thesis is confirmed, based on the actions of the majority of the actors involved; the packaging thesis is thereby rejected. To evaluate the cornerstone thesis, the social policy integration project must be reconstructed more precisely, since, although present from the outset, it can be only indirectly deduced. Only in this way can the further development of this policy area up until the Maastricht Treaty be understood and the supplement thesis be discussed.

The Delorist project

The 'European social area' project of Mitterrand and the then French government has already been described. Its adoption as part of the Luxembourg package was not achieved, and in 1986 France elected a new rightist government led by Jacques Chirac. Throughout the conflict-ridden *cohabitation* of a socialist president and a right-wing government, President Mitterrand was clearly restrained in his role as the most important promoter of social policy integration up to that time. The role of the Commission therefore became even more important. What was *its* project in this regard?

The goal pursued by the Delors Commission was a 'mixed' method

---

[17] Delors at a press conference, 27 November 1985 (Gazzo 1986: 87).
[18] See UNICE position paper, *The Social Dimension of the Internal Market*, 30 November 1988: 'The Single European Act rightly places emphasis on "dialogue". Dialogue . . . , not collective bargaining.'

'involving social regulation and harmonization of employment and working conditions, characterized by a combination of Directives and Regulations on the one hand and arrangements deriving from the social dialogue on the other'.[19] The social dialogue had a greater weight in the project of the Commission than it did in that of a 'European social area'.

The project can therefore be called *Delorist*, because not only was the Commission president its most important promoter and his cabinet[20] the most important producer of ideas and corresponding concepts, but he gave it its specific content. As shown in chapter 2, for Delors the concept of *concertation*, the involvement of 'social partners' in the formulation and implementation of political programmes, had always been a central part of his politics. It is therefore not surprising that Delors, shortly after taking office, invited representatives of the Union of Industrial and Employers' Confederations (UNICE), the European Centre of Public Enterprises (Centre Européen des Entreprises Publiques, CEEP) and the European Trade Union Confederation (ETUC) to talks at the 'Val Duchesse', a small palace on the outskirts of Brussels. The goals that Delors had pursued from the outset with the 'social dialogue' were reflected in the Venturini Report (see note 19). The dialogue of 'social partners' at the European level was supposed to lead later to the recognition by the 'social partners' of a 'joint responsibility to manage the changes deriving from the single market and adopt a more 'European' attitude by planning their strategy within the framework of a Europe without frontiers and by managing their own internal contradictions' (Venturini 1988: 63f). In the area of the legal regulation of labour relations, this meant subjecting European collective agreements to compulsory standardization and coordination with the various national levels (intersectoral collective agreements, sectoral agreements, company bargaining).

The thesis of an existing and specific European 'societal model', whose elements exist in all societies and their respective states (see chapter 2, p. 56), provides the background and argumentation for the Delorist project. As Delors often said, the social dimension is not an invention of the Brussels bureaucracy, nor does it depend upon the

---

[19] A formulation from the important Venturini Report (1988: 65). The Venturini Report (whose original title is *Un espace social européen à l'horizon 1992*) did not have the status of an official position paper of the Commission, but drew from earlier work and deliberations of the Commission.

[20] Delors' cabinet was the site of conceptual innovation in the area of social policy; central concepts and papers were drafted there, sometimes up to the point of detailed drafts. When necessary, his cabinet circumvented those of other Commissioners and established parallel networks to achieve the desired results.

personal convictions of the president of the Commission; rather, it is inherent in the form and manner in which the European nations have progressed for decades (Delors 1988b: 6).

More broadly stated: for the political left, the revitalization of European integration held the promise of recapturing political control of the economy through a new system of supranational governance as well as in industrial relations, internalizing the external effects that increasingly pre-empt the authority of individual national regimes and extricating European industrial relations from the dictates of competition among regimes and market forces. Their goal was the defence and continuation of the tradition of inclusion of unions and workers' interests in the shaping of industrial relations and political regulations in general. In this sense, current efforts to add a social dimension to the internal market are best understood as 'attempts to preserve, if only by default, the historical labour-inclusiveness of European industrial relations against strong economic and political pressures for deregulation by anchoring it in tripartite supranational institutions able to promote a new convergence among national regimes along labour-inclusive lines' (Streeck 1993: 89).

If we have correctly described the Delorist project, the question arises of why its advocates did not raise its realization to a *conditio sine qua non* from the beginning. If one reconstructs the prehistory of the Single Act, then the answer lies at hand: only through a strategic withholding of controversial areas could the blockade of integration be overcome. In this sense, we can understand the statement by EC Commissioner Lord Cockfield[21] that a linkage with social policy demands would have clearly slowed down the integration thrust, if not completely hindered it: 'Had "linkage" been accepted it would have resulted in intolerable delay being imposed on the Internal Market Programme and in the light of subsequent changes in the economic and political climate this delay could well have frustrated the programme altogether' (Cockfield 1994: 46).

Ross describes Delors' strategy as an attempt to seize the available opportunities for action from the area of all political possibilities, to accumulate through success the necessary resources and to invest these again in the expansion of this area. Here Ross compares Delors' strategy to a Russian doll, which consists of several dolls, each concealed inside the other: 'It was necessary to begin with proposals which would tap most of the open dimensions of the opportunity structure and create

---

[21] Compare the reference to Lord Cockfield in Fels (1989: 162, fn. 1), which cites the following: 'If we had linked the social questions with the economic regulations neither of the two would have moved ahead.'

forward momentum . . . Its success was immediately cashed in on new initiatives: the Russian dolls' (Ross 1995a: 46).

With this strategy, the transition from market-creating to state-building was supposed to be achieved. In the course of the integration process, elements of state-building would appear, that is, the transfer of sovereignty in the direction of the EC, whose weight would thereby become greater. Venturini (1988: 26) emphasizes the coherence of Delors' strategy: the decision to begin with the 'economic path', instead of with the other three alternatives under consideration (institutions, currency or defence), was outlined by Jean Monnet. After the adoption and the fixing of a timetable for the Single Market project, the subsequent strategy rested on the impetus provided by economic and social interest groups (ibid: 28). We will see that Venturini describes exactly the procedure Delors would follow in 1988.

The anchoring (albeit weakly) of social policy elements in the Act was extremely important for Delors' strategy. From this foundation one could push the development of this policy area (create a 'breach'). Delors constantly tried to attach the same significance to the Single Act as he did to the Treaty of Rome with respect to its quasi-constitutional legal status in terms of social policy and the 'concertation' process.[22] In any case, this step-by-step process became a politically risky path, considering the different goals of the national governments with respect to integration and the structural weakness of actors who favoured the development of social policy at the European level.

The situation after the Single Act – allies and opponents of the Commission

The administrative planning and management authorities within the EC are largely self-sufficient and only weakly influenced by the representative political bodies of the EC (Bach 1993b: 265). However, Delors cleverly recruited the support of the European Parliament and the Economic and Social Committee as part of his strategy. They were allies of the Commission insofar as they could be counted on as generally sympathetic to integration and to the area of social policy (see Springer 1992). However, Däubler (1989: 43) points out the inverse proportion operative here: the greater the advocacy of social policy in the drafts and pronouncements of the various EC organs, the less their own decision-making authority in that domain.

---

[22] Delors (1988c: 10f) in his preface to the Cecchini Report on the 'Cost of Non-Europe'.

The European Parliament

Since the 1960s the European Parliament has striven to turn the EC into a '*Grundrechtsgemeinschaft*' (community of fundamental rights) with respect to social policy issues as well (ibid.: 52f). In February 1984, the draft treaty of the European Parliament for a European Union emphasized a 'competing responsibility' within the proposed political union in the areas of social and health policy. Article 56 of the draft treaty regarding social and health policy included, among other things, the creation of comparable conditions for the preservation and creation of jobs, the need for the Community to take action in the area of rights of association and collective bargaining (particularly with regard to the conclusion of EC-wide wage agreements) and worker participation. Generally, the EC would have committed itself under Articles 2 and 4 of the draft to the maintenance and development of social rights, which follow from the national constitutions and the European Social Charter. However, the draft treaty was not seized upon as part of the integration relaunch in 1984–5 (see chapter 2, pp.46f, 64).

In November 1986 the European Parliament adopted by a large majority six reports on various aspects of the European social area, calling in general for a strengthening of the role of the Economic and Social Committee and the 'social dialogue'.[23] However, it was and is the case that the influence of the European Parliament is slight. This was illustrated in 1989, when the European Parliament adopted a resolution on the social dimension in which it considered the question of basic rights for employees, a resolution that was not taken up by the other EC bodies. It was further demonstrated by its lack of any role or influence in the negotiation process that produced the Social Charter, during which, despite its protests, the European Parliament was simply bypassed (see Falkner 1994: 184; Springer 1992: 90f).

The Economic and Social Committee

The Economic and Social Committee has a consulting function for the Commission and the Council of Ministers. It consists of representatives of national and European associations (employers, workers and different

---

[23] The Raggio Report proposed that the agreements of the 'social partners' achieved up to now at the Val Duchesse meetings could serve as a basis for a general directive laying out the fundamental rights of all workers. The demand for a 'Community framework agreement on the basic rights of workers' (as it was formulated in the Bachy Report) also emerged repeatedly in the reports. For the most important proposals of the European Parliament and a list of its most important reports between 1986 and 1988, see Venturini (1988: Annex 5).

interests such as craft workers, consumers and farmers), who are appointed by the Council on the basis of nominations from the national governments. One of its nine working parties covers the social policy area and compiles position papers as part of the general EC decision-making process or in response to specific enquiries on the part of the Council or Commission. It is noteworthy that the 'social dialogue' initiated by Delors, with its goal of the exchange of views and 'informal' agreement, has a somewhat unresolved relationship to the more formal Economic and Social Committee, with its specific position in the EC decision-making process. Streeck (1994: 16) speaks of a 'de facto replacement' and with it a displacement to 'softer', less binding forms of consultation.

The Economic and Social Committee, despite basically agreeing with the Internal Market programme, sharply criticized the fact that it did not contain concrete and approved proposals about a working programme for the realization of a European dimension in the social sphere. In September 1987 it decided to prepare a position paper on the social aspects of the internal market. The report by Beretta (*The European Social Area*), published in November of the same year, stated in paragraph 1.6, under the heading 'Making a Success of the Internal Market and European Social Area': 'Adoption of Community legislation guaranteeing basic social rights immune to competitive pressures is . . . a key stage in the creation of the single market.'[24] Both the European Parliament and the Economic and Social Committee advocated a broad interpretation of the social policy articles of the Single Act.

The European Court of Justice

To complete the picture we must mention the European Court of Justice. Its consistent broadening of EC jurisdiction (Falke 1993) contributed to a 'Europeanization' of various policy areas. In the domain of social policy, the Court emphasized the 'indication of a social responsibility of the Community' in the founding treaties of the EC and also the Single Act and raised this to the level of a quasi-constitutional welfare state principle.[25]

---

[24] In Venturini (1988: Annex 6, see pp. 74, 102ff); see Falkner (1994: 189).

[25] See Streil (1986); Schulte (1993b) and Everling (1990). The strategic position of the Court, particularly in terms of its social policy importance, is revealed by the fact that Thatcher was rarely able actively to include the Court in her blocking strategy. Her lawyers pointed out again and again to her that on questions of the Community and the competence of the Commission the ECJ would favour a 'dynamic and expansive' rather than a restrictive interpretation of the treaty articles: 'The dice were loaded against us' (Thatcher 1993: 743).

The 'social partners'

The realization of the Delorist project naturally counted on the actors who stood at the centre of the concept: the social partners. Through the 'social dialogue', they were supposed to be systematically tied in to the integration relaunch from the beginning. The European trade unions knew Delors' background and his earlier policies in France and accordingly had high hopes of the new Commission. In 1985, another unionist had become a member of the new Commission: Alois Pfeiffer, who represented the German trade union confederation (DGB) in the European Trade Union Confederation. Responsible for economic and regional policy, he fought long and hard for the social dialogue.

The European Trade Union Confederation, which in principle favoured further integration, followed the tying up of the Luxembourg package with some concern.[26] In fact, the ETUC had early on expressed itself in favour of the internal market project, but criticized the absence of a social dimension in the Commission's White Paper. The simultaneous development of a 'European social area' would be imperative in order to prevent social regression through social dumping and the lowering of standards for health and safety protection. During the Luxembourg intergovernmental conference, the ETUC warned that the Community, acting on the basis of the Commission's White Paper, could be tempted to pursue a one-sided and fundamentally faulty approach in its pursuit of the necessary greater European unity. The ETUC embraced the Single Act, although it was not satisfactory from its point of view, insofar as it did not always ensure a balance between the economic and social dimension.

The Union of Industrial and Employers' Confederations of Europe had actually declared itself in favour of 'social dialogue' on a Community level in principle.[27] It declined, however, to enter into binding decisions, in the sense of EC-wide agreements, arguing that the differences between the industrial relations and collective bargaining traditions in the individual member states made that impossible. Furthermore, social and labour market policies were deemed to be genuine domains of the nation-state, and the bargaining power of the national employers' associations would not have been sufficiently

[26] For ETUC's position concerning the integration relaunch, see its Activity Reports from 1985 onwards, especially its position paper on the internal market project of October 1985.

[27] For UNICE's position concerning EC social policy see the position paper *The Social Dimension of the Internal Market* (30 November 1988) and its monthly reports from 1985 onwards; see Kohler-Koch and Platzer (1986: 168ff), Tyszkiewicz (1989a) and Tiedemann (1989).

reflected. Some national member associations of the UNICE, such as those in Italy, Luxembourg and France (with some exceptions), were ready, primarily for domestic reasons, to lead the European 'social dialogue' with a higher degree of obligation and a broader spectrum of themes. However, the majority of the UNICE member associations declined the expansion of the dialogue. The UNICE favoured the process of 'natural convergence' as the main mechanism for the development of European social policy. From that point of view, the Commission was supposed to function as the centre for information on 'decentralized' initiatives that had been successful in promoting competitiveness and innovation.

Only in the area of occupational health and safety did the UNICE favour harmonization at the EC level. Tyszkiewicz, president of the UNICE, justified this as follows: 'Health and safety and equal opportunities are of direct benefit to all members of the work force. By supporting action in these fields, employers demonstrate their refusal to compete, within the EC, on humanitarian factors such as the health or safety risks to which workers may be exposed, or on the equal rights of women, or of minorities' (Tyszkiewicz 1989a: 73). These areas dealt with 'very specific cases where one could indeed argue the risk of unfair competition' (Tiedemann 1989: 93, vice-president of the UNICE Committee of Social Affairs). In other words, in the opinion of the employers' representatives, in the areas with 'humanitarian factors' no 'unfair' competition should exist, although in all other areas it should be given free rein (see Silvia 1991: 634).

In fact, the 'social partners' soon adopted common positions on questions of training, motivation, information on and consultation about the introduction of new technologies and on macroeconomic questions (Venturini 1988: Annex 4). The value of these early results was defended by DG V and other interested parties, often with reference to the importance of these positions for building mutual trust between employers and the trade unions. Relatively quickly, however, it became clear that the dynamic Delors had hoped for would not develop. This is no doubt connected to the very general formulation of Article 118b (Vogel-Polsky 1991: 32f); however, it is also simply an expression of the dramatically diverging projects and expectations that lay behind it.[28] After his initial optimism, Delors had to confess that after three-and-a-half years the results were rather sobering. In a speech at the ETUC Congress in 1988, he cited as reasons for this the fact that the involved

---

[28] On the phase of the revitalization of the social dialogue, see among others *Jahrbuch der Europäischen Integration 1985*: 291ff, Kohler-Koch and Platzer (1986), Siebert (1989) and Ross (1995a: 45).

parties did not have a real mandate for negotiation at their disposal; that from the standpoint of the 'social partners' the joint opinions did not amount to much for the countries that already were more developed in these areas; and moreover that this approach of collective bargaining was on the decline even at the national level in favour of bargaining at the level of the branch or company. In Delors' estimation there was also the danger that long-term fruitless activities undertaken as part of the 'social dialogue' could disguise the actual stagnation of social policy (Delors 1992: 77f, cf. 121). In view of this situation, some national governments indicated their impatience concerning the social policy stagnation, and the trade unions emphasized that, for them, the 'social dialogue' was not the only way to develop Community-wide social policy.[29]

The attempt at the subsequent creation of a social dimension

Most advocates of the supplement thesis make reference to the events of 1988, when fears about the consequences of the realization of the internal market spread among the trade unions, increasingly also among politicians, and above all among members of the European Parliament (see Berié 1992: 58; Mosley 1990: 154). Teague (1989: 75) emphasizes that an almost inexplicable shift took place in favour of the Commission and the other actors sympathetic to social policy integration. The following explanatory factors can be brought to bear to explain the new momentum in the social policy area from 1987 on.

First, from the viewpoint of the Commission, the regional policy components of the 'cohesion target' had been passed with the adoption of the 'Delors Package' in February 1988, and now it was time to deal with its more controversial social policy components. In order to generate a continuing dynamic, the level of pressure generated by workers' organizations, which had been too low, had to be increased, in particular with respect to governments that were still hesitant in this area. In 1988 the Commission president toured from labour union conference to labour union conference. In addition to his speech at the Stockholm conference of the ETUC, *Nourrir le dialogue sociale* ('Fostering the Social Dialogue', in Delors 1992: 71ff), in which he proposed the establishment of a '*Charte communitaire des droits des travailleurs*' ('Community Charter of Workers' Rights'), his visit to the Congress of

---

[29] Hinterscheid, secretary-general of the ETUC, as cited in 'Cohésion sociale et dialogue social européen dans la construction du marché intérieur' published by Fondation Europe et Société in *Cahiers de la Fondation*, no. 12–13, Paris, 1989, pp. 57ff.

the British TUC in Brighton was very important. Within the British trade unions, a strategic re-evaluation of the EC had already been under way for several months.³⁰ The renewed electoral victory of the Conservatives in Great Britain in the summer of 1987 and the ratification of the Single Act might have been decisive impulses for this. However, the convergence of the unions' EC policies led to an increase in their political weight at the European level. Thus the expansion of the groups of actors (a development promoted by the Commission) can also be regarded as a second factor.

A third factor was the constellation of member states. In 1987, with the accession of Spain and Portugal, the coordinates of the debate at the EC level about social policy shifted in a certain respect. On the one hand, the danger of 'social dumping' in a common market, considering the significantly enlarged disparities, assumed a new, intensified dimension. On the other hand, the current governments of these countries were comparatively pro-interventionist.

Another important factor was the ambitions of the Council presidencies of member states with a progressive position on social policy, particularly Belgium and Denmark (first and second halves, respectively, of 1987). In May 1987 the Belgian minister for social affairs, Hansenne, advanced the concept of a 'pedestal of social rights'.³¹ The Belgians' (improvised) proposal was designed to reactivate the Commission to get the 'social dialogue' back on track, that is, to put social policy on the agenda again.³² The Delors cabinet had also been discussing proposals regarding fundamental social rights as a possible way to concretize the 'European social area'.³³ From this point on, the core concept of the post facto social policy for cushioning the impact of the internal market

---

[30] See the TUC Report entitled *Europe 1992: Maximising the Benefits – Minimising the Costs* at the 1988 Congress; see *The Times*, 19 August 1988, p. 4, Silvia (1991: 632) and Springer (1992: 124f). Thatcher's still famous speech at the College of Europe in Bruges (20 September 1988) must be understood as a reaction to Delors's speech in Brighton. Against the growing pressure for social policy initiatives at the EC level she counter-posed the concept of the EC as 'a European Single Market with the minimum of regulations – a Europe of enterprise': 'We have not successfully rolled back the frontiers of the state in Britain only to see them reimposed at a European level, with a European super-state exercising a new dominance from Brussels' (Thatcher 1993: 745). This speech provoked serious protest on the part of many national governments and other political actors.

[31] The Belgian memorandum carried the title *La CEE va-t-elle craindre de garantir des droits sociaux fondamentaux à l'heure de la flexibilité?* (see Vogel-Polsky (1991: 154)).

[32] Interview with an official working for the Belgian Permanent Mission to the EC, 29 November 1995.

[33] Interview with Patrick Venturini (DG V), 19 September 1996. According to him, a '*socle des droits fondamentaux*' ('a pedestal of social rights') was an idea that had been floating around; see also Ross (1995a: 43).

Social policy 173

develops: the Community Charter of the Fundamental Social Rights, or Social Charter.[34]

The growing public pressure for a post facto social cushioning of the impact of the internal market implied the threat of withdrawing support for the European integration process and/or decreasing voter favour for socialist and Christian democratic governments. This had a clear effect on two important national governments: the French, again socialist since Spring 1988, and the German. The latter, particularly during the intergovernmental conference of 1985, had taken a very restrained position on European social policy. This now began to change, no doubt owing to the obvious irreversibility of the realization of the internal market, but also because its Christian democratic majority was receptive to public pressure for a social Europe.

All these factors have to be considered in context: 1988 was the year in which a wider European public first became aware of the Single Act, i.e. of the internal market project. A widespread publicity campaign undertaken by the Commission regarding 'Project 1992' no doubt contributed to this development. Moreover, as companies began to prepare themselves for the common internal market, a wave of restructuring measures, takeovers, and mergers confirmed the seriousness of the project. The nearer the realization of the Single Market came, the more the public debates intensified with respect to anticipated undesirable outcomes, in particular rising unemployment and the threat of 'regime shopping' and 'social dumping'.[35] According to the Eurobarometer surveys, the percentage of respondents who thought the internal market was a 'good thing' dropped 6–10 per cent from Autumn 1987 to Autumn 1988 in Belgium, Germany, France and the Netherlands.

At the European Council meeting in Hanover (June 1988)[36] it was emphasized that the internal market measures must not reduce the level of social protection in the member states. Moreover, the Single Market was also supposed to serve as the means for improving the living and

[34] In support of the 'precedents' set by the European Social Charter of 1965 and the entirety of the International Labour Organization (ILO) conventions, and reflecting its receptiveness to the proposal by the Belgian Council chair of May 1987 and the Economic and Social Committee position (the Beretta Report), the Venturini report stated: 'The idea of a body of guaranteed minimum social provisions–a charter of fundamental rights–is one of the possible short-term solutions to the problem presented by the existence of major disparities between the social legislation in force in the various Member States. It has the advantage of not recommending Community laws, unrealistic at the present time, but providing a framework, a joint minimum reference, for the national system' (Venturini 1988: 70).
[35] For the lines of argument, see, among others, Venturini (1988: 63) and Däubler (1989: 2), and additional literature cited in note 42.
[36] Final conclusions in *Europa-Archiv* 16/1988, D443ff; conclusions in the social policy area also in Venturini (1988: 69); see also Delors (1992: 69f).

working conditions and the work and health protection of all citizens. For the first time since 1974, the European Council thereby dealt extensively and centrally with social policy at European level and underlined the necessity of creating, simultaneously and in a balanced manner, the 'social dimension' of the Single Market 1992 (Berié 1992: 58; see Däubler 1989: 41).

Delors, whose mandate was extended for four years in Hanover, now put the Brussels apparatus into high gear in order to make the most of this new social policy momentum. He gave the Economic and Social Committee a mandate to draft a Social Charter. In September 1988, the Commission's social policy working programme was presented under the title *The Social Dimension of the Internal Market* (Venturini 1988: Annex 7). The trade unions thought this did not go far enough, while the UNICE reacted positively with respect to a number of its proposals (see Tyszkiewicz 1989a).

Evaluating the supplement thesis

In the first part of this chapter, the packaging thesis was essentially refuted, in that it could be shown that the 'social dimension' held great importance for key actors in the integration thrust, even though their concern bore relatively little fruit. The explanatory power of the supplement thesis is more difficult to judge. A part of the dynamic corresponds to the explanatory logic of neofunctionalist integration theory. The unions, initially overrun by the integration dynamic and additionally weakened through diverging EC policies, mobilized in response to the progress of integration and subsequently tried to implement a 'social dimension'. National governments came under pressure to extend integration 'sectorally'.

On the other hand, the supplement thesis is at least partially refuted through the confirmation of the cornerstone thesis: what happened was not simply an attempt at a subsequent creation of a social dimension, but the realization of what was regarded as the cornerstone of the integration project by several governments and the Commission. With the possible exception of the project of the German government, no prominent alteration of integration projects can be established in this sense. The dynamic in this area, the (temporal) development of the agenda, is mainly to be explained, as we have shown in this section, by shifting resources and the interplay of the tactics of actors who desired a European social policy from the beginning. Our argument is that 1988 signified that the postponed Delorist project was back on the agenda.

The Social Charter and the Maastricht Treaty

The creation of a subsequent 'social dimension' to the internal market concentrated increasingly on efforts to implement a charter of fundamental social rights. At the end of 1988, the European Trade Union Confederation presented a draft of a legally binding Social Charter,[37] a body of important social rights, modes of implementation and rights to sue for workers and/or unions. All thirty-six member unions of the ETUC supported this draft. The demand of the ETUC was formulated clearly: '1989 must become the year of social policy, just as 1985 was the year of the White Paper.' In a speech to the European Parliament in January 1989, Delors spoke of a Social Charter as the means to make concrete 'the European societal model' and to bring it to life (Delors 1992: 121). He connected this with the hope for a breakthrough in the 'social dialogue'. The UNICE spoke in favour of a Social Charter, but not in legally binding form; the UNICE preferred to think of it as a set of recommended standards, to which member states should aspire.

In March of the same year, the meeting of labour and social ministers in Seville made clear that, now as before, well-known fundamental differences remained. The British Employment Secretary Norman Fowler saw a Social Charter as 'unnecessary regulation'.[38] In February the Economic and Social Committee presented its opinion on an EC Social Charter.[39] In May the Commission put its proposal on the table, which recommended that the charter be given the character of a non-binding 'solemn declaration' (*EC Bulletin* 5-1989). Along with this, the Commission proposed an action programme for implementation of the points listed in the charter; these would have to be individually reviewed and adopted by the Council of Ministers. These proposals for non-binding status and the 'splintering' of the project resulted in furious criticism from the trade unions. The British government remained in fundamental disagreement with a Social Charter in any shape or form.

In the Spring 1989 Eurobarometer poll (March/April), a new question was taken up: 'There is talk of adopting a charter of fundamental social rights for the entire EC, that is, a set of common rules throughout all the member countries for matters concerning the rights and respon-

---

[37] ETUC, 'Community Charter of Social Rights: A Report by the Executive Committee', 1988; see also Silvia (1991: 632ff).
[38] As cited in *Jahrbuch der Europäischen Integration* (1989/90: 450).
[39] Economic and Social Committee, *Basic Community Social Rights: Opinion* (CES 270/89), February 1989.

sibilities of workers and employers. Do you think such a charter would be a good/bad thing?' The results indicated popular support for the EC Social Charter project. Approval of the idea was at or above 60 per cent in all countries except Denmark, with only 47 percent, and the Federal Republic of Germany, with only 57 percent. In France, Holland, Spain and Italy approval was over 70 percent; the average for the entire EC was 69 percent. In June, the socialist parties emerged as victors in the elections to the European Parliament, but this did not perceptibly influence the future fate of the Social Charter.

At the EC summit in Madrid during the same month, Thatcher put forward the argument that the voluntary Social Charter of the European Council was quite sufficient and that an EC document was not necessary. As she later explained, such a Community document 'I knew [would] be the basis of directives aimed at introducing the Delors brand of socialism by the back door' (Thatcher 1993: 751). Although the consent of the United Kingdom was not necessary for the adoption of a non-binding charter, the decision was postponed; this was due perhaps to the desire not to place the planned action programme into jeopardy through the exclusion of the United Kingdom.

During the second half of 1989, under the French Council presidency, the Social Charter became the main priority. In September the Commission presented a new proposal, which responded to its critics through simultaneously specifying and making flexible specific points in the Charter. Neither attempts to create political pressure on the part of the unions, which organized a demonstration in Brussels in October under the slogan 'For a Social Europe', nor further watering-down of the Charter by the labour and social ministers could move Fowler and the British government to agreement. Still, the Council of Ministers stood by the watered-down version, a fact that is sometimes taken as an indication that other national governments hid their own opposition to the Charter behind the British rejection.

Solemnly, but without obligation: the Community Charter of the Fundamental Social Rights of Workers

At the December 1989 meeting of the European Council in Strasbourg the *Community Charter of the Fundamental Social Rights of Workers* (*Social Europe* 1/1990) was adopted by eleven states as a political declaration of intent of an advisory nature. The following 'fundamental social rights of workers' were listed therein: freedom of movement; employment and remuneration; improvement of living and working conditions; social protection; freedom of association and collective bargaining; vocational training; equal treatment for men and women; information, consultation and participation for workers; health protection and safety at the workplace; protection of children and adolescents; and the integration of elderly and disabled persons. The content of the Social Charter essentially confirmed the original social policy conception of the EC, according to which social policy regulations at EC level were connected first of all to the realization of the fundamental freedoms of the internal market (see Schulte 1993b: xxxixf).

On no account should the legally non-binding Social Charter be mistaken for the fulfilment of the project for a 'European social area' or the 'social dimension of the internal market'.[40] The demand for a Charter of binding rights, as conceived and demanded by the unions and the European Parliament, whose enforcement would serve as the basis upon which all could appeal, had not been fulfilled. Many significant individual agreements that the Commission had proposed were discarded in the course of the negotiations; for example, agreements about questions of workers' rights with respect to transborder services, working hours and the introduction of a guaranteed minimum income. Additionally, the Council, in opposition to the Commission, had determined that the Charter applied only to workers (instead of to all citizens, as was originally proposed). Neither Community areas of responsibility nor the obligations of member states to guarantee these fundamental rights were approved; the Charter emphasized only their 'responsibility', and that only 'in accordance with national practices'.

Because of its non-binding character, the Charter was an act with predominantly symbolic meaning; it was known to all that any real disputes would arise in connection with the yet to be determined social policy action programme. According to Berié (1992: 60), the Social Charter, despite the fact that it had an indirect influence on social policy legislation, hardly fulfilled the expectations it had aroused. In particular, it represented no progress in terms of the status quo, that is, the position advocating minimal Community responsibilities in the area of social policy legislation.

It became increasingly clear during the Social Charter negotiations that, without a prior change in the treaty, no legal basis existed for significant social policy advances as part of European integration. The opportunity for such a change had been missed with the Single Act (see Berié 1992: 61), a consequence of the initial postponing of the

---

[40] See the statements on this in the Commission's programme for 1991 in *EC Bulletin*, Supplement 1–1991.

'social dimension'. The intergovernmental conference leading to the Maastricht Treaty offered a chance for catching up.[41]

Social policy in the Maastricht Treaty

At the EC summit in Maastricht in December 1991, eleven states decided, in light of British resistance, 'to continue along the path laid down in the 1989 Social Charter' and, leaving the United Kingdom aside, to finalize for this purpose a Protocol on Social Policy. The Dutch Council presidency had presented a more moderate draft than the first Commission draft in order to obtain the participation of the United Kingdom. When it became clear in the course of the negotiations that the UK would still not go along, the original draft was again taken up.

The Agreement on Social Policy provided for majority voting in the Council in the areas of working environment and conditions, information and consultation of workers, equality between men and women, and integration of persons excluded from the labour market (Article 2, paragraph 1). Explicitly reserved for unanimous voting in the decision-making procedure are the areas of social security and social protection of workers, protection of workers when their employment contract is terminated, representation and collective defence of the interests of workers and employers (including co-determination), conditions of employment for third-country nationals, and financial contributions for promotion of employment and job creation (Article 2, paragraph 3). Important areas of labour law are excluded from Community regulations, including 'pay, the right of association, the right to strike or the right to impose lock-outs' (Article 2, paragraph 6). Within the meaning of 'horizontal subsidiarity', the Agreement provides for an expanded role for the 'social partners' at both the national and EU levels (see Baumann 1995: 18ff). According to Article 2, paragraph 4, a member state may entrust management and labour, at their joint request, with the implementation of directives. Articles 3 and 4 regulate details of the 'social dialogue' and tripartite cooperation with the Commission. At the EU level, two consultations are provided for; the 'social partners' can thereby inform the Commission whether they are in agreement on the facts in a negotiation and want to conclude an agreement by means of social dialogue. The 'social partners' then have nine months to conclude this process. If this time limit is not sufficient to resolve the issues, the

---

[41] The negotiations of the intergovernmental conference regarding social policy cannot be presented here. On this point see, among others, Doutriaux (1992), Lange (1993), Ross (1995a) and Moravcsik (1998: 452ff).

Commission may use its own means according to the usual legislative process.

After Maastricht the social policy momentum dissipated. Just as it had during the negotiations, the issue of economic and monetary union continued to dominate. At the same time, results of the referenda in Denmark and France reflected a strong upswing for opponents of the integration process, at least in its existing form. The economic recession of the 1990s and rising unemployment in Western Europe also changed the social policy agenda of the EU: the social policy order of the day shifted from constructing social regulatory policies at the European level to reconfiguring labour market and other arrangements to allow the European economy to increase its competitiveness.

A ruling of the German Bundesverfassungsgericht (Federal Constitutional Court) in October 1993 is important for interpreting the Union treaty and assessing future possibilities. According to Kaufmann-Bühler (1994: 4) of the German Foreign Office, from this decision it was inferred that social policy remains in essence an issue for each of the member states; thus, the Community is limited to supportive activities, essentially with respect to minimum standards for occupational safety. Further, the decision maintained that there is no legal basis in the treaties for a common economic policy, much less a common social policy.

The judgment of the Bundesverfassungsgericht is significant not just as a restriction on a central actor, the German government. In addition, just like the anchoring of the subsidiarity principle in the Union treaty, it has the function of excluding the 'Monnet-ist' type of integration (see pp. 71f), and thus of restraining the Commission. If the 'Monnet' method can no longer be sustained, then this will become very evident with the further development of European social policy. Only an unambiguous expansion of the Community's areas of authority via the treaty can alter this picture.

The defeat of the Delorist project

The balance sheet of social policy development in the framework of the integration thrust of the 1980s is not simple to compile. The expert literature is divided; part of the discussion revolves around the 'Is the glass half empty or half full?' conundrum. Answers that point to successful harmonization in the area of occupational health and safety as the main evidence of a successful EC social policy are not convincing (for example, Eichener and Voelzkow 1994; see also Pierson and Leibfried 1995: 436). This area is uniquely entitled to a special status;

one goal of this chapter has been to explain why this is so. In the judgement of Wolfgang Streeck (1994, 1995), the second wave of social policy proposals in the 1980s (which followed a progressive phase in the 1970s) was turned back even more decisively than the first. Springer (1992: 121f) compares the body of social policies with the economic measures contained in the White Paper and comes to the conclusion that the two are in no way of equal weight.

With respect to the social dialogue at the European level, it is often emphasized that this was initiated during a time when strong efforts were (and indeed are still today) under way in most states towards dismantling or decentralizing collective bargaining. Against this unfavourable background, the argument goes, the mere existence of such negotiations and their anchoring in the treaties is important, and acts as a signal for actors at the national level. Nevertheless, success must be judged by the result, and this result does not correspond in large measure to the projects of most political actors. The objection is often made, and particularly by representatives of the Delorist project, that it is too early to draw up a balance sheet, and that it took a long time to satisfy the demand for successful institutionalization of corporatist negotiation models at the national level as well.

From our point of view, the Delorist project itself must be taken as a critical measuring stick for judging the development thus far of social policy. The renewed integration process should not only serve the goal of the preservation and improvement of the economic competitiveness of Europe but also prevent social regression. This could occur only in an *espace organisé*, an organized area with common social standards set at a high level. This has actually been true in only a few areas up to now; most areas are characterized by a competitive articulation of national standards (Ziltener 1999). The intensified intra-European competition in product markets, and also between locations with respect to investments and jobs, places heavy pressure on (expense) factors such as social standards, wage levels and taxation. This 'systems competition', sought after by some political actors, does not correspond to the Delorist concept of a balanced approach with the goal of achieving the primacy of politics (see Delors 1992). Trade union circles refer to the dynamic of deregulation and competition unleashed by the internal market project, which has encompassed the labour markets as well as national wage scales and social policy systems (see Kleinhenz 1990: 23f). Cases of social dumping,[42] the conscious exploitation of differ-

---

[42] See on this point Teague (1989: 77ff), Mosley (1990: 158ff), Hagen (1992), Mueller and Purcell (1992), Leibfried and Pierson (1996: 200f), and, for the example of the construction sector, Baumann (1995).

ences among national or regional regulations and the playing off of one workforce against the other within the Single Market by businesses have inflicted heavy damage on the 'social image' of the EU.

So far, no dynamic has developed from the 'social dialogue' that would mitigate the increasing pressure felt at the national level by achieving results at the European level.[43] From this a sceptical assessment also follows with respect to the main goal of the Delorist project: the preservation of the *modèle européen de société* (the 'European societal model') and the protection of its labour-inclusiveness. For Delors himself, what has been achieved up to now does not definitively preclude the possibility of the (backward) development of the EU into one big free-trade zone.[44]

Conclusion

Using the method of reconstructing the integration projects and the implementation strategies of the central actors in the social policy area, in this chapter we tested three theses regarding the role and weight of this policy area in the integration thrust of the 1980s. The cornerstone thesis received the greatest support from the evidence: from the beginning, the creation of a 'European social area' was a central demand of important actors in the revitalization of European integration. Articles 21 and 22 of the Single Act were not mere 'packaging' for the internal market project, although they are often interpreted as such; rather, they were the 'vestiges' of an ambitious social policy integration project, which for strategic reasons was postponed so as not to hinder the renewal of the integration process. By following this path, a departure was made from the simultaneous realization of the European social area explicitly demanded by Delors and the trade unions and from the policy insisted on by the French government of maximum homogenization of the social policy area as a precondition for an internal market.

In 1987-8, the representatives of the 'social area' project renewed their efforts at implementing it. These efforts had already been connected with Delors' relaunching of the 'social dialogue' in 1985 and his offer of an alliance with the trade unions for the purpose of pushing ahead with the 'social dimension'. A series of favourable factors (Council presidencies held by national governments that were progressive on

---

[43] See CEU (1995a); for the discussion about structural obstacles see Windolf (1993), Armingeon (1994) and Platzer (1994: 49).

[44] Delors, in an interview in *Die Zeit* of 2 February 1996 on the question: 'Do you exclude the development of Europe into a big free trade zone?': 'No, but I am against it. If the political leaders of Europe lack farsightedness, it could come to that' (our translation).

social policy issues, the reorientation of the British trade unions and the consequent strengthening of the European Trade Union Confederation as a European actor, and public debates about the social consequences of the Single Market project) reinforced the energy of the initiative(s). But, in contrast to the allies of the Commission in the other central areas of the integration package, this alliance was comparatively weak and it met with the greatest resistance.

The 'second try' started with the project of a charter of fundamental social rights; the 'one-sidedness' of the Single Act was supposed to be corrected by it. This second attempt led, via many conflict-ridden detours, to the Social Protocol of Maastricht, this time with the exclusion of the United Kingdom. However, in our view the social policy dimension of the Treaty on European Union cannot be regarded as the realization of the Delorist project.

If one reconnects this reconstruction of the development of the EC social policy with the earlier theoretical discussion, the following conclusions can be drawn. First, if one focuses on the intergovernmental conference of 1985 and the Single Act alone, an intergovernmentalist explanation seems plausible. The end result in the area of social policy was very close to the 'lowest common denominator' among the member states. The role of the Commission was restricted from the beginning; its suggestions failed owing to the resistance of some member states. In contrast to the regional policies, the Commission had to take on a lawyer-like function for the actors that could not participate at the intergovernmental conference and that had no possibility of blocking it. If one takes a wider view of the entire process up to the Maastricht Treaty, however, it is clear that analysing this policy area through the reductionist logic of intergovernmentalism and its variants is inadequate. From the beginning, the Commission pursued a policy of systematic inclusion and appreciation of interested actors. It successfully promoted a dynamic conceptualized by the neofunctionalist theory as *spillover* effect. The anchoring of an expanded role for the 'social partners' in the Union treaty brought a qualitatively new dimension to the Community decision-making processes. This expansion makes it possible to speak of a political multi-level system.

In this regard a comparison with the more successfull development of regional policy (as reconstructed in chapter 5) points up some commonalities between the two policy areas. However, there are also major differences that must be emphasized. The lack of any possibility for non-governmental actors to block further integration has already been mentioned. In addition, the 'social partners' constitute a completely different category from that of the 'cohesion countries'. Whereas the latter were in principle more united in the demand for an extension of Community regional policy, with few exceptions this was not the case for the 'social partners'. In particular, the European Trade Union Confederation can hardly be characterized as a homogeneous actor. A further difference is the comparatively higher level of development of regional policy prior to the integration thrust of the 1980s; here the necessary work of rebuilding the system should not be underestimated. A critical difference is also reflected in the different degree to which EC policy had repercussions in the nation-states. Cohesion payments may indeed be financially painful for net payers, but they do little to impair the formation of a nation-state's regulatory options and accordingly have few implications for sovereignty.

To summarize: in contrast to regional policy, in the social policy area there were no actors capable of blocking integration to be 'bought off' and in addition no new, uncontested, instruments for doing it. The establishment of common social standards (harmonization) as the sole measure against social regression touches in a profound way the core of the structure of 'historic compromise' of the involved states and societies.

III

Conclusions beyond the Single European Act of 1986

The signing of the Single European Act did not, however, make the internal market a *fait accompli*. Chapter 7 by Michael Nollert, in collaboration with Nicola Fielder, shows that this was also the view of the European Roundtable of Industrialists and that they continued to lobby for the goals set by the Act to be met. In studying the evolution of the Roundtable from the 1980s to the 1990s its extraordinary position becomes evident, especially when compared with the halfhearted EC policy of the main European umbrella business organizations. The Roundtables have been active ever since the early 1980s and even gained in membership as well as interlinked economic power. But, having successfully helped to push for the new European economic order, they had no comparable influence on other issues of the ongoing European integration.

Looking again beyond the Single Act, chapter 8 by Michael Nollert analyses the further development of European technology corporatism. He investigates in detail the European biotechnology policy – shaping an industrial branch predicted to be among the most dynamic of the twenty-first century. This chapter points to an enormous surge in funds provided by the Commission and to the established dialogue between the interest organizations and the Commission, which evidence the working of technology corporatism outside the information and communication sector where it was first established at the beginning of the 1980s. Yet, the limits of European technology corporatism already mentioned in chapter 4 by Simon Parker are also evident in Michael Nollert's chapter on biotechnology policy. The current challenges lie in transregional alliances of the leading enterprises and in the massive public reservations about EU biotechnology policy.

Chapter 9 by Patrick Ziltener looks at the Single European Act as a milestone that started to change the political economy of Europe, from the internal market project of the 1980s to the monetary union project of the 1990s. Furthermore the actors and alliances that have been addressed in the various chapters of this volume are briefly reviewed and reassessed. The conclusion of chapter 9 is important for a correct interpretation of our novel theoretical explanation of the events of the integration thrust. We do not suggest that the obvious central role of the Commission and the Roundtables in providing the decisive impulse for the Single Act is a model that can be generalized to other events of the now long history of European integration.

The final chapter, by Volker Bornschier, addresses the outcome of the processes that have been the topic of this volume: the puzzling nature of the governance structures embodied in the institutions of the European Union. Rather than looking at the EU as an unfinished federal state, it is suggested that the EU should be seen as representing a renewed compromise between old European processes – nationalism and liberalism – in an innovative multi-level composition of state power. What is the position of this European State of Nations vis-à-vis its competitors in the triad – the United States of America and Japan? With political union, the European state, which was the model for the world, is departing from the national framework it originally helped to create. Might it become a model for the world for reconciling the different manifestations of nationalism and liberalism in a multi-level system of governance?

7 Lobbying for a Europe of big business: the European Roundtable of Industrialists

Michael Nollert in collaboration with Nicola Fielder

'We value the fact that the ERT not only engages in lobbying, narrowly defined, but also makes general proposals and elaborates general projects. We have access on a higher level than all the associations, unions, etc.; we are not lost among the many partners in dialogue, we speak directly with Commission presidents, with the heads of government or at a minimum directly with the economic ministers.'

Helmut Maucher, President of the Board of Directors of Nestlé and chairman of the European Roundtable of Industrialists since 1996, interview, 11 July 1995

Introduction

The signing of the Single European Act did not make the internal market a *fait accompli*, a view shared by European Roundtable members, whose actions became more pronounced. A watchdog group, the Internal Market Support Committee, was formed in December 1986; its members met regularly with unions, heads of state and government, top government officials and key commissions of the European Community and emphasized the urgency of fulfilling the goals set by the Single European Act.[1] Nowadays, the European Roundtable of Industrialists (ERT) is still considered one of the most influential interest organizations in Brussels. The evidence for this consists not only of the self-description by the president of the Nestlé administrative council and interviews with representatives of European umbrella organizations but also in the very origins of the Single European Act (see chapter 3).

In this chapter, we want to sketch the organization and development as well as the financial and management interconnections of the Roundtable. First, the history and the activities of the Roundtable up to the passage of the Single European Act are outlined. Then we show that the success of the Roundtable is based not only on the goodwill of the

---

[1] All these findings lend further support to the theory presented in chapter 3 of this volume regarding the acceleration of the European integration process and the origins of the Common Market.

Commissioner responsible for the internal market and industrial affairs, but also on the inability of the public to influence these matters and on the low organizational capacity of European employers' associations. An overview of the development of the Roundtable in the first decade after the Single European Act follows, showing that today the Roundtable's goal of designing the internal market is a high priority. The final section offers network analyses of the financial and management interconnections of the Roundtable.[2] Here it appears that in the course of the 1980s the Roundtable began to transform itself into a transnational business network, one whose core is only slightly fragmented and is dominated by the German, Belgian and French member-businesses.

The origin of the ERT and its influence on the Commission

The European Roundtable of Industrialists was the result of a collaboration between Etienne Davignon, at the time Commissioner of the European Communities for the Internal Market and Industrial Affairs, and Pehr Gyllenhammar, the chief executive officer (CEO) of Volvo. Various CEOs were invited to join, and in April 1983 the first meeting took place in Paris. Since that first meeting, the European Roundtable has convened regularly. Regular meetings also take place between the European Roundtable and the Commission of the European Communities. The Roundtable's secretariat is now based in Brussels and has issued several publications on a variety of pan-European subjects.[3]

The history of the European Roundtable of Industrialists has been thoroughly researched by Maria Green Cowles (1995), who begins her study of the European Roundtable in 1982, when the *Economist* issued its obituary for the European Community in response to the Eurosclerosis of the 1970s and the European Council's failure to take decisive action.[4] In the same year, Gyllenhammar started calling for European business to take positive action in formulating industrial strategies for the future and to cooperate on a European level to promote these strategies. Gyllenhammar was influenced and supported by Commissioner Etienne Davignon. Their discussions led to the decision to create a cross-sectoral group of leading CEOs that would express its views on the European economic situation and the European Communities' industrial policy.

[2] For assistance with the data collection and analysis, we thank Carmen Baumeler.
[3] ERT publications: 'Missing Links: Upgrading Europe's Transborder Ground Transport Infrastructure' (1984); 'Changing Scales' (1985); 'Making Europe Work' (1986); etc.
[4] 'Alas, Poor Europe', *The Economist* 20 March 1982, pp. 11–12.

According to Green Cowles, the first list of potential members of such a group was drawn up in 1982 by Commission and Volvo staff. The planning group included Fernand Braun, Director-General for Internal Market and Industrial Affairs, Bo Ekman and Michael Hinks-Edwards, corporate planners with Volvo, and Pierre Defraigne, *chef de cabinet* to Commissioner Davignon. Seventeen of Europe's top businessmen[5] were recruited to the group and a preliminary meeting of top associates came up with six key areas for the agenda of the European Roundtable: the internal market, infrastructure, technology, jobs, environment and finance.

It should be noted here that many members of the Roundtable already knew each other prior to its formation. For example, Giovanni Agnelli (Fiat) – the brother of a co-founder of the Roundtable, Umberto Agnelli – was friends with the owner of Volvo, Peter Wallenberg. Pehr Gyllenhammar (Volvo) and Bernard Hanon (Renault) both belonged to the association of automobile manufacturers. The board of the Geneva International Management Institute is an important committee, and includes both Gyllenhammar and Stephan Schmidheiny (former Roundtable member). Gyllenhammar met Giovanni Agnelli and Kenneth Durham (Unilever) as advisers to the Chase Manhattan Bank. Finally, Gyllenhammar and Davignon were allied with the consulting firm of former US Secretary of State Henry Kissinger. One of the important clients of Kissinger Associates was Umberto Agnelli. Some members also met each other in the European Enterprise Group (Green Cowles 1997), which in the early 1980s played the role of a think-tank for the Union of Industrial and Employers' Confederations of Europe (UNICE).

Another venue of Roundtable members is the so-called 'Bilderberg Club', which retains its importance even today. The group was initiated by the British businessman Joseph H. Retinger, who was one of the founding members of the European Movement. In 1952 he proposed to his friend Prince Bernhard of the Netherlands, who at that time sat on the boards of Royal Dutch–Shell and the Belgian holding company Société Générale, that he summon a secret conference for the elites of

---

[5] Umberto Agnelli, Fiat, Italy; Sir Peter Baxendell, Shell, United Kingdom; Carlo de Benedetti, Olivetti, Italy; Wisse Dekker, Philips, the Netherlands; Kenneth Durham, Unilever, United Kingdom; Roger Faroux, Saint-Gobain, France; Pehr Gyllenhammar, Volvo, Sweden; Bernard Hanon, Renault, France; John Harvey-Jones, Imperial Chemical Industries, United Kingdom; Olivier Lecerf, Lafarge Coppée, France; Helmut Maucher, Nestlé, Switzerland; Hans Merkle, Bosch, Germany; Curt Nicolin, Asea, Sweden; Louis von Planta, Ciba-Geigy, Switzerland; Antoine Riboud, BSN, France; Wolfgang Seelig, Siemens, Germany; Dieter Spethmann, Thyssen AG, Germany.

the NATO member states. In the USA, this proposal was principally supported by the Rockefeller family, which controlled Chase Manhattan Bank and Standard Oil. The first meeting took place in 1954 at the Bilderberg Hotel in Oosterbeek. Usually approximately 115 people would take part in the annual discussions, of whom about 80 were from Europe. At the moment, representatives on the Steering Committee include Roundtable members and former Commissioners Etienne Davignon and Peter D. Sutherland, former Roundtable members Percy Barnevik and David De Pury (both Asea Brown Boveri), and Hilmar Kopper (Deutsche Bank), who links several Roundtable firms (see table 7.2 below). Giovanni Agnelli sits on the advisory committee. At the conference in 1996 in Toronto, participants included the Italian Commissioner Mario Monti, Giovanni Agnelli, Barnevik, Bertrand Collomb (Roundtable member, Lafarge Coppée) and Morris Tabaksblat (Roundtable member, Unilever).

Informal contacts were also made through the Trilateral Commission, in which Giovanni Agnelli, Etienne Davignon and Poul Svanholm participated in the early 1980s. The Trilateral Commission was convened for the first time in 1973 by members of the Bilderberg Club; it was designed to provide an opportunity for a selection of prominent politicians, business leaders and academics from Europe, North America and Japan to think about and discuss coordinated action on issues of world historical importance (Gill 1991). In contrast to the discussions of the Bilderberg Club, the results of the Trilateral Commission's proceedings were published.

In April 1983 the first Roundtable meeting was held. This was the 'first time that European CEOs organised themselves to address European policy matters publicly' (Green Cowles 1995: 505). At a press conference following the meeting, Gyllenhammar spoke of the meeting as a unique moment in European history, and indicated that there was a common feeling among the industrialists that something had to be done in Europe.

Shortly afterwards, at the second meeting of the European Roundtable, a memorandum to Commissioner Davignon was completed. It was entitled 'Foundations for the Future of European Industry' and spoke first and foremost of the need to promote a unified European market.[6]

The ideas and strategies of the European Roundtable were not only presented to the Commission, however. They were expressed in articles and press conferences by the newly formed European Roundtable

[6] ERT, 'Foundations for the Future of European Industry. Memorandum to Commissioner Davignon', 10 June 1983.

secretariat in Paris. Major European newspapers began to write about the European Roundtable and its plans and progress.

In January 1984 the first major European Roundtable project was launched: the European Venture Capital Association, which was intended to encourage transnational investments in Europe. The second European Roundtable project was announced by Gyllenhammar in December 1984: 'Missing Links: Upgrading Europe's Transborder Ground Transport Infrastructure.' These projects were well received and the 'Missing Links' project provided the foundation for future infrastructure work of not only the European Roundtable but also the European Community.

At the end of 1984, Karl-Heinz Narjes, the new Commissioner for the Internal Market and Industrial Affairs, presented his package of proposals for completing a European common market. The package has since been described by insiders, business leaders and European Community experts as unwieldy, uncoordinated and lacking a precise time-frame (see chapter 3). Business leaders decided that they needed to develop their own programme.

On 11 January, 1985, Wisse Dekker, the CEO of Philips and one of the first supporters of the European Roundtable, put forward his plan, 'Europe 1990',[7] to an audience of 500 people in Brussels, including Lord Cockfield, who later became the author of the 1985 White Paper[8] (see also Dekker 1996: 251–5). The paper contained a simple plan for a unified market with an exact timetable and was also sent to all the heads of state and government of the European Community.

European Roundtable contacts with the new Delors Commission and with government figures continued and strengthened in 1985. Jacques Delors called for a Europe without borders in his inauguration speech before the European Parliament only three days after the Dekker programme was presented. The creation of the Common Market was endorsed by the Council at its meeting in March 1985. At the same time, veiled threats by Wisse Dekker and other CEOs that European multinationals would take their companies overseas if the European leaders did not follow through with their plans for a united Europe appeared on the front page of the *Financial Times*.

In the following three months Cockfield and his associates produced the White Paper, a coherent programme with a definite time-frame. The Council decisions on the Single European Act were taken in Milan in June 1985 and in Luxembourg in December of the same year.

---

[7] 'Europe 1990. An Agenda for Action', Philips, 1984.
[8] According to a statement made by Lord Cockfield in an interview with Nicola Fielder in March 1993.

According to Green Cowles, the European Roundtable members did not seek to influence the intergovernmental conference negotiations, as these pertained mainly to powers and procedures of the European Parliament, which were of little interest to the industrialists. However, Dekker contacted over thirty CEOs to send a strong joint message to the European Council, which was to meet in Luxembourg for a final vote on the Single European Act. The message telexed to the Council members in the various languages of the European Community was straightforward: it told them to decide one way or another, but to decide. Industry would then make its own determinations as to the future of its investment and growth strategies in Europe or elsewhere. Although Green Cowles concedes that there is no evidence to suggest that these telexes actually influenced the final vote on the Single European Act, they without doubt represent the first time that leaders of European transnational businesses united to speak out determinedly on a treaty decision.

Organizational characteristics and bases of success

Undoubtedly, the founding of the European Roundtable is to a great extent a reflection of global economic changes and the personal commitment of Etienne Davignon and some prominent big businessmen who complained about the halfhearted Europe policy of the established European umbrella organizations. This was also the opinion of the former secretary-general of the Roundtable, Keith Richardson:[9] 'UNICE (the Union of Industrial and Employers' Confederations of Europe) was weak and above all else incapable of formulating a Europe policy' (Niggli 1989: 165). Nevertheless, the Roundtable's high degree of influence on policy formation in Brussels cannot be explained by these factors. The extraordinary position of the Roundtable becomes explicable only if one takes into consideration the clublike organization of the Roundtable, the democracy deficit in the European Union and the organizational problems of the employers.

The Roundtable: a Club lobbying for the interests of big business

Political and economic interests can be articulated to the legislative and executive powers directly or through the framework of associations. In the nineteenth century, businesses attempted to influence legislation

---

[9] As of March 1998, Wim Philippa is the new secretary-general. He has worked for Heineken and managed the European Union Relations office for Ciba-Geigy in Brussels for four years.

principally by means of informal contacts with those who were politically responsible. Thus, for example, representatives of interests sought contact with the then US President (1869–77) Ulysses S. Grant, who made himself available in the lobby of the Willard Hotel on Pennsylvania Avenue; this is how the concept of lobbying derived its name. Lobbying was also a popular method of big enterprises in Europe. Thus, Swiss economic policy in the nineteenth century was decisively shaped by Alfred Escher. As a banker and railroad industrialist, he had at his disposal extraordinary contacts within the Federal Council and, for a long time, had no parliamentary opposition representing the workers or competitors to fear. His opponents at the time therefore characterized this ingenious style of government as the 'Escher System' (Grossmann and Decurtins 1993: 108).

With the strengthening of the trade union movement, employers were forced to organize themselves collectively. The social clubs of the elite were fertile ground for the organization of such interests. Within these walls, leading business personalities were shielded from the public view and could discuss business and common political concerns.

However, the selective access criteria of the clubs resulted in political lobbying that covered only a limited spectrum of business interests. The political efficacy of the clubs was weakened above all by the expansion of the right to vote; indeed, decisions by the government that were friendly to business interests could be unilaterally overturned at the ballot box. In view of the vehement criticism of the opaque and informal exertion of influence by the clubs, businessmen were now under pressure to join together in associations and to make the effort to legitimize the concerns of employers in the eyes of the populace.

Nevertheless, such clubs have not disappeared. As a rule, they serve their members nowadays as a means for making and maintaining personal or business contacts. Such clubs still play a major role in Great Britain (Wendling 1991) and Japan. Comparative studies point out that British managers, in contrast to their German colleagues, still prefer to meet in prominent clubs (e.g. Marylebone Cricket Club, Brook's, White's, Pratt's, Boodle's, City of London, Carlton) rather than at board meetings (Useem 1984). The Japanese *shacho-kai* are similar to clubs. Here, informal monthly meetings of all the presidents of business groups (*keiretsu*) take place. According to Gerlach (1992: 107), informal meetings create a group identity and serve the formulation of political positions. Important service clubs that are connected transnationally, such as the Kiwanis, Lions Club and Rotary Club, as well as the Bilderberg Club and the Trilateral Commission (see above), offer big businessmen the opportunity for the informal exchange of information.

The European Roundtable combines elements of a club (Buchanan 1965; Useem 1984) and a conventional association. In fact, in comparison with business associations such as UNICE, it is comparatively exclusive and therefore cannot claim to be representative to any great extent. Moreover, the size of the membership is small, which results in members knowing each other personally and being able to formulate and sustain common political positions. It should be noted that the Roundtable, in comparison with the traditional British clubs, does not restrict itself to lobbying at the highest levels of government, but also has at its disposal an association-like infrastructure and disseminates its views to the public through its reports.

The structural bases of success

The strong political influence of the Roundtable on the Commission can be attributed, on the one hand, to the democracy deficit in the EU, which allows club-like and resource-rich organizations more influence than the European umbrella organizations (see Nollert 1996, 1997). Indeed, the Roundtable, like the nineteenth-century clubs, can assume that relying exclusively on lobbying will pay off as long as there is no danger that the measures thus obtained will be overturned later by a parliamentary veto. In the 1980s, the European Parliament still did not have veto power or the right to initiate legislation and was in a position only to reject unpopular proposals for the Commission. Club-like organizations are still in a privileged position when it comes to originating political measures, especially since the established Euro-associations are still characterized by ponderous, consensus-oriented decision-making mechanisms.

On the other hand, the success of the European Roundtable is based on the deficient organizational capacity of business at the European level. Olson (1968), Offe (1969) and Offe and Wiesenthal (1980) agree that employers, in comparison with employees, enjoy a structural advantage. Olson presumes that a greater heterogeneity of interests in the business community does not have an adverse effect on its organizational capacity, in that along with a broader heterogeneity the possibility increases that a single business will carry the bulk of the organizational costs. Streeck (1991) also suspects that there is a greater heterogeneity of interests among businesses, especially as he believes it is more difficult to unify product market interests than it is to unify labour market interests.

Traxler and Schmitter (1994) distinguish three dimensions of the organizational capacity of Euro-associations: (a) the generalizability of their claim to representation; (b) their capacity for control; and (c) their associational capacity. The two authors assume that, at the national and European levels, employers have less of a claim to representation and less capacity for control than employees, while at the same time employers enjoy a greater associational capacity. The organizational problem of the employers is further accentuated at the European level by the gap between export-oriented businesses, which are interested in a deregulation of the European product market, and internal market-oriented businesses supported by individual nation-states. That the employers are more capable as associations is demonstrated at the national level by the greater extent to which employers are organized. Conversely, employee associations, thanks to being fewer in number, can generalize their claim to representation and require less effort to commit their members to an agreement. The comparatively weak position of the European umbrella organization of businesses (the Union of Industrial and Employers' Confederations of Europe) supports the positions of both Olson and Streeck as well as Traxler and Schmitter. The large number of European business associations (see Nollert 1996, 1997) speaks of a greater heterogeneity of interests as well as a lower generalizability of their claims to representation. Further, the existence of the Roundtable supports Olson's assumption that a greater chance exists within a heterogeneous mass of businesses that individual businesses will take on the expenses of the collective representation of interests. Finally, the existence of the European Roundtable shows that large firms, by virtue of their resources, are not only capable but also ready to take control away from the national and European umbrella organizations.

Limited representativeness and internal disputes

However, it must be noted that the Roundtable did not offer a representative image of big business in the European Community. Thus, within the Roundtable, transnational businesses from small countries that are highly dependent on foreign trade were and still are overrepresented.

Furthermore, four businesses from countries that were not even members of the European Community – Asea Brown Boveri and Volvo (both based in Sweden) and Nestlé and Ciba-Geigy (both based in Switzerland) – have belonged to the Roundtable since its inception. In comparison, the large industries of the core countries (France, the United Kingdom and Germany) are weakly represented. This might not have been necessary because pluralistic models of the mediation of political-economic interests had dominated in the three countries

(Nollert 1992). In other words, their businesses gained privileged access to government in contrast to those that were joined together with labour unions in a corporatist circle.

The limited representativeness of the Roundtable is also substantiated through the network analyses in the anthology by Stokman et al. (1985). Their findings indicate that only Thyssen occupies a central position in the German network. However, Siemens, in contrast to Bosch, is extremely closely linked with Thyssen. It is also noteworthy that the German Deutsche Bank is involved with every Roundtable business. Of the three Dutch members (Royal Dutch–Shell,[10] Philips and Unilever), only Philips occupies a central position in their national network. However, both Nestlé and Ciba-Geigy belong to the core of the Swiss network. French industry too is only partially represented. In fact, Saint-Gobain and Danone (formerly BSN) are in the core, whereas Renault and Lafarge Coppée are not. Upon closer examination, it appears that the French businesses represented in the Roundtable are linked with holding company Compagnie de Suez (Lyonnaise des Eaux, Saint Gobain, and Total). The second-largest holding company, Paribas, is linked only financially with Danone. Belgian industry is also only partially represented. The businesses that sat at the Roundtable are primarily those linked with the Société Générale (Sofina, Petrofina and Solvay). The partner businesses of the Groupe Bruxelloise Lambert, the second-biggest holding company, are missing, however. Since the British network is only weakly centralized, founding members Imperial Chemical Industries and Royal Dutch–Shell cannot be regarded as its representatives. A parent holding company in the United Kingdom, namely the Prudential Corporation, is also overrepresented. The business network in Italy is fragmented regionally. Fiat and Olivetti, the two Roundtable members, belong to the 'Turin Group'. The state-controlled businesses in the region of Rome are not represented, nor are the Milanese businesses controlled by the Pesenti and Falck families, the state-controlled businesses in the Genoa region, or the businesses of the Ferruzi and Gardini families. We can summarize at this point that, in France, Belgium and Italy, the businesses of the Suez Group (e.g. Société Générale) and the de Benedetti holding companies are over-represented. Here it should be noted that Carlo de Benedetti (representative of Olivetti) even holds shares in Suez, which in turn controls the Société Générale. The European Roundtable primarily encompasses businesses that are globally active but at the same time are dependent on

[10] Royal Dutch–Shell has grown out of an alliance of the Royal Dutch Petroleum Company and the British Shell Transport and Trading Company, by which the two companies merged their interests on a 60:40 basis.

European consumers and which therefore are in favour of an expansion of the European internal market (see chapter 1).

The unity of the Roundtable businesses with respect to the internal market project should not blind us to the fact that there are substantial economic disputes among Roundtable members. Thus, for example, in the 1980s, Gyllenhammars' Volvo tried unsuccessfully to penetrate the sphere of the businesses controlled by Peter Wallenberg (including among others Asea, Ericsson and Electrolux) through the involvement of Atlas Copco and Stora Kopperberg. Conversely, Wallenberg for his part is presently trying to incorporate Volvo into his empire (*Weltwoche* 1997).

The aggressive business policy of the Olivetti representative was a major source of disputes. After a one-year guest appearance in the management of Fiat, which was rewarded with a large number of shares in Fiat, Carlo de Benedetti bought and redeveloped Olivetti's Turin typewriter factory in 1986 and later Triumph-Adler's German office equipment factory. Parallel to this manoeuvre he also tried to put together a European conglomerate of banks, insurance companies and food businesses, which did not sit well with other Roundtable members. De Benedetti succeeded in bringing in Europe's second-largest (after Bosch) auto parts supplier only after he indicated that he was prepared to separate out the domain of weapons and leave it under French control.

Even more vehement was the resistance to majority participation by de Benedetti in Société Générale. The Belgians asked the Parisian bank Indosuez for help. According to Sand (1992), the Wallonian Davignon, who became the head of the Société Générale after leaving the Commission, used his informal connections to Suez to ensure that Suez took over a majority share in Société Générale and defeated de Benedetti's 1988 takeover attempt. De Benedetti was supported by the Flemish André Leysen, the head of Gevaert, who sat on the boards of the Roundtable members Bayer, VEBA and Philips.

On 19 March 1997, it was made public that the German steel firm and Roundtable member Krupp (Gerhard Cromme) intended to take over a majority of shares in Roundtable member Thyssen. Dieter Vogel, the head of Thyssen, considered this a 'hostile takeover attempt' and accused Krupp of 'Wild West manners' (*Tages-Anzeiger*, 19 March 1997: 33).

Discord was also expressed on the occasion of the planned merger of Suez and Lyonnaise des Eaux, the business of then Roundtable president Jérôme Monod. Roundtable member Louis Beffa, president of Saint Gobain, complained in April 1997 that the merger took too little account of his participation in Suez and demanded a bonus. The merger was also awkward for Beffa because at the same time Saint Gobain was also involved with the two big French rivals Lyonnaise des Eaux and Générale des Eaux (CGE).

The ERT after the SEA: Constant Influence, New Goals

The activities of the European Roundtable of Industrialists during the time leading up to the signing of the Single European Act were very intense and the interest of its members in the matter at hand was certainly extremely high. With the passage of the Single European Act, the Roundtable had undoubtedly achieved its main goal. At that point it therefore would have been possible for the members to retreat into their businesses again and to engage future issues from within the framework of the European umbrella organizations. Indeed, many of its most prominent members have already departed. Among those who must be mentioned in this regard are Pehr Gyllenhammar (Volvo), Umberto Agnelli (Fiat), Wisse Dekker (Philips), Karl-Heinz Kaske (Siemens) and Hans Merkle (Bosch). Of the founders, only Antoine Riboud (Danone, formerly BSN), Helmut Maucher (Nestlé) and Carlo de Benedetti (Olivetti) remained.

But the European Roundtable is still an active lobbyist, with interests in various areas such as infrastructure and unemployment. In 1988 the secretariat was moved from Paris to Brussels. In the same year, Wisse Dekker took over the leadership from Gyllenhammar. Between 1992 and 1996, Jérôme Monod, the head of Lyonnaise des Eaux, held the office of chairman of the European Roundtable. In January 1996 Helmut Maucher of Nestlé became the new chairman. In 1997 he formalized relations between the Roundtable and the Union of Industrial and Employers' Confederations of Europe. The Roundtable meets regularly and holds regular discussions with the European Commission. Unlike associations such as UNICE, which must react to all regulations issued by the Commission affecting its members, the European Roundtable selects areas that it views as important, organizes task forces to research these areas, and then expresses its views based on the results of this research.

The Roundtable's Competitiveness Advisory Group, initiated by the 'Competitiveness' working group in its 1994 report 'European Competitiveness: The Way to Growth' (see below), has become a new and especially important body through which the Roundtable exercises influence. Thus, the advisory committee newly created by the Commission works closely with the policy advisory group and is responsible for reporting every six months to the Commission president (presently Sir Iain Vallance, chairman of Roundtable member British Telecom) on the competitiveness of European industry.

The members of the European Roundtable are also heard by their national governments and their views are highly respected. The Roundtable's continuously high level of political influence is illustrated by the fact that the former supporter of the European Roundtable, Etienne Davignon, as chairperson of the Société Générale, belongs to the Roundtable himself. Also indirectly linked to the Roundtable is the former General Director Fernand Braun, who presently advises the VEBA Group (Germany). As one member of the European Roundtable (Helmut Maucher) told us in an interview in November 1995, the members of the European Roundtable have access to and are heard by the president of the European Commission and by the heads of state or government. Unlike those of unions and associations, their contacts are made directly with the highest levels of government. It is no surprise therefore, that Roundtable member Heinrich von Pierer (Siemens) belonged to Helmut Kohl's closest circle of advisers (*Wirtschafts Woche* 1996). The view that the Roundtable in no way lost influence after the passage of the Single European Act is substantiated through our interviews with Wisse Dekker, Etienne Davignon, Herwig Kressler (chief expert of the Advisory Group for Social Relations and Industrial Policy), Fernand Braun (adviser to the VEBA Group) and Hannes Glatz (the head of the Daimler-Benz office in Brussels).

The membership structure of the Roundtable has certainly changed. Additions include businesses from the South European member countries including Turkey (Profilo). In 1995, the European Roundtable already included forty-six businesses from sixteen European countries (see table 7.1 below) that together account for an annual turnover of 550 billion ECU and employ more than 3 million people worldwide. The unequal representation of countries and industry branches has also remained. Electronics, energy, food and machinery (industry) are well represented; metals, banks, insurance companies, telecommunications and transportation are not.

In 1991, the European Roundtable published the report 'Reshaping Europe', (ERT 1991b), which defined its goals for the 1990s. It demanded a harmonization of the legal framework, a Community industrial policy, the creation of a monetary union, expansion to the east, and the promotion of world trade. Along with this, educational and infrastructural measures were demanded, which were supported by two brochures. In the brochure 'Rebuilding Confidence: An Action Plan for Europe' (ERT 1992) demands were made for modernization and increased competitiveness in the European Community and investments in the education, infrastructure, environment and technology sectors. The 'Missing Networks' catalogue (ERT 1991a) was a follow up to the 'Missing Links' brochure published in 1984. In 'Missing Links', the demand had been made to close three gaps in the European transportation system (a tunnel under the English Channel, a bridge connection between Denmark and Sweden, and an extension of Route Nationale 134 with a tunnel under Col du Somport); thus, 'Missing Networks' demanded an extension of the European highway network. In the years that followed, the Commission has also taken this demand into account. The responsible Commissioner, Karel van Miert, published four documents in 1993 in which he proposed to build 15,000 kilometres of new highways within the framework of the Trans European Network (TEN).

In November 1994, the White Paper of the Commission *Growth, Competitiveness, Employment* (CEU 1993) was subject to commentary in an ERT paper entitled 'European Competitiveness: The Way to Growth and Jobs'. The following demands are raised in it:

(1) with an eye toward lowering costs, energy, transportation and telecommunications markets should be liberalized;
(2) the cost of capital and business taxes should be drastically reduced;
(3) the Commission should form a Competitiveness Advisory Group and thereby institutionalize the dialogue between governments and industry;
(4) Community educational and technology policies should be developed. Moreover, the transfer of knowledge should be promoted between universities and businesses.

Prominent recent reports are 'Education for Europeans' (ERT 1995), calling for a reform of Europe's education system, 'Investing in Knowledge' (ERT 1997) and 'Job Creation and Competitiveness through Innovation' (ERT 1998).

At present, reports are generated by twelve working groups on policy issues (accounting standards, competitiveness, corporate governance, education and development, employment and social policy, environment, European company statute, export controls, EU enlargement, intergovernmental conference, informational society, and North–South relations), each of which is chaired by a Roundtable member.

Since March 1994, the work of the European Roundtable has been additionally supported through the European Centre for Infrastructure Studies (ECIS) in Rotterdam. A Centre for Businesses, Regional Bodies and Foundations will be financed. It is supposed to promote the exchange of scientific reports on infrastructure issues, the carrying out of smaller studies and the development of conferences and research networks.

The exchange of opinion among Roundtable members is no longer restricted to its sessions in Brussels and meetings in the context of the Trilateral Commission and the Bilderberg Club, which are largely concealed from public view. Many of the Roundtable members meet annually at the beginning of the year in Davos (Switzerland) to discuss world economic trends and problems together at the World Economic Forum with top politicians and representatives of international organizations. Members of the Roundtable are also present on the Executive Committee of the World Business Council for Sustainable Development, which was formed in January 1995 and includes 120 enterprises from 34 countries. These are Stephan Schmidheiny (former Roundtable member and founder of the council), Percy Barnevik (Asea Brown Boveri), Bertrand Collomb (Lafarge Coppée) and Helmut Maucher (Nestlé). Numerous Roundtable members also represent enterprises belonging to the World Business Council: Kymmene (Finland); Lafarge Coppée (France); Fiat and Pirelli (Italy); Philips and Unilever (Netherlands); Norsk Hydro (Norway); Volvo (Sweden); Asea Brown Boveri, Hoffmann-La Roche and Nestlé (Switzerland); Imperial Chemical Industries and Royal Dutch–Shell (Netherlands, United Kingdom).

Fertile ground for a transnational business network

Finally, we turn to the following question: to what extent are the informal contacts between the members of the European Roundtable reflected in the construction of a transnational European business network? The intermittently published 'Reports on the Competition Policy of the Commission' create the impression that, with the passage of the Single European Act, transnational mergers and acquisitions in the European Community increased tremendously (see Windolf 1993). In view of the growing competitiveness within the European internal market, the 'national champions' saw their power to acquire other businesses or to join with other firms increase. In fact, a pan-European cooperation between large firms does not presuppose an inevitable merger. It is sufficient to build strategic alliances or joint ventures, or to link together through mutual financial or management connections. A network analysis at two points in time – 1984 and 1994 – of the interconnections between the Roundtable businesses through financial participation and through managers who hold management or board responsibilities in at least two member businesses will help us answer the question.

According to an analysis of transnational interconnections in Europe in 1976 by Fenemma and Schijf (1985), we should expect that, above all, Belgian and French as well as Dutch and German businesses maintain close transnational contacts. A review of the economic and financial newspapers of the European Union (*WirtschaftsWoche* 1991) noted that Roundtable businesses are overrepresented in the network of boards of directors, which at the beginning of the 1990s was still quite weakly interconnected. Thus, among the seventeen people identified as having at least two seats, four Roundtable members and four non-members can be found who have two seats in Roundtable businesses. Included among those holding three or more seats are André Leysen (representative of Gevaert in the Roundtable) and Etienne Davignon (representative of the Société Générale in the Roundtable). Among those with two seats are Carlo de Benedetti (Olivetti) and Helmut Maucher (Nestlé). In addition, Roundtable businesses are connected through Hilmar Kopper (Solvay, Pilkington), Henry C. Bodmer (Fiat, Pirelli), François Laage de Meux (Olivetti, Société Générale) and Niklaus Senn (VEBA, Siemens).

In order to answer the question regarding the structure of and changes in the interconnections among Roundtable businesses, network analyses were performed for 1984 and 1994 and compared.[11] The types of connections taken into account were financial participation and connections via top managers who hold seats in at least two member businesses. The sources of data are the directories published by *Moody's International Manual* (1985 edition) and *Major Companies of Europe* (1996 edition). The only missing data are the business profiles of Olivetti in 1984 and of the Turkish holding company Profilo in 1994.

In contrast to the financial participation data, the census of management interconnections was impeded in two ways. First, corporate law varies considerably in Europe. In some countries, we find a one-board system, that is, no institutional separation between operational and supervisory functions (for example, in the United Kingdom). However, in Germany and the Netherlands, these two functions are performed by two different committees (two-board system). In order to guarantee comparability, and to simplify the coding process, in the case of the two-board system the two committees are seen as two parts of a single super committee. The second complication to be taken into account is that Roundtable businesses become connected through more than just other Roundtable members. It is possible that a manager of a non-member business might sit on the boards of several Roundtable businesses.

---

[11] Reviews of social network analysis methods are presented in Scott (1991) and Wasserman and Faust (1994).

Similarly, a Roundtable representative might sit on the board of a non-member business. In our analysis here, those links caused by a non-Roundtable member are also taken into account. We do not analyse links among non-Roundtable businesses.

A principal finding of the network analyses is that the interconnections among members increased over the decade. In contrast to 1994, the founding members of the Roundtable in 1984 were sparsely interlocked. We found not a single financial interconnection and only fifteen managerial interconnections; the latter involved at least indirect connections involving only five business (Unilever, Siemens, Thyssen, Asea Brown Boveri, Volvo). The central business in 1984 was Unilever (Roundtable representative: Kenneth Durham), which was directly interconnected with Volvo (Pehr Gyllenhammar), Siemens (Wolfgang Seelig) and Thyssen (Dieter Spethmann). This centrality was primarily attributable to Spethmann from Thyssen, who held seats with Siemens and Unilever. Of the remaining managers with two seats, we mention here only Tore Browaldh, who is not a Roundtable member but who is linked with Unilever and Volvo and thereby serves as a bridge between German and Swedish industry.

In 1994 we can observe a comparatively greater number of financial and management interconnections. Bayer was financially linked with the Belgian firm Gevaert (100 per cent), while Gevaert has a 1 per cent share in Bayer. VEBA was financially linked with the British Cable & Wireless (10.5 per cent). Davignon's Société Générale and Sofina held shares in Petrofina (12.7 per cent and 1.3 per cent respectively); Société Générale and the Lyonnaise des Eaux were linked with Total (3.6 per cent and 1 per cent respectively). Finally, the Fiat holding company Ifial had a 5.8 per cent financial involvement with Danone (formerly BSN).

As expected, the greatest number of financial links are found in Belgium, where the French holding company Compagnie de Suez, one of the parent companies of the Société Générale, had indirect interconnections to French Roundtable firms. Suez was thus linked through its 5 per cent share in Saint Gobain and its 17 per cent share in Lyonnaise des Eaux. For its part, Saint-Gobain controlled over 6.3 per cent of the stock and 10 per cent of the voting rights in Suez. On 11 April 1997, the boards of Suez and Lyonnaise des Eaux finally approved a merger, thus deepening the interconnectivity. The apparently weak interconnection among German businesses may be deceptive; the three large banks Deutsche Bank, Commerzbank and Dresdner Bank were represented in advisory bodies of Roundtable firms and were shareholders of Roundtable firms, thus forging indirect personal and financial connections between the German member firms. Not to be forgotten is Peter Wallenberg's Investor AB, which controlled two Roundtable firms: Asea Brown Boveri and Ericsson. The new chairperson of the board of Investor AB is Percy Barnevik, the former head of the Asea Brown Boveri conglomerate. According to *Weltwoche* (1997), the nomination of the former head of Wallenberg's Electrolux as the head of Volvo went too far even for Wallenberg, a founding member of the Roundtable, who complained: 'Sweden appears to occupy a rather unique position if one considers how unilateral and monolithic we have become, and how highly power is concentrated with us' (ibid.: 24).

Since 1994, the joint venture between former members Volvo and Renault has been dissolved. In 1990, both firms had decided to work together in divisions devoted to automobile, truck and bus production, a deal cemented by an exchange of shares and the creation of three joint committees. During the 1980s, a cartel also existed between Solvay and Imperial Chemicals but in 1990 this soda ash cartel was outlawed and fined by the Commission. In addition, several contract joint ventures – such as that between Daimler-Benz and Siemens on traffic control and information systems – and a number of capital joint ventures between Roundtable businesses still exist: between Nestlé and Danone (chocolate production: Cokoladovny); between Daimler-Benz and Asea Brown Boveri (transport system: Adtranz), between Thyssen and Lyonnaise des Eaux (water: Eurawasser), between Thyssen and VEBA (mobile telephones: E-Plus Mobilfunk) and between Bosch and Siemens (household appliances: Bosch-Siemens Hausgeräte).

The top board interconnections among Roundtable firms also increased between 1984 and 1994 from 15 to 122. However, the density and centralization (see table 7.1), when compared with the values in national networks, were still low. Thirty-three member businesses were at least indirectly connected to one other member through their management in 1994 (that is, have a 'degree' score of 1). The only businesses not connected with this group of thirty-three were the members from Spain (CEPSA, Telefónica and Iberdrola are themselves interconnected), Portugal (Amorin), Finland (Kymmene), Denmark (Carlsberg), Norway (Norsk Hydro, Statoil), Ireland (Jefferson Smurfit), Greece (Titan) as well as the British firms Cable & Wireless and GKN.

In the centre of the network were the German firms VEBA (nine interconnections) and Bayer (eight) and the Belgian firm Solvay (eight). The German, Belgian and French firms were the most central. Volvo was no longer on the list, owing to the departure of Gyllenhammar. Unilever exhibited only an average level of centrality. What is more,

Table 7.1. *The centrality of Roundtable companies in 1994*

Company (branch)	Degree	Norm	Links	Betweenness norm
VEBA (energy)	9	20.45	19	8.34
Bayer (chemistry)	8	18.18	20	4.35
Solvay (chemistry)	8	18.18	15	*18.13*
Danone (food)	7	15.91	10	5.38
Société Générale (holding)	7	15.91	14	5.38
Saint-Gobain (glass)	7	15.91	10	7.70
Daimler-Benz (holding)	6	13.64	12	7.12
Petrofina (energy)	6	13.64	13	0.94
Sofina (holding)	6	13.64	16	*12.29*
Lyonnaise des Eaux (holding)	5	11.36	9	0.64
Philips (electronics)	5	11.36	6	5.04
Pilkington (building materials)	5	11.36	8	3.28
British Petroleum (energy)	4	9.09	5	7.59
Thyssen (machines)	4	9.09	12	7.17
Fiat (Automobile)	3	6.82	3	6.34
Gevaert (photo)	3	6.82	3	0.00
Krupp (machines)	3	6.82	3	0.00
Siemens (electronics)	3	6.82	13	0.74
Total (energy)	3	6.82	4	1.88
Unilever (food)	3	6.82	5	4.85
Nestlé (food)	3	6.82	7	9.41
Asea Brown Boveri (engineering)	2	4.55	8	3.28
Bertelsmann (publishing)	2	4.55	4	0.49
Bosch (electronics)	2	4.55	2	1.42
Lafarge Coppée (building mat.)	2	4.55	5	4.37
Pirelli (tyres)	2	4.55	4	3.28
Royal Dutch–Shell (energy)	2	4.55	3	1.48
B.A.T. Industries (tobacco)	1	2.27	2	0.00
British Steel (metals)	1	2.27	1	0.00
Ericsson (electronics)	1	2.27	4	0.00
Imperial Chemicals (chemistry)	1	2.27	3	0.00
Iberdrola (energy)	1	2.27	2	0.00
Olivetti (computers)	1	2.27	3	0.00
Hoffmann-La Roche (chemistry)	1	2.27	2	0.00
Telefónica de España (telecom)	1	2.27	2	0.00
Centralization		14.6%		15.6%

Solvay and Sofina had unexpectedly high 'betweenness' scores.[12] That is, both businesses, in comparison with Bayer and Petrofina, had

---

[12] Unlike the measurement of 'degree', 'betweenness' indexes the extent to which an actor is located between unlinked actors. Actors who are linked only with actors who are connected to each other get a 'betweenness' score of 0 (see Wasserman and Faust 1994: 188ff).

Table 7.2. *Connectors between Roundtable companies, 1994*

Name	Management	Advisory body	Total
Hilmar Kopper	Deutsche Bank	Bayer, D.-Benz, Pilkington, Solvay, VEBA	5
Yves Boël (ERT)	Sofina, Petrofina	Danone, Petrofina, Sofina, Solvay	4
Et. Davignon (ERT)	S. Générale	Petrofina, S. Générale, Sofina, Solvay	4
André Leysen (ERT)	Gevaert	Bayer, Gevaert, Philips, VEBA	4
Hermann Strenger	Bayer, VEBA	Bayer, Siemens, VEBA	3
Jean Gandois		Danone, Lyonn. des Eaux, S. Générale	3
Gérard Mestrallet	Suez	Lyonn. des Eaux, Petrofina, S. Générale	3
Gérard Worms		Lyonn. des Eaux, S.Générale, St. Gobain	3

Note: Chairpersons of advisory bodies are also counted as members of management. ERT = members of the Roundtable.

comparatively few redundant connections. The high number of links reflects the fact that the firms in general and Siemens and Thyssen in particular had multiple connections to the same firms. In contrast to 1984, in 1994 the non-members of the Roundtable were the most active as connectors. This trend is also documented by table 7.2, which shows that the central person was no longer a Roundtable member but the chairperson of the management of Deutsche Bank, Hilmar Kopper. The most central Roundtable members were the Belgians: Boël, Davignon and Leysen. From the list of the firms we can see that the boards of Solvay, Sofina, Petrofina, Société Générale, VEBA and Lyonnaise des Eaux were the most popular venues of Roundtable members.

A familiar concept that designates the subgroups of a network is the 1–clique (see Wasserman and Faust 1994: 253ff). This refers to groups of actors that are all directly interconnected. In 1994, seven 1–cliques could be identified with at least three companies. Four of these involved five companies: (1) Bayer, Daimler-Benz, Pilkington, Solvay, VEBA; (2) Danone, Lyonnaise des Eaux, Petrofina, Société Générale, Saint-Gobain; (3) Danone, Petrofina, Société Générale, Saint-Gobain, Sofina; and (4) Danone, Petrofina, Société Générale, Sofina, Solvay. In addition, comparatively large 2–cliques can be identified, i.e. groups of actors linked at least indirectly by a maximum of two paths. The biggest 2–clique had ten companies; along with Bosch, Daimler-Benz, Gevaert, Krupp, Philips, Pilkington, and Siemens, this group included the three most central firms: Bayer, Solvay and VEBA.

The stability of the cliques is substantiated by the block procedure and N-core analysis. Blocks designate components that do not disintegrate into two subcomponents after the rejection of one actor. In other words: all block members connect to each other by at least two paths. The block contains no communicatively privileged 'bridges' (Burt

1992). The only block with more than three Roundtable members involved the following twenty-four companies: Bayer, Bertelsmann, Bosch, British Petroleum, Daimler-Benz, Danone, Fiat, Gevaert, Krupp, Lafarge Coppée, Lyonnaise des Eaux, Petrofina, Philips, Pilkington, Royal Dutch–Shell, Société Générale, Saint-Gobain, Siemens, Sofina, Solvay, Thyssen, Total, Unilever and VEBA. The central firms were therefore not only directly linked but also interconnected through numerous other paths. Thus, the network itself would not fall apart with the exit of the representatives of Sofina and Solvay, the two firms with the outstanding 'betweenness' scores. Nestlé, which also distinguished itself through a comparatively high 'betweenness' score, was not contained in the block however. Indeed, the Swiss food conglomerate formed a bridge between the network's centre (Solvay) and the peripheral businesses Asea Brown Boveri and Hoffmann-La Roche. Here it should be noted that the link between Solvay and Nestlé is to be attributed not to Roundtable member Maucher, but rather to the president of the board of the Credit Suisse bank, Rainer Gut.

Another measurement of the cohesion of a subnetwork is the N-core. This is a group of actors who are directly connected with at least N members of the group. In the present data set we identified a 4–core, which involved the following nine firms: Bayer, Danone, Daimler-Benz, Lyonnaise des Eaux, Petrofina, Pilkington, Société Générale, Solvay and VEBA. In other words, each of the listed nine businesses was directly connected with at least four other businesses.

These different analyses of cohesion show that the central firms of the network did not constitute separate, weakly connected subnetworks. In other words: The centre of the network of Roundtable firms is only slightly fragmented and is dominated by German, Belgian and French businesses. The division of the presidency of the Roundtable reflects the two axes that had already become visible in the research of Fennema (1982) and Fennema and Schijf (1985). Thus, president Monod represents firms linked to the Suez Group (French and Wallonian-Belgian businesses) and vice-president Leysen represents those firms linked to the Deutsche Bank (German, Dutch and Flemish-Belgian businesses). As second vice-president, Maucher plays the role of a neutral 'old boy'.

Conclusion and outlook

In summary, we can say that the founding of the European Roundtable reflected the halfhearted Europe policy of the main European umbrella organization of the employers, the Union of Industrial and Employers' Confederations of Europe. Dissatisfied heads of export-dependent firms considered it more effective to form an exclusive club and advance the internal market project through it. However, the founding of the European Roundtable is attributable not only to the business personalities involved (Gyllenhammar, Dekker, Maucher) and the active support of the then Commissioner Davignon, but also to the general organizational weakness of the employers at a pan-European level. Thus, the establishment of the European Roundtable confirms the assumption that large firms, thanks to their resources, can directly control the representation of their own interests, without being dependent on a European umbrella organization. This weakening of the system of associations also becomes increasingly visible at the national level. Indeed, thanks to weakened unions, firms no longer require the support of an association. In other words, informal contacts with the government have regained their meaning (see also *WirtschaftsWoche* 1996).

Even after the passage of the Single European Act, the European Roundtable is still among the most influential protagonists in Brussels. However, in the 1990s its interest was focused more on particular issues than on the project of European integration. The Roundtable considers the principal challenges of the present to be lagging competitiveness, the low job creation potential of European industry, the completion of the Single Market project and, last but not least, the eastward expansion of the European Union. In a message on 12 January 1997, to the fifteen heads of state of the member states signed by its new chairman Helmut Maucher (Nestlé) and Percy Barnevik (Asea Brown Boveri),[13] the Roundtable also indicated its willingness to cooperate with expansion efforts and underscored at the same time its demand for a reform of the decision-making structures of the Union in light of its future expansion to twenty-five member states. In 1998 the Roundtable also began to send a number of messages to European governments about the Millennium Bug.

The Roundtable will serve as fertile ground for the development of transnational business interconnections that will influence the European integration process well into the twenty-first century. Thus, by 1994 more than 70 per cent of the forty-six businesses were linked via interlocking boards. Here we must also note that the German, Belgian, British and French firms were financially linked with financial firms that had good relationships at the national level with political representatives. It is foreseeable that the network will condense even further. Thus, in April 1997 a merger was initiated between Lyonnaise des Eaux and the Compagnie de Suez, which is linked with the Société Générale and

---

[13] The message, 'EU Enlargement', can be read in its entirety at the following world wide web address: http:/www.ert.be/2_activ/eu_enlargement.html.

Saint-Gobain. Moreover, Monod proposed to the head of the new conglomerate and president of the Roundtable that Cromme (Krupp) and Davignon (Société Générale) as well as a representative of Nestlé (Reto Domeniconi) be appointed to the board of Lyonnaise des Eaux–Suez. Operationally, the new conglomerate is led by the former chairperson of Suez, Mestrallet, who already holds seats in Roundtable firms (see table 7.2). Finally, the relations between Roundtable firms could pave the way for capital joint ventures or even mergers such as that between Krupp and Thyssen in 1998 after which Heinz Kriwet (Thyssen) had to leave the Roundtable.

Although the Roundtable is still principally concerned with European affairs, a number of its member enterprises (for example, in biotechnology, discussed in chapter 8) are tied into transnational alliances and within the framework of the Transatlantic Business Dialogue support free trade and free movement of investments between Europe and North America. This dialogue was initiated by the two Commissioners Martin Bangemann and Sir Leon Brittan and the American president Bill Clinton in November 1995. In addition to representatives of the US government and the Commission of the European Union, leading managers from Europe and North America also take part in the annual meetings, among them Peter Sutherland, former Commissioner and present Roundtable representative of British Petroleum. The dialogue is also supported by the European–American Business Council, an association to which approximately eighty European and American major corporations and banks belong. It is surely no coincidence that Roundtable members Philips and Ericsson were among the founders of this body, and that presently sixteen Roundtable member businesses also belong to it.[14] Likewise it is hardly surprising that the Council currently favours a bilateral trade agreement between the European Union and the United States of America. In light of the successful military integration of the two triad members through NATO, it would also be no big surprise if in the end the Council – analogous to the role of the Roundtable in the 1980s in Europe – becomes the driving force for transnational economic integration at the beginning of the twenty-first century.

[14] Airbus Industrie, B.A.T. Industries, British Petroleum, British Telecom, Daimler-Benz, Ericsson, Hoffmann-La Roche, Imperial Chemical Industries, Nestlé, Nokia Group, Norsk Hydro, Philips, Pirelli, Siemens, Unilever, VEBA.

8 Biotechnology in the European Union: a case study of political entrepreneurship

Michael Nollert

'Just as "telematics" and its various areas of application were the focal point of technological, scientific, and human activities in the 1980s, experts believe that the biological revolution unleashed by discoveries of biotechnology will become the greatest challenge of the 1990s.'
Etienne Davignon (1981: 189f, my translation)

Introduction

In this chapter we examine the question of whether technology corporatism – established at the beginning of the 1980s – also flourishes beyond the domain of information technology, where it was initiated (see chapter 4). Moreover, we consider whether it shaped Europe's competitive position in biotechnology, an industry widely considered to be among the most dynamic in the twenty-first century.

The starting point of a European biotechnology policy was the Commission's insight at the beginning of the 1980s that the Community displayed a technological backwardness with respect to the USA and Japan and that bio-industry could make a decisive contribution to resolving the employment problem. Therefore, by the middle of the 1990s, the advancement of biotechnology was to become – as Davignon predicted above – an established goal of the technology policy of the European Union. Consequently, the Commission pushed for research programmes and a corporatist policy formulation process that included the participation of the interest organizations of bio-industry.

In contrast to information technology, however, the 'national champions' in the chemical and pharmaceutical industries were not very interested in European research programmes similar to Esprit (see chapter 4). Indeed, they had already established transregional alliances even before the first programme was launched and preferred competitive to pre-competitive research. Yet, during the 1990s their industry associations closely cooperated with the Commission because they regarded existing regulations as too restrictive.

The first sections that follow sketch out the continuous ascent of biotechnology and genetic engineering in the agenda of the European Union using (a) official positions taken by the Commission; (b) research programmes and regulative acts; and (c) the dialogue between the Commission and European biotech organizations.[1] This chronology of the events broadly supports the view that the Commission acted as a political entrepreneur (see chapter 1), while the European bio-industry organizations have always been reactive rather than proactive. In the final section, however, we suggest that two facts limit the establishment of a biotechnology corporatism. First, the interest of the Commission in increasing the competitiveness of European bio-industry is only partially compatible with the global thinking of European chemical and pharmaceutical firms. Secondly, whereas information technologies have been broadly adopted by the population, large segments of the population and members of the European Parliament do not share the Commission's euphoria about genetic engineering.

Diagnoses and proposals of the Commission

Biotechnology in the broader sense includes all instruments for the alteration of living organisms and plants by means of biological organisms, systems and processes. According to the definition of the European Federation of Biotechnology (the European umbrella organization of scientists), biotechnology is 'the integrated use of biochemistry, microbiology and engineering sciences in order to achieve the technological application of the capacities of microorganisms, cultured tissue cells and parts thereof'.[2] Economically, the newest branch of biotechnology, genetic engineering, is the most promising. In 1973, Stanley Cohen and Herbert Boyer, both Americans, succeeded for the first time in extracting genes from DNA molecules and transferring them to bacteria. This recombinant DNA technology was the cornerstone for the industrial use of genetically modified organisms and plants.

Proceeding from the assessment that European industry exhibited considerable backwardness in the development of key technologies

[1] My thanks to Albert Klepsch (DG XII Science, Research and Development, Department of Biotechnology and Society: Public Perception and Socioeconomic Impacts, Brussels), Jens Krazek (CEAT, Bund für Umwelt und Naturschutz, Bonn), Stefan Ryser (Hoffmann-La Roche, Senior Advisory Group Biotechnology, Basel), Kristin Schreiber (DG III Internal Market and Industrial Affairs, Department of Agroindustry and Biotechnology, Brussels), Christof Tannert (member of the European Parliament, Socialist group, Berlin), Kathleen Vandendael (European Federation of Pharmaceutical Industry Associations, Public Relations and Vaccines, Brussels) for information.
[2] *EFB Newsletter*, No. 4 (December 1981): 2.

when compared with the USA and Japan (Servan-Schreiber 1968), the memorandum 'The Industrial Policy of the Community' (CEC 1970) and later the resolution of the Council of the European Community of 17 December 1973, regarding a common industrial policy urged the member countries to promote their high-tech enterprises. Only two years after Boyer's and Cohen's discovery the Commission concretized its plans with respect to the collective advancement of biotechnology in that it proposed a research programme, the Biomolecular Engineering Programme, to the Council of Ministers. In that same year, the German Commissioner responsible for science and technology, Ralf Dahrendorf, created a 'Europe Plus Thirty' study group, whose recommendations led to the first programme, 'Forecasting and Assessment in Science and Technology' (FAST, 1978–83). The first provisional report of FAST's ten-member group of experts (1982), which was summarized in the book *Eurofutures: The Challenge of Innovation* (1984), contained among other things a section on the prospects of a 'bio-society' and a strategic recommendation for the development of European bio-industry.

Proposals by the Commission to reduce the technological gap

As a result of the first FAST report, the Commission emphatically and repeatedly recommended biotechnology as a key technology and a growth engine for the 1990s (see Davignon 1981). Thus, on 8 February 1983, Gaston Thorn, the president of the Commission, mentioned in a speech that biotechnology should be stimulated just as information technology had been previously. As a result, Directorate General III (Internal Market and Industrial Affairs) and Directorate General XII (science, technology and research) began negotiating a scientific sponsorship programme. The Commission also communicated to the European Council on 3 June 1983 its report 'Biotechnology: The Task of the Community' (CEC 1983a), which included a list of the most important defects of the European bio-industry:

(1) fragmentation of research efforts in basic biotechnology and in some specific areas, namely agricultural foodstuffs, the chemical industry and public health;
(2) a shortage of engineers and scientists with experience in modern biotechnology;
(3) a lack of sufficient European support for the infrastructure and legislation for biotechnology.

After the Council of Ministers called on the member states to register all biotechnology and genetic engineering research projects in its 1982 Recommendation 82/472, the European Council responded to the

Commission at the summit in Stuttgart with an appeal to create a European network of scientific activity in the individual member states and to develop a collective research programme. The appeal was further supported by the Commission's report to the Council on 29 September 1983, 'Biotechnology in the Community' (CEC 1983b), which concretized the recommended measures that had already been announced in the Commission's earlier communication (CEC 1983a). In this document, the scientific importance of biotechnology is laid out, and the competitive weakness and technological deficiencies of European bio-producers with respect to their American and Japanese counterparts, as well as the danger of migration by scientific specialists, are noted. In this connection, the diagnosis of the American Task Force of the White House Office of Scientific and Technology Policy is mentioned, according to which Japan and not Europe will become the strongest competitor to the US bio-industry. Thus, the European bio-industry was seen to be suffering from a shortage of qualified scientists and engineers (particularly in process technology), a lack of satisfactory cooperation between enterprises and universities and insufficient research and development resources. Accordingly, the Commission called for an increase in European competitiveness in the global biotech markets by means of the following six Community actions in the period 1984–9:

(1) research and training programmes;
(2) harmonization of biotechnology policies;
(3) new regulations about agricultural production for industrial purposes;
(4) a European concept for regulations in the area of biotechnology;
(5) European law for securing intellectual property rights in the field of biotechnology;
(6) demonstration projects.

For the financing of these actions, 200 million ECU were demanded, most of which was aimed at the research and training programmes, which were to receive 106 million, and the demonstration projects in the final phase of the programme, which were to receive 80 million. By contrast, only 6.6 million ECU were demanded for the harmonization efforts and the activities of the committee for supervising the risks and developing the regulations. Further intersectoral and transnational unions of enterprises and associations were explicitly endorsed. Thus the report mentioned Biogen, a medium-sized enterprise headquartered in Geneva that belongs to a group of transnational companies, and the European Federation of Biotechnology, as well as the national ad hoc coordinating committees.

Under Karl-Heinz Narjes, who replaced Etienne Davignon in 1985 as vice-president of the Commission and Commissioner for Science, Technology and Research, the technology-friendly posture of the Commission continued. However, although he prophesied in a 1989 article that biotechnology would advance, along with information technology, telematics, new materials, aeronautics and new energy sources as the most important European growth industries in the twenty-first century, in the second half of the 1980s the Commission focused its efforts on information technology (see chapter 4).

Assessments and proposals after the Single European Act

In a speech on 17 January 1990, Commission President Jacques Delors reinforced the request of the Community to support bio-industry by calling for more basic research in the areas of the automotive industry, air and space travel, electronics and biotechnology. Consequently, a further communication by the Commission to the European Council and the European Parliament followed in 1991 entitled 'Promoting the Competitive Environment for the Industrial Activities based on Biotechnology within the Community' (CEC 1991b). International distribution strategies, the legal protection of inventions and the construction of centralized and incomplete bio-databanks were identified as the bases for the current lack of competitiveness of European bio-industry. Particularly problematic was the fact that the Community *could not* protect the research results of its producers through patents. The emphases on bio-sciences in the recently concluded Third Framework Programme was also reinforced. Finally, an adjustment of the existing guidelines, biotechnology statistics, a standardized test process, mandatory research efforts and public relations work as well as the institutionalization of the ethical advisory group established in 1991 were also demanded.

Biotechnology was emphasized even more in the *White Paper 'Growth, Competitiveness, Employment'* (CEU 1993). Section B on the economic prospects of biotechnology (pp. 100ff) recapitulates the efforts up to the present: 'The Community has taken a number of initiatives, on the one hand, to promote the competitiveness of bio-industries and, on the other hand, to ensure the safe application of biotechnology. It implies mainly funding of research and development and the putting into place of a regulatory framework' (CEU 1993: 100). The lack of competitiveness was once again deplored and along with it the loss of potential jobs as well as the sceptical and critical posture of the population toward biotechnology:

Measuring innovative activity by patents filed for relevant products in the USA, the Community and Japan show[s] that patents filed have increased from 1,100 per annum in the early 1980s to 3,350 per annum in 1990. In 1980 the Community was in leading position, by 1990 the USA was filing 50 per cent more patents than the Community. European Patent Office (EPO) statistics reveal a similar evolution: between 1980 and 1991 biotechnology patents filed with the EPO increased by a factor of 10, the most being filed by US-based companies . . .

. . . Current global indicators of the growth prospects of the biotechnology industry are the following: in the USA the industry based on modern biotechnology had a turnover of over US$ 8 billion in 1992, a growth rate of 28 per cent with employment growing at 13 per cent. It is estimated on the basis of the observed rates of diffusion of biotechnology that the US biotechnology industry's revenues will grow at an average rate of 40 per cent to reach US$ 52 billion by the year 2000. The current industry size in Japan is officially put at US$ 3.8 billion and is estimated by the Ministry of International Trade and Industry to reach US$ 35 billion by the end of the century. In the Community, despite the emergence of a significant number of firms and a substantial growth in markets, primarily of bio-pharmaceuticals, to over US$ 3 billion, at the current rate of growth, the value of output and employment is about the same as that in Japan. It is therefore clear that by the year 2000 with an estimated world market of ECU 100 billion for the biotechnology industry, the Community growth rate will have to be substantially higher than at the present to ensure that the Community will become a major producer of such products, thereby reaping the output and employment advantages while at the same time remaining a key player in the related research area. (CEU 1993: 101)

The Commission fears that the Community will become merely a leading future market for bio-pharmaceuticals but not a leading future producer, because technology hostility and social inertia with respect to biotechnology have been more pronounced in the Community in general than in the United States or Japan (CEU 1993: 102). In other words, the Commission recommends: (a) deregulation of the biotech sector: b) the creation of a scientific committee; c) the establishment of science parks; d) investment incentives; e) public relations work for biotechnology; and f) a more vigorous discussion of the ethical aspects (p. 102).

On 1 August 1994, the communication of the Commission to the European Council, the European Parliament, and the Economic and Social Committee finally appeared: 'Biotechnology and the White Paper on Growth, Competitiveness and Employment' (CEU 1994). In this report, a recapitulation and assessment of the recommendations of the White Paper are followed by suggestions for modifying Directive 90/219/EEC regarding the application of genetically modified micro-organisms in closed systems and Directive 90/220/EEC regarding the deliberate release of genetically modified organisms in the environment. Thus, the goals of the communication of the Commission (CEC 1991b) and the White Paper are underlined once again. Both small and medium-sized enterprises on the one hand and the ethical aspects of gene research on the other are accentuated.

At the conference of the European Council in Corfu in June 1994, Delors highlighted once again the role of biotechnology as a growth engine whose own growth should be accelerated through a relaxation of the existing directives. Thus, the Commission conceded for the first time since the early 1980s the outstanding role of biotechnology as a growth engine and at the same time kept in view the fact that European bio-industry exhibits a drastic technological backwardness compared with the United States and Japan. According to its documents, the root of the competitive weakness of European biotech producers lies in the lack of support from member states; a fragmented research landscape, defective legal protection of biotechnological innovations, as well as the lack of acceptance of genetic engineering among the population. Accordingly, demands are made for strengthened research efforts; a bio-patent Directive; and, since the White Paper (CEU 1993), a general deregulation in the area of genetic engineering and a higher level of acceptance among the population. Only a few member states doubted the rationality of a collective technology policy. The United Kingdom, the Netherlands and Germany expressed regulatory concerns regarding the project of supporting private enterprises through public means.

The assessments and proposals of the Commission were then supported by several surveys conducted by Ernst & Young of enterprises in Western Europe. The first Ernst & Young biotech report (1994), for example, indicated that Europe's total turnover in bio-industry had already reached approximately 38 billion ECU. The branches of health, then 15 billion ECU, foods, with 10 billion ECU, and diagnosis, with 8 billion ECU, had the largest commercial potential. Although bio-industry employed only a total of 184,000 people, 6 per cent of the enterprises surveyed – above all small and medium-sized enterprises – expected a 10–25 per cent increase in employment; 20 per cent expected an increase of 25–50 percent; and 51 per cent expected an increase of over 50 percent. According to the second Ernst & Young report, *Biotech 95* (1995), by the year 2000 total turnover might reach 90 billion ECU, despite stable and strong competition from the United States and Japan. However, in Europe more is invested in absolute terms than in the United States or Japan, although of course the rate of increase in investment is rather small.

The pillars of European biotechnology policy

In retrospect, one could argue that the aforementioned documents of the Commission probably exaggerated the backwardness of European biotechnology (Junne 1992). Thus, the often mentioned indicator for the technological state of development – the number of patents – is of only limited value, because, on the one hand, numerous inventions will not be patented for reasons having to do with establishing power in the market and, on the other hand, others of course will be patented but may ultimately not be marketed or may serve exclusively to defend against competitive products (Archibugi 1992). However, the pessimistic assessments by the experts of the Commission successfully pushed first for research programmes and then for a revision of European biotech regulation.

European research programmes

As we have already noted, in a 1973 resolution on a common industrial policy the Council of the European Community recommended that enterprises with progressive technology be advanced. This intent was institutionalized in Article 130f–q of the Single European Act (see also chapter 4), wherein Article 130q forms the basis for the support for research facilities, universities and enterprises for the implementation of common projects. The multi-year Framework Programmes and research institutes, which are directed jointly by the Community, the member countries and the involved institutes and enterprises, are the main political support for research. The frameworks are guided by a jointly compiled catalogue of goals, by the principle of competitiveness and by the principle that research projects are exclusively composed of teams from member countries or associated states.

The value of furthering biotechnology research was still controversial in the 1970s. From the beginning, it was mainly France that advocated Community support for this effort (Moreau and Richonnier 1983; Boissière and Warusfel 1991), while the United Kingdom, Germany and the Netherlands placed their faith in the research efforts of their 'national champions'.[3]

---

[3] According to Sharp (1986: 183) in the 1980s France was initially the main state supporting bio-industry and by far the most active EC member. In 1982–3, expenditures for state biotechnology programmes in France totalled approximately US$ 117 million; in the United Kingdom US$ 43.9 million; in Germany US$38 million; in the Netherlands US$9.4 million; and in Italy US$4.6 million.

Thus, it was not until 1975 that the Commission was able to control the dissent among member countries and to arrive at an agreement on the first biotech research programme, the Biomolecular Engineering Programme (BEP), for the period 1982–5. Because of successful protests against the project of supporting medical research, the programme limited itself with respect to gene technology research projects to the areas of agriculture and foodstuffs, which was supposed to permit the networking of the greatest number of research teams and laboratories from the various member states.

Having carried out the Engineering Programme, with a budget of 15 million ECU, in 1985 the second programme, the Biotechnology Action Programme (BAP), with a budget of 55 million ECU, was launched. With the linking of Spanish and Portuguese labs to this project in 1987, this budget was increased by an additional 20 million ECU. The Action Programme was designed principally to support projects that serve the improvement of scientific infrastructure and education. Thus, the infrastructure was to be expanded by means of bio-databanks and 'concerted actions' as well as by dialogue between science, industry and the population. European Laboratories Without Walls (transnational networks of university and private laboratories) were supposed to delve deeply into specific questions and thus promote the understanding of biotechnological processes in Europe. Altogether thirty-five laboratories were formed with an average of six research teams from universities and enterprises. As a rule, the teams met every six months in one of the involved laboratories to exchange experiences. In addition, the academics visited one of the associated partner laboratories for a few weeks.

The Engineering and the Action Programmes were not elements of the First Framework Programme, which was adopted in 1983 by the Council and supported for the period 1984–7 with 3.75 billion ECU. Against the recommendations of the Commission, which reserved 80 million ECU in the programme budget for biotechnology, the Council of Ministers favoured a slight increase in the budget for information technology and ultimately appropriated only 37.1 million ECU for biotechnology (Ridinger 1991: 202). The biotech programme module in the Second and Third Framework Programmes was the Biotechnological Research for Innovation, Development and Growth in Europe (BRIDGE), which ran from 1989 to 1993 and absorbed 100 million ECU. In contrast to the Action Programme, larger projects were now given preference. Additionally, research teams from European non-EC member countries were considered. However, large enterprises were still to be prevented from participating in any projects other than those that were part of the European Research Coordination Agency (EUREKA) research programme, which was started in 1985.

Two agriculturally oriented programmes with concentrations in biotechnology and genetic engineering were running parallel to BRIDGE. The programme European Collaborative Linkage of Agriculture and Industry through Research (ECLAIR), endowed with 80 million ECU, was approved by the member states on 23 February 1989; it furthers the agro-industrial use of biotechnological knowledge. The programme Food Linked Agro-Industrial Research (FLAIR), endowed with 25 million ECU, was approved on 20 June 1989, and generally promotes biotechnological research in the food sector. In addition, on 29 June 1990, a human genome analysis programme was approved, which ran over three years and was supported by the Community with 15 million ECU.

In March 1992 the programme module BIOTECH I was approved by the Council, to run from 1992 to 1994 and with a budget of 164 million ECU. The goal of the programme was the production of biotechnological knowledge that can be utilized in the agricultural, industrial, health and environmental sectors. For this purpose, molecular research was to be particularly promoted, including such topics as protein structures and antibody–antigen interactions, cell and organism research and studies of the ecological as well as demographic aspects, that is, problems of the release and conservation of genetic resources.

In the Fourth Framework Programme biotechnology gained ground. The Commission considered henceforth the areas of information science, telecommunications, material sciences and biotechnology as key technologies deserving promotion. A further change of course was expressed in the effort to intensify cooperation with non-European, principally American and Japanese research teams. The programme module BIOTECH II, endowed with 552 million ECU, supports the coordination of resources, in particular of national research programmes, horizontal activities in the sense of demonstration projects, and investigations of the ethical, social and legal aspects and the socio-economic consequences of biotechnology as well as the promotion of dialogue among scholars, users and the public. The first announcement of the BIOTECH II programme on 17 July 1995, was completed after the filing of 294 proposals. Fifty-six proposals were temporarily selected; of these the 'cell factories' module, with twenty projects, is the largest area. Projects with biotechnological or gene technology content are also being carried out as part of the biomedicine and health research programmes (BIOMED I and II), with an emphasis on human genome analysis and the agriculture and fishery programme (Fisheries and Agro-Industrial Research).

Table 8.1. *Expenditure on the biosciences in the EU, 1984–98 (ECU million)*

	Framework Programme			
	I 1984–87	II 1987–91	III 1990–94	IV 1994–98
Biotechnology	37	120	164	552
Agro-industrial technologies	–	105	333	684
Agricultural competitiveness	–	55	–	–
Biomedicine and health	–	133	336	–
Biosciences and technologies for developing countries	–	–	111	–
Total for biotech	37	280	741	1,572
Grant total for all research	2,797	5,396	5,700	12,300

Source: various publications of the Commission

Table 8.1 shows that expenditures for EC research on biosciences in the period 1984–98 doubled in the Second and Fourth Framework Programmes when compared with the programmes that preceded them. In contrast, the increase in the Third Programme, prepared during the second half of the 1980s, was not very impressive. In sum, the expenditures for biotechnology in the narrow sense of the term (row 1 in table 8.1) rose from 37.1 million ECU in the First Framework Programme to 552 million ECU in the Fourth Framework Programme. Biotechnology gained ground at the expense of information technology in both relative and absolute terms. Thus, the share of expenditures for biotechnology in the broad sense of the term (all rows in table 8.1) rises from under 1.4 per cent in the First Framework Programme to 12.8 per cent in the Fourth. The opposite is true for the proportional expenditures for information and communications technology, which declined considerably from the Second to the Fourth Framework Programme, from 42 per cent (2,275 million ECU), to 28 per cent (3,405 million ECU), respectively. The Commission's proposal (9 April 1997) for the Fifth Framework Programme (1998–2002), which demands a budget of 16,300 million ECU, underlines the importance of biotechnology and will probably preserve its role in the European research agenda.

A prime example of an intensive use of the research programme is the Belgian agricultural biotechnological enterprise, Plant Genetic Systems (PGS). The enterprise was founded in 1982 by the University of Gent and employs 135 staff members; it participates in numerous joint ventures with North American and Indian enterprises and is a member of the Senior Advisory Group Biotechnology. From the beginning, PGS specialized in the manufacture of new kinds of grains, seed oils and vegetables for the European and Asiatic markets. It currently holds 43 patents and has an additional 142 worldwide patent proposals under examination. Its pioneer project was the development of a plant that is resistant to attack by insects. The plant was developed by inserting a gene that tells the plant cells to produce proteins that are poisonous to insects. Since the mid-1980s PGS has participated in every biotechnology programme of the Community and cooperated additionally in two EUREKA projects. PGS has also taken part in training programmes of the European Union (Human Capital and Mobility, 1990–4) and supports students by means of research scholarships.

Projects with biotechnological and gene technology content are also supported by two European research programmes, COST (European Cooperation in the field of Scientific and Technical Research) and EUREKA. Both programmes leave the content and financing of the projects to the participants; the programme office examines only the worthiness of each project and its term. Despite the minimal attractiveness of COST to private enterprises, the number of projects rose continuously from 7 (1971) to 115 (January 1995), thanks not least to an increase in the number of member countries. The 13 projects with biotechnological content (as of January 1995) concentrate on the agricultural sphere. EUREKA, which covers nine technological areas altogether, is more competitive and thus more attractive to the chemical and pharmaceutical industries. According to the 1989 annual report by the EUREKA secretariat (EUREKA 1989), since 1985 the number of new projects with a biotechnological content increased four times more than the number of new projects in the information technology sector. In 1989, of the total of 241 projects, only 24 per cent were in the area of information technology, and at that point already 19 per cent were in biotechnology and 18 per cent were in the field of robotics and automation. By the end of 1994, the sphere of medicine and biotechnology included more than 120 active and 30 completed projects. In October 1994, the completed biotech projects represented about 14 per cent (28 projects) of the total of 202 completed projects. Of the 657 active projects, 18.5 per cent were in the field of genetic engineering (EUREKA 1994). The high proportion of projects with biotechnological content should not obscure the fact, however, that the cost of these projects (730 million ECU) measured as a share of the total costs of all active projects (11,660 million ECU) was at the time a modest 6.3 percent. It is approximately the same in the Fourth Framework Programme.

Arrangements, directives and regulations

Since the early 1980s the Commission has willingly soothed critics of genetic engineering research and products with reference to the fact that European enterprises are subject to comparatively more instruction than their American and East Asian competitors. In fact, in its 1983 communication (CEC 1983b) the Commission had already insisted upon mandatory legal boundaries for genetic engineering research. By 1988 three directives had been presented to the Council of Ministers and the European Parliament for examination and subsequent approval in 1990: European Union Directive 90/219 regarding the application of genetically modified organisms in closed systems (lab Directive); Directive 90/220 regarding the intentional release of genetically altered organisms into the environment (deliberate release Directive); and Directive 90/679 regarding protection from the dangers of working with biological agents (protection Directive). Directive 93/39, which demands a uniform authorization process for bio-high-tech products, followed in 1993.

On 1 September 1994, Regulation 2100/94 on Community protection of the genetic resources of plants and animals came into effect. Since 1 October 1994, member states must also deal with the changes of Directive 93/114, which replaces Directive 70/524/EEC regarding additives in animal feed. Additives that consist of genetically modified organisms are also now being newly reconsidered. In the second half of the 1990s other measures were also being debated, including a directive proposed by the Commission (91/414) regarding the evaluation of the dangers of genetically modified pesticides, amendments to Directives 70/457/EEC (seed traffic) and 70/458/EEC (catalogue of sorts) and a regulation of the Council regarding Community protection of plants' and animals' genetic resources. Also under discussion is a bio-ethics convention of the Council of Europe.

As controversial now as then is the evaluation of products containing the growth hormone bovine somatotropin. The determining factor in the decision by the Commission to forbid the use of this gene-technology-based animal medication in member states is Directive 87/22, whereby all high-grade gene technology medicines are to be examined before their use is authorized by the Community. After years of clarification of the after-effects (a moratorium) through the Committee for Veterinary Medicine Products and the Ethical Advisory Group, in 1993 the Commission certified two products from Monsanto and Eli Lilly, with the implication that their use would be unobjectionable. Taking into account the planned agricultural reform, which argues against further expansion of meat and milk production, the Commission, however, has up to now forbidden the use of bovine somatotropin products and in December 1995 extended the moratorium for five more years. Moreover, on 1 January 1995, Directive 93/41/EEC superseded the standard Directive 87/22/EEC regarding the authorization of technologically high-grade medicines.

In 1986, the Council of Ministers had already recommended Community regulation and acceleration of the test process for biotechnological medicines. With the opening of the European Medication Evaluation Agency (EMEA) on 26 January 1995, this recommendation was realized. As a result, all medicines developed in the European Union are now subjected to a standardized authorization process. This process is supposed to last 300 days, considerably less than the 500 days required in the USA. Until now, European pharmaceutical enterprises had to announce a newly developed product in all countries, and in the most unfavourable case the authorization process could take up to six years.

Since summer 1997, a regulation on 'novel food' (258/97/EC) has been in effect. It requires obligatory labelling for all European Union states of any genetically modified foods and food ingredients including the genetic engineering procedure if the genetic modification can be proved. This regulation was put forward as early as 1992, but because of furious opposition on the part of consumer associations and ecologically oriented powers in the Council of Ministers and in the mediation committee of the European Parliament no consensus could be reached on it. After lengthy negotiations between the Commission, the Parliament (which had to consider no fewer than sixty-three amendments), and the member countries, the first compromise proposed by the mediation committee of the Council of Ministers failed on 6 June 1995. Sweden, Denmark, Germany and Austria and the majority of the Parliament pleaded for a restrictive labelling requirement, whereas the Commission, the Group of Advisers on the Ethical Aspects of Biotechnology and the biotech enterprises as well as the United Kingdom, France, Belgium, Finland, Italy and Ireland considered such a conspicuous declaration to be hostile to consumers and wanted to label only materials that could cause allergic reactions.

The views of enterprises and environmental groups with reference to the content of the so-called bio-patent Directive are still incompatible. The European Patent Convention of 5 October 1973, which seventeen West European countries including Switzerland have signed, anticipated that animals and plants are themselves patentable. Patent protection is granted, however, only for species and plant varieties that are not marked with breed- and/or variety-specific characteristics. According to Article 53 of the Convention, patenting of inventions is also forbidden if 'their publication or utilization would offend the public order or morals'. The Council of Europe's European agreement for the protection of vertebrates used in testing and for other scientific purposes, which was also ratified in 1993 by Switzerland, allows gene technology experiments with animals only if the terms of the agreement regarding animal testing are observed. Since 6 February 1994, the European agreement for the protection of animals employed in agriculture has contained a protective clause for working animals that are the result of either traditional animal breeding or genetic operations. Natural and artificial breeding methods as well as food additives that cause the animals pain and suffering are forbidden.

In 1983 the Commission moved to create mandatory legal protection within the Community for intellectual property in biotechnology processes, following the American model (see CEC 1983b). This demand was later emphatically strengthened by the Commission and has been renewed since then in all official documents. The directive was intended to contain mandatory patent regulation, to guarantee the rights of research institutions, to harmonize the permission procedures for bioproducts on the European domestic market and thereby to promote gene technology research. From the point of view of the Commission, the employers' associations and the Group of Advisers on the Ethical Aspects of Biotechnology (see below), a regulation based on the American model was indispensable and ethically justifiable. Enterprises would be ready to invest in research only if biotechnological inventions were protected for a certain period from access by the competition. In 1988, Directorate General III for Internal Market and Industrial Affairs published a directive entitled 'Proposal for a Council Directive on the legal protection of biotechnology inventions' (COM (99) 496 final – SYN 159).

Under the terms of the European patent agreement, the corresponding patent applications are currently examined by the European Patent Office in Munich. By the end of 1995, the Office had approved the first two patents for animal cells: one for the 'Harvard cancer mouse', which had been patented in 1988 in the United States, and one for a type of cell that produces tumour-forming proteins. Altogether, 300 registrations for genetically modified organisms are currently being processed. In November 1995 a three-day hearing took place at the Patent Office in Munich regarding the 1992 approval of the so-called cancer mouse patent (patent No. 0 169 672). This was the first patent for a genetically altered animal – a mouse that easily becomes ill with cancer.

Despite massive propaganda on the part of the Commission, on 1 March 1995, the European Parliament rejected the first bio-patent proposal put forward jointly by the Council and a parliamentary delegation, by a vote of 240 to 188, with 23 abstentions. Representatives of the parliamentary majority – Socialists, Greens, and Communists – supported by Greenpeace and expert opinion from the Freiburg Ecology Institute argued that genetically modified life forms must be seen not as inventions but as discoveries, and as such are not subject to protection. For the first time, the European Parliament exercised its veto power in the decision-making process over recommendations of the Commission. Opponents of bio-patents spoke accordingly of a 'historic' decision, while representatives of the Commission and the Council suspected that with this decision the technological gap between Europe and the USA and Japan would only increase. However, on 6 July 1998, the European Parliament ended its opposition and adopted the revised Directive for Patents in Biotechnology (98/44/EC), which harmonizes national laws on biotechnological inventions but also provides that plant and animal varieties and the processes of cloning human beings are not patentable.

A further victory for environmentalist organizations was the de facto moratorium on the approval of genetically manipulated organisms, on 24 June 1999, in Luxembourg. In their declarations the ministers of environment of Denmark, France, Greece, Italy, Luxembourg, Austria, Belgium, Finland, Germany, the Netherlands and Sweden demanded a more rigorous and transparent legal framework concerning potential risks to health and the environment.

The dialogue between the Commission and the interest organizations

From the beginning the Commission has attempted to incorporate representatives of economic interests into its policy formulation process. Thus, the formation of European umbrella organizations was actively promoted and their experts were invited to participate in the advisory bodies of the Commission. In contrast to diverse economic and cultural interests, which primarily make use of informal channels of communication (lobbying), at the moment the biotech interests are well articulated in these advisory bodies. Nevertheless, European biotechnology corporatism has remained fragmentary until now. This is due to a weakly centralized system of associations and to narrow and selective accessibility of the corporatist committees (corporatism without ecological interests), but also to an unreadiness on the part of the Commission to institutionalize dialogue with interest groups.

Interest organizations in the biotechnology sector

The biotechnology policy of the European Community is influenced by a variety of interest organizations. Whereas European industrial branch associations, large enterprises and agricultural associations are working for deregulation, environmentalists, consumer organizations and the chemical workers' unions are fighting for restrictive directives and regulations.

Biotech producers' associations

The interests of the biotech manufacturers at the level of the European Union are manifested principally through the large umbrella organizations of the agrochemical and pharmaceutical industries. In addition, the large European pharmaceutical manufacturers have their own lobbyists in Brussels and, since 1989, an organization that pursues biotech interests exclusively.

Prior to the conclusion of the Single European Act the interests of the biotech departments of large enterprises were principally represented by the European umbrella organizations of the chemical and pharmaceutical industries. In 1972 the European Chemical Industry Council (CEFIC) was founded, which today includes umbrella organizations from the EU member states and from Switzerland and Norway. In light of the growing influence of the ecology movement on national legislation, the chemistry industry expected that its association would advocate industry-friendly regulation at the European level: 'The hope is that at the European level the legislation can either be halted by opposition from other states or, at least, can be significantly modified in an intergovernmental arena at a distance from the intrusion of domestically powerful environmental groups' (Grant et al. 1989: 182).

The European Federation of Pharmaceutical Industry Associations (EFPIA), founded in 1979, became the second important biotech lobbyist alongside the CEFIC during the 1980s. Umbrella organizations from fourteen Community member countries (with the exception of Luxembourg) and from Switzerland and Norway belong to it. Thus, some umbrella organizations, such as the Swiss Gesellschaft der Chemischen Industrie, are members of the organizations of both the chemical industry and the pharmaceutical industry. In contrast to CEFIC, however, the spectrum of activities of EFPIA is limited to research, production and the marketing of medicines. Close contacts exist therefore between it and Directorates General III, XII and XI, which are responsible for the proposals for Directives 90/219, 90/220 and 90/679. Other important points of contact include: Directorate General XV, which is concerned with the patenting of medicines; Directorate General I (External Relations), which is concerned with expansion to the east; and Directorate General V, which deals with health issues. Above all, EFPIA advocates the deregulation of the biotech industry and a simplification of the medicine testing process.

The European Federation of Animal Health (FEDESA), founded in 1987, is also in favour of deregulation. This organization was founded in response to the 1985 EC Regulation 89/649, which forbids the use of hormone preparations in cattle-raising. Ten umbrella organizations from EU member states and Switzerland belong to this association of hormone producers. Similar to the composition of the CEFIC, there are also twenty-three associated enterprises with offices in Europe and the United States. The association is mainly focused on attaining an all-European authorization for the use of the growth hormone bovine somatotropin and/or a suspension of the moratorium on its use passed by the Commission. For this purpose the association seeks to maintain a high profile in the committees of Directorate General VI (Agriculture). Additionally it is a member of the committee for the formation of the European medicine testing institute of Directorate General III (Internal Market and Industrial Affairs).

The European agricultural association, COPA, and the association of agricultural cooperatives, COGECA, also work closely with the association of hormone producers (Burkhardt-Reich and Schumann 1983). The main goal of both agricultural associations is the promotion of biotechnological and gene technology processes, which result in animals with more meat as well as rot- and pest-resistant plants.

The representation of biotech interests by CEFIC, EFPIA and FEDESA became channelled and coordinated by the Forum for European Bioindustry Coordination (FEBC), founded in 1993. According to its own statements, the Forum represents enterprises with altogether 5 million employees, of whom approximately 184,000 are working directly in modern biotechnology. The main goals of the Forum are the revision of Directives 90/219 and 90/220 (see above) and the patenting of biotechnological and gene technology processes. The Forum represents only matters that are supported by all member associations. Therefore, the industrial branch associations pursue additional lobbying on their own.[4]

The Forum was the successor organization to the European

---

[4] Thus the Association of Microbial Food Enzyme Producers in Western Europe (AMFEP) demands, for example, in connection with the 1989 guideline proposal on food additives, that the role of enzymes in food production has also to be considered.

Biotechnology Coordination Group (EBCG), which was founded at the wish of Directorate General XII in 1985 and originally included the following branch organizations: chemicals (CEFIC), pharmaceuticals (EFPIA), food and feed enzymes (AMFEP), food (CIAA), pesticides (GIFAP), patents (EBPG), agrochemicals (ECRAB), plant breeders (COMASSO), animal health products (FEDESA) and plants and seeds (GIBIP). New additions during the 1990s include the Euro-associations of feedstuff additives producers (FEFANA), compound feed producers (FEFAC), plant protection products (ECPA), diagnostic products (EDMA), EuropaBio (Senior Advisory Group Biotechnology) and the Farm Animal Industrial Platform (FAIP). In the meantime, the patents association, the producers of agrochemicals and the producers of pesticides had all left the Forum.

During this period (1989–91) eight national organizations (Belgium, Spain, Denmark, France, Italy, the Netherlands, Portugal, the United Kingdom) also belonged to the Coordination Group. However, in 1992 they left the Forum and formed the European Secretariat of National Biotechnology Associations (ESNBA), headquartered in Brussels. According to the Secretariat, the Forum was neglecting the interests of the small and medium-sized enterprises. Although dialogue between the Forum and the Secretariat is only rudimentary, close contacts exist between the plant breeders, the plants and seeds producers and Directorate General XI (Environment, Consumer Protection and Nuclear Safety).

Discontented with Directives 90/219 and 90/220 and with lobbying through the European Biotechnology Coordination Group, seven large biotech enterprises (Ferruzi Group, Hoechst, ICI, Monsanto Europe, Rhône-Poulenc, Sandoz and Unilever) founded a committee within the umbrella organization of the chemical industry in 1989, known as the Senior Advisory Group Biotechnology (SAGB). In their opinion, the Coordination Group proved strikingly ineffective during the 1980s, and suffered above all from the fact that the small and medium-sized enterprises, thanks to the memberships of the national biotech associations, carried more weight. In addition, for most of the industrial branch associations, biotechnology was just one focal point among many. The rapid increase in membership and the expansion of the scope of activity led in June 1991 to the organizational separation of the Advisory Group from CEFIC. The first president of the Group was Peter Doyle, general director of British Zeneca. On 23 November 1993, Jürgen Drews, a member of the medical faculty of the University of Heidelberg and a staff member of Swiss Hoffmann-La Roche, assumed the chairmanship.

By 1995 the Advisory Group already had thirty-two member enterprises, which together accounted for approximately 2 million employees and over US$305 billion in turnover, and invested approximately US$17 billion in research and development. The Group works closely with the Forum for European Bioindustry Coordination, which is expressed, among other ways, by the fact that both organizations have their general secretariats in the same building.

The model for the Group is the influential US Biotechnology Industry Organization (BIO), to which approximately 800 enterprises and university research institutes belong. Along with the Japan Bioindustry Association (JBA) and the Industrial Biotechnology Association of Canada (IBAC), both organizations belong to the International Bioindustry Forum (IBF), founded in 1990. The Group is a member of a Steering Committee, an executive body to which the managements of the member enterprises belong, and a Strategic Committee, which bolsters its arguments through position papers developed by work teams.

The main goal of the Senior Advisory Group is the creation of a positive regulatory climate in Europe. According to the Group, Europe suffers from a lack of acceptance of biotechnology and genetic engineering by the public and by the various governments. If this did not change in the course of the 1990s, the Senior Advisory Group feared a massive shift in production, which would be accompanied by a loss of jobs and taxes. Therefore, the Group demands from the European Union that it revise the existing directives and make them more friendly to enterprises. Research policy is of secondary importance for Group members, since they have sufficient capacity for conducting their own research and want to use their research results privately. Moreover, the EU programmes basically promote only competitive research and thus, in comparison with the EUREKA programme, are comparatively unattractive.

In addition, the Senior Advisory Group compiles position papers on European biotechnology policy. In 1990 three position papers were published, which provide information on the direction of their representation. In the first paper, published in January 1990, *Community Policy for Biotechnology: Priorities and Actions* (SAGB 1990a), the economic significance of biotechnology for the pharmaceutical, agricultural, food and environment sectors was highlighted. Because of the neglect of European bio-industry it was to be expected that the United States and Japan would expand their current advantage even further. The demand made to the European Community, therefore, was that it create a single legal framework and industry-friendly boundaries for research. The discussion of corresponding directives and regulations was to be transparent and accompanied by formally institutionalized consultation with affected interest groups. It was noted that the member enterprises of the Senior Advisory Group were already part of such consultation processes in their home countries. More general suggestions followed for improving the competitiveness of European bio-industry. For example, it was suggested that biotechnology research in the European Union adopt a more distinctly European profile and that it support more ambitious projects and research topics.

In July 1990 the paper *Economic Benefits and European Competitiveness* (SAGB 1990b) was published. Once again, it called attention to the economic significance of biotechnology and the competitive weakness brought on by over-regulation. This weakness is also expressed by the asymmetrical flow of investment from Europe to the United States and the comparatively few European patent registrations. This state of affairs was blamed not only on over-regulation and a lack of public acceptance of biotechnology, but also on comparatively meagre public research resources and, compared with the United States, decentralized research activities at the level of the member states. Thus the demand was made for biotechnology research in Europe to be coordinated analogously to the United States at the federal level.

In October 1990 the interest expressed in January for an institutionalized dialogue was concretized. In the paper *Creation of a Community Task Force and an Independent Advisory Body* (SAGB 1990c), two new (quasi-)corporatist institutions were demanded. Analogously to the areas of information technology and small and medium enterprises, whose Task Forces were later transformed into independent Directorates General, the Community was to create a committee with representatives of the Commission, bio-industry and bioscience, in order to elaborate mandatory political measures on the basis of a coherent programme and to bring about the implementation of these measures. Along with this, an independent commission of experts was to be formed to deal with the ethical aspects of biotechnology.

In 1993 the Commission published a White Paper in which biotechnology was granted a central role as future engine of growth (see the first section of this chapter). According to statements by Stefan Ryser, a member of the Strategic Committee, the Senior Advisory Group had not collaborated on the text, although it was made aware of pre-publication drafts of passages relevant to biotechnology and was permitted to comment on them. Thus the Group commented very favourably on the suggestions of the White Paper. In April 1994, the paper *Biotechnology Policy in the European Union. Prescriptions for Growth, Competitiveness and*

Employment: A Response to the Union's 1993 White Paper on Growth, Competitiveness and Employment (SAGB 1994a) was published. As supporting measures, the Group demanded a dismantling of regulations and investment barriers, tax privileges for enterprises that invest in biotechnology, education and training programmes for small and medium-sized enterprises, as well as better management of biotechnology policy by means of a Biotechnology Task Force.

Similarly, in April 1994 the paper *Biotechnology Policy in the European Union: Competitiveness, Investment and the Cycle of Innovation* (SAGB 1994b) predicted that European enterprises would be inclined to shift their research and development elsewhere. This process could only be stopped if the research potential in the EU could be preserved and readiness of enterprises to engage in research and development was not hindered through regulation. Additional demands were made that gene technology processes and inventions be granted patent rights and that research and education at a European level be strengthened.

On 17 May 1994, the Senior Advisory Group commented on the Commission's 1993 White Paper and proposed a plan of action containing the following points (*Agence Europe*, cited in Reuters EU Briefings):

(a) The creation of an ad hoc, high-level task force for biotechnology, which would deal with questions related to the economy and competitiveness. This unit would include representatives of the national authorities (ministries of economics and industry), the European Commission (Biotechnology Coordination Committee), industry, the world of finance, employers, the agricultural sector and academia. As an advisory body, its main task would be to develop goals and concrete measures that the Community should take in this field. The decision to set up this high-level group was expected to be taken prior to the Industry Council in November; the Senior Advisory Group hoped that this matter would be addressed at the European summit in Corfu at the end of June.

(b) The implementation of a five-point plan of action to improve the competitiveness of Europe's biotechnology industry: (1) ensure more effectiveness, greater transparency and more predictability regarding Community regulations; (2) encourage and facilitate investment in the biotechnology sector, notably by creating dynamic small and medium-sized enterprises – to this end, there must be better protection for intellectual property, measures must be taken to stimulate the European capital markets, public aid must be granted to innovative basic research, etc.; (3) encourage risk investment in biotechnology innovation (tax incentives, alleviation of costs and other constraints that weigh on enterprises, especially small and medium-sized enterprises, etc.); (4) improve the qualifications and flexibility of workers (more political and financial support for the training of workers, mutual recognition of qualifications, etc.); (5) provide broad-based leadership for biotechnology competitiveness in key sectors: industry, agriculture, political leaders, academia.

In 1995 the Senior Advisory Group, representing large firms, and the European Secretariat of National Bioindustry Associations, representing small and medium-sized enterprises, decided to share their offices in Brussels. In late 1996, both organizations even decided to create a new association, EuropaBio, which represents forty-seven big companies (including seven member enterprises of the European Roundtable of Industrialists: Akzo Nobel, Bayer, Danone, Nestlé, Solvay, Rhône-Poulenc and Unilever)[5] and twelve national associations representing some 700 biotech companies (as of June 1999). In 1998, Pol Bamelis (Bayer) succeeded its first chairman Jürgen Drews (Hoffman-La Roche). According to its report *Benchmarking the Competitiveness of Biotechnology in Europe* (EuropaBio 1997), Europe's position in biotechnology improved during the 1990s. However, the USA had still been more successful than Europe in terms of turnover, research and development expenditures, number of companies and number of employees. The report therefore recommends governments, media, universities and research institutes to take actions to create a more positive business environment.

Scientists, conservationists, consumers and unions

The most important interest group of scientists is the European Federation of Biotechnology (EFB), founded in 1978 in Interlaken. The Federation has its main office in Frankfurt and includes about sixty groups. The Federation is committed to the use of biotechnology in environmental protection and is in close contact with Directorate General XI. As part of the Task Group on Public Perceptions of

---

[5] The membership list, as of 1999, is as follows: Advanta, AgrEvo, Akzo Nobel, Ares-Serono, BASF, Bayer, Biogen, Bioresearch Ireland, Boehringer Ingelheim, Boehringer Mannheim, British Biotechnology, Cargill, Celltech, Centocor, Danone, Dekalb Genetics, Dompé Biotec, Dow AgroSciences, DSM-Gist, DuPont, Eli Lilly, Evotec BioSystems, Hoffmann-La Roche, Genencor, Genset, Genzyme, Hoechst, Innogenetics, KWS, Limagrain, Monsanto, Nestlé, Novartis, Novo Nordisk, PepsiCo, Pharmacia, Pharming, Pioneer Genetique, Procter & Gamble, Rhône-Poulenc, Rothschild Asset Management, Schering, Smithkline Beecham, Solvay, Transgene, Unilever, Zeneca.

Biotechnology, founded in 1991, its chairman, John Durant, is in charge of the Eurobarometer items on biotechnology and documents them on behalf of the Commission (Durant 1992; Durant, Bauer and Gaskell 1998).

Environmental protection interests perceive the four principal organizations reflecting their interests to be: the European Environmental Bureau (EEB), the Coordination Européenne des Amis de la Terre (CEAT), the Worldwide Fund for Nature (WWF) and Greenpeace. The most active are Greenpeace and the CEAT, a network of thirty independent, national environmental organizations in twenty-nine countries. At the beginning of 1995, the EU unit of Greenpeace declared itself in opposition to the bio-patent proposal compromise of the mediation committee of the European Parliament and the Council of Ministers. In a communication directed to the parliamentarians, Greenpeace labelled the patenting of genetically modified creatures 'immoral'. In addition, Greenpeace pointed out that bio-patents would not solve the global hunger problem, since the patent owners would logically like to sell their products at the highest possible price. According to Greenpeace, bio-patents should not serve to further the industry and their desire for profits – at the expense of more moral, socially beneficial and environmental values.

Owing to a shortage of financial and personnel resources, in 1991 the four environmental organizations formed the Biotechnology Clearinghouse, which obtains information about technology policy projects of the Commission. Although the Clearinghouse was financially supported by the Concertation Unit of Biotechnology in Europe (CUBE; see below), it was dissolved in 1995. It was replaced by the office of Friends of the Earth Biotechnology Europe (FEBE), which both obtains information and develops common positions in the policy formation process. In contrast to the Clearinghouse, Friends of the Earth initially employed three people and was supported financially by the national Friends of the Earth organizations. In this division of financial support, the German Bund für Natur und Umwelt (BUND) is responsible for the area of biotechnology.

Consumer interests are currently represented by the Bureau of European Consumers' Organizations (Bureau Européen des Unions des Consommateurs: BEUC). The most important national consumer associations belong to the Bureau; however, the office in Brussels is financially supported by the Community and thus engages in only moderate criticism of the proposals of the Commission. The Bureau advocated the most restrictive kind of obligatory labelling as part of the novel food Regulation, although it does not fundamentally oppose novel food. In a press release of 14 February 1994, the Bureau stated that it is not opposed to research into, or the production of, novel foods and novel food ingredients. Indeed, it recognized the potential benefits that these could have for consumers and the environment. The Bureau did demand, however, a highly visible and recognizable label for genetically modified organisms and a declaration of all ingredients manufactured with gene technology. The Bureau is also critical of the position of the Ethics Group of the European Biotechnology Coordination Committee (see below), according to which consumers need only be informed that a product contains genetically manipulated ingredients.

In comparison with the environmental protection and consumer organizations, up to now the trade unions have played a subordinate role in biotech affairs. The European Federation of the Chemical Unions (FESCID), founded in 1988, is a union committee of the European Trade Union Confederation (ETUC). It primarily advocates workplace protection in bio-industry; thus, it welcomed Directive 90/679 on protection from dangers associated with working with biological agents (the protection Directive). Because of limited financial, personnel (fewer than five staff positions) and specialized resources, up to now the Federation has limited itself to the demand for safety measures. Moreover, in contrast to the environmental protection organizations, the trade unions are comparatively biotechnology friendly; in fact, they fear that strict regulation will lead to a shift of research and production sites and thus in the long run threatens those jobs.

Levels of corporatist dialogue

The most important level of the dialogue between members of the European Union and biotech organizations are the committees, which can be convened on an ad hoc basis by officials of the Commission with regard to planned directives and regulations. The paramount importance of these committees for the European biotech producers is an expression of the extraordinary role of the Commission in the legislative process. According to the Community statutes (Article 155 of the original agreement founding the EEC), EU norms are initiated not by the Council of Ministers, but rather by the Commission. Article 152 anticipates, of course, that the Commission must take into consideration the suggestions of the Council. However, the fact remains that the Council of Ministers has no right of initiative. Thus, in the event of passivity on the part of the Commission, the Council's only recourse under Article 175(1) is to file a complaint for inactivity.

Interest groups are therefore forced to make their presence known at the initiation of a directive or regulation. The starting point for a proposal from the Commission to the Council of Ministers is a draft text, which as a rule is initiated by one of the higher officials in the affected Directorate General and is drawn up by a competent specialist. After that, the draft will be discussed with all interested Directorates General and Commission agencies and in the committees, in which both representatives of member states as well as private interests sit. Often Commission officials also travel to the capitals of the member countries to sound out the level of acceptance of the proposal. After an initial revision, the text is delivered to the cabinet of the Commissioner responsible for the matter. After a second revision by the cabinet, the text ultimately reaches the Commissioner. If the text is approved by this Commissioner, the General Secretariat will be asked to present the draft to the Commissioners. Next, the cabinet members discuss the draft at their weekly meeting. If no further differences of opinion exist, the text is recommended to the Commissioners for acceptance, that is, for publication. If disagreements still exist, the Commissioners will debate further and, if need be, the text is sent back to the responsible Directorate General for another revision.

Since in the second phase the text of draft directives and regulations will be examined by the European Parliament and possibly by the Economic and Social Committee, the views of interest groups, professional lobbyists, politicians, officials of the Committee of Permanent Representatives (COREPER) and the responsible committees of the Parliament and the Economic and Social Committee will be sought out in informal conversations and in the committees.

After publication the text is transferred to the Council of Ministers, which presents it to the European Parliament and the Economic and Social Committee for examination. In both main consulting bodies of the European Union the text will now be discussed in the responsible committees, criticized, and, if necessary, revised. In this way, positions are taken on the issue after a period of six to twelve months.

The committee structure involves more than 300 standing committees and more than 1,000 issue-specific ad hoc advisory bodies. According to Grote (1990: 243) between 1980 and 1989 the number of standing committees increased from 197 to 248. Here it must be understood that in the period 1980–4 the number increased from 197 to 241, then declined to 225 in 1985, only to rise again to its current number. The most extensive Directorate General is the one responsible for agriculture (DG VI), with fifty-eight standing committees in 1989. It is followed by Directorate General III (Internal Market and Industrial Affairs) with thirty-three; and Directorate General V (Employment, Social Affairs, Education) and Directorate General XI (Environment, Consumer Protection and Nuclear Safety) with twenty-six standing committees each. In addition to these Commission committees, on an annual basis there are more than 1,000 unspecified meetings of Commission authorities with representatives of public and private institutions and organizations (Budget of the EC, Article 250).

In addition, there are numerous committees in which an exchange of experience and opinion occurs between the Commission and interest groups. One example is Committee 233 on biotechnology of the European Committee of Standardization. The committee is concerned with creating uniform technical norms and instructions in the interest of consumers. Participation in the committee is particularly important for national associations, since manufacturers always seek to protect the norms of their production location, especially from foreign competition. The starting point for this committee was the view expressed in the White Paper (CEC 1985: 19) that the danger of damage and accidents could be decreased by means of uniform technical instructions. The infrastructure for Committee 233 is provided by Directorates General III and XII; it is currently charged with formulating the technical safety requirements of the three biotechnology Directives. Since the adoption of the novel food Regulation in 1997, the committee has also been discussing the manner in which genetically modified foods and food ingredients should be labelled.

To coordinate the work of all the sections in the Commission that deal with biotechnological questions, the Inter-service Biotechnology Steering Committee was formed in 1984. This committee of departmental representatives was charged with implementing the stated goals of the 1983 EC summit in Stuttgart. In light of strong differences of opinion and problems of coordination among the various Directorates General, in 1985 the committee proposed the formation of the European Biotechnology Coordination Group.

Faced with widespread public scepticism regarding genetic engineering, the BRIDGE programme (see above) was supposed to contribute to 'an increase of public awareness and understanding of biotechnology'. The task of creating public acceptance was entrusted to the Concertation Unit of Biotechnology in Europe (CUBE). CUBE was formed in 1984 as a section of DG XII and served as the secretariat for the Biotechnology Steering Committee. CUBE maintained close contact with the bio-industry associations and supported the dissolution of the Coordination Group, which it reproached for its inability to create consensus.[6] As the result of furious criticism on the part of the environmental organizations that CUBE was conducting free public relations work in favour of biotech production, it was dissolved in 1992 (Dreyer 1993).

The central forum for the exchange of experience and opinion between interest groups and the Commission is currently the issue-specific biotechnology roundtables, to which a selection of representatives are invited by Euro-associations and industry. On 11 July 1992, the general secretary of the European Biotechnology Coordination Group succeeded for the first time in conducting a general discussion with representatives of industry, labour unions and environmental organizations. On 29 September 1993, a discussion was conducted on the regulatory aspects of biotechnology. In a communication of the Commission to the Council, the European Parliament and the Economic and Social Committee explicit reference is made to the dialogue with the biotech interests: 'They will make further efforts, as they have in the past, to conduct roundtable discussions' (COM (1992) 219 final: 2). According to statements by EU officials, however, the Commission does not intend to institutionalize roundtable discussions. Thus, in 1996 the Coordination Group renounced the 'table talks' with interest organizations. Instead, a so-called 'Trialogue' was held in March 1996, in which the Council, the European Parliament and the Commission jointly discussed how to proceed in light of the failed bio-patent Directive.

Interest groups are also contacted by the independent Group of Advisers on the Ethical Implications of Biotechnology working for the Commission since November 1991. In the mandated periods 1991-3 and 1994-6 the Ethics Group consisted of eight scientists, who provide non-binding expert opinion regarding ethically controversial projects at the request of EU sections. Chair of the group is Mrs Noëlle Lenoir, chair of the UNESCO International Bioethics Committee. In the course of their work, they also consult with representatives of industry. Beginning in 1998 the Ethics Group was integrated into the European Group on Ethics in Sciences and New Technologies, which henceforth concerned itself with the ethical aspects of biotechnology as well as information technology.

Since 1995, Directorate General XII has included a Task Force on Vaccines and Viral Diseases. This committee is authorized to coordinate among agencies of the Commission that deal with vaccines and viruses with respect to the development of industry projects in the Community. The basis for this committee is Articles 130k, l, n of the Single

---

[6] *European Biotechnology Information Service*, No. 4 (July 1991).

European Act, which allows the European Union to work together with individual member states in the field of research. The task force has two assignments: (1) to provide an overview of the research situation in Europe; and (2) to elaborate a 'research action plan' to improve the position of European industry.

Figure 8.1 shows the different levels of dialogue between the Commission and the interest organizations. Above the thick dotted line are located the committees and Directorates General of the European Union that are directly involved with biotechnological questions. Below the dotted line are the main organizations with biotech interests. On the left and upper right side are the producers' associations and on the lower right side the environmental organizations. It should be noted that in the mid-1990s the office of Friends of the Earth Europe worked for the member organizations of CEAT, Greenpeace and the WWF at the same time. On the upper right side is the umbrella organizations of environmentalists and scientists as well as EuropaBio, the new common federation of the Senior Advisory Group Biotechnology and the European Secretariat of National Bioindustry Associations.

In addition to these formal connections, all organizations below the thick dotted line have informal contacts with the listed Commission committees. Thick lines denote especially close relationships between committee members and/or members of interest organizations. Thus, producer associations have close contact with the DG III (Internal Market and Industrial Affairs) as well as with the European Biotechnology Coordination Committee.

Bio-industry interests flow together even further in the formation of the research programmes. Thus DG XII consults not only with independent scientists, but also with experts from industrial enterprises regarding the content of the research programme. There are of course numerous issue-specific committees in the European Union in which independent scientists examine the proposals for the research programme. However, these committees become involved only after the directive of the research has already been initiated and exclusively developed by scientists and associations (Tulder and Junne 1986; Ridinger 1991). The body responsible for the biotechnology module in the Framework Programmes is department E 'Bioscience and Biotechnology' in DG XII. It is incumbent on the department to disseminate the programme documents, to appraise the project proposals and to supervise the projects.

The central research policy committee, to which the representatives of bio-industry have access, is the Industry Research and Development Advisory Committee (IRDAC). This committee is convened by the

Biotechnology in the European Union

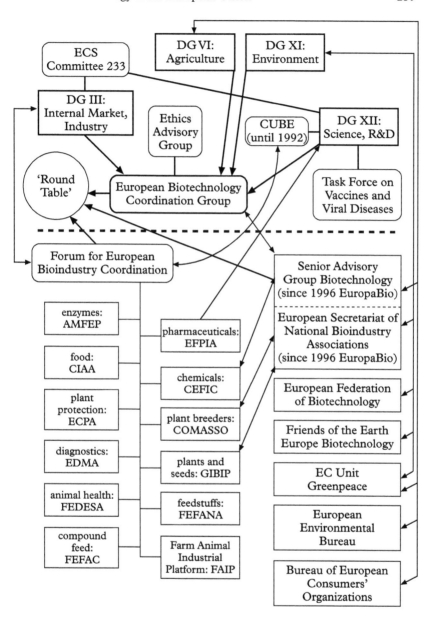

Figure 8.1 Dialogue committees of the Commission and interest organizations

Commission. Its diverse teams debate the individual parts of the current research programme and ultimately make a proposal regarding the content of the programme to the cabinet of the Commissioner responsible for research, technology and development. Before the cabinet's detailed proposal reaches the Council, the European Parliament and the Economic and Social Committee, it will be evaluated by the Committee of Experts of Science and Technology (CODEST), to which scientists from public and private enterprises belong. The practice of the consultation process shows, however, that a cabinet proposal does not as a rule encounter any serious opposition, although the budget proposed by the Commission is often modified by the Council.

A further possibility for contacts with responsible officials in DG XII is afforded by the 'industry platforms', that is, branch-specific events, at which possible commercial applications of the results of the research are demonstrated. Thus, since 1997 a Structural Biology Industrial Platform (not shown in fig. 8.1) meets in members' companies or in association with other events.

Current challenges: transregional enterprise alliances and the lack of legitimacy

Although the recent report by EuropaBio (1997) and the reader by Senker (1998) suggest that Europe's bio-industry has improved its technological performance, European biotech producers still argue that the efforts of the Commission are not sufficient to increase their competitiveness. Thus large firms, unlike the university institutes, have been only moderately interested in offers of pre-competitive research. This is not surprising, given that companies such as the large European pharmaceuticals producers, for example, have sufficient research capacities and would not want to relinquish their results to any potential competitor. Also, European enterprises do not appear any more favourably disposed to inevitable cooperation with European rather than with American or Japanese enterprises (see Tulder and Junne 1986; Junne 1992; Ohmae 1985; Esser 1993). Although the Commission is participating meanwhile in an EU–US task force for biotechnological research, which conducted a workshop on 'Methods of Communicating Biotechnology with the Public' in March 1992 and a conference on the application of biotechnology to environmental protection in October 1994, now, as before, the idea of global competition between Europe, the USA and Japan prevails in the Commission.

Nevertheless, one cannot overlook the fact that many 'European champions' have already formed numerous alliances with American and

Japanese enterprises while at the same time competing with other European champions. According to Hagedoorn and Schakenraad (1990: 177), of a total of 980 agreements signed in the field of biotechnology prior to 1988, 24 per cent (229) were between European enterprises, 1 per cent (188) were between European and American enterprises, and 3 per cent (30) were between European and Japanese enterprises. This finding is corroborated by my network analysis of joint ventures between the forty-five biotech enterprises, which are listed by Hagedoorn and Schakenraad in the appendix of their article (p. 190). Thus we can identify twenty-five groups of actors, all of whom directly interact with each other (1-cliques; see Wasserman and Faust 1994: 253ff), sharing at least three enterprises. However, only two of these cliques include enterprises exclusively from EU member countries: (a) Akzo Nobel (the Netherlands), Gist-Brocades (the Netherlands) and Royal Dutch–Shell (the Netherlands/Great Britain), and (b) Bayer (Germany), Hoechst (Germany) and Kabivitrum (Sweden). An additional clique includes Rhône-Poulenc (France), Royal Dutch–Shell and Ciba-Geigy from non-EU Switzerland, while three cliques are purely American and one is purely Japanese. In other words, eighteen of the twenty-five cliques (72 percent) include enterprises from different continents.

A second challenge lies in massive public reservations about biotechnology policy. Despite costly public relations campaigns by the Commission, now as before a widespread scepticism regarding gene technology processes and products prevails among the population of the member countries. Meanwhile, according to Eurobarometer 1993, a majority are in favour of the promotion of biotechnology and genetic engineering. A more refined survey, however, shows that application of this technology to livestock and the manufacture of foods is opposed by the majority, just as it had been previously (Seifert and Torgersen 1996). The scepticism among the population is the result not of a lack of knowledge, as the Commission and bio-industry like to assume, but rather of better knowledge about biotechnological processes. Thus, the Eurobarometer investigations show that the well-informed Danes, Dutch and Germans demand strict state controls over biotechnology and genetic engineering, when compared with the poorly informed Spaniards, Portuguese and Austrians.

Doubts are also expressed about the rationale of the research programmes. The subsidizing of the programmes by private enterprises through their research contributions undermines the competition policy of the EU (Starbatty and Vetterlein 1990; Sturm 1992). Indeed, the programmes support – although not as blatantly as in the 1980s – the so-called 'European champions'. At the end of 1995, the audit division of the European Union issued a complaint that evaluators of the projects are at the same time laying claim to project monies (*Neue Zürcher Zeitung*, 6 December 1995). Enterprises from large countries also profit disproportionately. Thus the research programme serves to cement the North–South technological cleavage (Junne 1992).

The massive public reservations about the European Union's biotechnology policy cannot be eliminated simply by costly 'information campaigns'. Rather, the Commission needs to orient itself to the proposals of its *groupe de rélexion* (CEU 1995b) and make the committee work of the Commission more transparent, formalizing it and giving critical voices more of an audience. In fact, European interest groups are still primarily dependent on informal contacts with EU officials, particularly with respect to sponsoring their efforts, and for procuring (a) information about planned projects and committees; and (b) access to the relevant committees. This demand for a democratization of policy formation is not new. In the early 1980s, the Economic and Social Committee and the European Parliament complained about the lack of transparency of the Commission's work (e.g. the selection of experts, the process of discussions). In 1985, the 'Boserup Report' of the European Parliament reminded the Commission that, according to the Treaty of Rome, it was not the expert committees but rather the Economic and Social Committee that was envisioned as the organ for the representation of economic interests. The report further criticized (a) the absence of clearness and transparency with regard to the consultation activities of the Commission; (b) the fact that the Commission embodied no effective mechanisms and centralized control systems for its committee activities; and (c) that the consultation process in large measure has assumed an autonomous character and can no longer simply be described as having occurred somehow under the care of the Commission.

Owing to the process of co-decision-making, the European Parliament still has the possibility in the meantime to block the Commission's proposals. If, for example, it was impossible in the 1980s for the environmental organizations to inform themselves about impending biotechnological projects of the Commission through the individual Directorates General and thereafter to seek seats on the relevant advisory bodies, today they can attempt to block the proposals of the Commission through lobbying the Parliament and the national ministries of environment. Thus critics of genetic engineering were able to celebrate their first successes, namely the rejection of the bio-patent Directive on its third reading and the de facto moratorium on the approval of genetically manipulated organisms. So that such debacles do not recur, the Commission must incorporate environmental organizations more fully in the process of policy formation, whether it likes it or not.

The chronology of events presented above shows that from the early 1980s the Commission proceeded on the assumption that biotechnology and genetic engineering would advance to become the growth industry of the twenty-first century. In addition, the Commission assumed that European bio-industry displayed a technological backwardness compared with the USA and Japan, and acted (in line with Bornschier's argument) as a political entrepreneur for the creation of an industry-friendly legal environment and research programmes. Moreover, the Commission actively promoted a positive image of genetic engineering and bio-industry and expanded the dialogue with its leading organizations. From this perspective it can be understood why the criticism of the leading employers' organizations has been moderate up to now. The positive outlook of the responsible Commissioners is unanimously appreciated.

Looking to the future, it is apparent that the dialogue between the biotechnology producers and the Commission will have different focal points from that between the producers of information technology and the Commission. In particular, the large chemical and pharmaceutical firms, in light of their transregional alliances with primarily smaller, specialized research firms, will not be enthusiastic about 'research corporatism' *à la* Esprit. Of far greater interest to the biotechnology firms is the dialogue concerning directives and regulations regarding genetic technology research and production; this concern is already reflected by the public relations work of the European Union in favour of genetic technology. Briefly stated, the interests of the biotechnology firms are substantially different from those of the information technology firms. Correspondingly, in their dialogue with the Commission, it is not questions of research policy or programmes that are of primary interest to biotechnology firms, but rather the development of an industry-friendly regulatory framework based on the American model.

9 European integration after the Single Act: changing and persisting patterns

Patrick Ziltener

Introduction

With and through the integration thrust of the 1980s, a qualitative change in the interaction between economic and political actors has developed in Western Europe. The Single European Act, now more than a dozen years in force, marks the beginning of this process. The massive underestimation of the meaning of the Single Act on the part of most observers as well as actors involved in the integration process remains nothing less than astounding. In retrospect, the assessment of the actors who understood the Single Act as the first result of a far-reaching dynamic has been confirmed. This is true on the economic level, where a fundamental structural change was set in motion in anticipation of the internal market, as well as on the political level. First, elements of integration projects that had been set aside were put back on the agenda in the 1980s, in particular the project of a European monetary union, which became the core of the next policy package, the Maastricht Treaty. The political dynamic after 1986 can also be traced back to changes in the decision-making process at European level that were effected through the Single European Act, especially the further erosion of the 'veto culture'. In addition, the Commission was able to develop and maintain a strong, proactive role in many areas. Along with this came successive expansions of the circle of involved political actors. The new transnational forms of cooperation, without which the new integration dynamic cannot be explained, developed further. This did not lead to an end of the central position of the individual roundtables of industrialists in Brussels, but they increasingly became one voice among others. In sum, our analyses confirm that a more and more complex multi-level political system[1] has developed in Western Europe.

---

[1] A concept that an increasing number of integration researchers tend to use; see the influential essay by Scharpf (1994), Jachtenfuchs and Kohler-Koch (1996) and the volumes edited by Marks et al. (1996), Hooghe (1996) and König, Rieger and Schmitt (1996).

Not all actors were equally successful, and not all policy areas became 'Europeanized' to the same extent. For many observers, the European integration process still has a certain bias. It poses the question of the future design of 'statehood in Europe', especially its welfare state elements, which have barely been incorporated by the political integration dynamic up to now. The elite pact between transnational and supranational actors, which for us is the prominent element in our explanation of the integration thrust of the 1980s, was the result of specific historical conditions. It would therefore be incorrect to elaborate a general theory of integration based on this phenomenon.

The effects of the Single European Act and the continuing integration dynamic

The internal market as project and reality

Between 1985 and 1990, a process of economic adaptation occurred in anticipation of the internal market in Western Europe. Investment in the EC grew at a rate of 5.2 percent, clearly surpassing the 3 per cent growth rate of GDP.[2] Mergers and acquisitions within the EC increased enormously (see Windolf 1993). Moreover, the project produced economic stimuli and served as a strong magnet for foreign investments, especially from countries of the European Free Trade Association (EFTA). The EC's proposal to create a European Economic Area (EEA) represented an attempt to extend the internal market to the territory of the EFTA nations. Negotiations got under way in 1990 and led to the signing, on 22 October 1991, of a corresponding treaty, which like the internal market was to take effect on 1 January 1993.

In light of these effects of the internal market project and the public attention given to it, which the Commission cleverly promoted, far-reaching changes also occurred in the political landscape of Western Europe. In the EFTA nations in particular, joining the EC increasingly became understood as something unavoidable. For these predominantly social democratic governments, the new levels of integration and membership in the EC were finally accepted as prerequisites for political action when the social dimension was placed on the agenda during 1988 (see chapter 6). The European Economic Area initiative was also used by the EC for shielding the political dynamic within the Community from a new round of expansion. Deepening integration had first priority.

Alas, the ominous deadline that was linked with the internal market

---

[2] According to Union Bank of Switzerland, *Wirtschaftsnotizen*, Nov./Dec. 1991.

project could not be kept. The delays in translating the White Paper into action were less the work of the Commission than of the Council, as well as the slow process of the adaptation and translation of its measures into national law by the member states. A deficit in actually executing the project exists in all member states, although to considerably varying degrees. The first day of the year 1993 was nevertheless celebrated as the 'birthday' of the internal market, although it was overshadowed by the post-Maastricht crisis. At the Amsterdam summit of July 1997, the concluding session of the intergovernmental conference approved what was probably the last *Action Plan for Completing the Internal Market*.

In 1993, in its *White Paper on Growth, Competitiveness, Employment* (CEU 1993: 3), the Commission drew up the following balance sheet under the title 'The 1992 Objectives: A Tangible Reality':
(1) 9 million jobs created between 1986 and 1990;
(2) 0.5 per cent extra growth each year;
(3) a 3 per cent saving on the costs of international transport;
(4) investment up by one third between 1985 and 1990;
(5) three times more company mergers and acquisitions in the Community over the period in question;
(6) twice the number of European companies involved in mergers and acquisitions in the rest of the world;
(7) a doubling of trade in the Community in sectors previously regarded as sheltered from competition;
(8) 70 million customs documents done away with.

The continuing integration dynamic: the monetary union project

An important part of the continuing integration dynamic of the 1980s can be traced back to the efforts of different actors belatedly to develop a 'social dimension', which had initially largely failed in the Single Act (chapter 6). However, this did not become the centrepiece of the next policy package; that role was played by the economic and monetary union (EMU) project. Some actors saw monetary union as a logical extension of the realization of the internal market; it was the cornerstone of their integration project from the outset. In this category we would include, in addition to the Commission, countries such as France[3] and Belgium; in fact both were dominated by German monetary policy, without being able to really influence it. Indeed, monetary policy

---

[3] See Secrétariat d'Etat auprès du Premier Ministre and Commissariat Général du Plan (1983): ch. 3. This report sees the strengthening of the 'monetary identity of Europe' as an absolutely essential part of concerted macroeconomic regulation at the European level. The establishment of an EMU was described at the time as a 'pipe dream'. The

proposals were among the most controversial at the intergovernmental conference of 1985; proportionally speaking, monetary policy content in the Single Act was minimal, although strategically important (see chapter 2, p. 68).

The monetary union project as such is older, having been a Community goal since 1969. The establishment of the European Monetary System envisaged a monetary union. The central motive for a European currency at the time, namely to provide a regional answer to world monetary instability, was no longer as prominent in the second half of the 1980s. The long phase of stability of the European Monetary System had begun in 1987, after final realignments; until 1991, it functioned as a true fixed-rate system. This was an expression of sustained economic convergence in Western Europe. These factors formed the background to the negotiations that led to the Maastricht Treaty (see Krägenau and Wetter 1994: 68f).

Following a once successful method, in 1987 EC corporate officials founded the Association for Monetary Union to lobby for a European monetary union. Its leaders came from such companies as Philips, Société Générale de Belgique, Fiat, Total-CFP, Rhône-Poulenc and Agfa-Gevaert. The smaller Committee for the Monetary Union of Europe, chaired jointly by Valéry Giscard d'Estaing and Helmut Schmidt, was founded in late 1986 and brought together government officials, industrialists and bankers (including a Deutsche Bank chairman) to push EC governments toward monetary union (Sandholtz 1993: 24). It is difficult to assess the influence of these groups. In any case, the development of the monetary union project cannot simply be seen as being parallel to the internal market project; the weight of 'political' motives (in the narrower sense of the term) was clearly greater than that of the 'economic' ones. However, at the Hanover summit in June 1988, the heads of state and government reaffirmed the goal of a monetary union. A committee under the leadership of Delors was created to examine and develop concrete steps toward the realization of a monetary union.[4]

It is historically incorrect to describe the change in the German government's position as the 'price' of German reunification.[5] The

---

centrepiece of the report's proposals was the establishment of a European monetary fund.

[4] It consisted of the central bank presidents of the member states, the general director of the Bank for International Settlements, Alexandre Lamfalussy, as well as other experts. The committee's task was not to discuss the goal of a monetary union as such but only to submit a plan for attaining one.

[5] For a (self-)description of the role of the German foreign secretary, see Genscher (1995: 387). He justifies the initiative on the basis of the necessary and desirable (further)

so-called Genscher Memorandum of February 1988 had already advocated the creation of a European monetary area and a European central bank. According to the memorandum, a monetary union was no longer the final stage or 'coronation' of economic convergence (the previous official position) but a necessary catalyst for it. The change in the German federal government's position might have taken place in the fall or winter of 1987, after the approval of the Single Act, when the implementation of the internal market was secured. In April 1988, the German Christian democratic party (CDU) and the German Social Democratic Party (SPD) voiced their approval of a European monetary union. Economic policy circles in Germany, especially the Bundesbank, were openly sceptical about a monetary union. They would be won over to it only if the European central bank were to represent a superelevation of the Bundesbank, that is, make absolute the principles underlying its policy.

Although two separate, parallel intergovernmental conferences (one on the monetary union and one on the political union) prepared for 'Maastricht', it was *one policy package*.[6] The core of the package was the German 'yes' to the monetary union (and with it the surrender of the Deutsche Mark) and a solid timetable for it. The German conditions – the anchoring of an absolute policy orientation towards monetary stability, the independence of the European central bank and the so-called convergence criteria as well as a (albeit minimal) strengthening of the political dimension (the rights of the European Parliament) – were fulfilled. The (heterogeneous) policy package was supplemented in Maastricht with another reinforcement of the cohesion policy and the deepening of intergovernmental political cooperation (common foreign and security policy, cooperation in the fields of justice and domestic affairs).

The Luxembourg Compromise – requiescat in pace?

In the recent literature, the Single Act's main effect is nearly unanimously said to be the overcoming of the Luxembourg Compromise. The Commission's secretary-general Noël (1987), pointed out that the

---

development of European integration, which increasingly inserted itself into a predictable East–West rapprochement. The prospect of German reunification allowed the pressure by France and Italy to increase, which clearly greatly accelerated the process.

[6] See Stavenhagen (1991), Lipp and Reichert (1991), Doutriaux (1992), Artis (1992), Corbett (1992), Krägenau and Wetter (1993) and Ross (1995a) on the Maastricht negotiations. See in particular the collection of documents and analyses of the intergovernmental conference on the political union in Laursen and Vanhoonacker (1992).

Luxembourg Compromise was *not* included in the negotiations regarding the Single European Act; the latter makes no reference to it at all. However, he did express his hope at the time that majority decisions could eventually be enforced 'whenever necessary and desirable'. In his influential critique of the Act, Pescatore (1986), a former judge at the European Court of Justice, emphasized that the most important unanimity clauses not only would remain untouched but would even be strengthened, especially with respect to the free movement of persons, rights of employees, fiscal harmonization and economic and monetary policy. For the first time, this represented the embodiment of the partial veto power of individual governments.

In the opinion of the British government, the Luxembourg Compromise was still valid after the adoption of the Single Act, as it stated in its reports to the House of Commons.[7] The British Foreign Affairs Committee, however, was very sceptical about whether the Luxembourg Compromise was still intact.

The fear that the member states would continue to assert 'vital national interests' under the Luxembourg Compromise or that regulations similarly based on the mutual acceptance of such interests would emerge was not confirmed in the following years. Instead, a number of cases have shown that the member states prefer to go to the European Court of Justice and file a suit against the legal basis of a decision rather than to assert 'vital interests' during negotiations in the Council. Nevertheless, many decisions were still decided unanimously, whereas the pressure exerted by the threat of a majority vote did lead to an increased willingness to consent (Engel and Borrmann 1991: 262). Teasdale (1993) also concludes that the Luxembourg Compromise actually disappeared in the course of the 1980s, even though some governments still refer to it, and that it no longer has any significant bearing on the way the Community functions. The 'veto culture' has even been eroded in areas that are not formally covered by the qualified majority principle.

In actual fact, since that time there has been only one attempt by a member state to refer to the Luxembourg Compromise. In 1988 the Greek government asserted its 'vital national interest' when fighting against a decision concerning the agricultural price system. However, the other member states did not accept this, and the Greek government, completely isolated, gave way.

---

[7] See especially 'The Single European Act: Observations by the Government' (Third Report from the Foreign Affairs Committee, Session 1985–86, Cmnd. 9858); see also Howe (1994: 458).

Beyond intergovernmentalism

The most important argument against neorealism is that 'national interests' are increasingly being defined within the EU context. Membership in the EU has become part of the interest calculation for governments (and other actors). Even in non-integrated areas, the power of the nation-state is more and more restricted and embedded in a tight network of legal and institutional regulations owing to its EU membership. Economic integration, as well as political and legal integration, at least of the EU's core, have reached a vast extent that meanwhile can hardly be revised anymore (see Cameron 1992: 36ff). Therefore, the question of maintaining national sovereignty, which is emphasized by neorealism, has different implications for EU members. The fact that giving up (formal) national sovereignty is seen as a chance to regain real sovereignty, at least partially, is only seemingly a paradox. It is the only explanation for the French pressure towards a monetary union, for example. German foreign policy is governed by historically caused restrictions that at least partially oppose neorealist assumptions. The analysis of such historically determined 'structural conditions' is decisive for understanding integration projects.

Moravcsik (1991: 42; see also 1998: 365) interprets the Single Act negotiations in accordance with the three basic principles of his approach (intergovernmentalism, lowest-common-denominator bargaining, protection of sovereignty) as a 'process of limiting the scope and intensity of reform – a process necessary to gain the acceptance not only of Britain but also of other member states who, when it came to drafting a document, suddenly proved quite jealous of their sovereignty. The maximalist programme of broad reform was progressively sacrificed in favour of the minimalist programme limited to those procedural and substantive changes needed to liberalize the internal market.' From our point of view, it is more sensible to interpret the Single Act as a compromise between different integration projects of (admittedly unequally strong) national, transnational and supranational actors than to compare it to a hypothetical 'maximalist programme'. It is also not clear which project corresponds with or is equivalent to this 'maximalist programme': the project of the Commission or the project of the federalists? Moreover, the lowest common denominator as a result would have been the implementation of the Single Market project through an agreement without institutional reform, practically a European GATT, as proposed by the British government. The Single Act already encompassed two core areas with elements of supranationality: the internal market and technology corporatism; the expanded integration process after 1986 addressed the many areas in which 'strategic postponing' had taken place. A remarkable feature of the Act is that it is also the consequence of the integration projects of many national governments, which were prepared to transcend the actual result and thus give up (formal) sovereignty. The erosion of the 'veto culture' after the Single Act confirms that the vast majority of national governments were ready for a new political praxis at European level.

Repercussions on the political systems of the member states

The decline of the Luxembourg Compromise had repercussions on the domestic politics of the member states. As a consequence, the focal point of the lobbying by interest groups has changed. It no longer suffices to put one's 'own' government under pressure in order to prevent an undesirable decision by means of its veto power in Brussels. This now requires a transnationally coordinated campaign in several countries. The incentive to undertake (supranational) lobbying in Brussels has also increased.

With majority voting in the Council, the possibility of determining political accountability has been removed; the possibilities for individual governments to justify decisions made in Brussels that have unpleasant consequences for domestic politics have increased. There are reasons one might describe the national governments and bureaucracies as in fact intrastate winners in the integration process, rather than as losers, although they are commonly characterized as losers, usually with reference to the supranationalization of policy areas. This effect is reinforced by the fact that there is no comparable parliamentary control of the Council at the European level. The former president of the European Parliament called the integration process 'an intrastate shifting of authority': the national parliaments lost essential possibilities for influence and initiative, while the national governments won the right to create European legislation (Hänsch 1989: 218).

From the point of view of Europe's nation-states, European integration itself represents a complex process, one that includes the partial replacement (supranationalization) of what are perceived as functions of the national state, and the partial abolition, restriction and insidious undermining of these functions or their gentle transformation through incentives. In many respects, the process also represents the competitive articulation of these functions with other levels and areas of government, as well as with other mixed state–private sector committees or completely private organizations (see Ziltener 1999).

The underlying trend of this process is development in the direction of what has been described as the 'Schumpeterian workfare state' (Jessop 1995) or the 'competition state' (*Wettbewerbsstaat*, Hirsch 1995). In this sense, a process of convergence of state forms and regulation is taking place in Europe. Convergence under these conditions, however, signifies the implementation of the logic of spatial competition, and consequently the fragmentation and differentiation of spaces within the societal whole.

There is a great deal of evidence that national political elites use the European level in the implementation of projects that are domestically difficult or impossible to implement. In some of these efforts, argumentation based on the 'practical constraint of Europe' can be constructed without being conditioned on the particular case or interests involved. However, there is often a traceable strategic calculation that in effect incorporates the European level. This applies in particular to cases in which national governments and/or big business pursuing their own projects are confronted with strong, well-elaborated, balanced political arrangements of a corporatist nature and/or with predominantly negative public opinion. Insofar as formal and/or actual regulatory authority is removed from the national parliaments and interest mediation systems (as a result of negotiations among national governments and transnational and supranational actors), the resistance of interest groups established in the previous systems of regulation is overcome at a national level. The argument also applies to the case in which a certain government finds itself in a situation in which it 'must' contravene the articulated interests of its own clientele.

Actors and alliances evaluated

A central finding of our analyses of the dynamic of European integration in the 1980s is that the reality of the political processes at the European level, despite the still dominant position of the Council, cannot be reduced to an intergovernmentalist explanatory model. In some policy areas, the central initiatives can be traced back to non-governmental actors, while in others the number of actors involved expanded in the course of or as a result of the thrust toward integration. In many areas, non-governmental actors, especially the roundtables of high-ranking representatives of large European firms, and the supranational bodies, in particular the Commission, played an important role.

In what follows we take a somewhat broader view of these two groups of actors, which were central for forging the European elite pact. The fact that we concentrate on these does not mean that they were the only important actors or that the integration thrust can be explained *in toto* by looking at the interactions of these two alone. From our point of view, this is justified by the fact that these new forms of cooperation constitute what is new and particular about this stage of integration.

The Delors Commission as political entrepreneur

The analyses in this volume unequivocally indicate that the Commission was the most important supranational body in the integration relaunch. This is not surprising if we compare the role of other supranational institutions, such as the European Parliament, whose role we assess as marginal, or the European Court of Justice, although its rulings were very significant for certain policy areas (e.g. the *Cassis de Dijon* decision for the internal market project or the judgments regarding the social dimension). It should be emphasized that here we can speak accurately of an actual *rebirth of the EC Commission* as both a prerequisite for and a consequence of the push for integration in the 1980s (chapter 2, pp. 52ff). The impact of the Commission on the process leading to the Single Act and beyond – especially with regard to initiating projects, mediating and mobilizing actors – has to be admitted even from a neorealist point of view, as in Moravcsik's (1998) recent contribution.

All our interviewees emphasized the strength and leadership function of the Delors Commission. The unanimous assessments of the Committee of Permanent Representatives (COREPER) members were especially informative in this regard, since they are independent of the Commission but at the same time very directly affected by its activity. The Delors Commission is often compared with the first Commission under Walter Hallstein (who held office from 1958 to 1967). One of the founding fathers of integration theory, Ernst B. Haas (1964: 87ff), defined three critical determinants of effective supranational leadership in his account of its successful activity: (1) the definition of an 'organizational ideology' (priority goals, strategy); (2) a bureaucracy that is committed to this ideology ('cohesive and loyal staff'); and (3) supporting coalitions and alliances among individuals, groups and organizations in the members' national systems, organized around the ideology and the specific action proposals of the supranational leadership.

The 'Delorist leadership system' (Ross 1995a: 158ff) successfully connected these elements. In comparison with the Hallstein Commission, however, the Commission formed in 1984 was saddled with other less favourable conditions at its inception. The Hallstein Commission faced a newly formulated founding treaty with clearly defined roles for the supranational organs. The Delors Commission, on the other hand, had first to recapture the space for its praxis (see Ehlermann 1988: 58) while simultaneously partially reorganizing the bureaucracy. To put it another way, the wheels of the train had to be changed while it was still moving. The counter-argument – that conditions also did not favour its predecessor's construction of a bureaucracy – is only partially right. The available resources may have been fewer at the beginning, but the unity of the bureaucracy and thus the possibilities for its instrumental use were disproportionately greater.

The activity of the Delors Commission was overlaid by the 'heritage' of earlier years, which again and again hindered its initiative and impeded the opening of new areas of activity. The budgetary problems and the question of the member states' contributions are examples of this, which were resolved in a compromise within the Delors Package of 1988 (chapter 5, pp. 142f) Nevertheless, the Commission was able unequivocally to strengthen its position as 'ruler of the process' in the course of the 1980s, as shown in this volume for several policy areas. As a consequence, a new, intensified network relationship developed between the Community organs.[8]

The Delors Commission, building on the activity of the previous Commissions, demonstrated particular skill with respect to assembling supporting coalitions and alliances. This pertains specifically to the support of transnational interest groups, from the various roundtables of industrial interests to the trade unions. We have reviewed how this process (a mixture of push and pull elements) developed in certain areas, and indicated how it may be understood theoretically in terms of the supply of and demand for order (see chapter 1). In addition, one must also keep in mind that the integration thrust would hardly have been possible without the excellent relationships between the Delors Commission and political actors at the national level and in the national administrations.

The (continued) pact with the European transnational business elite

The area of research and technology policy was actually the first in which a qualitative breakthrough in forms of transnational cooperation took place; this occurred some time prior to the Single Act and even before the actual 'take-off' phase of the integration thrust in 1984. The research findings from the areas of information technology (and biotechnology) presented in this volume confirm the important role of the Commission and how successfully it took the initiative.

[8] See the particularly detailed and informative account by Engel and Borrmann (1991) and the contributions in Engel and Wessels (1992).

The origins of the initiatives in the information technology area can be traced to the late 1970s and are closely connected with the name of Commissioner Etienne Davignon (chapters 1 and 4). The Esprit programme that was approved in 1984 not only was the first result of these efforts, but has also served decisively as the 'flagship' of the entire European research and development policy since then (see Grande and Häusler 1994). In particular, through this programme, cooperation between the Commission and a roundtable – the European Information Technology Industry Roundtable (EITIRT) – was institutionalized for the first time. This new form of cooperation proved very successful and thus became the strategic model for many other projects of the Commission. With regard to the further development of this European technology corporatism, we must note that there are indications that the former clearly dominant position of the EITIRT has rather weakened in the course of the past ten years primarily owing to the proliferation of voices in Brussels and the intent of the Commission to include more interests (chapter 4). In general we can say that there has been a perceptible expansion of these forms of cooperation.

In the area of biotechnology the Commission has also tried from the beginning to channel interests by means of the formation of European umbrella organizations. However, this proved to be difficult in light of the low degree of centralization among the corresponding interest groups and thus the absence of any 'internal' method of interest mediation. Nevertheless, the lobbyists and technical experts of big business successfully influence policy formulation in the advisory bodies of the Commission (chapter 8).

The European Roundtable of Industrialists (ERT), whose initiative was the crucial weight behind the creation of a European Single Market (chapter 3), is still one of the most influential interest organizations at European level, as also stressed by Green Cowles (1997: 131): 'the most powerful industrial coalition in Brussels.' It has successfully expanded its base (numbers, range and reciprocal interconnection of the represented businesses; chapter 7) and the scope of its activities and still has at its disposal the most important avenues of influence. Of particular importance is the newly created Competitiveness Advisory Group, whose duties are connected with the argumentation regarding general industrial policy and competitiveness in the 'Europe 1990' paper (Dekker 1984, 1985b) and the White Paper of 1985 (CEC 1985). That said, we must add that it is also true that, with the increased number of European actors in the political landscape, the ERT's weight has also diminished somewhat in relative terms. The ERT as well as the other roundtables suffered not so much a decrease in centrality but rather a loss in exclusiveness.

The increasing significance of these more direct political interventions on the part of big business, without taking the 'detour' through the corresponding umbrella organizations, is also detectable at the national level. This is especially effective at the European level, since, with the exception of some specific areas (agricultural policy), there are still no strong umbrella organizations and no system for the mediation of interests that one could describe as corporatist (see Streeck and Schmitter 1991). At the same time, it is also true that lobbyists profit from the fact that the comparatively weak resource base of the Brussels state apparatus makes it dependent on external expertise. The large European firms systematically and successfully take advantage of the specifics of the supranational level within the European multi-level system. In two policy areas – information technology and biotechnology – the efforts of the Commission are currently aimed at overcoming its all too exclusive cooperation with the roundtables of leading European firms. It is difficult to judge to what extent this can be attributed to an increasingly critical attitude of the public with respect to a one-sided 'Europe of big business' and thus can be described as a reaction by the Commission to its legitimation problems. However, the thesis that these new forms of cooperation might represent only a short-term and limited transition phase on the road to an extensive corporatist European interest mediation system based on the model of the national political systems of the postwar era seems to us implausible.

A new social compromise at European level?

A Commission without strong allies

The Commission did not have comparably strong allies at its disposal when it came to certain projects beyond the realization of a single market or European technology policy. Where there was no strong economic and political 'demand' for supranational regulations, the Commission tried on its own to obtain these in the interest of the enforcement of its overall integration project. The most obvious example of this was social policy, when Delors tried to arouse the public and possible allies in the summer of 1988. In areas of inferior 'demand' or relatively weak actors, the Commission was clearly less successful. From the point of view of the Commission's project, the balance sheet with respect to social policy and the coordination of economic policy is mixed. The path to harmonization of political regulations at the European level ran into too much resistance, except for a few areas such as occupational health and safety.

Generally speaking, most of the integration research emphasizes the predominance of market-creating as opposed to market-correcting measures. In many areas, there is in fact a 'competition of (national) systems', which does not correspond to the concept of an *espace européen organisé* as advanced by Delors at the beginning of 1985 (chapter 2, pp. 54ff, chapter 6, pp. 163ff).

From the point of view of the Commission, the balance sheet for the second central dimension of the 'cohesion target' that was envisioned from the inception of the integration thrust – the extension and rebuilding of regional balance – is clearly more positive. EC regional policy was not only provided with more resources; it became elaborated in the direction of a supranational mode of regulation. The functions of the Commission were strengthened and a greater variety of actors were drawn into the process.

On the one hand, the reasons for the varying degrees of success in these two policy areas are due to their political nature (deep-seated divergences of interests among the involved actors and differences with respect to their ability to block the integration process). On the other hand, they also have a deeper structural dimension, namely the divergences between the West European societies and nation-states as well as the basic institutional structure of the EC. With respect to the latter, we refer not only to the imbalance among the European institutions (for the debate on the democracy deficit, see chapter 10, pp. 266f) but also to a dramatic inequality among the political actors regarding the 'utility' of the European level for their projects.

Thus, the trade unions, for example, despite the efforts of the Delors Commission to the contrary, are without a doubt still holding the short straw. While the competitive articulation of national regulations promotes a deregulatory dynamic, pro-active efforts aimed at re-regulation quickly come to a standstill in the face of polymorphous EC decision-making. The unions have much to fear from the 'regulation gap' between insufficient EU regulatory authority and the national governments, which are increasingly under pressure. In this light, actors who are not interested in social policy integration can easily pursue a reactive strategy.

But the weaknesses of the unions at European level can also be traced back to 'internal' problems resulting from variability in the traditional conflict structures in the member states, patterns of social mobilization and forms of internal mediation of interests. Furthermore, the varying degrees to which industrial relations are regulated, the variety of trade union and political party goals, alliances and resources of power in the different member states also contribute to the resulting relative weakness (see Ebbinghaus and Visser 1994). The same applies to social movements, which still find the logic of influence in Brussels heavy going.

Generally speaking, one can say that the new style of integration, as developed from the integration thrust of the 1980s, favours the heavyweights, that is, the organizations of particular interests that are not burdened by lengthy internal processes for mediating multiple interests. The 'slow' representative organizations and movement-based actors, as well as diffuse general interests that are difficult to organize, are discriminated against.

Legitimation without welfare?

For many theories of the state, the legitimacy of state order is connected with the organization of social security and relative social balance between the classes in society. In view of the far-reaching absence of such elements at European level and the simultaneously relatively successful construction of a European regional policy, the question is posed: Is this a substitute for or indeed 'the' social policy of the EU?

Only in a limited sense can regional policy be equated with social policy. On the one hand, it contributes to the equalization of life chances. However, it is not a substitute for regulatory harmonization, nor does it provide claims to payments (entitlements based on citizenship) on the part of individuals or regions. Rather, regional policy is concerned with the promotion of infrastructural investments and an opening of regions, from which the entire European economic area potentially profits.

In one respect, there is an important 'compensatory' connection between the absence of harmonization and financial balance. The cohesion payments to countries with a low level of regulation have surely contributed to the fact that these countries did not react to the intensified competition from the core with a decrease in this level of regulation. In this sense, the regional policy elements of the integration relaunch of the 1980s have become the most significant instruments for pre-empting any 'race to the bottom' in labour standards and labour market regulation. This made it possible, as Ross (1995b: 364) puts it, 'to buy backward EC regions into the "European model of society"'. Anderson (1995b: 149) poses the question, 'Why, at critical junctures in the development of the EC, have member states and the Commission selected this particular approach to uneven regional economic development over plausible entitlement-based social options?' and answers it with three interrelated reasons. First, the structural funds insert themselves into the fundamental institutional characteristics and broader aims of the EU, and, once in place, they have presented EU policy-makers with pre-existing frameworks for interpretation and action. Secondly, as a result, the costs of addressing the negative effects of integration through the structural funds are lower in comparison with new social policy approaches and programmes. Anderson finds a third reason in the increasingly strong support networks at the national and subnational levels, which support and even increase the demand for such regional policy measures. The reasons named by Anderson correspond with our explanation of the differential success of the two policy domains.

Whether regional policy payments will in fact prevent regulatory competition in the long term is more than questionable. The middle- and long-term effect of the fully realized internal market will reinforce the temptations. What is more, it already appears that this competition works even more strongly between the European *core countries*, for example with business taxation. This fact, along with the monetary union and the expansion of the EU to East Central Europe, will inevitably raise anew the related questions about the basic regulatory structure of the EU in the near future. The disputes over questions regarding harmonization, competition and competitiveness will be revived again, just as they were in 1987–8.

Will the EU itself at some point in the future become the institutional centre of socially necessary welfare state functions in (Western) Europe? Our research, like the vast majority of research on integration, suggests a negative answer to this question.[9] From this assessment, two evaluations are possible: that the nation-state will continue to play the central role in this area, or that this development points in the direction of a general reduction of state functions in this area.

In the future, impulses toward the further development of the welfare functions of the EU will also emanate from the Commission. Especially important in this regard is its policy with respect to the expansion of the circle of involved actors. In March 1996, about 1,000 representatives of non-governmental organizations met for the first time in Brussels with the Commission. The 'European Social Forum' aimed to broaden the scope of interaction between the EU institutions and those actors

---

[9] Streeck (1996) sketches the new form of governance under the concept of neo-voluntarism: 'Unlike neo-corporatism, where strong quasi-public organizations of social groups are enabled by an interventionist public policy to negotiate and correct market outcomes, neo-voluntarism returns allocational decisions to private actors in private markets, with no possibility previously to readjust their political and organizational resources' (Streeck 1996: 83; see also Lange 1992: 256). For Flora (1993) as well, a European welfare state will be characterized by institutional fragmentation, subsidiarity and parastatist organization.

involved at the grassroots level in the fields of economic and social action and social cohesion (CEU 1996b). To what extent this policy will be successful depends not only on the (momentary) constellation of actors, but also quite pivotally on whether the contradictions that arise from European integration itself are resolved in favour of the nation-state or in favour of 'Europe'.

In this context, certain tendencies that result from a fully realized internal market must be discussed. The increasing mobility of intra-European labour would have serious organizational consequences for national welfare regimes (see Flora 1993; Guild 1999). Intensified locational competition forced by the internal market, displacements of businesses on the basis of cost factors and regulatory competition will not be readily accepted by the political publics in Europe: National responses to these issues, however, would fragment the internal market such that European solutions could conceivably appear as the cheaper ones.

Much will also depend on the perception of the development of the structure of social inequality. If in the future the distribution of the costs and benefits of European integration is judged to be unequal, then pressure will increase in favour of a European system as the guiding mechanism of this distribution. The older neofunctionalist scholars have already spoken on this matter;[10] then as now the threat of the alternative, namely a sudden shift to nationalist fragmentation, was not sufficiently taken into account.

These problems cannot be avoided, much less solved, through an exclusive elite pact of the type previously described. Even if the initiatives always proceed from above – 'L'initiative vient toujours d'en haut!', the conclusion reached by the politically sobered Frédéric Moreau in Flaubert's *Education sentimentale* – their results are sustainable in the long term only if at the very least they do not destroy a minimum of social cohesion.

The future of elite bargaining

In a certain sense, the situation in the mid-1980s was unique. The surprisingly powerful capabilities of the alliance between transnational companies and the Commission were based on a series of prerequisites:

---

[10] See Schmitter's analysis of the tension-producing conditions of integration processes. As 'basic contradictions' he includes, among others, 'uncertainty in regard to the capacity to guarantee relative equality of perceived benefits once new productive and distributive forces are unleashed (equity)' and 'heightened sensitivity to the comparative performance of one's partners generated by higher transactions and available information (envy)' (Schmitter 1971: 235f).

(a) convergence of the policies of the national governments in Western Europe after the failure of the final attempt to revitalize the Keynesian societal model; (b) the capacity for action of the political elites in the context of the permissive consensus, that is, the widespread lack of interest of the political publics in Western Europe in the negotiations at European level; (c) the relative 'shelteredness' of the European integration process with respect to world politics; and, last but not least, (d) the coincidence of the integration thrust and a conjunctural economic upswing phase.

These conditions have now changed extensively. First, the 'shelteredness' of the elite bargain has for the most part dissolved. In the course of the 1980s new economic and political actors whom the elite bargain had largely bypassed now pushed their way into the negotiation system. These included long-established Brussels business interest organizations, the European trade unions, the governments of the EFTA states and subnational and non-governmental organizations. The inclusion of these forces was welcomed, promoted and in some cases even initiated by the Commission. However, in this way it was the Commission itself that contributed to the undermining of the elite bargaining model that was so successful in the 1980s.

That the national governments are still not ready to give up their position as the strongest actors in the increasingly complex multi-level political system is demonstrated by the negotiations at both the Maastricht and Amsterdam intergovernmental conferences. The Delors Commission was increasingly restricted in its late phase, and the approval of the successor to the Commission president was unambiguously intended to create a more 'comfortable partner' for the national governments.

The permissive consensus among the West European populations has been eroded in the course of the post-Maastricht crisis. This is connected to the economic recession, and also to the fact that the populations were repeatedly asked to make adjustments that were justified in the name of 'Europe'. Moreover, few have failed to notice that the orientation of national policies toward the convergence criteria for monetary union has deepened the economic recession. Widespread opinion holds that the 'fruits' of integration have thus far remained elusive.

The external conditions have also changed. Throughout the 1980s, the USA successfully exercised political pressure in alliance with the traditionally free-trade-oriented European countries in such a way as to connect the new integration thrust externally with steps toward economic liberalization. The General Agreement on Tariffs and Trade

(GATT) negotiations continued parts of the Single Market liberalization on a world scale. For many *dossiers* a close connection between these two processes can be shown: a series of measures for the dismantling of non-tariff and regulatory barriers to trade are to be found on both agendas. In many cases the actions for completing the internal market served as 'test and laboratory cases for solving difficult liberalization tasks' (Wegner 1991: 201, our translation) that existed in new areas such as the liberalization of services, which were also being debated in GATT. This strengthened the trend toward the completion of transatlantic strategic alliances between companies, and, moreover, the inclusion of Japanese firms in these alliances; the area of biotechnology illustrates this. In this way, the meaning of the European level for transnational business became relative.

As a result of the world political changes that accompanied the collapse of the Soviet Union, new demands were placed on the European institutions, which led to an obvious system overload. The pressure for a rapid expansion of the European Union to the east was increased by certain actors in order to hamper or at least slow down the deepening of the integration process. In 1994, despite the accelerated integration process, Delors noted in response to the question of the basis for Europe's falling relatively behind: 'The world has changed more quickly than we.'[11]

The fact that the European elite pact, whose many facets we have described in this volume, could come into effect only in the context of specific historical conditions was clear to us from the outset. It was never our intention to advance a general theory of integration that would replace existing general theories. If we placed the elite pact between transnational business and the supranational political entrepreneur at the centre of our analysis of the integration relaunch, this does not signify that this alliance was also decisive for earlier (and later) events in the long history of European integration. Although stressing different conditions for successful political entrepreneurship, we agree with Moravcsik (1998, 1999) that there was indeed a unique 'window of opportunity' for the alliance of supranational and transnational actors in the 1980s. There are good arguments for his claim that 'informal entrepreneurs enjoy brief successes and long periods of failure' (Moravcsik 1999: 285). Yet these 'brief successes' can and did set the course of economic and political trajectories.

For us, the point was to analyse what was qualitatively new in the integration thrust of the 1980s and to show that this was the central

[11] Delors in a TV interview, ARTE, 26 April 1994.

precondition for the integration relaunch and, therefore, for the development of a historically new multi-level political system in Europe. This development is not complete, and the logic of the multi-level polity in the 1990s was already quite different from that of the elite pact of the 1980s. The integration process provoked the transformation of the relationship between politics and economics and of the meaning of statehood in Europe, and continues to pose new theoretical questions.

Concluding remarks

The Amsterdam Treaty, the result of the intergovernmental conference of 1996–7, is widely regarded as insufficient with respect to institutional reform. It is plausible to think that the EU is heading for a situation in which the gap between the deficiencies of its ability to formulate policy and the internal and external requirements for action becomes even bigger.

There are a number of indications that the type of integration pursued up to now has definitely reached its limit in view of new conditions; the Amsterdam Treaty itself is evidence of this fact. A qualitatively new dynamic can be expected only if the EU can be reshaped as a political arena. But grand designs or even concrete projects aimed at the institutional reorganization of the EU are not on the agenda at the moment.

In any case, we think that there are good reasons to abandon the idea of the EU as an 'unfinished federal state', as it was seen by Hallstein (1969), the first Commission president. Moreover, some puzzling elements of contemporary statehood at European level may be not of a temporary nature but rather the central characteristics of a new hegemonic form. As we suggest in chapter 10, this notion is based on a new composition of tendencies in European history.

10   The state of the European Union

Volker Bornschier

What kind of state?

Having reassessed the integration thrust of the 1980s and the events that it set in motion, we have summarized our findings on the structure of the policy areas that set the tone of the political economy of the Union. We would now like to comment on the form of state that developed out of this process. The curious nature of this state is widely acknowledged by scholars; we would like to add that the puzzling nature of the governance structures embodied in the institutions of the European Union is due to a renewed compromise between two old European processes – nationalism and liberalism.

What exactly is 'odd' about the form of state called the European Union?

The European Union, which evolved from the renewed drive for European integration in the mid-1980s and which officially assumed this new name through the Treaty on European Union (agreed to at the end of 1991 and in effect since the completion of its ratification in 1993), is something new in the recent history of European state-building. This new form of state remains, as we termed it in chapter 1, a somewhat strange hermaphrodite – something between a confederation of states and a federal state. One important difference between the two is that a federal state unites several states within the framework of a single state in a single nation and is the exclusive subject of international law. By contrast, a confederation of states does not constitute a subject of international law on its own (Scholz 1995: 116f). The latter is formally the case of the EU insofar as its member states have remained sovereign in terms of international law. But even de jure the status of the EU is beyond a confederation, because the sovereignty that the member states retain is substantially truncated by the self-binding treaties to which they have agreed. Community law – the *acquis communautaire* – is indeed supranational, binding all member states in the sense that the regulation is directly applicable.

Yet, despite these ambiguities, the EU de facto represents a respected and powerful actor on the international stage. For example, during the renegotiations of the General Agreement on Tariffs and Trade (GATT), which led to the foundation of the World Trade Organization (WTO), the EU was an accepted party to the fierce bargaining that took place with the USA. Furthermore, the EU is regularly represented by the president of the European Commission when the famous Group of Seven gathers. Finally, 'international politicians have added Brussels to their itinerary when on world tours', as Beverly Springer (1996: 274) puts it.

We used the metaphor of a hermaphrodite to indicate that conventional social science categories fail to come to terms with what the EU actually is. This view is shared by scholars studying the nature of the state in the European Union, regardless of their theoretical approach (see, for example, Münch 1993: 133–81). Klaus Dieter Wolf (1996: 3) stated it concisely: 'The governance structure embodied in the institutions of the European Union is of a puzzling nature, no matter which theoretical perspective is applied to it.' Beverly Springer, reflecting on the 'March toward Monetary Integration', concluded that the EU is neither an international organization nor a fully sovereign state: 'Attempts to compare it to a federal system, such as that of the United States, are as flawed as attempts to compare it to the North American Free Trade Agreement (NAFTA)' (1996: 274).

It was Raymond Vernon (1994, see Springer 1996: 273) who poetically decribed the European Union as 'an historical aberration smuggled into the family of nations'. Although poetic, this is an ultimately inaccurate characterization. The European Union is indeed a strange novelty when compared with other products of mainstream state formation, which culminated in the full establishment of nation-states in the nineteenth century. But, in historical perspective, the EU represents something that was rare but not uncommon in the history of European state-building, and the EU has at least one very influential and eminent European forerunner, which we discuss below. However, in its present form, the EU represents a reconciliation between two mighty European forces that was seldom achieved in mainstream European development.

The compromise and its price

It is obvious that, for its member states, the EU restricts their sovereignty and preserves their jointly exercised sovereignty. Keohane and

Hoffmann (1991: 7f, 16f) describe it aptly as the 'pooling and sharing of sovereignty' rather than the transfer of sovereignty to a higher level. Indeed – as all scholars of EU affairs acknowledge – the Council of Ministers and the European Council[1] represent the real political power in the EU. Member states wield ultimate authority through these Councils: they negotiate and agree on treaties and their amendments, extensions or modifications, which then become law in the European Union.

In this context, Klaus Dieter Wolf (1996) has drawn our attention to yet another puzzle. The member states – normally very proud of the democratic achievements and forms of political participation in their respective nation-states – obviously refuse to allow similarly strong forms of democracy to develop at the level of the Union. They are the only formally authorized actors who could jointly agree to let such forms arise. Obviously, the nation-states do not want to do so or cannot do so owing to restrictions placed upon them by their electorates.

This leads to what is commonly referred to as a deficit of democracy at the level of the EU (see, for example, Lepsius 1991; Bach 1999; Buchmann 1999). Fully democratic procedures at the EU level would certainly legitimate that supranational governance structure, which would then gain power at the expense of the member states. Faced with this prospect, the member states have preferred to supply the EU with only indirect democratic legitimation since they – as democratically elected and controlled governments – have the last say on treaty matters.

The so-called deficit of democracy, although often referred to in both public as well as academic discourse, is often not fully understood. Several dimensions to this problem need to be distinguished. First, democratic governance requires not only that majorities legitimately decide on political action but that at the same time minorities are protected against the arrogance of majorities. In the latter respect the EU's track record is not bad, provided of course that the interests of minorities find a way to be represented by a nation-state.

Secondly, an important criterion of the degree of democratic governance is the equality of each individual vote. However, the quota system

[1] The Council of Ministers consists of a representative of each member state at ministerial level, authorized to commit the government of that member state (see the Treaty on European Union, signed in Maastricht on 7 February 1992, Article 146). The European Council brings together the heads of state or government of the member states and the president of the Commission. They are assisted by the ministers of foreign affairs of the member states and by a member of the Commission. The European Council meets at least twice a year, under the chairmanship of the head of state or government of the member state that holds the presidency of the Council. The European Council provides the EU with the necessary impetus for its development and defines the general political guidelines thereof (ibid., Article D).

through which the assembly of the European Parliament is constituted poses a severe problem in this respect because it violates the principle of equality in franchise (see also Scholz 1995: 120): the number of seats for a country is not directly proportional to the size of its population. A vote for a representative of the European Parliament in Ireland or Greece, for example, has more impact on the distribution of seats in the assembly than a vote in France or even more so in Germany.

Thirdly, the lack of separation of powers is also a serious drawback. Since only the Council can create EU law by amending, extending and renegotiating the treaties binding on all member states, this body simultaneously also creates supranational law. In this way, the Council forces the national parliaments automatically to ratify this change in EU law, i.e. by incorporating it into their national laws. This, however, clearly violates the democratic principle that only legitimized parliaments have the power to legislate (see also Vaubel 1995: 131).

Fourthly, the EU is characterized by a lack of democratically constituted control. The Commission wields de facto executive power rather extensively in the sense that it transforms EU law into decrees and specific regulations that affect the life of many if not all EU citizens (see also Bach 1992), something that is, of course, the very intention of the treaties. Under strictly democratic conditions, such executive power should be responsible to parliamentary control and parliamentary investigating committees, which, as noted above, are not available in a legitimized form at the EU level.

These are several relevant aspects of what is called the democracy deficit. Since the democratically constituted governments of the nation-states have reserved for themselves the right to legislate EU matters, the trade-off between the sovereignty of member states and democracy at the EU level has been resolved in favour of joint implementation of national sovereignty at the expense of democracy at the highest level of European statehood.

Nationalism meets liberalism

Despite the nationalist element present in the governance of the European Union discussed above, liberalization in the form of deregulation of formerly quite heavily segmented national economies was successfully implemented through the programme of 'completing the internal market'. This was the 'Europe 92' initiative approved via the Single European Act of the mid-1980s. The so-called four freedoms – capital, labour, trade and services – and the establishment of a common governance structure for economic matters through harmonization and/or mutual recognition of regulations correspond to a liberal economic programme advocating the removal of barriers to trade and a homogenized market as a basis for and benefit to prosperity and growth. There is no doubt that the transition of formerly nationally regulated and thus quite substantially segmented markets into a single, common market represents an important step in institutionalizing economic liberalism throughout Europe. Indeed, it is the largest and most far-reaching deregulation project in economic history.

We can thus conclude that the form of state in the European Union represents a compromise between nationalism and liberalism. This conclusion is hardly novel; Streeck (1996: 305) has already described this state as an 'alliance of nationalism and neoliberalism'. Nevertheless, we would like to add that this compromise between divergent forces present throughout European history should be acknowledged as a reconciliation of forces that – to the detriment of Europe – has been quite rare.

In chapter 1 we reflected briefly on state-building in Europe. Here we would like to acknowledge the two key social forces that acted on this process throughout European history. During the first phase of modernity, i.e. until the beginning of the nineteenth century, European states became more dissimilar. On the one hand, the absolutist state projects accentuated war, while, on the other hand, decentralized social systems emphasized trade. Important predecessors of the latter included Venice, the Hanseatic League, the United Provinces of North Holland, and later England and the United States. Over centuries, this polarization in state-building was accompanied by a dramatic process of concentration, reducing the number of states from about five hundred to twenty-five (Tilly 1975: 27).

The historical roots of contemporary processes

Which exactly were the forces acting on state formation over these centuries? They consisted primarily of two quite contradictory forces that emerged following the dissolution of the medieval world of Catholic European society. Each represented a new 'absolutism', albeit in ways that were diametrically opposed to one another. One emphasized collectivism, whereas the other promoted individualism (see also Coleman 1974). The first was expressed in the theory of the absolute power of the state, the second through a theory of individualism in which the individual is of paramount importance.

Absolute power of the state and individual pre-eminence clashed not only with each other but also with the medieval idea of a fixed position for each social agent within the whole. Power exercised on the basis of the absolutist claim of the state or the individual claim to pre-eminence thus needed new justifications to convince the public that order beyond collective and individual egoisms was possible. In collectivism the exercise of power was legitimated over time through the claim that this power was deployed 'for the people'. This justification remained inherently problematic since power exercised in favour of one group of people easily clashed with the claims of other people, and thus engendered belligerent competition between the emerging states of Europe. In the end, attempts at creating order through mutual recognition of the territorial power base of others and the promise of non-intervention in the internal affairs of sovereign states were only a kind of temporary truce.

In the case of individualism, the prescribed form of legitimation seemed much more elegant. Adam Smith provided the well-known justification of individualism: while egoistically pursuing their own ends, humans are led by an invisible hand in such a way as to promote an end that was never part of their intentions. The mysterious alchemy of the market thus transforms individual egoism into a social good – if and only if the market is given free rein. Thus, laissez-faire, i.e. restricting the state to a minimal role, is an integral part of this alchemy. This evolved into the doctrine of economic liberalism, which assumed – just as in case of the other absolutism – a quasi-religious status.

Yet, liberalism has always been more than that. Although it is true that the ideology of liberalism started to spread throughout Europe after the French Revolution, the central ideas and social movements that became liberalism are in fact much older. A very early example that demonstrates the roots of liberalism as a manifestation of individualism is the preamble of a law promulgated in Florence in the year 1289 – five hundred years (!) before the French Revolution – which proclaimed: 'Because liberty as the basis of will cannot be conditional upon alien criteria but must be based on self-determination; because personal freedom derives from natural right – the same that protects peoples from oppression, that protects and elevates their rights – we are determined to preserve and enhance it' (quoted in Raith 1979: 29, our translation). Thus, declarations of human rights came into being long before the Dutch, English, American and French revolutions. They are manifestations of an old and powerful European social movement and theory – individualism – that became elaborated in the European Enlightenment with its programme of self-empowerment and nourished diverse forms of liberalism.

The term 'liberalism' as such, however, appeared late. It first came into use in the political sphere at the beginning of the nineteenth century (i.e. *los liberales* in the Spanish Cortes) and signified a plea for the liberty of the individual and his/her right to self-expression.

Each of the two aforementioned 'absolutisms' – collectivism and individualism – became manifest in diverse and even conflicting movements. With respect to individualism, we mention here only three of the often conflicting manifestations of individualism: economic, political and social liberalism. Collectivism was an emerging consequence of the claim to absolute power by the state. The expansion of state power in Europe ultimately created a very powerful ideology – nationalism – in order both to legitimate and to limit through democratization the exercise of this absolute power of the state. At the same time, the territorial expansion of state power produced its own collective enemy, based also on collective bonds, i.e. regionalism. Regionalism, which can be seen as a lower-level nationalism, opposed the centralization implied by modern state-building, which abolished or restricted older identities that included patriotism and the right to self-governance at the regional level. This opposition between regionalism and the central state is a consequence of the key feature of European state-building, i.e. the aforementioned shrinking of five hundred state-like entities to only twenty-five over the past five hundred years of European history.

Socialism, although in theory an internationalist movement, is collectivist in orientation but also oriented toward a strong state. The programme of revolutionary socialism was to conquer state power and exercise a new and more just rule prior to the withering away of the state. Even when the reformist, social democratic version of the movement triumphed, socialism was still interested in a strong state with an extended role in economic and social matters whose purpose was to improve the destiny of the people. In this respect socialism and nationalism had a common interest; although in severe conflict with each other, they were both hostile towards liberalism.

The two conflicting historical movements (collectivism and individualism) are still found today in rather different notions of the state present in political science (Wolf 1996: 8). In the realist approach, the state is mystified as a single unitary rational actor trying to maximize its autonomy within a system of states. By contrast, the liberal perspective on the state sees the state as a subsystem of national or international society, which reflects societal needs based on people's preferences and which produces a public good. Here the state is seen as the problem-solver instead of a mystified, glorious and autonomous actor.

Both currents of thought have been influential in terms of political practice as well as political theory. Thus, the two opposing theories were also embedded as conflicting principles in the Charter of the United Nations, which establishes both the rights of nations (along with a non-intervention clause) and the human rights of the individual. Today, the clash between the principle of territoriality, established on the basis of social groups within a certain area, and the capitalist logic of the free use of economic opportunities in markets, which are fundamentally trans-territorial, has become clearly evident. To some observers this appears to be a *new* feature of global capitalism. But the battle between these principles has been going on in Europe for centuries. Unlike today, these forces were represented in conflicting state projects prior to the convergence that began in the nineteenth century.

An early form of reconciling the two conflicting forces was the United Provinces of North Holland, which developed at the end of the sixteenth century. This state was highly atypical for its time but seems very up-to-date when we compare it with the European Union (see chapter 1). In the provinces of North Holland, the most fully urbanized area at that time, civilian rule had for the first time in European history created a state structure that was also able to dominate its territory, which became the home of civil liberalism. The balance between the patriotic forces of the sovereign provinces and the newly emerging liberalism sheds new light on what has been called the curious form of state that is the present-day European Union.

To conclude this section, let us make the following points. First, the conflictive compromise between nationalist claims of sovereignty and liberalism, which we observe in present-day Europe at the level of the European Union, is not as new as it might seem. Even the democracy deficit can be found in its historical forerunner. Secondly, during the process of reconciling nationalism and liberalism in the competitive setting that was Europe, the modern state was ultimately more strongly influenced by the 'trade and economic state' as a 'contract of association' than by the colossal, rapacious states founded on domination and military power that represent the European tradition of war. The formation of the European Union is consistent with this trend toward peace. This aspect of European cooperation is not simply a recent occurrence, but was intended from the beginning, when, on the fifth anniversary of the end of the Second World War (9 May 1950), the French minister of foreign affairs, Robert Schuman, proposed a common organization in Europe.

Shifts in the composition of nationalism and liberalism

Compromise – even if conflictive – is not such a bad thing. More often in European history, the supremacy of collectivism was imposed at the expense of liberalism. To be sure, the forerunners of the capitalist project in Europe, which over time were situated in very different places (Venice, the Hanseatic League, North Holland and the United Kingdom), were always more liberal than their historical counterparts. But apart from this, the composition of nationalism and liberalism in Europe as a whole shifted in considerable waves which mark distinct phases.

In order to understand the different phases of nationalism and liberalism in the twentieth century we must briefly turn to the previous one. The nineteenth century started with an initial surge and ended with a resurgence of nationalism. Nevertheless, it was also the century in which liberalism triumphed for the first time in large parts of Western Europe. Liberalism then began to lose strength during the 1880s, both within as well as between countries (see Mommsen 1969). The new nationalism after 1870 was an attempt at ideologically mending societal ruptures without having to undertake more fundamental reforms. European imperialism from 1885 until the end of the First World War can be seen as an extreme form of nationalist thinking, not only in the continental countries but also under liberal imperialism in England.

Extreme nationalism, popular arrogance and accompanying racism and xenophobia were reactions to an insufficient compromise in the class-polarized societal model around the turn of the century. Once again, during the 1920s and the 1930s, such attitudes could be observed in many European countries (and something similar, although much weaker, took place during the 1980s and the 1990s). These ideologies were used to divert attention from domestic conflicts. In this respect Hitler's race hatred and lust for conquest are directly related to this imperialist phase.

The various Europes in the twentieth century

The first phase of the composition of nationalism and liberalism in Europe in the twentieth century is actually the continuation of the resurgence of nationalism in the last third of the nineteenth century which ended in the Thirty Years War of the twentieth century, 1914–45. In the course of the second part of this phase, hyper-nationalism and imperialism triggered the world wars of the twentieth century, in the course of which dramatic changes in economic and political positions within Western core society became evident. By the end of this phase, Europe had lost its leadership position to the United States. After 1945, in the second phase of the composition of nationalism and liberalism in the twentieth century, Europe, under the hegemony of liberal Keynesianism and US liberalism, recovered. But liberalism remained restricted – 'The state is the solution' was the key phrase to characterize the societal model – and national alliances of the state, business and the labouring classes for recovery and growth kept a tight rein on liberalism. The third phase of the recomposition of nationalism and liberalism started with the decay of the Keynesian societal model.

As the 1960s drew to a close, liberalism experienced a resurgence. In one respect, this was obviously evidenced by the renewed absolutism of neoliberalist doctrine, which became hegemonic during the 1970s. But in important respects there was more to it than that. Political liberalism was strengthened, as evidenced by the anti-authoritarian youth movements and the subsequent broad wave of progressive political and social movements, which, in addition to their specific themes, had a strong and common focus on basic democratic procedures. It was not only the anti-authoritarian and autonomous movements that evidenced a fresh and radical claim to freedom throughout the Western world; wider segments of society were also increasingly affected. The greater desire of citizens to assume responsibility for organizing their own lives was clearly evident. These citizens demanded a society of multiple choices that makes possible an individualized lifestyle. 'Individualization' is the term sociologists have created for this concept. Even those who do not like the quasi-religious nature of economic neoliberalism have been forced to admit that it is only part of a broad current of resurgent individualism.

In sociology and political science this remarkable shift, which altered both the themes of political discourse and the forms of interest articulation, has been labelled by Ronald Inglehart (1977) as *The Silent Revolution*. But this term does not tell the whole story. When institutionalized value priorities and those manifest at the level of citizens begin to diverge, society is on the move. Political potentials can be defined as value priorities among citizens that – given appropriate political opportunity structures and framing through theories – feed oppositional movements expressing discontent and opposition. The decay of the Keynesian compromise, however, triggered not just one new political potential (the so-called new social movements) but two. Since the beginning of the 1970s, these two emerging political potentials have become increasingly polarized in Western countries. This is shown by the detailed empirical research of Stefan Sacchi (1998) covering the past quarter of a century. Indeed the 'silent revolution' represented both the rebirth of oppositional (and universalist) liberalism and the rebirth of a regressive and authoritarian political potential that nourished the renewed identification with forms of 'nationalisms' at the regional and nation-state level.

The move toward political union: did liberalism eventually beat nationalism?

The modern push towards European integration, which started as early as the beginning of the 1950s, persisted through two phases of Europe in the twentieth century – the Keynesian era and the resurgence of liberalism. But it was only the revitalization of the European Community in the 1980s that changed the very nature of integration by adding a considerably extended political dimension to it, one that was continued but in no way fundamentally altered by the Treaty on European Union, which came into effect in 1993.

In this volume we have argued that the European transnational corporations were the decisive protagonists behind the move towards the European Union. This could be falsely interpreted as a triumph of deregulationist philosophy over the state, but this is in fact not the case. Even for the European transnational corporations themselves, a compromise between protective nationalism and liberalism is evident. To be sure, this new type of nationalism is a social force that transcends the established nation-states. It seems less emotional and more instrumental in kind, and its frame of reference is competition in the world system. The European business elite and the political elite in Brussels were and are the early, influential spokespeople of this Euro-nationalism. Among the latter, the political Euro-entrepreneur Jacques Delors has always been a strong advocate of this new form of Euro-nationalism and one willing to project European brilliance into the future. Therefore he used to warn: 'We must move quickly otherwise Europe will become an archaeological excavation site, where Americans and Japanese seek for lost ideas and ways of life' (Delors 1991).

But Euro-nationalism was in no way restricted to the elite who managed the integration thrust of the mid-1980s. A significant minority of Community citizens belongs to this group, too. Unfortunately, despite continuing efforts at monitoring European public opinion, we cannot say whether this group has increased in size over time. At least we know that in 1982 – before the push for integration – slightly more than 20 per cent of the Community's citizens could be classified as

Euro-nationalists, i.e. often self-identifying as 'Europeans' and expressing mistrust of extra-European powers (Krummenacher 1997).

We now must acknowledge the varieties of 'nationalism' in Europe. At present, nationalism as a powerful historical manifestation of a collective ideology assumes different and opposing forms: regionalism, nationalism and Euro-nationalism. Patriotism rooted in local or regional bonds may easily reactivate resentments against the nation-state, since the victory of that very nation-state originally put an end to their forms of self-government. Therefore, this kind of nationalism is most often opposed to classical nationalism, although it might well seek alliances with Euro-nationalist forces against the nation-state in order to regain more independence. Classical nationalism is rooted in historically constructed bonds that are based on entitlements, political and social rights that became institutionalized at the level of the nation-state during the past two centuries. It may regard regional bonds as forms of backwardness while at the same time perceiving Euro-nationalism as threatening established political and social rights. Euro-nationalism is progressive in a historical sense in so far as it seeks protection at a level beyond the nation-state, a collectivity large enough to provide competitive advantages in a world system in which smaller political units increasingly feel the threat of falling behind.

Unfortunately, we have little empirical evidence on the shifts in size of the different kinds of collective identities over time and on their exclusiveness. Even if we have little information on changes over time, we can say that up to 30 per cent of EU citizens can be classified as distinct nationalists, and about 20 per cent can be termed marked Euro-nationalists in the above-mentioned sense (Krummenacher 1997). Another finding for two time points at the beginning of the 1990s suggests that about 55 per cent of EU citizens feel very attached to their region (Rothenbühler 1997). The latter study suggests that nationalist and regionalist identification are of about the same size, whereas the identification with Europe or the EU is clearly lower and declined between 1991 and 1995.

From recent research we can conclude that a distinct nationalist orientation does not represent a serious threat to European integration. The expression of national pride and support for European integration are not mutually exclusive alternatives; in fact, there is a very small but positive correlation between the two. Less spectacular is the finding that Euro-nationalists on the average are more favourable toward integration than the rest of the population and would regret it more if it failed (Krummenacher 1997). In the 1990s, citizens of the EU seemed to be increasingly attached to smaller units such as the region or city while the corresponding figures for feelings of attachment to the European Union fell. But there is no hint at all that identification with one's own region is affecting attitudes towards European integration (Rothenbühler 1997).

A compromise – no victory of liberalism

Interpreting the form of the state in the European Union as a compromise between nationalism and liberalism must acknowledge not only the tensions between the underlying forces of collectivism and individualism, but also the fact that the European reality is a bit more complex than that. Indeed, in the case of different forms of nationalism, it is a multi-level compromise. Modern-day liberalism quarrels with nationalism, but different forms of collective identity also quarrel among themselves: regionalism, classical nationalism and Euro-nationalism. The same is true for the various manifestations of liberalism, although to a lesser extent. While economic liberalism is quite well established at the Union level, the key claims of political liberalism are not – as evidenced by the democracy deficit to which we have referred.

Looking back at European history, the various manifestations of collective identity have changed considerably in terms of their impact. Regionalism has always been opposed to the centralization implied by state-building, which restricted or abolished older rights and forms of self-government of smaller political units. Nationalism and the creation of a nation became a strategy to legitimate the authority of the nation-state. This in turn triggered the extension of citizens' rights (see Marshall [1950] 1965). At the EU level this process is repeated. Nationalism now seems to be playing the role of an oppositional force with respect to the Union project much as regionalism once did vis-à-vis the emerging nation-states. However – and this is quite important – contemporary regionalism has not become weakened by the process of European integration; quite the contrary. Thus regionalism and nationalism have become two distinct forces in opposition to the centralization of authority, while at the same time both are in opposition to each other.

The European nation-state has thus come under pressure to compromise from two sides: from the quest for more regional autonomy, and from being forced to give away regulatory authority to the supranational body of the EU. The European nation-states reacted to these pressures by maintaining ultimate control over the matters of the Union. However, the binding nature of the EU treaty is at the same time significant and transfers considerable executive power from the nation-states to the new supranational European state. The price of this overall compromise is the not insignificant deficit of democracy in European politics. Given the complicated forces behind the compromise, this deficit will not be easy to overcome.

Empirical evidence for the compromise is suggested by the mentioned findings: contrary to general opinion, classical nationalism as well as regionalism – in their present forms at least – are not endangering European integration, although they do help to shape it.

Given the weight of the multi-level compromise of collective identities embodied in the overall governance structures of European institutions, one can hardly say that liberalism took over in Europe. Yet, it increased its impact at the same time. Without question, the deregulation project in Europe is of historic dimensions and was pushed by a forceful ideology. We should not however make neoliberalism a comic figure. This is only one aspect of the resurgence of liberalism, which has become accepted by wider segments of the population in the realm of politics (grassroots democracy, referenda) and everyday life (individualization). Thus we have to accept, even if we do not admire, that European citizens have become more liberal and seek to democratize their freedom. This is why opposition to economic liberalism has been limited.

The European Union – an untimely undertaking?

The political dimension of European integration developed during an era of dramatic change in information technologies and intensified economic globalization. Many observers have contended that the state is in decline or even that states are withering away precisely because of these two factors. If this were true, the EU would indeed be an untimely undertaking. However, we question the myth of the decline and/or withering away of the state and suggest two arguments in support of our view.

Our first argument relates to the emerging era of telematics (the fusion of telecommunications with information technologies under the aegis of digitalization). Views of discontinuous technological development have changed since the early 1980s. Whereas the original approach of Joseph Schumpeter was to explain innovation thrusts by reference to changes in the economic sphere alone, Carlota Perez and those who followed her line suggested an important revision, to which we have already referred in chapter 1. Both the technological style and the politico-economic regime – the techno-economic and the socio-institutional subsystems – need to adjust to each other in order to make a long-term economic upswing viable. Since the adjustment of the socio-institutional subsystem is a necessary part of the evolution and diffusion of a new technological style, the institutional infrastructure that is able to support a new technological style is subject to a political logic. This needs to be defined, and new institutions need to be created through political struggles, not only within nation-states but also in the world market and the world polity.

We contend that the new political institutions that will be necessary in the age of telematics imply that the state sphere is not becoming obsolete but will be an indispensable element for making the new technological style viable. The need for social and material infrastructure at the national as well as at the international level will increase, especially with regard to information technology. And with this comes an increasing need for international cooperation. Although these developments will alter the nature of state sovereignty, they will not make states and leadership in the global community obsolete. Those states that take the lead in providing the infrastructure for the global information system will be in a position to exert dominance in setting the norms and standards of the new infrastructures.

The EU as a supranational state is unique in meeting this present challenge. In developing the infrastructure for the emerging technological style of the telematics era, the EU did something that no nation-state was willing or able to do on that scale. There may be debate about how well it has performed in this regard (see Bornschier 1994; Mytelka 1995), but this is not the point here. What is important to note is that the state sphere is not becoming obsolete in the era of the new technological style.

Our second argument regarding economic globalization seems to have invited considerable misunderstanding. In comparison with the time prior to and following the turn of the nineteenth century, the expansion of economic globalization that began in the 1980s is not so exceptional, as we have already noted in chapter 1, and during this earlier expansion the state survived quite well. This should make us cautious about predicting the withering away of the state any time within the twenty-first century. Beyond this historical analogy, wishes for or fears of the withering away of the state in the world political economy are not warranted.

In order to explain why, one has to consider that states and business in the capitalist world political economy are inextricably interrelated. States provide territorially bounded public goods which – if of good quality – help economic enterprises to prosper. This applies not only to the average firm that normally does business only within the framework of a single state, but more importantly – and this is a point neglected in the recent debate on globalization – to transnational corporations. In order to compete successfully, these corporations, although economically active around the world, need a strong base of operations allowing for economies of scale as well as shared economic regulation. They prosper if backed by strong governments that protect their interests both at home and abroad.

Even in an era of flourishing free trade ideology, protective state action continues to be important. One recent example is the EU protecting European aerospace from the merger of two gigantic US aerospace corporations, Boeing and McDonnell Douglas: an EU antitrust panel found that the US$15 billion merger would strengthen Boeing's existing dominant position and therefore should be prohibited. Under EU law, the European Commission can block mergers – even of non-European enterprises – if it feels these will harm fair trade in the Union. Yet, in completely blocking the merger the EU Commission would have seriously collided with the US government, which had already approved the deal between the two aircraft giants without conditions. Eventually the case was settled by an agreement with conditions when it came to a decision in July 1997. Another example from the competition in the triad is that 'the EU will reintroduce minimum prices on some computer chips exported by Japan and South Korea. The antidumping move will be phased in over the next three months, a slower pace than the European chip industry has sought' (*Wall Street Journal Europe*, 11 March 1997, p. 1).

We can find many other examples in favour of the proposition that states regulating a huge market command considerable market power and weight in the world political economy. The same relationship between size and power applies, of course, also to currencies. Indeed, this was the underlying rationale for the European monetary union established through the Treaty on European Union. Ironically, the rigid timetable and convergence criteria ultimately had the negative side-effect of tying the hands of European governments (owing to limits on public debt) when it came to overcoming sluggish growth and persistent unemployment in the mid-1990s through anti-cyclical public spending.

States not 'withering away' and state alliances in no way novel

The recent debate on globalization and telematics rests in our view on fatally flawed premises in so far as it falsely suggests that the state is withering away. This will certainly not be the case, since strong states and big business go hand in hand in the world political economy. This is a lesson perhaps lost on the authors of present-day economics textbooks although not on students of history.

What seems true, however, is that political middleweights, such as the old European powers, as well as political lightweights will increasingly suffer a loss of impact in comparison with the Keynesian era. Strong and – via measures to enhance solidarity – solidly integrated states are very likely to have a clear advantage in the twenty-first century in effectively competing for shares in the world political economy.

As we have witnessed, since the 1980s several integration projects have been launched – the North American Free Trade Agreement (NAFTA), the Asean Free Trade Area (AFTA) and Asia-Pacific Economic Cooperation (APEC), to mention only those involving members of the triad. European integration served as a trigger for these, although thus far it remains unique. One might well argue that alliances aimed at aggregating state power would not compare favourably to well-established nation-states; as units of power they are hardly as effective. Although this seems a plausible argument, it neglects the role alliances have played in the history of the world political economy.

Alliances between states are in no way novel. Just as firms can and do merge, so it is with states; indeed states have done so in the past. Consider, for example, the last three hegemons in the world political economy following the first Thirty Years War; all were in fact alliances of states: the United Provinces of North Holland, the United Kingdom of England, Scotland and Northern Ireland, and the United States of America.

The EU and the other big players in the world political economy

The role of the European Union in the world political economy is often too narrowly analysed in terms of economic aggregates. This omits the fact that economic competition is also intrinsically a form of competition between institutional solutions. One complex set of such institutions relevant to the topic of this volume is the state, an institutional set that, as we have concluded, will surely not become obsolete in the near future. Before addressing the competing forms of the state in the core of the world system, let us begin by reciting some important economic figures.

We start with the year 1992, when the internal market project was realized. In terms of share of world trade and world share of foreign direct investment, the EU clearly leads Japan and the USA, the other two nation-states making up the triad (see also chapter 1). Moreover, the jurisdiction of the Union encompasses the largest ever single high-income market; the combined population of the EU's fifteen members is 368 million, compared with a population of 255 million in the USA and

125 million in Japan. Even though per capita income (corrected for purchasing power parities) in the EU ranks only third to its rivals in the triad (USA: US$ 23,120; Japan: US$ 20,160; EU: US$ 17,424), total market size is somewhat larger in the EU (US$ 6,417 billion) than in the USA (US$ 5,898 billion), while Japan ranks a distant third (US$ 2,510 billion) (figures computed from World Bank 1994: 201, 259).

Of course, a huge market like the one under EU jurisdiction cannot be equated with a leading position in high-tech industries; here Europe does not command positions commensurate with its market size. Yet, one should not dismiss huge markets as an effective source of power in itself. Here the EU is in a strong position, which it wants to consolidate through the new Euro-currency (a heavyweight in the world economy), and anxieties about its decline seem premature if not far-fetched.

Let us proceed to the second half of the 1990s. Two decades after the time when, to many observers, the USA seemed to be in decline and Japan's economic growth was actually challenging Europe's position, the situation in the triad had changed very considerably. The revitalized American position has become clearly evident. Without a doubt, the new technological style of the telematics era has put both US firms and US standards in leading positions. This pertains not only to information technologies but also to biotechnology.

Japan, whose spectacular economic growth made it the big challenger of the 1970s and 1980s, featured in very different newspaper headlines in the 1990s. The crisis in Japan has affected societal self-confidence and exposed the rotten pillars of its postwar order. The years of extreme self-confidence are over, and Japan has entered a phase of deep self-doubt. Japan is moving from its position as a special case in the postwar era to being a normal case of discontinuous development in the core.

Western Europe, hit by worrisome levels of unemployment and fears of further job losses, now shares with Japan the fate of being second to the USA in terms of economic soundness. Yet, in contrast to Japan, Western Europe has already carried out much of the task of deregulation, and despite the currently sluggish economy has produced a timely vision. This vision is evidenced by the White Paper of December 1993 entitled *Growth, Competitiveness, Employment – The Challenges and Ways Forward into the 21st Century*. This report calls for a 'new model of European society' and for 'sustainable development': 'It is important to develop a societal project for a higher quality of life in the Community, which can motivate people and hence can generate the required human energy' (EU 1993: 15, 150f).

Leadership

The present economic ranking in the triad – the United States as number one, followed by the European Union, and both rather unchallenged by Japan in third place – is also present in ideological leadership in shaping global concerns.

Even if the United States is no longer the world's premier economic power, as it was from the end of the Second World War until the 1960s, its recent come-back is remarkable and it remains the ideological and military leader. The European Union has undoubtedly gained stature in economic policy circles. Together with the United States, the European Union facilitated the agreement establishing the World Trade Organization (WTO), while Japan remained in the background. The United States is frequently able to gain support for its positions in the WTO. Although the United States is no longer the world's biggest exporter, it does successfully export its values: America's passion for deregulation and free trade. At the beginning of 1997, the United States brought seventy countries to agreement on its position regarding the deregulation of telecommunications. The chief US negotiator immodestly stated in press releases that this made the American style of competition the norm. For telecommunications, the world's third-largest industry today, and one which until recently was dominated by state monopolies (even in the United States), this unleashes a revolution.

In other areas of global concern, the European Union is ideologically the overall leader. Take, for example, protection of the atmosphere. At the Rio conference as well as at the subsequent conferences of the parties to specify the climate convention, the European Union was showing leadership, while the United States was the biggest hindrance among the developed countries (Missbach 1999). At the various preparatory meetings for the third conference of the parties in Kyoto at the end of 1997 this became obvious from the EU proposal, which aimed to find broad support among developing countries too. The European Union proposed that industrialized countries should reduce their greenhouse gas emissions by 15 per cent by 2010 from 1990 levels while developing countries were exempted from reductions. Notwithstanding that the results of the Kyoto conference fell short of this initial EU position, it is noteworthy that in the end the European Union succeeded in pushing the United States and Japan to a first binding agreement for protecting the atmosphere from greenhouse gases.

There is another remarkable point to the EU initiative. A special strength of the European Union lies in the fact that it can focus the diverging positions of its fifteen member countries beforehand, thus increasing its odds of success at large international conferences. The forging of a common position for external consumption is made possible through internal compensation. In this respect the European Union could be a model for the world. The EU environmental ministers succeeded in creating an equitable system of internal compensation between the rich and poor member states. The total reduction for the Union is realized through an extremely unequal internal formula: whereas the rich countries must reduce their production of greenhouse gases, the poorer ones can even produce more greenhouse gases than in the reference year of 1990.

The European state of nations – a model for world society?

The heading above is not a product of arrogance or Euro-centrism; it is quite obvious that previous European social innovations have been models for the world. The cultural legacy of the Atlantic West – the roots of which lie in Europe – shaped the institutions that incontrovertibly determine core status in world society: the market, social egalitarianism and the rule of law, along with the sharing of power and political checks and balances, economic enterprise and modern schools. To be sure, within that globally dominant social praxis Europe does not play the role it once did. But it is far from being on the decline, as evidenced by its revitalization since the 1980s and its proven ability to continue to contribute innovatively to the future shape of world society – the supranational state being the case in point here.

At present two quite different kinds of state alliances are preparing for leadership in the twenty-first century: the United States of America as a federal nation-state and the European state of nations. Even if different, the two are actually not independent, a point made obvious by the NATO alliance linking the Atlantic West under American leadership and military might. Despite this joint leadership, which is facilitated by a strong common cultural heritage, the differences in the two forms of state are important and will not wither away in the course of time.

It has become clear from what we and others have already said (see, for example, Lepsius 1991) that there will not be a United States of Europe, since that would imply a melting pot of groups from different nations – although admittedly this was an admirable historical accomplishment in the case of the USA. In contrast to this, the European state project rests, and needs to rest, on the acknowledgement of its constituent nations, which have developed in the course of its history. What the Union contributes to this is an increasingly European identity – not as a replacement for, but as an addition to, national, regional and local bonds. Such an overarching European identity has existed for a long time in Europe's history, albeit to varying degrees and restricted to elites.

Does the specific type of alliance of state power that recently developed in Europe imply that the resulting state will be a comparatively weak one? What is a strong state and what is a weak one? A strong state is one that is able to institutionalize cohesion and social balancing – an obvious strength of postwar European state-building – and can reconcile the different forces (nationalism and liberalism) in a productive compromise that represents more than a stalemate. This does not seem impossible in the case of the European Union – for efforts see 'target cohesion' and 'social and economic convergence' in chapters 5 and 6. But will such a state configuration also be successful in taking part in peaceful world economic competition? This remains to be seen, but the history of Europe suggests that pessimism is not appropriate. The aforementioned example of the state of North Holland seems to be relevant to the debate. Here we recall Braudel's question (see chapter 1): Can the United Provinces of North Holland be called a 'state'? No matter how that question is answered, there is no doubt that during its time the novel system of governance in North Holland achieved pre-eminence in the emerging world economy for at least one century and that this societal system was astonishingly liberal compared with its contemporary rivals.

Thus, what has been termed the 'odd nature' of the form of state represented by the European Union and what has even been called 'an historical aberration' must be reinterpreted in a rather different light. The present-day uniqueness of this European social innovation (which follows that earlier European innovation, the nation-state) may become a model to the world for reconciling the different manifestations of nationalism and liberalism in a multi-level system of governance. We hope that such an interpretation (see Bornschier 1996: 368; and Therborn 1997: 586) does not seem too optimistic to the reader.

Appendix: List of interview partners (1993–1996)

EU COMMISSION AND DIRECTORATES GENERAL

Lord Cockfield	Commission
E. Davignon	Commission
F. Braun	DG/VEBA
K. Schreiber	DG III
M. Rüte	DG IV
C. Savoini	DG V
P. Venturini	DG V
A. Klepsch	DG XII
J.-P. Masson	COST/DG XII
R. Hüber	DG XIII

COMMITTEE OF PERMANENT REPRESENTATIVES (COREPER)

Two British senior officials
Two German senior officials
J. Vandamme   Counsellor of the Belgian COREPER delegation

EUROPEAN PARLIAMENT

Chr. Tannert	Socialist group
J. Moreau	Former chairman of the Economic and Monetary Affairs Committee; president of the Economic and Social Committee

EMPLOYERS, BUSINESS ASSOCIATIONS, ROUNDTABLES OF INDUSTRIALISTS

W. Dekker	Philips/European Roundtable of Industrialists
F. Braun	DG/VEBA
H. Maucher	Nestlé/European Roundtable of Industrialists

H. Glatz	Daimler-Benz
H. Kressler	Unilever/European Roundtable of Industrialists
S. Ryser	Hoffmann-La Roche, Senior Advisory Group Biotechnology
R. Verschueren	UNICE
K. Vandendael	EFPIA
W. Wagner	European Information Technology Industry Roundtable
J. Moritz	Siemens
N. Hazewindus	Philips
J. Vanhumbeeck	Siemens, Liaison Office to the European Union

TRADE UNIONS

F. Bisegna	ICEF
T. Jenkins	TUC/ETUC, also Economic and Social Committee
W. Bergans	ETUC

NON-GOVERNMENTAL ORGANIZATIONS

J. Krazek	Friends of the Earth Europe, BUND

OTHER INFORMANTS

Prof. S. George	University of Sheffield
Prof. M. Sharp	University of Sussex
Prof. J. Pelkmans	Centre for European Policy Studies, Brussels

Bibliography

I. OFFICIAL PUBLICATIONS OF THE COMMISSION OF THE EC/EU

CEC 1970. *Die Industriepolitik der Gemeinschaft*. Memorandum der Kommission an den Rat.
1981a. *Communication from the Commission to the Council on the State of the Internal Market*. Strasbourg, 17 June 1981, COM (81) 313 final.
1981b. *A Policy for Industrial Innovation – Strategic Outlines of a Community Approach*. COM (81) 620 final.
1982a. *Commission Communication to the Council on Re-Activating the European Internal Market*. Brussels, 15 November 1982, COM (82) 735 final.
1982b. *On Laying the Foundations for a European Strategic Programme of Research and Development in Information Technology: The Pilot Phase*. COM (82) 486 final/2.
1982c. *Towards a European Strategic Programme for Research and Development in Information Technologies*. COM (82) 287 final.
1983a. *Biotechnologie: Die Aufgaben der Gemeinschaft*. COM (83) 328 final.
1983b. *Biotechnologie in der Gemeinschaft*. COM (83) 672 final.
1984a. 'Eurofutures: The challenges of innovation'. *Futures* (Special Edition).
1984b. *Communication from the Commission to the Council: Consolidating the Internal Market*. Brussels, 13 June 1984, COM (84) 305 final.
1985. *Completing the Internal Market. White Paper from the Commission to the European Council*. June 1985, COM (85) 310 final.
1991a. *Informations- und Kommunikationstechnologien. Die Rolle Europas*. General Directorate XIII.
1991b. *Promoting the Competitive Environment for the Industrial Activities Based on Biotechnology within the Community*. SEC (91) 629.
1991c. 'Förderung eines wettbewerbsorientierten Umfeldes für die industrielle Anwendung der Biotechnologie in der Gemeinschaft'. *EC Bulletin*, Suppl. No. 3.
1992. *Europe on the Move. The European Community in the 1990s*. Booklet for the Universal Exposition in Seville 1992. Publications Unit.
CEU 1993. *White Paper: Growth, Competitiveness, Employment: The Challenges and Ways Forward into the 21st Century*. COM (93) 700 final. Luxembourg: Office for Official Publications.
1994. *Biotechnologie und das Weissbuch über Wachstum, Wettbewerbsfähigkeit und Beschäftigung. Vorbereitung der nächsten Phase*. COM (94) 219 final.

1995a. 'Der soziale Dialog in der Gemeinschaft 1995: eine Bestandesaufnahme'. *Social Europe* No. 2. Luxembourg: Office for Official Publications.

1995b. *Intergovernmental Conference 1996. Commission Report for the Reflection Group.* Luxembourg: EUR–OP.

1996a. *First Report on Economic and Social Cohesion.* Luxembourg: Office for Official Publications.

1996b. *Die Weiterentwicklung der europäischen Sozialpolitik – Bericht über die Arbeiten des Forums.* Luxembourg: Office for Official Publications.

II. OTHER REFERENCES

Agnelli, Giovanni. 1989. 'The Europe of 1992'. *Foreign Affairs* 68(4): 61–70.

Allen, David. 1992. 'European Union, the Single European Act and the 1992 Programme'. In D. Swann (ed.), *The Single European Market and Beyond. A Study of the Wider Implications of the Single European Act.* London and New York: Routledge.

1996. 'Cohesion and Structural Adjustment'. In H. Wallace and W. Wallace (eds.), *Policymaking in the European Union.* Oxford: Oxford University Press.

Alter, Karen J. 1996. 'The European Court's Political Power'. *West European Politics* 19(3).

1998. 'Who are the "Masters of the Treaty"? European Governments and the European Court of Justice'. *International Organization* 52(19).

Alter, Karen J., and Sophie Meunier-Aitsahalia. 1994. 'Judicial Politics in the European Community. European Integration and the Pathbreaking Cassis de Dijon Decision'. *Comparative Political Studies* 26(4).

Anderson, Jeffrey J. 1995a. 'The State of the (European) Union: From the Single Market to Maastricht, from Singular Events to General Theories'. *World Politics* 47: 441–65.

1995b. 'Structural Funds and the Social Dimension of EU Policy: Springboard or Stumbling Block?' In S. Leibfried and P. Pierson (eds.), *European Social Policy: Between Fragmentation and Integration.* Washington DC: Brookings.

Archibugi, Daniele. 1992. 'Patenting as an Indicator of Technological Innovation: A Review'. *Science and Public Policy* 19: 357–68.

Armingeon, Klaus. 1994. 'Die Regulierung der kollektiven Arbeitsbeziehungen in der Europäischen Union'. In W. Streeck (ed.), *Staat und Verbände.* Special issue of *Politische Vierteljahresschrift,* No. 25. Opladen: Westdeutscher Verlag.

Artis, M.J. 1992. 'The Maastricht Road to Monetary Union'. *Journal of Common Market Studies* 30(3).

Attali, Jacques. 1993. *Verbatim. Tome 1: Chronique des années 1981–1986.* Paris: Fayard.

1995. *Verbatim. Tome 2: Chronique des années 1986–1988.* Paris: Fayard.

Bach, Maurizio. 1992. 'Eine leise Revolution durch Verwaltungsverfahren. Bürokratische Integrationsprozesse in der Europäischen Gemeinschaft'. *Zeitschrift für Soziologie* 21.

1993a. 'Vom Zweckverband zum technokratischen Regime: Politische Legitimation und institutionelle Verselbständigung in der Europäischen Gemeinschaft'. In H.A. Winkler and H. Kaelble (eds.), *Nationalismus – Nationalitäten – Supranationalität*. Stuttgart: Klett-Cotta.

1993b. 'Integrationsprozesse in der Europäischen Gemeinschaft: Vom Zweckverband zum technokratischen Regime?' In H. Meulemann and A. Elting-Camus (eds.), *26. Deutscher Soziologentag. Lebensverhältnisse und soziale Konflikte im neuen Europa, Tagungsband II: Sektionen, Arbeits- und Ad hoc-Gruppen*. Opladen: Westdeutscher Verlag.

1999. *Die Bürokratisierung Europas. Verwaltungseliten, Experten und politische Legitimation*. Frankfurt/Main: Campus.

Bairoch, Paul. 1996. 'Globalization Myths and Realities: One Century of External Trade and Foreign Investment'. Pp. 173–92 in Robert Boyer and Daniel Drache (eds.), *States against Markets: The Limits of Globalization*. London and New York: Routledge.

Baumann, Hans. 1995. *Von nationalstaatlichen zu europäischen Arbeitsbeziehungen? Möglichkeiten und Grenzen der sozialen Dimension in Europa nach Maastricht: Das Beispiel der Bauwirtschaft*. Basler Schriften zur europäischen Integration No. 11, Basel: Europa Institut.

Begg, Ian, and David Mayes. 1993. 'Cohesion, Convergence and Economic and Monetary Union in Europe'. *Regional Studies* 27(2).

Berié, Hermann. 1988. 'Deutsche EG-Präsidentschaft: Erfolg für den europäischen Sozialraum'. *Bundesarbeitsblatt* 9.

1992. 'Maastrichter Beschlüsse / Auf dem Weg zur Sozialunion'. *Zeitschrift für Sozialreform* 8.

Bieber, Roland, Jean-Paul Jacqué and Joseph H.H. Weiler (eds.). 1985. *L'Europe de demain. Une Union sans cesse plus étroite. Analyse critique du projet de traité instituant l'Union européenne*. Brussels: Collection perspectives européennes.

Bieber, Roland, J. Pantalis and J. Schoo. 1986. 'Implications of the Single European Act for the European Parliament'. *Common Market Law Review* 23.

Biehl, Dieter. 1988. 'Ein substantielles, aber begrenztes Reformpaket – Zum Brüsseler Reformgipfel'. *Integration* 2.

Boissière, Jean-Baptiste, and Bertrand Warusfel. 1991. *La nouvelle frontière de la technologie européenne*. Paris: Calman-Levy.

Bornschier, Volker. 1988. *Westliche Gesellschaft im Wandel*. Frankfurt/Main: Campus.

1994. 'The Rise of the European Community. Grasping towards Hegemony? Or Therapy against National Decline?' Pp. 55–82 in Max Haller and Rudolf Richter (eds.), *Towards a European Nation. Political Trends in Europe*. New York: Sharpe.

1996. *Western Society in Transition*. New Brunswick, NJ: Transaction Publishers.

Bornschier, Volker, and Christopher Chase-Dunn. 1999. 'Technological Change, Globalization and Hegemonic Rivalry'. Chapter 14 in Volker Bornschier and Christopher Chase-Dunn (eds.), *The Future of Global Conflict*. London: Sage.

Bornschier, Volker, and Christian Suter. 1992. 'Long Waves in the World

System'. Pp. 15-49 in Volker Bornschier and Peter Lengyel (eds.), *Waves, Formations, and Values in the World System*. Vol. 2 of World Society Studies. New Brunswick and London: Transaction Publishers.

Bornschier, Volker, and Patrick Ziltener. 1999. 'The Revitalization of Western Europe and the Politics of the "Social Dimension"'. In P. Boje, B. van Steenbergen and S. Walby (eds.), *European Societies: Fusion or Fission?* London: Routledge.

Braudel, Fernand. [1979] 1984. *The Perspective of the World.* Vol. 3 of *Civilization and Capitalism 15th-18th Century.* New York: Harper & Row.

Buchanan, James M. 1965. 'An Economic Theory of Clubs'. *Economica* 32: 1-14.

Buchmann, Marlis. 1999. 'European Integration: Disparate Dynamics of Bureaucratic Control and Communicative Participation', In P. Boje, B. van Steenbergen and S. Walby (eds.), *European Societies: Fusion or Fission?* London: Routledge.

Bullmann, Udo. 1994. *Die Politik der dritten Ebene. Regionen im Europa der Union.* Baden-Baden: Nomos.

Bulmer, Simon, and William Paterson. 1987. *The Federal Republic of Germany and the European Community.* London: Allen & Unwin.

Burkhardt-Reich, Barbara, and Wolfgang Schumann. 1983. *Agrarverbände in der EG.* Kehl-Strassburg: Engel.

Burt, Ronald S. 1992. *Structural Holes.* Cambridge, Mass.: Harvard University Press.

Busch, Klaus. 1978. *Die Krise der Europäischen Gemeinschaft.* Frankfurt/Main: Europäische Verlagsanstalt.

Butler, Michael. 1986. *Europe - More than a Continent.* London: Heinemann.

Cameron, David. 1992. 'The 1992 Initiative: Causes and Consequences'. Pp. 23-74 in Alberta M. Sbragia (ed.), *Euro-Politics: Institutions and Policy-making in the EC.* Washington DC: Brookings Institution.

Cini, Michelle. 1996. *The European Commission. Leadership, Organization and Culture in the EU Administration.* Manchester: Manchester University Press.

Cockfield, Lord. 1990. 'The Real Significance of 1992'. In C. Crouch and D. Marquand (eds.), *The Politics of 1992. Beyond the Single European Market.* Oxford and Cambridge: Basil Blackwell.

1991. 'From Genesis to Revelation: The Emergence of the Vision of a New Europe'. In A. Clesse and R. Vernon (eds.), *The European Community after 1992: A New Role in World Politics?* Baden-Baden: Nomos.

1992. '1992 - Bilan d'une renaissance. Le Programme 92: Objectifs et méthodes'. Address by the Rt. Hon. The Lord Cockfield at the Séance Academique in Brussels on 17 December 1992. Reprinted in Lord Cockfield, *The European Union. Creating the Single Market.* Chichester: Wiley Chancery Law, 1994.

1994. *The European Union. Creating the Single Market.* Chichester: Wiley Chancery Law.

Colchester, Nicholas, and David Buchan. 1990. *Europower. The Essential Guide to Europe's Economic Transformation in 1992.* New York: Times Books and Random House.

Coleman, James S. 1974. *Power and the Structure of Society*. New York: Norton.
1990. *Foundations of Social Theory*. Cambridge, Mass.: Belknap Press.
Corbett, Richard. 1992. 'The Intergovernmental Conference on Political Union'. *Journal of Common Market Studies* 30(3).
Cox, Robert. 1993. 'Structural Issues of Global Governance: Implications for Europe'. Pp. 259–89 in Stephen Gill (ed.), *Gramsci, Historical Materialism and International Relations*. Cambridge: Cambridge University Press.
Cutler, Tony, et al. 1989. *1992 – The Struggle for Europe: A Critical Evaluation of the European Community*. New York: Berg.

Dahrendorf, Ralf (ed.). 1981. *Trendwende: Europas Wirtschaft in der Krise*. Vienna: Molden.
1992. *Der moderne soziale Konflikt*. Stuttgart: Deutsche Verlags-Anstalt (extended version of the English-language edition, *The Modern Social Conflict*, 1988).
Däubler, Wolfgang. 1989. 'Sozialstaat EG? Notwendigkeit und Inhalt einer Europäischen Grundrechtsakte'. In Wolfgang Däubler (ed.), *Sozialstaat EG? Die andere Dimension des Binnenmarktes*. Gütersloh: Bertelsmann Stiftung.
Davignon, Etienne. 1981. 'Europa am Ende oder vor einem neuen Aufschwung'. Pp. 167–91 in Ralf Dahrendorf (ed.), 1981. *Trendwende: Europas Wirtschaft in der Krise*. Vienna: Molden.
Dekker, Wisse. 1984. *Europa 1990*. Lecture at the Centre for European Policy Studies in Brussels, 13 November 1984.
1985a. *Die Zukunft einer Europäischen Informationstechnologie im internationalen Wettbewerb*. Lecture at a conference of the 'Statistisch-Volkswirtschaftliche Gesellschaft' in Basel, 4 February 1985.
1985b. *Europa 1990: Ein Massnahmen-Katalog – Fortschritte und Fortsetzung*. Lecture to the 'Deutsche Gesellschaft für Auswärtige Politik e.V'. In Bonn, 9 October 1985.
1989. 'The American Response to Europe 1992'. *European Affairs* No. 2: 105–10.
1996. *Levenslang Philips*. Amsterdam: Balans.
Delapierre, Michel, and Jean-Benoît Zimmermann. 1994. 'The Computer Industry: Reshaping European Competitiveness in a Global Industry'. Pp. 217–36 in U. Muldur and R. Petrella (eds.), Directorate-General Science, Research and Development. *The European Community and the Globalization of Technology and the Economy*. Brussels: Commission of the European Communities.
Delors, Jacques. 1981. 'Frankreich zwischen Reform und Gegenreform'. In R. Dahrendorf (ed.), *Trendwende. Europas Wirtschaft in der Krise*. Vienna: Molden.
1988a. *La France par l'Europe*. Paris: Clisthène-Grasset (*Our Europe*. London: Verso, 1991).
1988b. 'Für ein soziales Europa'. *Bundesarbeitsblatt* 11.
1988c. Preface to the Cecchini-Report, *EUROPA '92. Der Vorteil des Binnenmarktes*. Baden-Baden: Nomos.
1991. 'Wir müssen Grossmacht werden'. Interview in *Der Spiegel*.

1992. *Le Nouveau Concert Européen*. Paris: Editions Odile Jacob.
1993. 'Entwicklungsperspektiven der Europäischen Gemeinschaft'. *Aus Politik und Zeitgeschichte* 1.
Deppe, Frank, and Michael Felder. 1993. *Zur Post-Maastricht-Krise der Europäischen Gemeinschaft (EG)*. Arbeitspapier No. 10, Forschungsgruppe Europäische Gemeinschaften (FEG) am Institut für Politikwissenschaft der Philipps-Universität Marburg, Marburg.
De Ruyt, Jean. 1989. *L'Acte Unique Européen*. Brussels: Editions de l'Université de Bruxelles.
De Zwaan, J.W. 1986. 'The Single European Act: Conclusion of a Unique Document'. *Common Market Law Review* 23.
Doutriaux, Yves. 1992. *Le Traité sur l'Union Européenne*. Paris: Colin.
Dreyer, Marion. 1993. *Akzeptanzmodelle der EG-Politik zur Bio- und Gentechnologie. Ein (soziologischer) Nachruf auf CUBE*. Florence: Europäisches Hochschulinstitut.
Durant, John (ed.) 1992. *Biotechnology in Public. A Review of Recent Research*. London: Science Museum.
Durant, John, Martin Bauer and George Gaskell. 1998. *Biotechnology in the Public Sphere: A European Source Book*. London: Science Museum.

Ebbinghaus, Bernhard, and Jelle Visser. 1994. 'Barrieren und Wege "grenzenloser Solidarität": Gewerkschaften und Europäische Integration'. In W. Streeck (ed.), *Staat und Verbände*. Special issue of *Politische Vierteljahresschrift*, No. 25. Opladen: Westdeutscher Verlag.
Ehlermann, Claus-Dieter. 1987. 'The Internal Market Following the Single European Act'. *Common Market Law Review* 24.
1988. 'Die Beschlüsse des Brüsseler Sondergipfels: Erfolg einer Gesamtstrategie der Delors-Kommission'. *Integration* 2.
Eichener, Volker, and Helmut Voelzkow. 1994. 'Europäische Regulierung im Arbeitsschutz: Überraschungen aus Brüssel und ein erster Versuch ihrer Erklärung'. In V. Eichener and H. Voelzkow (eds.), *Europäische Integration und verbandliche Interessenvermittlung*. Marburg: Metropolis.
EITIRT (European Information Technology Industry Roundtable). 1995. *Europe and the Global Information Society: Proposals for the Implementation of Priority Applications by the European IT Industry*. Brussels: EITIRT, January.
Elias, Norbert. [1969] 1977. *Über den Prozess der Zivilization. Wandlungen der Gesellschaft*. Frankfurt/Main: Suhrkamp, 3rd edition.
Endo, Ken. 1998. *Political Leadership in the European Community: The Role of the Commission Presidency under Jacques Delors, 1985–1995*. New York: St. Martin's Press.
Engel, Christian. 1991. 'Regionen in der Europäischen Gemeinschaft: Eine integrationspolitische Rollensuche'. *Integration* 1.
Engel, Christian, and Christine Borrmann. 1991. *Vom Konsens zur Mehrheitsentscheidung. EG-Entscheidungsverfahren und nationale Interessenpolitik nach der Einheitlichen Europäischen Akte*. Bonn: Europa Union Verlag.
Engel, Christian, and Wolfgang Wessels (eds.). 1992. *From Luxembourg to Maastricht: Institutional Change in the European Community after the Single European Act*. Bonn: Europa Union.

Ernst & Young. 1994. *Biotechnology's Economic Impact in Europe: A Survey of Its Future Role in Competitiveness.* Brussels: SAGB.
1995. *Biotech 1995.* Brussels: SAGB.
ERT (European Roundtable of Industrialists). 1984. 'Missing Links: Upgrading Europe's Transborder Ground Transport Infrastructure'. Brussels: ERT.
1985. 'Changing Scales'. Brussels: ERT.
1986. 'Making Europe Work'. Brussels: ERT.
1991a. 'Missing Networks: A European Challenge'. Brussels: ERT.
1991b. 'Reshaping Europe'. Brussels: ERT.
1992. 'Rebuilding Confidence. An Action Plan for Europe'. Brussels: ERT.
1994. 'European Competitiveness. The Way to Growth and Jobs'. Brussels: ERT.
1995. 'Education for Europeans – Towards the Learning Society'. Brussels: ERT.
1997. 'Investing in Knowledge – The Integration of Technology in Europe'. Brussels: ERT.
1998. 'Job Creation and Competitiveness through Innovation'. Brussels: ERT.
Esping-Andersen, Gösta. 1990. *The Three Worlds of Welfare Capitalism.* Cambridge: Polity Press.
Esser, Josef. 1993. 'Technologieentwicklung in der Triade. Folgen für die europäische Technologiegemeinschaft'. Pp. 21–42 in Werner Süss and Gerhard Becher (eds.), *Politik und Technologieentwicklung in Europa.* Berlin: Duncker & Humblot.
ETUC (European Trade Union Confederation). 1988. *Anhang zum Tätigkeitsbericht 85/87.* Brussels.
1991. *Anhang zum Tätigkeitsbericht 88/90.* Brussels.
EUREKA. 1989. *Annual Report.* Brussels: EUREKA Secretariat.
1994. *Annual Report.* Brussels: EUREKA Secretariat.
EuropaBio. 1997. *Benchmarking the Competitiveness of Biotechnology in Europe.* Brussels.
Everling, Ulrich. 1990. 'Von der Freizügigkeit der Arbeitnehmer zum Europäischen Bürgerrecht?' in G. Nicolaysen and H.-J. Rabe (eds.), *Europäisches Arbeits- und Sozialrecht.* Europarecht-Beiheft 1. Baden-Baden: Nomos.
1993. 'Die Entwicklung des europäischen Wirtschaftsrechts'. In H.A. Winkler and H. Kaelble (eds.), *Nationalismus – Nationalitäten – Supranationalität.* Stuttgart: Klett-Cotta.

Falke, Josef. 1993. 'Von der Implementation zur Selbstimplementation? Zur Kontrolle der Anwendung des Gemeinschaftsrechts in den Mitgliedstaaten'. In H. Meulemann and A. Elting-Camus (eds.), *26. Deutscher Soziologentag. Lebensverhältnisse und soziale Konflikte im neuen Europa. Tagungsband II: Sektionen, Arbeits- und Ad hoc-Gruppen.* Opladen: Westdeutscher Verlag.
Falkner, Gerda. 1994. *Supranationalität trotz Einstimmigkeit: Entscheidungsmuster der EU am Beispiel Sozialpolitik.* Bonn: Europa Union.
FAST (Forecasting and Assessment in Science and Technology). 1984. *Eurofutures: The Challenge of Innovation.* London: Butterworths.

Fels, Gerhard. 1989. 'Die Sozialcharta ökonomisch gesehen'. In W. Däubler (ed.), *Sozialstaat EG? Die andere Dimension des Binnenmarktes*. Gütersloh: Bertelsmann Stiftung.
Fennema, Meindert. 1982. *International Networks of Banks and Industry*. The Hague: Nijhoff.
Fennema, Meindert, and Huibert Schijf. 1985 'The Transnational Network'. Pp. 250–66 in Fram N. Stokman, Rolf Ziegler and John Scott, *Networks of Corporate Power*. Cambridge: Polity Press.
Ferrera, Maurizio. 1993. *EC Citizens and Social Protection. Main Results from a Eurobarometer Survey*. Brussels.
Fielder, Nicola. 1997. *Western European Integration in the 1980s. The Origins of the Single Market*. Bern, Frankfurt, New York: Peter Lang.
Flora, Peter. 1993. 'Europa als Sozialstaat'. In B. Schäfers (ed.), *Lebensverhältnisse und soziale Konflikte im neuen Europa. Verhandlungen des 26. Deutschen Soziologentages in Düsseldorf 1992*, Frankfurt/Main: Campus.
Franzmeyer, Fritz, Bernhard Seidel and Christian Weise. 1993. *Die Reform der EG-Strukturfonds von 1988. Konzeption, Umsetzung, Weiterentwicklung aus deutscher Sicht*. Berlin: Duncker & Humblot.

Garrett, Geoffrey, and Barry R. Weingast. 1993. 'Ideas, Interests, and Institutions: Constructing the European Community's Internal Market'. In J. Goldstein and R.O. Keohane (eds.), *Ideas and Foreign Policy: Beliefs, Institutions, and Political Change*. Ithaca, NY: Cornell University Press.
Gazzo, Marina (ed.). 1985. *Towards European Union. From the 'Crocodile' to the European Council in Milan (28–29 June 1985)*. Brussels, Luxembourg: Agence Europe.
—— 1986. *Towards European Union II. From the European Council in Milan to the Signing of the European Single Act*. Brussels, Luxembourg: Agence Europe.
Genscher, Hans-Dietrich. 1981. 'Jetzt die Europäische Union schaffen!' Speech on 12 December 1981 to the XXVII Congress of the Europa-Union Deutschland in Bremen. Bonn: Europa-Union Deutschland.
—— 1995. *Erinnerungen*. Berlin: Siedler.
George, Stephen. 1990. *An Awkward Partner. Britain in the European Community*. Oxford: Oxford University Press.
—— 1991. *Politics and Policy in the European Community*. Oxford: Oxford University Press, 2nd Edition.
—— 1992. 'Intergovernmentalism, Supranationalism and the Future Development of the European Community'. Paper presented to the Pan-European Conference on International Relations, Heidelberg, September.
—— 1993. 'Supranational Actors and Domestic Politics: Integration Theory Reconsidered in the Light of the Single European Act and Maastricht'. Paper presented to the Political Studies Association Annual Conference, University of Leicester, April.
Gerbet, Pierre. 1995. *La France et l'intégration européenne*. Bern: Lang.
Gerlach, Michael. 1992. *Alliance Capitalism. The Social Organization of Japanese Business*. Berkeley: University of California Press.
Gill, Stephen. 1991. *American Hegemony and the Trilateral Commission*. Cambridge: Cambridge University Press.

Grande, Edgar, and Jürgen Häusler. 1994. *Industrieforschung und Forschungspolitik. Staatliche Steuerungspotentiale in der Informationstechnik.* Frankfurt/Main: Campus.
    1996. 'Demokratische Legitimation und europäische Integration'. *Leviathan* 3: 339–59.
Grant, Charles. 1994. *Delors. Inside the House that Jacques Built.* London: Nicholas Brealey Publishing.
Grant, Wyn. 1989. *Government and Industry. A Comparative Analysis of the US, Canada and the UK.* Aldershot: Edward Elgar.
    1990. 'Industrial Policy'. Pp. 25–42 in James Simmie and Roger King (eds.), *The State in Action: Public Policy and Politics.* London: Pinter Publishers.
Grant, Wyn, William Paterson, and Charles Whitson. 1989. *Government and the Chemical Industry. A Comparative Study of Britain and West Germany.* Oxford: Clarendon Press.
Green Cowles, Maria L. 1994. 'The Politics of Big Business in the European Community: Setting the Agenda for a New Europe'. Dissertation, American University, Washington DC.
    1995. 'Setting the Agenda for a New Europe: The ERT and EC 1992'. *Journal of Common Market Studies* 33(4): 501–26.
    1997. 'Organizing Industrial Coalitions: A Challenge to the Future?' Pp. 116–40 in Helen Wallace and Alasdair R. Young (eds.), *Participation and Policy-Making in the European Union.* Oxford: Clarendon Press.
Grosser, Alfred. 1989. *Frankreich und seine Aussenpolitik. 1944 bis heute.* Munich: Deutscher Taschenbuch Verlag.
Grossmann, Susi, and Daniela Decurtins. 1993. 'Die Bedeutung sozialer Vernetzung für die Gründung der Zürcher Kantonalbank'. In Jakob Tanner and Youssef Cassis (eds.), *Banken und Kredit in der Schweiz (1850–1930).* Zurich: Chronos.
Grote, Jürgen-R. 1990. 'Steuerungsprobleme in transnationalen Beratungsgremien. Über soziale Kosten unkoordinierter Regulierung in der EG'. *Jahrbuch für Staatswissenschaften* 4: 227–56.
Guild, Elspeth (ed.). 1999. *The Legal Framework and Social Consequences of Free Movement of Persons in the European Union.* The Hague: Kluwer Law International.
Gulman, Claus. 1987. 'The Single European Act – Some Remarks from a Danish Perspective'. *Common Market Law Review* 24.

Haas, Ernst B. 1958. *The Uniting of Europe. Political, Social, and Economic Forces 1950–1957.* Stanford, Calif.: Stanford University Press.
    1964. *Beyond the Nation-State: Functionalism and International Organization.* Stanford, Calif.: Stanford University Press.
Hagedoorn, John, and Jos Schakenraad. 1990. 'Strategic Partnering and Technological Co-operation'. Pp. 171–91 in Ben Dankbaar, John Groenewegen and Hans Schenk (eds.), *Perspectives in Industrial Organization.* Boston: Kluwer.
Hagen, Kare. 1992. 'The Social Dimension: A Quest for a European Welfare State'. In Z. Ferge and J.E. Kolberg (eds.), *Social Policy in a Changing Europe.* Frankfurt/Main and Boulder, Colo.: Campus and Westview.

Hallstein, Walter. 1969. *Der unvollendete Bundesstaat. Europäische Erfahrungen und Erkenntnisse*. Düsseldorf and Vienna: Econ.
Hänsch, Klaus. 1989. 'Die auswärtige Innenpolitik. Zum Demokratiedefizit der Europäischen Gemeinschaft'. In H. Elsenhans, G. Junne, G. Kiersch and B. Pollmann (eds.), *Frankreich – Europa – Weltpolitik. Festschrift für Gilbert Ziebura*. Opladen: Westdeutscher Verlag.
Haywood, Elizabeth. 1993. 'The European Policy of François Mitterrand'. *Journal of Common Market Studies* 31(2).
Hirsch, Joachim. 1995. *Der nationale Wettbewerbsstaat. Staat, Demokratie und Politik im globalen Kapitalismus*. Berlin: Edition ID-Archiv.
Hooghe, Liesbet (ed.). 1996. *Cohesion Policy and European Integration: Building Multi-level Governance*. Oxford: Oxford University Press.
Hort, Peter. 1988. 'Eine Bilanz der deutschen EG-Präsidentschaft'. *Europa-Archiv* 15.
House of Lords Select Committee on the European Communities. 1984. Session 1984–5. 8th Report: Esprit. London: Her Majesty's Stationery Office.
Howe, Geoffrey. 1984. 'Grossbritannien und die Bundesrepublik Deutschland als europäische Partner'. *Europa-Archiv* 21.
1985. 'Europa – unsere Zukunft'. *Europa-Archiv* 29.
1994. *Conflict of Loyalty*. London: Macmillan.
Hrbek, Rudolf. 1982. '"Relance Européenne" 1981?' *Integration* 1.
1996. 'Kommission'. Pp. 180–87 in Beate Kohler-Koch and Wichard Woyke (eds.), *Die Europäische Union*. Munich: Beck.

Inglehart, Ronald. 1977. *The Silent Revolution: Changing Values and Political Styles among Western Publics*. Princeton, NJ: Princeton University Press.

Jachtenfuchs, Markus, and Beate Kohler-Koch. 1996. 'Regieren im dynamischen Mehrebenensystem'. In M. Jachtenfuchs and B. Kohler-Koch (eds.), *Europäische Integration*. Opladen: Leske & Budrich.
Jessop, Bob. 1995. 'Die Zukunft des Nationalstaats: Erosion oder Reorganization? Grundsätzliche Überlegungen zu Westeuropa'. In *Europäische Integration und politische Regulierung – Aspekte, Dimensionen, Perspektiven*, Study of the Forschungsgruppe Europäische Gemeinschaften (FEG), No. 5, University of Marburg, Marburg.
Jones, Erik. 1993. 'Small Countries and the Franco-German Relationship'. In P. McCarthy (ed.), *France–Germany 1983–1993*. New York: St. Martin's Press.
Junne, Gerd. 1992. 'Konfrontation zwischen Europa und Japan?' Pp. 287–98 in Klaus W. Grewlich (ed.), *Europa im Technologiewettlauf. Der Weltmarkt wird zum Binnenmarkt*. Gütersloh: Bertelsmann.

Kasakos, Panos. 1991. 'Die neue EG-Agenda und die griechische Europa-Politik'. *Europa-Archiv* 7.
Kaufmann-Bühler, Werner. 1994. 'Deutsche Europapolitik nach dem Karlsruher Urteil: Möglichkeiten und Hemmnisse'. *Integration* 1.
Kennedy, Kevin. 1989. 'Competitiveness and Technology Policy'. *International Journal of Technology Management* 4(3).

Keohane, Robert O., and Stanley Hoffmann. 1991. 'Institutional Change in Europe in the 1980s'. Pp. 1–39 in R. Keohane and S. Hoffmann (eds.), *The New European Community. Decisionmaking and Institutional Change*. Boulder, Colo.: Westview.

Kleinhenz, Gerhard. 1990. 'Die sozialpolitische Bedeutung der Verwirklichung des Binnenmarktes'. In R. Birk (ed.), *Die soziale Dimension des Europäischen Binnenmarktes*. Baden-Baden: Nomos.

Kleinknecht, Alfred. 1987. *Innovation Pattern in Crisis and Prosperity: Schumpeter's Long Cycle Reconsidered*. New York: St. Martin's Press.

Kohler-Koch, Beate. 1992. 'Interessen und Integration. Die Rolle organisierter Interessen im westeuropäischen Integrationsprozeß'. In M. Kreile (ed.), *Die Integration Europas*. Special issue of *Politische Vierteljahresschrift*, No. 23: 81–119.

Kohler-Koch, Beate, and Hans-Wolfgang Platzer. 1986. 'Tripartismus – Bedingungen und Perspektiven des sozialen Dialogs in der EG'. *Integration* 4.

König, Thomas, Elmar Rieger and Hermann Schmitt (eds.). 1996. *Das europäische Mehrebenensystem*. Frankfurt/Main and New York: Campus.

Konstanty, Reinhold, and Bruno Zwingmann. 1989. 'Europäische Einigung und Gesundheitsschutz in der Arbeitsumwelt'. *WSI. Mitteilungen* 10.

Krägenau Henry, and Wolfgang Wetter. 1993. *Europäische Wirtschafts- und Währungsunion – vom Werner-Plan zum Vertrag von Maastricht. Einführung und Dokumentation*. Baden-Baden: Nomos.

  1994. 'Europäische Wirtschafts- und Währungsunion (EWWU) – Vom Werner-Plan bis Maastricht'. In R. Caesar and H.-E. Scharrer (eds.), *Maastricht: Königsweg oder Irrweg zur Wirtschaft- und Währungsunion?* Bonn: Europa Union.

Kramer, Heinz. 1985. 'Die Europäische Gemeinschaft auf neuen Wegen?' *EG-Magazin* 8.

Kreile, Michael (ed.). 1991. *Europa 1992. Konzeptionen, Strategien, Auswirkungen*. Baden-Baden: Nomos.

Krummenacher, Franz. 1997. 'Nationalismus und europäische Einigung'. MA thesis, University of Zurich, Sociological Institute.

Lange, Peter. 1992. 'The Politics of the Social Dimension'. In A.M. Sbragia (ed.), *Europolitics. Institutions and Policymaking in the 'New' European Community*. Washington DC: Brookings Institution.

  1993. 'Maastricht and the Social Protocol: Why Did They Do It?' *Politics and Society* 21(1).

Laursen, Finn, and Sophie Vanhoonacker (eds.). 1992. *The Intergovernmental Conference on Political Union. Institutional Reforms, New Policies and International Identity of the European Community*. Maastricht: European Institute of Public Administration.

  1994. *The Ratification of the Maastricht Treaty. Issues, Debates and Future Implications*. Maastricht: European Institute of Public Administration.

Lederman, Leonard. 1985. 'Science and Technology in Europe: A Survey'. *Science and Technology Policy* 12(3).

Leibfried, Stephan, and Paul Pierson (eds.). 1995a. *European Social Policy: Between Fragmentation and Integration*. Washington DC: Brookings.

1995b. 'Semi-Sovereign Welfare States: Social Policy in a Multi-Tiered Europe'. In Stephan Leibfried and Paul Pierson (eds.), *European Social Policy: Between Fragmentation and Integration*. Washington DC: Brookings.

1996. 'Social Policy'. In H. Wallace and W. Wallace (eds.), *Policymaking in the European Union*. Oxford: Oxford University Press.

Lepsius, M. Rainer. 1991. 'Nationalstaat oder Nationalitätenstaat als Modell für die Weiterentwicklung der Europäischen Gemeinschaft'. In R. Wildenmann (ed.), *Staatswerdung Europas? Optionen für eine Europäische Union*. Baden-Baden: Nomos.

Lequesne, Christian. 1989. 'Europapolitik unter Mitterrand: Die französische Präsidentschaft als Etappenziel'. *Integration* 4.

1993. *Paris – Bruxelles. Comment se fait la politique européenne de la France*. Paris: Presses de la Fondation nationale des sciences politiques.

Lindberg, Leon N., and Stuart A. Scheingold. 1970. *Europe's Would-Be Polity*. Englewood Cliffs, NJ: Prentice Hall.

Lipp, Ernst-Moritz, and Horst Reichert. 1991. 'Konfliktfelder auf dem Weg zur Europäischen Währungsunion'. In M. Weber (ed.), *Europa auf dem Weg zur Währungsunion*. Darmstadt: Wissenschaftliche Buchgesellschaft.

Lodge, Juliet. 1985. 'European Union: A Qualitative Leap Forward?' *The World Today*, 41(11).

Louis, Jean-Victor, and Denis Waelbroeck (eds.). 1989. *La Commission au coeur du système institutionnel*. Brussels: Editions de l'Université de Bruxelles.

Lowe, Philip. 1988. 'The Reform of the Community's Structural Funds'. *Common Market Law Review*: 25.

Ludlow, Peter. 1982. *The Making of the European Monetary System: A Case Study of the Politics of the European Community*. London: Butterworth Scientific.

1991. 'The European Commission'. In R. Keohane and S. Hoffmann (eds.), *The New European Community. Decisionmaking and Institutional Change*. Boulder, Colo.: Westview Press.

McAleavey, Paul, and James Mitchell. 1994. 'Industrial Regions and Lobbying in the Structural Funds Reform Process'. *Journal of Common Market Studies* 32(2).

McDonald, Robert. 1985. 'Greece after Pasok's Victory'. *The World Today* 41(7).

Marks, Gary. 1992. 'Structural Policy in the European Community'. In A.M. Sbragia (ed.), *Europolitics. Institutions and Policymaking in the 'New' European Community*. Washington DC: Brookings Institution.

Marks, Gary, Fritz W. Scharpf, Philippe C. Schmitter and Wolfgang Streeck (eds.). 1996. *Governance in the European Union*. London: Sage.

Marshall, Thomas H. [1950] 1965. *Class, Citizenship and Social Development*. Garden City, NY: Anchor Books.

1975. *Social Policy*. London: Hutchinson.

Mayes, David G. (ed.). 1997. *The Evolution of the Single Market*. Cheltenham: Edward Elgar.

Mertes, Alois. 1983. 'Die Europapolitik der Bundesregierung – Kontinuität und Aufbruch'. *Integration* 1.

Middlemas, Keith. 1995. *Orchestrating Europe. The Informal Politics of the European Union 1973–1995*. London: Fontana Press.
Missbach, Andreas. 1999. *Das Klima zwischen Nord und Süd. Eine regulationstheoretische Untersuchung des Nord-Süd-Konflikts in der Klimapolitik der Vereinten Nationen*. Münster: Westfälisches Dampfboot.
Møller, Ørstrøm J. 1988. 'The Nordic Angle III: The Single European Act – A Danish View'. *The World Today*, November.
Mommsen, Wolfgang J. 1969. *Das Zeitalter des Imperialismus*. Frankfurt/Main: Fischer.
Moravcsik, Andrew. 1991. 'Negotiating the Single European Act: National Interests and Conventional Statecraft in the European Community'. *International Organization* 45(1): 19–56.
   1993. 'Preferences and Power in the European Community: A Liberal Intergovernmentalist Approach'. *Journal of Common Market Studies* 31(4).
   1998. *The Choice for Europe. Social Purpose and State Power from Messina to Maastricht*. Ithaca, NY: Cornell University Press.
   1999. 'A New Statecraft? Supranational Entrepreneurs and International Cooperation'. *International Organization* 53(2): 267–306.
Moreau, Jacques, and Michel Richonnier. 1983. *Quelle stratégie européenne pour la France dans les années 80?* Paris: La Documentation Française.
Mosley, Hugh G. 1990. 'The Social Dimension of European Integration'. *International Labour Review* 129.
Moynot, Jean-Louis. 1987. 'The Left, Industrial Policy and the Filière Électronique'. Pp. 263–90 in George Ross, Stanley Hoffmann and Sylvia Malzacher, *The Mitterrand Experiment*. Cambridge: Polity Press.
Mueller, Frank, and John Purcell. 1992. 'The Europeanization of Manufacturing and the Decentralization of Bargaining: Multinational Management Strategies in the European Automobile Industry'. *International Journal of Human Resource Management* 3(1).
Müller, Joachim. 1990. *European Collaboration in Advanced Technology*. Amsterdam: Elsevier.
Münch, Richard. 1993. *Das Projekt Europa. Zwischen Nationalstaat, regionaler Autonomie und Weltgesellschaft*. Frankfurt/Main: Suhrkamp.
Mytelka Krieger, Lynn. 1993. 'Strengthening the Relevance of European Science and Technology Programmes to Industrial Competitiveness: The Case of ESPRIT'. Pp. 56–63 in Marc Hubert (ed.), *The Impact of Globalization on Europe's Firms and Industries*. London: Pinter Publishers.
   1995. 'Dancing with Wolves: Global Oligopolies and Strategic Partnerships'. Pp. 182–204 in John Hagedoorn (ed.), *Technical Change and the World Economy. Convergence and Divergence in Technology Strategies*. Aldershot: Edward Elgar.
Mytelka Krieger, Lynn, and Michel Delapierre. 1987. 'The Alliance Strategies of European Firms in the Information Technology Industry and the Role of ESPRIT'. *Journal of Common Market Studies* 26(2): 231–53.

Narjes, Karl-Heinz. 1988. 'Europe's Technological Challenge: A View from the European Commission'. *Science and Public Policy* 15(6): 395–402.
Nicolaysen, Gert. 1991. *Europarecht I*. Baden-Baden: Nomos.

Niggli, Peter. 1989. 'Auf den Tisch klopfen'. *Bilanz* No. 3: 164–8.
Noël, Emil. 1987. 'The European Community Today'. *Government and Opposition* 22(1).
Nollert, Michael. 1992. *Interessenvermittlung und sozialer Konflikt. Über Bedingungen und Folgen neokorporatistischer Konfliktregelung.* Pfaffenweiler: Centaurus.
  1996. 'Verbandliche Interessenvertretung in der Europäischen Union: Einflußressourcen und faktische Einflußnahme'. *Zeitschrift für Politikwissenschaft* 6(3): 647–67.
  1997. 'Verbändelobbying in der Europäischen Union – Europäische Dachverbände im Vergleich'. Pp. 107–36 in Ulrich von Alemann and Bernhard Wessels (eds.), *Verbände in vergleichender Perspektive*. Berlin: Sigma.
Nye, Joseph S. 1971. 'Comparing Common Markets: A Revised Neo-Functionalist Model'. In L.N. Lindberg and S.A. Scheingold (eds.), *Regional Integration. Theory and Research*. Cambridge, Mass.: Harvard University Press.

Offe, Claus. 1969. 'Politische Herrschaft und Klassenstrukturen. Zur Analyse spätkapitalistischer Gesellschaftssysteme'. Pp. 155–89 in Gisela Kress and Dieter Senghaas (eds.), *Politikwissenschaft. Eine Einführung in ihre Probleme*. Frankfurt/Main: Europäische Verlagsanstalt.
Offe, Claus, and Helmut Wiesenthal. 1980. 'Two Logics of Collective Action. Theoretical Notes on Social Class and Organizational Form'. *Political Power and Social Theory* 1: 67–115.
Ohmae, Kenichi. 1985. *Macht der Triade. Die neue Form des weltweiten Wettbewerbs.* Wiesbaden: Gabler.
Olson, Mancur. 1968. *Die Logik des kollektiven Handelns. Kollektivgüter und die Theorie der Gruppen.* Tübingen: Mohr.

Padoa-Schioppa, Tommaso. 1987. *Efficiency, Stability, and Equity: A Strategy for the Evolution of the Economic System of the European Community: A Report.* Oxford: Oxford University Press.
Perez, Carlota. 1983. 'Structural Change and Assimilation of New Technology in the Economic and Social Systems'. *Futures* 15(5): 357–75.
  1985. 'Microelectronics, Long Waves and World Structural Change: New Perspectives for Developing Countries'. *World Development* 13(3): 441–63.
Pescatore, Pierre. 1986. 'Die einheitliche Europäische Akte. Eine ernste Gefahr für den Gemeinsamen Markt'. *Europa-Recht* 2.
Peterson, John. 1991. 'Technology Policy in Europe: Explaining the Framework Programme and Eureka in Theory and Practice'. *Journal of Common Market Studies* 29: 269–90.
Pierson, Paul. 1998. 'The Path to European Integration: A Historical-Institutionalist Analysis'. In W. Sandholtz and A. Stone Sweet (eds.), *European Integration and Supranational Governance*. Oxford: Oxford University Press.
Pierson, Paul, and Stephan Leibfried. 1995. 'The Dynamics of Social Policy Integration'. In S. Leibfried and P. Pierson (eds.), *European Social Policy: Between Fragmentation and Integration*. Washington DC: Brookings.
Platzer, Hans-Wolfgang. 1994. 'Sozialpolitik und soziale Integration in der

Europäischen Union – Bedingungen, Perspektiven und Grenzen im Spannungsfeld von Markt- und Politikintegration'. In B. Dietz, J. Bardelmann and T. Schäfer (eds.), *Die Soziale Zukunft Europas. Bedingungen und Perspektiven einer Europäischen 'Sozialen Integration'*. Giessen: Focus.

Raith, Werner. 1979. *Florenz vor der Renaissance. Der Weg einer Stadt aus dem Mittelalter*. Frankfurt/Main: Campus.

Ridinger, Rudolf. 1991. *Technologiekooperation in Westeuropa. Die Suche nach grenzübergreifenden Antworten auf technologiepolitische Herausforderungen*. Hamburg: R. Kraemer.

Ringrose, Marjorie Anne. 1994. 'The Bureaucratic Imperative: Esprit and the Making of British Foreign Policy'. Thesis submitted for the PhD in International Relations, London School of Economics and Political Science, University of London.

Robinson, Jeffrey J. 1995. 'The State of the (European) Union. From the Single Market to Maastricht, from Singular Events to General Theories'. *World Politics* 47: 441–65.

Rokkan, Stein. 1975. 'Dimensions of State Formation and Nation-Building'. Pp. 562–600 in Charles Tilly (ed.), *The Formation of National States in Western Europe*. Princeton, NJ: Princeton University Press.

— 1981. 'Territories, Nations, Parties: Toward a Geoeconomic-Geopolitical Model for the Explanation of Variations within Western Europe'. Pp. 70–95 in Richard L. Merritt and Bruce Russett (eds.), *From National Development to Global Community. Essays in Honor of Karl W. Deutsch*. London: Allen & Unwin.

Ross, George. 1995a. *Jacques Delors and European Integration*. Cambridge: Polity Press, and Oxford: Blackwell.

— 1995b. 'Assessing the Delors Era and Social Policy'. In S. Leibfried and P. Pierson (eds.), *European Social Policy: Between Fragmentation and Integration*. Washington DC: Brookings.

Ross, George, Stanley Hoffmann and Sylvia Malzacher (eds.). 1987. *The Mitterrand Experiment*. Cambridge: Polity Press.

Rothenbühler, André. 1997. 'Regionale Identität und europäische Integration'. MA thesis, University of Zurich, Sociological Institute.

Sacchi, Stefan. 1998. *Politische Potentiale in modernen Gesellschaften. Zur Formierung links-grüner und neokonservativer Bewegungen in Europa und den USA*. Frankfurt/Main and New York: Campus.

SAGB (Senior Advisory Group Biotechnology). 1990a. *Community Policy for Biotechnology: Priorities and Actions*. Brussels.

— 1990b. *Economic Benefits and European Competitiveness*. Brussels.

— 1990c. *Creation of a Community Task Force and Independent Consultative Body*. Brussels.

— 1994a. *Biotechnology Policy in the European Union. Prescriptions for Growth, Competitiveness and Employment*. Brussels.

— 1994b. *Biotechnology Policy in the European Union. Competitiveness, Investment and the 'Cycle of Innovation'*. Brussels.

Sand, Stephanie. [1990] 1992. *Das Europa der Konzerne*. Munich: Heyne.

Sandholtz, Wayne. 1992. *High-Tech Europe: The Politics of International Cooperation*. Berkeley: University of California Press.

Sandholtz, Wayne, 1993. 'Choosing Union: Monetary Politics and Maastricht'. *International Organization* 47(1): 1–39.

Sandholtz, Wayne, and Alec Stone Sweet (eds.) 1998. *European Integration and Supranational Governance*. Oxford: Oxford University Press.

Sandholtz, Wayne, and John Zysman. 1989. '1992 – Recasting the European Bargain'. *World Politics*. 42(1), October.

Savoini, Carlo. 1984. 'Der soziale Dialog in der Gemeinschaft'. *Soziales Europa* 2.

Scharpf, Fritz. 1994. 'Community and Autonomy: Multi-Level Policy-Making in the European Union'. *Journal of European Public Policy* 1(2).

Schlecht, Otto. 1990. *Grundlagen und Perspektiven der Sozialen Marktwirtschaft*. Tübingen: Mohr.

Schmid, Josef. 1995. *Wohlfahrtsstaaten im Vergleich. Stand, Perspektiven und Probleme der Organization und Finanzierung sozialer Sicherungssysteme*. Opladen: Leske & Budrich.

Schmidt, Susanne K. 1998. *Liberalisierung in Europa. Die Rolle der Europäischen Kommission*. Frankfurt/Main and New York: Campus.

Schmitter, Philippe C. 1971. 'A Revised Theory of Regional Integration'. In L.N. Lindberg and S.A. Scheingold (eds.), *Regional Integration. Theory and Research*. Cambridge, Mass.: Harvard University Press.

Schneider, Volker, and Raymund Werle. 1989. 'Vom Regime zum korporativen Akteur. Zur institutionellen Dynamik der Europäischen Gemeinschaft'. In B. Kohler-Koch (ed.), *Regime in den internationalen Beziehungen*. Baden-Baden: Nomos.

Schnorpfeil, Willi. 1993. *Europäische Sozialpolitik und industrielle Beziehungen seit der Einheitlichen Europäischen Akte (EEA). Policies, Netzwerke und Entscheidungsverfahren*. Mannheimer Zentrum für Europäische Sozialforschung (MZES), Arbeitspapier AB II/No. 1, Mannheim.

1994. *Die Europäisierung sozialpolitischer Teilbereiche in der Europäischen Gemeinschaft*. Mannheimer Zentrum für Europäische Sozialforschung (MZES), Arbeitspapier AB II/No. 4, Mannheim.

Scholz, Rupert. 1995. 'Europäische Union – Voraussetzung einer institutionellen Verfassungsordnung'. Pp. 113–27 in Lüder Gerken (ed.), *Europa zwischen Ordnungswettbewerb und Harmonisierung*. Berlin: Springer.

Schulte, Bernd. 1993a. 'Die Entwicklung der europäischen Sozialpolitik'. In H.A. Winkler and H. Kaelble (eds.), *Nationalismus – Nationalitäten – Supranationalität*. Stuttgart: Klett-Cotta.

1993b. 'Einführung'. In *Soziale Sicherheit in der EG*. 2. Auflage, Munich: Beck.

Schumpeter, Joseph. 1939. *Business Cycles*, 2 vols. New York: McGraw Hill.

Scott, John. 1991. *Social Network Analysis. A Handbook*. Beverly Hills and London: Sage.

Secrétariat d'Etat auprès du Premier Ministre and Commissariat Général du Plan. 1983. *Quelle stratégie européenne pour la France dans les années 80? Rapport du groupe de travail sur l'Europe*. Paris: La documentation française, April.

Secrétariat d'Etat au Plan. 1989. *La France, l'Europe. Xe Plan 1989–1992*. Paris: La documentation française.
Seifert, Franz, and Helge Torgersen. 1996. 'Die Bewertung der Bio- und Gentechnologie. Österreich im EU-Vergleich'. *SWS-Rundschau* 36: 47–72.
Seitz, Konrad. 1985. 'SDI – Die technologische Herausforderung für Europa'. *Europa-Archiv* 13.
— 1991. *Die japanisch-amerikanische Herausforderung*. Munich: Bonn Aktuell.
Senker, Jacqueline (ed.). 1998. *Biotechnology and Competitive Advantage. Europe's Firms and the US Challenge*. Cheltenham: Edward Elgar.
Servan-Schreiber, Jacques J. 1968. *Die amerikanische Herausforderung*. Hamburg: Hoffmann & Campe.
Sharp, Margaret. 1986. 'Biotechnology: Watching and Waiting'. Pp. 161–212 in M. Sharp (ed.), *Europe and the New Technologies*. Ithaca, NY: Cornell University Press.
— 1989. 'The Community and the New Technologies'. Pp. 202–20 in Juliet Lodge (ed.), *The European Community and the Challenge of the future*. New York: St. Martin's Press.
Sharp, Margaret, and Keith Pavitt. 1993. 'Technology Policy in the 1990s: Old Trends and New Realities'. *Journal of Common Market Studies* 12(2): 129–51.
Sidjanski, Dusan. 1992. *L'avenir fédéraliste de l'Europe. La Communauté européenne, des origines au traité de Maastricht*. Paris: Presses Universitaires de France.
Siebert, Gerd. 1989. 'EG-Binnenmarkt und Gewerkschaften'. In Gerd Siebert (ed.), *Wenn der Binnenmarkt kommt. Neue Anforderungen an gewerkschaftliche Politik*. Frankfurt/Main: Nachrichten.
Silvia, Stephen J. 1991. 'The Social Charter of the European Community'. *Industrial and Labor Relations Review* 44.
Springer, Beverly. 1992. *The Social Dimension of 1992: Europe Faces a New EC*. New York: Greenwood Press.
— 1996. 'The March toward Monetary Integration: Europe and the Maastricht Treaty'. Pp. 272–87 in C. Roe Goddard, John T. Passé-Smith and John G. Conklin (eds.), *International Political Economy. State-Market Relations in the Changing Global Order*. Boulder, Colo.: Lynne Rienner.
Stadlmann, Heinz. 1984. 'Die Europäische Gemeinschaft nach der französischen Ratspräsidentschaft. Die Bedeutung der gemeinsamen Rolle Frankreichs und der Bundesrepublik Deutschlands'. *Europa-Archiv* 15.
Starbatty, Joachim, and Uwe Vetterlein. 1989. 'Spitzentechnologie oder innere Kohäsion: Ein technologiepolitischer Zielkonflikt in der Europäischen Gemeinschaft'. *Europa-Archiv* 5: 145–54.
— 1990. *Die Technologiepolitik in der Gemeinschaft. Entstehung, Praxis und ordnungspolitische Konformität*. Baden-Baden: Nomos.
Stavenhagen, Lutz G. 1991. 'Durchbruch zur Politischen Union – Vor dem Maastrichter Gipfel'. *Integration* 4.
Stokman, Frans, Rolf Ziegler and John Scott. 1985. *Networks of Corporate Power*. Cambridge: Polity Press.
Stone Sweet, Alec, and Wayne Sandholtz. 1998. 'Integration, Supranational Governance, and the Institutionalization of the European Polity'. In

W. Sandholtz and A. Stone Sweet (ed.), *European Integration and Supranational Governance.* Oxford: Oxford University Press.
Streeck, Wolfgang. 1991. 'Interest Heterogeneity and Organizing Capacity'. Pp. 161-98 in Roland Czada and Adrienne Windhoff-Héritier (eds.), *Political Choice.* Frankfurt/Main: Campus.
— 1993. 'The Rise and Decline of Neocorporatism'. In L. Ulman, B. Eichengreen and W.T. Dickens (eds.), *Labor and an Integrated Europe.* Washington DC: Brookings Institution.
— 1994. 'Neo-Voluntarism: A New European Social Policy Regime?' Paper presented at a Conference on European Law in Context: Constitutional Dimensions of European Economic Integration, European University Institute, Law Department, Florence, 14–15 April 1994.
— 1995. 'From Market Making to State Building? Reflections on the Political Economy of European Social Policy'. In S. Leibfried and P. Pierson (eds.), *European Social Policy: Between Fragmentation and Integration.* Washington DC: Brookings.
— 1996. 'Neo-Voluntarism: A New European Social Policy Regime?' In G. Marks, F.W. Scharpf, P.C. Schmitter and W. Streeck (eds.), *Governance in the European Union.* London: Sage.
Streeck, Wolfgang, and Philippe C. Schmitter. 1991. 'From National Corporatism to Transnational Pluralism: Organized Interests in the Single European Market'. *Politics and Society* 19: 133–64.
Streil, Jochen. 1986. 'Der Beitrag des Gerichtshofes der Europäischen Gemeinschaften zur Entwicklung des Sozialrechts in der Gemeinschaft'. In H. Lichtenberg (ed.), *Sozialpolitik in der EG. Referate der Tagung des Arbeitskreises Europäische Integration e.V. In Augsburg vom 18. – 20. Oktober 1984.* Baden-Baden: Nomos.
Sturm, Roland. 1992. 'Konkurrenz oder Synergie? Nationale und europäische Industriepolitik'. Pp. 234–53 in Michael Kreile (ed.), *Die Integration Europas.* Special issue of *Politische Vierteljahresschrift*, No. 23. Opladen: Westdeutscher Verlag.
Sutcliffe, John B. 1995. 'Theoretical Aspects of the Development of European Community Regional Policy'. *Schweizerische Zeitschrift für Politische Wissenschaft* 1(2/3).
Swann, Dennis (ed.). 1992. *The Single European Market and Beyond. A Study of the Wider Implications of the Single European Act.* London and New York: Routledge.
— 1996. *European Economic Integration. The Common Market, European Union, and Beyond.* Cheltenham: Elgar.

Taylor, Paul. 1989. 'The New Dynamics of EC in the 1980s'. In J. Lodge (ed.), *The European Community and the Challenge of the Future.* New York: St. Martin's Press.
Teague, Paul. 1989. *The European Community: The Social Dimension. Labour Market Policies for 1992.* London: Kogan Page.
Teasdale, Anthony L. 1993. 'The Life and Death of the Luxembourg Compromise'. *Journal of Common Market Studies* 31(4).
Thatcher, Margaret. 1993. *The Downing Street Years.* London: HarperCollins.

Therborn, Göran. 1997. 'Europas künftige Stellung – Das Skandinavien der Welt?' Pp. 573–600 in Stefan Hradil and Stefan Immerfall (eds.), *Die westeuropäischen Gesellschaften*. Opladen: Leske & Budrich.
Thorn, Gaston. 1984. 'Die Europäische Gemeinschaft – war es ein Irrtum?' *Europa-Archiv* 8.
Tiedemann, W.A. 1989. 'Comments'. In Lammy Betten (ed.), *The Future of European Social Policy*. Deventer and Boston: Kluwer Law and Taxation Publishers.
Tilly, Charles (ed.). 1975. *The Formation of National States in Western Europe*. Princeton, NJ: Princeton University Press.
Timmermann, Heiner. 1995. 'Das Europa der Regionen nach den Maastrichter Beschlüssen: Motive und Wirkungen'. In Heiner Timmermann (ed.), *Die Kontinentwerdung Europas, Festschrift für Helmut Wagner*. Berlin: Duncker & Humblot.
Tömmel, Ingeborg. 1994. *Staatliche Regulierung und europäische Integration: Die Regionalpolitik der EG und ihre Implementation*. Baden-Baden: Nomos.
Toth, A.G. 1986. 'The Legal Status of the Declarations Annexed to the Single European Act'. *Common Market Law Review* 23.
Traxler, Franz, and Phillippe C. Schmitter. 1994. 'Perspektiven europäischer Integration, verbandlicher Interessenvermittlung und Politikformulierung'. Pp. 45–70 in Volker Eichener and Helmut Voelzkow (eds.), *Europäische Integration und verbandliche Interessenvermittlung*. Marburg: Metropolis.
Tsoukalis, Loukas. 1993. *The New European Community. The Politics and Economics of Integration*. Oxford: Oxford University Press, 2nd revised edition.
Tulder, Rob van, and Gerd Junne. 1986. *European Multinationals in Core Technologies*. Chichester: Wiley.
Tyszkiewicz, Zygmunt. 1989a. 'European Social Policy – Striking the Right Balance'. *European Affairs* 4.
  1989b. 'Trouver le bon niveau pour le dialogue social'. In Fondation Europe et Société, Cahiers de la Fondation No. 12–13, *Cohésion sociale et dialogue social européen dans la construction du marché intérieur*. Paris.

Ulman, Lloyd, Barry Eichengreen and William T. Dickens (eds.). 1993. *Labor and an Integrated Europe*. Washington DC: Brookings.
UNCTAD (United Nations Conference on Trade and Development). 1994. *World Investment Report 1994: Transnational Corporations, Employment and the Workplace*. New York and Geneva.
  1996: *Investment, Trade and International Policy Arrangements*. New York and Geneva.
Ungerer, Werner. 1983a. 'Europa-Politik unter deutscher Präsidentschaft im Rückblick'. *Aussenpolitik*, No. 1.
  1983b. 'Deutsche EG-Präsidentschaft im Rückblick'. *Aussenpolitik*, No. 4.
  1984. 'Europäische Perspektiven nach Fontainbleau'. *Aussenpolitik*, No. 2.
United Nations. Transnational Corporations and Management Division. 1993. *From the Common Market to EC 92. Regional Economic Integration in the European Community and Transnational Corporations*. New York.
Useem, Michael. 1984. *The Inner Circle*. London: Oxford University Press.

Uterwedde, Henrik. 1988. *Die Wirtschaftspolitik der Linken in Frankreich. Programme und Praxis 1974–1986*. Frankfurt and New York: Campus.

Vandamme, Jacques (ed.). 1985. *New Dimensions in European Social Policy*. London: Croom Helm.

Vaubel, Roland. 1995. 'Diskussionsbeitrag'. Pp. 129–34 in Lüder Gerken (ed.), *Europa zwischen Ordnungswettbewerb und Harmonisierung*. Berlin: Springer.

Védrine, Hubert. 1996. *Les mondes de François Mitterrand. À l'Élysée 1981–1995*. Paris: Fayard.

Venturini, Patrick. 1988. *1992. The Social Dimension*. Luxembourg: Office for Official Publications of the European Communities.

Vernon, Raymond. 1994. Speech to the Academy of International Business Conference, Boston, 4 November 1994.

Vogel, Jean. 1991. 'Analyse socio-politique'. In Eliane Vogel-Polsky and Jean Vogel, *L'Europe social 1993: Illusion, alibi où réalité?* Brussels: Editions de l'Université de Bruxelles.

Vogel-Polsky, Eliane. 1991. *Die Sozialpolitik im europäischen Integrationsprozess*. Ed. European Parliament. Luxembourg: Office for Official Publications.

1994. 'Maastricht ou la voie étroite du social'. In M. Telò (ed.), *Quelle Union sociale européenne? Acquis institutionnel, acteurs et défis*. Brussels: Editions de l'Université de Bruxelles.

Volle, Angelika. 1989a. 'Der Wandel Grossbritanniens vom zögernden Aussenseiter zum widerspenstigen Partner in der Europäischen Gemeinschaft'. *Politik und Zeitgeschichte* 3: 89.

1989b. *Grossbritannien und der europäische Einigungsprozess*. Forschungsinstitut der Deutschen Gesellschaft für Auswärtige Politik. Arbeitspapier zur Internationalen Politik No. 51, Bonn: Europa Union Verlag.

Wallace, Helen. 1988. 'Europäische Integration: Auf dem Weg nach 1992'. *Europa-Archiv* 120.

1996a. 'Politics and Policy in the EU: The Challenge of Governance'. In H. Wallace and W. Wallace (eds.), *Policymaking in the European Union*. Oxford: Oxford University Press.

1996b. 'The Institutions of the EU: Experience and Experiments'. In H. Wallace and W. Wallace (eds.), *Policymaking in the European Union*. Oxford: Oxford University Press.

Wallace, Helen, and William Wallace (eds.). 1996. *Policymaking in the European Union*. Oxford: Oxford University Press.

Wallace, William. 1996. 'Government without Statehood: The Unstable Equilibrium'. In H. Wallace and W. Wallace (eds.), *Policymaking in the European Union*. Oxford: Oxford University Press.

Walsum-Stachowicz, Judith Margaretha van. 1994. 'Corporate Diplomacy and the European Community Information Technology Policies: The Influence of Multinationals and Interest Groups, 1980–1993'. Thesis submitted for PhD in International Relations, London School of Economics and Political Science, University of London.

Ward, Hugh, and Geoffrey Edwards. 1990. 'Chicken and Technology: The

Politics of the European Community's Budget for Research and Development'. *Review of International Studies* 16: 111–29.
Wasserman, Stanley, and Katherine Faust. 1994. *Social Network Analysis.* Cambridge: Cambridge University Press.
Wegner, Manfred. 1991. *Die Entdeckung Europas. Die Wirtschaftspolitik der Europäischen Gemeinschaft. Ein Grundriss.* Baden-Baden: Nomos.
Weltwoche. 1997 'Die neue 'Sphäre' des Percy Barnevik'. No. 17, 24 April.
Wendling, Peter. 1991. *Die Unfehlbaren.* Zurich: Schweizer Verlagshaus.
Wessels, Wolfgang. 1984. 'Der Vertragsentwurf des Europäischen Parlaments für eine Europäische Union. Kristallisationspunkt einer neuen Europa-Debatte'. *Europa-Archiv* 8.
  1991. 'The EC Council: The Community's Decisionmaking Center'. In R. Keohane and S. Hoffmann (eds.), *The New European Community. Decisionmaking and Institutional Change.* Boulder, Colo.: Westview Press.
Wessels, Wolfgang, and Elfriede Regelsberger (eds.). 1988. *The Federal Republic of Germany and the European Community: The Presidency and Beyond.* Bonn: Europa-Union.
Windolf, Paul. 1993. 'Codetermination and the Market for Corporate Control in the European Union'. *Economy and Society* 22: 137–58.
Winkler, Heinrich August, and Hartmut Kaelble (eds.). 1993. *Nationalismus – Nationalitäten -Supranationalität.* Stuttgart: Klett-Cotta.
WirtschaftsWoche. 1991. 'Grenzenlose Kontrolle: Aufsichtsräte – die Machtverflechtungen in Europa'. No 33, 9 August: 46–8.
  1996. 'Kleines Kunststück'. No. 46, 7 November.
Wolf, Klaus Dieter. 1996. 'Defending State Autonomy. Intergovernmental Governance in the European Union'. Working Paper No. 5, World Society Research Group, University of Darmstadt and University of Frankfurt.
World Bank. 1994. *World Development Report.* Washington DC: IBRD.
Wurm, Clemens. 1993. 'Die Integrations- und Europapolitik Frankreichs und Grossbritanniens seit 1945 im Vergleich'. In H.A.Winkler and H. Kaelble (eds.), *Nationalismus – Nationalitäten – Supranationalität.* Stuttgart: Klett-Cotta.

Ysmal, Colette. 1993. 'France'. *European Journal of Political Research* 24: 425–34.

Ziltener, Patrick. 1999. *Strukturwandel der europäischen Integration. Die Europäische Union und die Veränderung von Staatlichkeit.* Münster: Westfälisches Dampfboot.

Index

absolutism, 268–70
acquis communautaire, 264
Ad Hoc Committee for Institutional Affairs, *see* Dooge Committee
Adtranz, 204
Advanta, 232 n.5
AEG, 107
aeronautics industry, 214, 279
Agnelli, Giovanni, 79, 189–90
Agnelli, Umberto, 189, 198
Agreement on Social Policy, *see* Treaty on European Union, Social Protocol
AgrEvo, 232 n.5
agricultural associations, 226, 227
agricultural policy, 138, 256
  reform, 140, 143
agricultural sector, 144, 219
  United Kingdom, 126
agricultural subsidies, 125, 126, 136, 140
agro-industrial technologies, 220
  see also biotechnology
Airbus Industrie, 209 n.14
Akzo Nobel, 232, 241
America, *see* United States of America
American Chamber of Commerce, 114
Amigo Group, 56
Amorin, 204
Amsterdam Treaty, 263
Anderson, Jeffrey, 258–9
Andreotti, Giulio, 60 n.33
Andriessen, Frans, 139
anti-trust panel, 279
  see also competition policy
Ares-Serono, 232 n.5
Asea AB, 189 n.5, 197
Asea Brown Boveri (ABB) Ltd., 190, 195, 201, 203–5, 207, 208
Asean Free Trade Area (AFTA), 280
Asia-Pacific Economic Cooperation (APEC), 280

Association of Microbial Food Enzyme Producers in Western Europe (AMFEP), 227 n.4, 228, 239
Association for Monetary Union, 247
Atlas Copco, 197
Attali, Jacques, 53
austerity, 41 n.5
Australia, transnational corporations, 25
Austria
  and biotechnology, 223, 225
  public opinion, 241
  transnational corporations, 23
automotive industry, 17, 214

Badische Annilin- und Soda-Fabrik (BASF) AG, 232 n.5
Bamelis, Pol, 232
Bangemann, Martin, 209
Bank for International Settlements (BIS), 247 n.4
banks, 199
Barnevik, Percy, 190, 201, 204, 208
barriers
  to investment, 23
  to trade, 23, 89, 268
  see also non-tariff barriers to trade
Baxendell, Sir Peter, 189 n.5
Bayer AG, 197, 203–7, 232, 241
Beffa, Louis, 197–8
Belgium
  big business, 188, 196–7, 202–4, 206–7, 208
  and biotechnology, 223, 225
  Council presidency, 138 n.22, 172, 173 n.34
  currency policy, 44
  and intergovernmental conference 1985, 66–7, 68, 157–8
  and monetary union, 246
  public opinion, 173
  and regional policy, 144

Index

and social policy, 157–8
  see also Benelux countries
Benedetti, Carlo de, 189 n.5, 196–7, 198, 202
Benelux countries, 43
  and intergovernmental conference 1985, 61, 64, 66–7, 132
Beretta report, *see* Economic and Social Committee
Bernhard, Prince of the Netherlands, 189
Bertelsmann, 205, 207
bilateral meetings, 51, 143
Bilderberg Club, 189–90, 201
Biogen, 213, 232 n.5
Biomolecular Engineering Programme, 218
Bioresearch Ireland, 232 n.5
biotechnology, 18, 103, 185, 210–43, 254–6, 262, 281
  acceptance problems, 215–16, 222–5, 229, 241–3
  definition, 211
  ethical aspects, 215, 237
  see also Group of Advisers on the Ethical Implications of Biotechnology
Biotechnology Action Programme, 218
Biotechnology Clearinghouse, 233
Biotechnology Industry Organization (BIO, United States), 229
Bodmer, Henry C., 202
Boehringer, 232 n.5
Boeing Corp., 279
Boël, Yves, 206
Bosch, 189 n.5, 196, 197, 198, 204–7
Boyer, Herbert, 211–12
Braudel, Fernand, 13, 284
Braun, Fernand, 189, 199
Bretton Woods, *see* exchange rates
Britain, *see* United Kingdom
British American Tobacco (B.A.T.) Industries, 205, 209 n.14
British Biotechnology, 232 n.5
British Cable & Wireless, 203–4
British Petroleum (BP), 205, 207, 209
British Steel, 205
British Telecom, 199, 209 n.14
Brittan, Sir Leon, 209
Browaldh, Tore, 203
BSN, 189 n.5, 196, 198, 203
Bund für Natur und Umwelt Deutschland (BUND), 233
bureaucracy, 6, 251, 253–4
  see also Directorates General; European Commission

Bureau Européen des Unions des Consommateurs (BEUC; Bureau of European Consumers' Organizations), 233–4, 239
business elite, 193, 252
  European transnational, 29, 32, 36, 78, 189, 192, 254
  see also European Roundtable of Industrialists
business organizations, 185
  see also European Roundtable of Industrialists; employer organizations

Canada
  biotechnology, 229
  transnational corporations, 23, 25
cancer mouse (EPO patent), 224
capital
  cost reduction, 200
  and labour, 15
  market, 136
  movement liberalization, 146
  and state, 26, 93, 96
capitalism, 5, 7, 8, 271, 278
Cargill, 232 n.5
Carlsberg, 204
Catholic social doctrine, 55
Celltech, 232 n.5
Centocor, 232 n.5
Centre Européen des Entreprises Publiques (CEEP), *see* European Centre of Public Entreprises
CESPA, 204–5
Chaban-Delmas, Jacques, 55
Chandernagor, André, 154
Chase Manhattan Bank, 189–90
chemical industry, 212, 221
  see also biotechnology; European Chemical Industry Council
Chevènement, Jean-Pierre, 103
Cheysson, Claude, 53
child protection, 177
Chirac, Jacques, 140, 163
Christian democratic governments, 150–1, 173
Christian democratic party, German, 173, 248
Christopherson, Henning, 139
Ciba-Geigy AG, 189 n.5, 192 n.9, 195–6, 241
CII, 105, 107
citizenship, 9
class, 122, 258, 272
climate convention (Rio 1992), 282
Clinton, Bill, 209

clubs, 192–4
Cockfield, Lord, 5, 11, 29, 69, 77, 79 n.1, 82, 83–4, 86–7, 89, 146, 165, 191
cohabitation (France), 163
Cohen, Stanley, 211–12
Cohesion Fund, 148
cohesion policy, 12, 63, 66, 133–5, 162
  see also regional policy; social policy
cohesion regime, 74, 146
cohesion target, 122, 149, 171, 257, 284
Cokoladovny, 204
Coleman, James S., 268
collective bargaining, 158–9, 163, 164, 169
collectivism, 268–70, 276
Collomb, Bertrand, 190, 201
Colombo, Emilio, 45
Commerzbank, 203
Committee for the Monetary Union of Europe, 247
Committee for Veterinary Medicine Products, 222
Committee of Experts of Science and Technology (CODEST), 240
Committee of Permanent Representatives, *see* COREPER
Committee of the Regions, 148
  see also Consultative Council of Regional and Local Authorities
Communist Party, France, 50
Compagnie Générale des Eaux (CGE), 107, 198
competition
  policy, 108, 201, 241
  state, 252
competitive advantages, 99
competitiveness, 12, 31, 86, 109 n.7, 126, 148, 179, 180, 199–201, 259
  and social policy, 155
  technological, 102, 214, 217, 230–2
computer integrated manufacturing, 97
computers, 15
  see also information technology
concertation, 54–5, 56, 164, 166
confederation, 13, 264
Confédération française et démocratique du travail (CFDT), 49, n.17, 55, 57
Confédération générale du travail (CGT), 55
conservation of genetic resources, 219
conservative governments, 41
Conservative Party, United Kingdom, 172
Consultative Council of Regional and Local Authorities (CCLRA), 145, 146
  see also Committee of the Regions

consumer organizations, 168, 226, 233–4
consumer protection, 161 n.12
convergence, 40–2, 247, 252, 261, 284
  criteria for monetary union, 261
  of living standards, 131
  see also regional policy
  of social policy, 170
  of social security systems, 156 n.7
Coordination Européenne des Amis de la Terre (CEAT), *see* Friends of the Earth
COREPER (Committee of Permanent Representatives), 59, 76, 81, 85, 86, 90, 235, 253
corporate law, 202
COST (European Cooperation in the field of Scientific and Technical Research), 221
Council of Europe
  bio-ethics convention, 222
  European agreement for the protection of animals employed in agriculture, 224
  European agreement for the protection of vertebrates used in testing and for other scientific purposes, 224
Council of Ministers, 10, 36–7, 78, 86, 167–68, 234–5, 240, 252
  and biotechnology, 212, 218, 223, 233
  and capital movement liberalization, 146
  environmental ministers, 283
  and Esprit, 96–7, 110–12
  and European Commission, 90
  and information technology, 105, 218
  industry ministers, 231
  internal market (trade ministers), 82
  lack of parliamentary control, 251
  legislative power, 266–7
  majority voting, 12, 42, 49, 58, 60, 65, 66, 76, 133–4, 156–7, 161, 162, 178, 249, 251
  presidency, 42, 44, 58, 181
    Belgium 1987, 138 n.22, 172, 173 n.34
    Denmark 1987, 172
    France 1984, 50–1, 53, 129, 155
    France 1989, 176
    Germany 1983, 45–6
    Germany 1988, 142–3
    Ireland 1984, 155
    Italy 1985, 59–61
    Luxembourg 1985, 59, 136
    Netherlands 1991, 178
    United Kingdom 1986, 139
  and regional policy, 127, 133–4, 136, 137, 141, 144

Index   311

research ministers, 103, 110
social affairs ministers, 155, 175–6
and social policy, 155–6, 161–2, 175–7
unanimity principle, 40, 66–7, 127, 133, 136, 137, 178
craft workers' organizations, 168
Craxi, Bettino, 61, 158
creative destruction (Schumpeter), 16
Credit Suisse, 207
Crocodile Group, 46
Cromme, Gerhard, 197, 209
cultural policy, 67

Dahrendorf, Ralf, 13, 18, 212
Daimler-Benz AG, 199, 204–7, 209 n.14
Dankert, Piet, 56
Danone, 196, 198, 203–7, 232
Davignon, Etienne Vicomte, 5, 11, 18–19, 41 n.5, 53, 82, 83, 86, 87, 89, 91, 94, 101–2, 104, 106–10, 112, 113, 188–90, 192, 197, 199, 202–3, 206, 208–9, 210, 213
  cabinet, 189
  'The Telematics Revolution', 18–19
deficit spending, 279
Defraigne, Pierre, 189
Dekalb Genetics, 232 n.5
Dekker, Wisse, 5, 11, 29, 82, 89, 189 n.5, 191, 198–99, 208
Delorism, Delorist project, see European Commission, integration project
Delors, Jacques, 4–5, 10, 33, 41, 44, 49 n.17, 52 n.22, 53–8, 62, 65, 70, 71, 83–4, 86, 87, 132–3 n.14, 133–4, 136, 138, 139, 142, 153, 154, 157–8, 163, 164–6, 170, 171–2, 174, 175, 181, 191, 214, 216, 247, 256–7, 262, 274
  cabinet, 57, 164 n.20, 172
  preface to the Cecchini report, 166 n.22
  speech at TUC Congress in Brighton 1988, 172
  tour of the capitals 1987, 139–40
  see also European Commission, presidency
democracy, 9, 113
  deficit in EC/EU, 192, 194, 266–7, 271, 276
  grassroots/direct, 277
  see also social movements
Denmark, 45
  big business, 204
  and biotechnology, 223, 225
  Council presidency, 172
  and intergovernmental conference 1985, 59–60, 63–4, 66–7, 157–8

public opinion, 176, 241
referendum on Union Treaty, 179
and Single European Act, referendum on, 70
and social policy, 49, 154, 157–8, 160–1
deregulation, 54, 165, 180, 195, 267–8, 282
  in biotechnology, 216, 226–7, 231
  winners and losers, 30
  see also liberalization
Deutsche Bank AG, 190, 196, 203, 206–7, 247
Directives
  70/457, 222
  70/458, 222
  70/524, 222
  87/22, 222–3
  90/219, 215, 222, 226, 228
  90/220, 215, 222, 226, 228
  90/679, 222, 227, 234
  91/414, 222
  93/39, 222
  93/41, 223
  93/114, 222
Directorates General, 57, 238, 242
  DG I, 227
  DG III, 81, 82, 83, 106, 108 n.5, 212, 224, 226, 236, 238–9
  DG V, 227, 236
  DG VI, 235, 239
  DG XI, 226, 228, 232, 236, 239
  DG XII, 98, 106, 108 n.5, 212, 226, 228, 236, 238–40
    Concertation Unit of Biotechnology in Europe (CUBE), 233, 236–7, 239
    Department E, 238
    Task Force on Vaccines and Viral Diseases, 237, 239
  DG XIII, 112, 114–15
    see also Information Technology Task Force
  DG XV, 82, 227
  DG XVI, 145
  DG XXI, 82
division of labour, European, 151 n.40
dollar–gold parity, 32
Domeniconi, Reto, 209
Dompé Biotec, 232 n.5
Dondelinger Group, 62
Dooge Committee, 52, 61
  final report (1985), 59, 67, 131, 154, 157
Dow AgroSciences, 232 n.5
Doyle, Peter, 228
Dresdner Bank AG, 203
Drews, Jürgen, 228, 232

312   Index

DSM-Gist, 232 n.5, 241
Dumas, Roland, 50
DuPont Inc., 232 n.5
Durant, John, 233
Durham, Kenneth, 189, 203

East–West conflict, 3
ECLAIR (European Collaborative Linkage of Agriculture and Industry through Research), 219
ecology movement, 226
  see also environmental organisations
economic and monetary union (EMU), see monetary union
economic and social cohesion, see cohesion policy; regional policy; social policy
Economic and Social Committee, 49 n.17, 126, 128 n.5, 131, 141, 142, 145 n.29, 159, 166–8, 174, 175, 235, 240, 242
  Beretta report, 162, 168, 173 n.34
economic competition among states, 26, 28
economic policy, 179
  convergence of, 50
  coordination, 256
economic recession (1990s), 179, 261
economies of common governance, 12
economies of scale, 5, 23–4, 25, 86, 99, 100, 118, 279
education, 200
Ekman, Bo, 189
Electrolux, 197, 204
electronics industry, 199
Elias, Norbert, 8
Eli Lilly, 222, 232 n.5
employer organizations, 155, 167, 169–70, 188, 192–5, 224, 243
  see also Union of Industrial and Employers' Confederations of Europe (UNICE)
employment policy, 154, 159, 178, 200
energy
  industry, 199
  market liberalization, 200
enlargement of EC/EU, 200, 208
  Eastern Europe, 259, 262
  first round (1973), 126
  second round (1981/1986), 117, 128
Enlightenment, 269
enterprise alliances, 240
environmental compatibility, 147 n.33
environmental organizations, 223, 225, 226, 233–4, 237, 243
  see also biotechnology, acceptance problems

environmental policy/protection, 12, 59, 64, 67, 68, 161 n.12, 189, 200, 219, 225, 232, 233–4, 240, 282–3
E-Plus Mobilfunk, 204
equal opportunities, 170, 177, 178
Ericsson, 197, 204–5, 209
Ernst & Young
  biotech reports, 216
Escher, Alfred, 193
Esprit (European Strategic Programme of Research and Development in Information Technology), 53, 66, 83, 103, 104, 114–21, 210, 243
  Advisory Board, 112–13
  genesis, 93–7, 107–12
  Management Committee, 112–13
  phase 1, 111
  Steering Committee, 113
  decision-making structure, 112–14
Ethical Advisory Group, see Group of Advisers on the Ethical Implications of Biotechnology
Eurawasser, 204
EUREKA, 42, 66, 110, 219, 221, 229
Eurobarometer surveys, 34, 36–7, 173, 175–6, 233
Euro-centrism, 283
Euro-nationalism, 274–6
  see also federalism, European
EuropaBio, see European Secretariat of National Biotechnology Associations; Senior Advisory Group Biotechnology
European Agricultural Guidance and Guarantee Fund (EAGGF), 125, 144
  see also structural funds
European–American Business Council, 209
European Assembly, 125
European Biotechnology Coordination Group (EBCG), 227–8, 236–7, 239
European central bank (project), 248
European Centre for Infrastructure Studies (ECIS), 200
European Centre of Public Enterprises (CEEP), 142, 164
European Chemical Industry Council (ECIC), 226–8
European Coal and Steel Community (ECSC) Treaty, 125
European Commission, 36, 102, 185–6, 194, 279
  and biotechnology, 210–25, 236–43, 255
  Biotechnology Coordination Committee, 231, 234, 238
  Biotechnology Steering Committee, 236

Index

Communications to the Council
  Biotechnology and the White Paper on Growth, Competitiveness and Employment (1994), 215
  Biotechnology in the Community (1983), 213
  Biotechnology: The Task of the Community (1983), 212–13
  Consolidating the Internal Market (1984), 77–8, 80
  on the State of the Internal Market (1981), 78, 80
  on Re-activating the European Internal Market (1982), 78, 80
  Promoting the Competitive Environment for the Industrial Activities based on Biotechnology within the Community (1991), 214
  Towards a European Strategic Programme for Research and Development in Information Technologies (1982), 110
cooperation with European Roundtable of Industrialists, 1, 58, 73, 75, 84–92, 188–91, 194, 198–201, 255
cooperation with European Information Technology Industry Roundtable, 73, 95, 107, 111–12, 113, 114–20, 121, 255
cooperation with transnational corporations, 93–4, 106, 109, 254–6, 260, 262
and Council of Ministers, 90
decline of influence in early 1980s, 46
decision-making process, 235, 242
and Esprit, 96–7, 110–12
executive power, 267
extension of competences, 146
and federalism, 149
and high-tech industry, 98–9, 105–6, 109–10
inception, 29
The Industrial Policy of the Community (1970), 212
Industry Research and Development Advisory Committee, 238, 240
integration project, 74, 91, 152, 154, 164–71, 174, 179–81
and intergovernmental conference 1985, 62–3, 66–7, 68, 70, 132–5, 156–8
leadership role in the Single Market project, 83–7
monopoly on initiatives, 71, 84, 140, 234–5
presidency, 187

Delors, 10, 34, 40, 56–8, 83 n.3, 84, 132, 145, 149, 163, 253–4, 257, 261
Hallstein, 83 n.3, 84, 253
Jenkins, 52 n.22
Thorn, 52, 83 n.3, 91
Programme 1985, 80, 155
publicity campaign for Single Market, 173, 245
rebirth in 1980s, 39, 52–8, 253
and regional policy, 124–51, 156, 257
  see also European Regional Development Fund, reform of 1988
Report on Regional Policy (1965), 125
in Single European Act, 65, 67
and social policy, 139, 152–82, 256
standing committees, 235–6, 242
as supranational actor, 2, 90, 136–37, 145, 262
and triad competition, 240
Venturini report (1988), 133 n.15, 164, 166, 170, 173 n.34, 174
White Papers, 76
  Completing the Internal Market (1985), 10, 11, 61, 76, 77, 79 n.1, 80–1, 82, 84, 92, 145, 153, 156, 169, 175, 180, 191, 246, 255
  Growth, Competitiveness, Employment (1993), 31, 200, 214, 216, 230–1, 246, 281
European Council (summit meetings), 10, 77–9, 124, 127, 146, 188, 266
  1981 June, 80
  1986 June, 138
  Amsterdam 1997, 246
  Athens 1983, 46
  Brussels, March 1984, 46 n.12, 51
  Brussels, March 1985, 81, 191
  Brussels, February 1988, 142
  Copenhagen 1982, 77, 80–1, 82
  Corfu 1994, 216, 229
  Dublin 1984, 77, 80–1
  Fontainebleau 1984, 48, 52, 77, 80–1
  Hanover 1988, 142–43, 173–4, 247
  London 1986, 139
  Luxembourg 1985, 2, 65, 128, 135, 158, 161, 191–2
  Maastricht 1991, 54, 128, 147–8, 178–9
  Madrid 1989, 176
  Milan 1985, 60–2, 66–7, 81, 156, 191
  Paris 1972, 126
  resolution on industrial policy 1973, 212, 217
  Strasbourg 1989, 176
  Stuttgart 1983, 212, 236

314   Index

European Council (summit meetings) (*cont.*)
   see also Solemn Declaration
   summit meetings of 1987, 142
   Versailles 1982, 97
European Court of Justice, 12, 37, 161, 249
   Cassis de Dijon decision, 53, 253
   directive on working hours, 162
   and social policy, 168
European Economic Area (EEA), 245
European Economic Community (EEC)
   Treaty, 11, 61, 85, 89, 166, 242
   Art. 92, 125
   Art. 152, 234
   Art. 155, 234
   Art. 175, 234
   Art. 235 (general clause), 110, 124, 127
European Enterprise Group, 189
European Environmental Bureau, 239
European federal state, 122, 263
European federalism, *see* federalism, European
European Federation of Animal Health (FEDESA), 227–8, 239
European Federation of Biotechnology, 211, 213, 232, 239
European Federation of the Chemical Unions (FESCID), 234
European Federation of Pharmaceutical Industry Associations (EFPIA), 226–8, 239
European Free Trade Association (EFTA), 245, 261
European Group on Ethics in Sciences and New Technologies, 237
European identity, *see* multi-level identities
European Information Technology Industry Roundtable (EITIRT), 66
   cooperation with European Commission, 73, 95, 107, 111–12, 113, 114–20, 121, 255
   decline of influence, 114–20, 121
European industrial area, 58
European Investment Bank (EIB), 125
European Laboratories Without Walls, 218
European Medication Evaluation Agency (EMEA), 223
European monetary fund (project), 247 n.3
European Monetary System, 138, 247
   establishment, 127–8
   in Single European Act, 12, 66
European Movement, 189
European norms and standards, 18
European Parliament, 9–10, 37, 175, 192, 235, 240
   and biotechnology, 211, 223, 225
   Boserup report, 242
   budgetary authority, 12
   Committee on
      Economic and Monetary Affairs, 49, n.17
      Institutional Problems, 46
   communist group, 225
   draft treaty on European Union (1984), 47, 51 n.19, 60, 62, 167
   and economic and social policy, 139
   elections of 1989, 176
   electoral system, 266–7
   extension of competences, 58, 60, 67, 140, 248
   green representatives, 225
   legislative power(lessness), 12, 251
   mediation committee, 223, 236
   and regional policy, 127 n.3, 131, 141, 145 n.29
   in Single European Act, 65, 69–70
   socialist group, 49, 225
   and social policy, 159, 162, 166–8, 171, 177
   as supranational actor, 145 n.29, 253
   veto power, 194
European Patent Convention, 223–4
European Patent Office (EPO), 215, 224
European Regional Development Fund (ERDF), 132 n.14
   establishment, 126–7
   at intergovernmental conference 1985, 132–4
   reform of 1979, 127–8
   reform of 1988, 123, 137–46
      content, 144–5
   regulation of 1984, 129
      Art. 5, 129
   in Single European Act, 136
   see also structural funds
European Roundtable of Industrialists (ERT), 1, 10, 32, 36, 74, 76, 81, 83, 96, 185–86, 187, 207–9, 232
   Advisory Group for Social Relations and Industrial Policy, 199
   characteristics, 194–5
   Competitiveness Advisory Group, 198–9, 255
   cooperation with European Commission, 58, 73, 75, 84–92, 188–91, 194, 198–201, 255
   'Education for Europeans' (1995), 200
   'Europe 1990: Agenda for Action' (1984), 29, 82, 191, 255
   'European Competitiveness: The Way to Growth and Jobs' (1994), 198, 200

founding, 48, 82, 87, 89, 188, 192, 207–8
'Foundations for the Future of European Industry' (1983), 190
historical development, 89
'Investing in Knowledge' (1997), 200
'Job Creation and Competitiveness through Innovation' (1998), 200
membership, 195–7, 202–7
'Missing Links: Upgrading Europe's Transborder Infrastructure' (1984), 89, 191, 200
'Missing Networks' (1991), 200
Policy Memorandum (1983), 29–30, 88
'Rebuilding Confidence: An Action Plan for Europe' (1992), 199–200
'Reports on the Competition Policy of the Commission', 201
'Reshaping Europe' (1991), 199
and Single Market, 66
European Secretariat of National Biotechnology Associations (ESNBA), 228, 232, 238–9
European social area, 49, 58–9, 63, 66, 154–8, 160, 163–4, 167, 169, 172, 181
European Social Charter (Council of Europe, 1965), 167, 173 n.34, 182
European Social Forum, 259
European Social Fund (ESF), 125 n.2, 144
see also structural funds
European societal model (*modèle européen de société*), 5, 19, 34, 56, 164, 181
European standardization organization (CEN/CENELEC), 162 n.16, Committee 233, 236, 239
European Trade Union Confederation (ETUC), 141, 142, 155, 164, 169–70, 182–3, 234
and intergovernmental conference 1985, 169
Social Charter draft, 175
Stockholm conference 1988, 171
see also trade unions
European Venture Capital Association, 89, 191
Europe Plus Thirty study group, 212
Euroscepticism, 97
Eurosclerosis, 1, 31, 75
Evotec BioSystems, 232 n.5
exchange rates
fixed, 32, 247
floating, 32
exemption regulations, 43
export controls, 200

Fabius, Laurent, 103
fair return, *see juste retour* principle
Falck family, 196
Farm Animal Industrial Platform (FAIP), 228, 239
farmers' organizations, 168
Faroux, Roger, 189 n.5
FAST (Forecasting and Assessment in Science and Technology) group, 106–7, 212
first provisional report (*Eurofutures: The Challenge of Innovation*, 1982/4), 212
federalism
European, 44, 149, 250
failure of integration projects, 47
and Single European Act, 57 n.28, 69, 71
see also Euro-nationalism; European Movement; Genscher–Colombo initiative; supranationality
United States, 265, 283
see also regions
Ferruzi
family, 196
group, 228
Fiat, 79, 189, 196–7, 198, 201, 202–3, 205, 207, 247
financial jurisdiction, 10
Finland
big business, 204
and biotechnology, 223, 225
transnational corporations, 23
fiscal crisis, 122
fisheries sector, 144, 219
FLAIR (Food Linked Agro-Industrial Research), 219
flanking measures, 54, 63, 133
see also regional policy; Single Market, negative effects; social policy
Flaubert, Gustave, 38, 260
Florence, republic, 269
food industry, 199
see also biotechnology
Fordism, 31
see also societal model, Keynesian
foreign direct investment (FDI), 20–4, 245
inside EU, 23
foreign policy cooperation, 64, 67
foreign trade, 20
inside EU, 23
Forum for European Bioindustry Coordination (FEBC), 227–9, 239
Fowler, Norman, 175–6
Framework Programmes, 217–21, 238
BRIDGE, 218–9, 236

France, 35, 42, 45, 51, 75
  and agricultural policy, 140
  big business, 188, 195, 196–8, 202–4, 207, 208
  and biotechnology, 217, 223, 225
  Commissariat du Plan, 48, 55
  Council presidency, 50–1, 53, 155, 176
  Deuxième Gauche, 55–6
  employers' organization, 170
  foreign ministry, 48
  and Germany, 43, 52
    see also French–German axis/tandem
  and industrial decline, 144
  integration project, 69
  and intergovernmental conference 1985, 61, 64–5, 66–7, 68, 132, 134, 157–8
  intergovernmentalist position, 51 n.19
  Keynesianism, 48
  Members of European Parliament, 47
  memorandum for a European social area, 49
  and monetary union, 246, 250
  as net payer, 145
  political culture, 160
  public opinion, 173, 176
  referendum on Union Treaty, 179
  and regional policy, 130, 134, 142, 144, 145, 151
  revolution, 269
  right-wing government, 140, 151, 163
  science and technology policy, 102–4, 105
  and Single Market project, 54
  socialist government, 41, 173
  and social policy, 154–55, 157–8, 163
  state-owned industry, 105, 116
  trade unions, 55, 57
  transnational corporations, 189 n.5
free trade, *see* liberalization of trade
Freiburg Ecology Institute (Öko-Institut Freiburg), 225
French–German axis/tandem, 41 n.5, 49, 64, 71, 126, 142
Friends of the Earth, 233, 238–9
functional integration, 9
Fusion Treaty, 10
  Art. 15, 90

Gandois, Jean, 206
Gardini family, 196
Gaulle, Charles de, 38 n.1
GEC, 107
Genencor, 232 n.5
General Agreement on Tariffs and Trade (GATT), 20, 261–2, 265

genetically modified organisms
  and food, 223, 233–4, 236
  release in the environment, 215
  see also biotechnology
genetic engineering, *see* biotechnology
Geneva International Management Institute, 189
Genscher, Hans-Dietrich, 45–6, 50, 52, 104, 247 n.5
Genscher–Colombo initiative, 45, 62, 67
Genscher Memorandum, 248
Genset, 232 n.5
Genzyme, 232 n.5
George, Stephen, 85, 91
Germany, 35, 75
  agricultural policy, 140
  big business, 188, 193, 195, 196, 202–4, 207, 208
  and biotechnology, 216, 217, 223, 225
  central bank (Bundesbank), 248
  Constitutional Court (Bundesverfassungsgericht), 179
  corporate law, 202
  Council presidency, 45–6, 142–3
  environmental organizations, 233
  and Esprit, 111
  and European Social Fund, 125 n.2
  foreign policy, 250
  and France, 43, 52
    see also French–German axis/tandem
  and industrial decline, 144
  integration project, 146, 174
    see also Genscher–Colombo initiative
  and intergovernmental conference 1985, 59, 64–5, 66–7, 68, 132, 173
  and Italy, 45
  Members of European Parliament, 47
  monetary policy, 246, 248
  neocorporatism, 55
  as net payer, 43 n.7, 146
  public opinion, 173, 176, 241
  and regional policy, 126, 143, 144
  reunification, 3, 148, 247
  science and technology policy, 102, 104
  and Single Market, 146
  trade unions, 169
  transnational corporations, 189 n.5
Gevaert, 197, 202, 203, 205–7, 247
Giscard d'Estaing, Valéry, 64, 155 n.4, 247
Glatz, Hannes, 199
globalization, 1, 5, 20–6, 277–9
Grant, Ulysses S., 193
Greece, 45, 46
  and agricultural policy, 140, 249
  big business, 204
  and biotechnology, 225

integration project, 131–2
and intergovernmental conference 1985, 59–60, 63, 66–7, 132–34
and regional policy, 128–34, 140, 144
and Single European Act, approval, 70
socialist government, 48, 130
trade balance, 150 n.40
and underdevelopment, 144
see also enlargement of EC, second round; Mediterranean countries
Greenpeace, 225, 233, 238–9
Groupe Bruxelloise Lambert, 196
Group of Advisers on the Ethical Implications of Biotechnology, 222–4, 237, 239
Group of Seven (G7), 265
Gut, Rainer, 207
Gyllenhammar, Pehr, 89, 188–91, 197, 198, 203–4, 208

Haas, Ernst B., 253
Hallstein, Walter, 83, 263
see also European Commission, presidency
Hanon, Bernard, 189
Hanseatic League, 268, 272
Hansenne, Michel, 172
harmonization
 biotechnology policies, 213
 occupational health and safety, 179
 regulation, 50, 156, 161, 256, 258–9, 267
 social protection, 159, 164, 183
 taxes, 44, 64
Harvey-Jones, John, 189 n.5
heads of state and government, 187, 191
see also European Council
health policy, 167
see also biotechnology; occupational health and safety
hegemony, 21, 36
 hegemonic transition, 4
 non-hegemonic cooperation, 40
 post-hegemonic competition, 1, 34
see also United States of America
Heineken, 192 n.9
Hinks-Edwards, Michael, 189
Hinterscheid, Mathias, 171 n.29
Hintze, Otto, 25
Hirsch, Joachim, 252
Hitler, Adolf, 272
Hobbes, Thomas, 13
Hoechst AG, 228, 232 n.5, 241
Hoffmann-La Roche AG, 201, 205, 207, 209 n.14, 228, 232
Holland, *see* Netherlands

Honeywell-Bull, 103, 105
see also CII
Hong Kong, transnational corporations, 23
Howe, Geoffrey, 51, 60, 69
Hüber, Roland, 108
human rights, 271

Iberdrola, 204–5
IBM Corp., 105
ICL, 107
Ifial, 203
Imperial Chemical Industries (ICI), 189 n.5, 196, 201, 204–5, 209 n.14, 228
imperialism, 272
India, biotechnology, 220
individualism, 268–70, 273, 276
Indosuez bank, 197
Industrial Biotechnology Association of Canada (IBAC), 229
industrial change, 144
industrial decline, 144
industrial policy, 50, 188
see also technology policy
industrial relations, 165, 257
see also collective bargaining; employer organizations; trade unions
informal negotiations, 76
information society, 19, 119, 200
information technology (IT), 20, 83 n.3, 94, 96–121, 210–11, 214, 218, 221, 230, 243, 254–6, 277–8, 281
 Big 12, 107–8, 110, 115
 ethical aspects, 237
see also Esprit; European Information Technology Industry Roundtable
Information Technology Task Force (ITTF), 106–7, 112–13
Inglehart, Ronald, 273
Innogenetics, 232 n.5
insurance companies, 199
Integrated Mediterranean Programmes, 130, 141
integration blockade, 165, 257
integration crisis (1965–6), 126
integration project, 39–40, 44, 71, 123, 250–1
 European Commission, 74, 91, 152, 154, 164–71, 174, 179–81
 France, 48–50, 69
 German–Italian, 47
see also Genscher–Colombo initiative
 Germany, 146, 174
 Greece, 131–2
 United Kingdom, 60, 250

318   Index

integration relaunch/thrust, 6, 27, 38, 41, 48–50, 56, 72, 75, 122–3, 147, 148, 150, 152, 154, 163, 174, 181, 186, 187 n.1, 244, 254, 258, 262–3, 264, 274
integration theory, 245, 253, 257, 262
  neofunctionalist, 27–8, 123, 149, 152, 174, 260
  neorealist, 27–8, 123, 250, 253
  network theory (S. George), 85
  see also convergence; package deal; political entrepreneurship; spillover
intellectual property rights, 213–15, 217, 223–5, 233, 237, 242–3
  see also European Patent Office
intergovernmental conferences, 1, 61, 71, 200
  Amsterdam 1996–7, 246, 261, 264
  Luxembourg 1985, 38, 62–70, 94, 182
  preparation, 59–61
  and regional policy, 132–5, 147, 156
  and social policy, 153, 156, 158, 161, 163, 169, 173
  Maastricht 1991, 123, 178, 248, 261
intergovernmentalism, 35, 123, 146 n.31, 148, 182, 244, 250, 252
internal logic of integration, 27
internal market, see Single Market
Internal Market Support Committee (IMSC), 89, 187
International Bioindustry Forum (IBF), 229
International Labour Organization (ILO), 173 n.34
international law, 264
  direct applicability, 265
international organizations, 265
international regime, 36
International Standardization Organization (ISO), 20
International Telecommunications Union (ITU), 20
interstate financial transfer, 124
interstate negotiations, 123
Investor AB, 204
Ireland, 45
  and agricultural policy, 140
  big business, 204
  and biotechnology, 223
  Council presidency, 155
  employers' organization, 170
  and intergovernmental conference 1985, 59, 61, 63, 66–7, 132, 134
  neutrality, 132
  and regional policy, 126–8, 132, 134, 140–1, 144
  and underdevelopment, 144

Italy
  big business, 196
  and biotechnology, 217 n.3, 223, 225
  Council presidency, 59–61
  and Germany, 45
  and industrial decline, 144
  and intergovernmental conference 1985, 63, 64, 66–7, 132
  Members of European Parliament, 47
  Mezzogiorno, 125, 143
  public opinion, 176
  and regional policy, 126–8, 130, 142–43, 144
  and Single European Act, approval 70
  state-owned industry, 196
  transnational corporations, 189 n.5
  and underdevelopment, 125, 144
  see also Mediterranean countries

Japan, 4, 18, 78, 86, 190, 212, 279, 280–2
  biotechnology, 210, 213–16, 219, 225, 229, 240–1, 243
  elite clubs, 193
  information technology, 96–7, 106, 107
  market size, 88
  Ministry of Trade and Industry (MITI), 101, 109, 215
  rise as a trading power, 1, 21, 31, 281
  technology corporatism, 94, 97, 101–2
  transnational corporations, 22–5
Japan Bioindustry Association (JBA), 229
Jefferson Smurfit, 204
Jenkins, Roy, 52 n.22
Jessop, Bob, 252
Joint European Submicron Silicon Initiative (JESSI), 115
juste retour principle, 127–8, 131, 132 n.14, 147

Kabivitrum, 241
Kant, Immanuel, 13
Kaske, Karl-Heinz, 198
Kissinger, Henry, 189
Kohl, Helmut, 64, 85, 143, 199
Kopper, Hilmar, 190, 202, 206
Kressler, Herwig, 199
Kriwet, Heinz, 209
Krupp, 197, 205–7, 209
KWS, 232 n.5
Kymmene OY, 201, 204

Laage de Meux, François, 202
labour market, 180
  policy, 125 n.2, 169, 179, 258
Labour Party, United Kingdom, 42

Index 319

Lafarge-Coppée, 189 n.5, 190, 196, 201, 205, 207
Lamfalussy, Alexandre, 247 n.4
Lamy, Pascal, 57
Lane, Frederic C., 25
Lecerf, Olivier, 189 n.5
Lederman, Leonard, 102
legitimacy, 26
Lenoir, Noëlle, 237
Leysen, André, 197, 202, 206–7
liberalism, 186, 264, 267–8, 269–77, 284
  see also societal model, liberal
liberalization, 267
  of capital movement, 146
  of energy markets, 200
  of services, 262
  of telecommunications markets, 200, 282
  of trade, 132, 150 n.40, 209, 260–1
  of transportation markets, 200
  see also deregulation; Single Market
Limagrain, 232 n.5
lobbying, 192–4, 225, 242, 251
locational competition, 260
Luxembourg
  and biotechnology, 225
  Council presidency, 59, 62
    see also intergovernmental conferences
  employers' organization, 170
  and intergovernmental conference, 66
  see also Benelux countries
Luxembourg Compromise, 38 n.1, 45, 49, 127, 128, 248–9, 251
Lyonnaise des Eaux, 196–98, 203–7, 208–9

Maastricht, see European Council; intergovernmental conferences; Treaty on European Union
McDonnell Douglas Corp., 279
machinery industry, 199
majority voting, see Council of Ministers
market economy, 9, 56
market failure, 99
Marshall Plan, 147 n.32
Martens, Wilfried, 53
materials science, 103, 214
Maucher, Helmut, 187, 189 n.5, 198–9, 201, 202, 207, 208
Mauroy, Pierre, 41 n.5, 154
Mediterranean countries, 141
member states, legislative power, 13
mergers and acquisitions, 201, 245, 246
Merkle, Hans, 189 n.5, 198
Mestrallet, Gérard, 206, 209
metals industry, 199

micro-electronics, 15, 18
Middle Ages, 268
middle classes, enlargement, 15
Miert, Karel van, 200
migration, 260
  of scientific specialists, 213
military integration, 209
Millennium Bug, 208
Mitterrand, François, 41 n.5, 50–3, 56, 64, 85, 103, 143, 155, 163
  speech to the European Parliament 1984, 51
modèle européen de société, see European societal model
Møller, Ørstrøm J., 61
monetarism, 15, 31
monetary policy, 66, 68, 158, 246–7
monetary union (EMU), 44, 66, 126, 127 n.3, 128, 147, 185, 199, 244, 246–8, 250, 259, 261, 265, 279, 281
Monnet, Jean, 71, 166
Monnetist type of integration, 179
Monod, Jérôme, 197, 198, 207, 209
monopoly, national, 29
Monsanto, 222, 228, 232 n.5
Monti, Mario, 190
Moravcsik, Andrew, 27, 35, 43, 68 n.37, 88, 159, 250, 253, 262
Moreau, Jacques, 49–50, 56
multi-level governance, 124 n.1, 149, 182, 186, 244, 261, 263, 284
multi-level identities, 276–7, 283–4

Narjes, Karl-Heinz, 41 n.5, 83, 191, 213
  cabinet, 108 n.5
national interest, 27, 81, 250
  see also sovereignty; veto
national markets, 30, 100
national parliaments, 251–2
national sovereignty, see sovereignty
nationalism, 186, 264, 267–8, 270–7, 284
nation-state, see state; state-building
negative integration, 150
neocorporatism, 14, 55, 259 n.9
neofunctionalism, see integration theory
neoliberalism, 15, 273, 277
  see also liberalism; monetarism; supply-side economics
neorealism, see integration theory
neo-voluntarism, 259 n.9
Nestlé SA, 187, 189 n.5, 195–6, 198, 201, 202, 204–5, 207, 208–9, 232
Netherlands
  and agricultural policy, 140
  big business, 202, 207
  and biotechnology, 216, 217, 225

Netherlands (cont.)
  corporate law, 202
  Council presidency, 178
  currency policy, 44
  and intergovernmental conference, 66–7
  public opinion, 173, 176, 241
  and regional policy, 126
  revolution, 269
  science and technology policy, 102
  transnational corporations, 189 n.5, 196
  see also Benelux countries; United Provinces of North Holland
net-payer countries, 145, 148, 149
network theory, see integration theory
New Zealand, transnational corporations, 25
Nicolin, Curt, 189 n.5
Nixdorf, 107
Noël, Emil, 52, 137, 248
Nokia OY, 209 n.14
non-governmental organizations (NGOs), 259, 261
  see also consumer organizations; environmental organizations; social movements; trade unions
non-tariff barriers to trade, 12, 29, 49, 262
Norsk Hydro, 201, 204, 209 n.14
North American Free Trade Agreement (NAFTA), 265, 280
North Atlantic Treaty Organisation (NATO), 190, 209, 283
North–South cleavage inside EC, 242
North–South relations, 200
Norway
  big business, 204
  transnational corporations, 25
Novartis AG, 232 n.5
Novo Nordisk, 232 n.5

occupational health and safety, 64, 159–62, 169–70, 177, 179, 234, 256
occupational training, 155
Offe, Claus, 194
Olivetti, 107, 189 n.5, 196, 198, 202, 205
Olson, Mancur, 194–5
organizational capacity, 194–5
Ortoli, François-Xavier, 11, 55, 91

package deal, 40, 43–4, 70, 123, 124, 126, 128, 134, 136
Padoa-Schioppa, Tommaso, 138
  Padoa-Schioppa report (1987), 138
Papandreou, Andreas, 46, 130
Papantoniou, Iannis, 131
parastatist organization, 259 n.9
Paribas, 196

patents, see European Patent Office; intellectual property rights
Pelkmans, Jacques, 53 n.23
PepsiCo, 232 n.5
Perez, Carlota, 16, 277
peripheral countries (in EC), 149, 150 n.40, 151
peripheral regions, 151 n.40
Permanent Representatives, see COREPER
Pescatore, Pierre, 249
Pesenti family, 196
Petrofina, 196, 203, 205–7
Pfeiffer, Alois, 169
pharmaceutical industry, see biotechnology; chemical industry; European Federation of Pharmaceutical Industry Associations
Pharmacia, 232 n.5
Pharming, 232 n.5
Philippa, Wim, 192 n.9
Philips Electronics N.V., 5, 11, 82, 83, 89, 105, 107, 189 n.5, 191, 196–7, 198, 201, 205–7, 209, 247
Pierer, Heinrich von, 199
Pilkington, 202, 205–7
Pioneer Genetique, 232 n.5
Pirelli, 201, 202, 205, 209 n.14
Planta, Louis von, 189 n.5
Plant Genetic Systems (PGS), 220–1
Plessey, 107
Political Committee for 'political cooperation', 62
political culture(s), 160
political entrepreneurship, 4, 28, 40, 42–3, 58, 70, 74, 87, 92, 93, 96, 109, 136, 148, 151, 152; 211, 243, 253, 262
political participation, 6
political public, 261
political union, 1, 186, 248
Pompidou, Georges, 55
Portugal
  and agricultural policy, 140
  big business, 204
  public opinion, 241
  and regional policy, 132, 140, 144, 146
  and social policy, 172
  trade balance, 150 n.40
  transnational corporations, 23
  and underdevelopment, 144
  see also enlargement of EC, second round; Mediterranean countries
post-Fordism, 100
power, 8, 269
  see also separation of powers
pre-competitive research, 108–10, 111, 210

Index

Procter & Gamble, 232 n.5
production technology, 103
productivity advance, 15
Profilo, 199, 202
property rights, 25–6
protection, 25–6, 278
  standards, 68
Prudential Corporation, 196
public goods, 10, 12, 13, 278
Pury, David de, 190

racism, 272
Ramaer, J.C., 89
rationalization, 17, 137
Reagan, Ronald, 34
redistribution, 6, 137, 147 n.33
  see also regional policy
Regional Fund, *see* European Regional Development Fund
regionalism, 270, 275–7
regional policy, 2, 73–4, 117, 122–51, 154, 171, 182–3, 257, 258
  at intergovernmental conference 1985, 132–5, 147, 156
  internal reform dynamic, 137
  see also European Regional Development Fund
regions, 128 n.5, 135, 143, 145, 149, 259, 261
  see also Committee of the Regions; Consultative Council of Regional and Local Authorities; regional policy
regulation, 41
  economic, 5, 279
  gap, 257
  harmonization, 50, 156, 161, 256, 258–9, 267
  interstate, 28, 36
  labour market, 258
  mutual recognition, 268
  Regulation 2100/94, 222
  Regulation 258/97, 223, 236
  regulatory capacity of nation-states, 70, 72, 183 252
  regulatory competition, 44, 138, 161, 165, 180–1, 259
  see also social dumping
  regulatory style, 161
Renault, 189, 196, 204
RENAVAL programme, 144
research and development (R&D), 12, 19, 53, 97, 99–102, 109, 111, 162, 231–2
  see also biotechnology; Esprit; information technology; technology policy
research networks, 201

RESIDER programme, 144
Retinger, Joseph H., 189
Rhône-Poulenc SA, 228, 232, 241, 247
Riboud, Antoine, 189 n.5, 198
Richardson, Keith, 192
Ripa Di Meana, Carlo, 56, 138, 139
Rockefeller family, 190
Rokkan, Stein, 6, 8
Rothschild Asset Management, 232 n.5
Royal Dutch–Shell, 189, 196, 201, 205, 207, 241
rule of law, 283

Saint-Gobain, 189 n.5, 196–7, 203, 205–7, 209
Sandholtz, Wayne, 102, 104
Sandoz AG, 228
Santer, Jacques, 136
Schering, 232 n.5
Schmidheiny, Stephan, 189, 201
Schmidt, Helmut, 64, 247
Schuman, Robert, 271
Schumpeter, Joseph, 16
Schumpeterian workfare state, 252
Schweizerische Gesellschaft der Chemischen Industrie, 226
science, 94, 213, 232–3
  see also biotechnology; information technology; technology policy
security cooperation, 59
Seelig, Wolfgang, 189 n.5, 203
Seitz, Konrad, 98, 104
Senior Advisory Group Biotechnology (SAGE), 220, 228–32, 238–9
  Benchmarking the Competitiveness of Biotechnology in Europe (1997), 232
  Biotechnology Policy in the European Union: Competitiveness, Investment and the Cycle of Innovation (1994), 231
  Biotechnology Policy in the European Union: Prescriptions for Growth, Competitiveness and Employment (1994), 230–1
  Community Policy for Biotechnology: Priorities and Actions (1990), 229–30
  Creation of a Community Task Force and an Independent Advisory Board (1990), 230
  Economic Benefits and European Competitiveness (1990), 230
Senn, Niklaus, 202
separation of powers, 267, 283
Sheehy, Patrick, 89
Shell, *see* Royal Dutch–Shell
Siemens AG, 105, 107, 117, 118, 189 n.5, 196, 198–9, 202–7, 209 n.14

Singapore, transnational corporations, 23
Single European Act (SEA), 2, 3, 5–6, 9, 10, 33, 46 n.12, 66–7, 73–4, 85, 132, 145, 148, 185–6, 187–8, 198–9, 201, 208, 244, 248–9, 250, 254
   adoption, 38, 70, 75, 192
   Annex Declarations, 66–7
      No. 7, 158
   Arts. 6–12, 67
   Art. 13, 66, 75
   Arts. 14–19, 66
   Arts. 20–24, 66
      Arts. 21–22, 152, 157–9, 181
      Art. 23, 135, 142
      Art. 24, 104–5, 116
   Art. 25, 67
   Art. 30, 67
   Commission's view, 133 n.15
   content, 11–2, 65–70
   Delors' view, 166
   and democratization, 33
   ETUC's view, 169
   genesis, 36–7, 66–7, 164
      role of industry, 89
   influence of big business on, 187–8, 192
   negotiations, 58, 250
   Preamble, 157–8
   ratification, 172
   and regional policy, 123, 135–6, 137, 147, 149
   and Single Market, 88, 142, 250
   and social policy, 152–3, 157–8, 168, 182
   and technology policy, 93, 96, 104–5, 250
   UNICE's view, 141
   see also intergovernmental conferences, Luxembourg; Single Market; Treaties on the European Communities
Single Market / internal market, 3, 61, 66, 70–1, 73, 75–6, 83, 85–92, 110, 141–2, 145–6, 162, 185, 189, 201, 236, 244, 250, 256
   and economies of scale, 100
   and Esprit, 118
   and harmonization of regulation, 161
   negative effects, 63, 152, 180, 259–60
   project / programme, 2, 12, 54, 57, 59, 78–81, 84, 93, 101, 122, 147, 165–6, 168, 180, 181–2, 208, 247, 255, 267–8
   and regional policy goals, 135
   safeguard clauses, 65
   and social policy, 152, 155, 156 n.6, 171–4, 177

   spatial effects, 150 n.38
   and structural policy, 138, 150
   Thatcher's view, 172 n.30
   and trade liberalization on a world scale, 262
   see also social dimension
small and medium-sized enterprises, 113, 114, 118, 119, 157–9, 228, 230–1
Smith, Adam, 269
SmithKline Beecham, 232 n.5
Social Charter of EC (Community Charter of the Fundamental Social Rights of Workers), 154, 173–4, 175–7
social compatibility, 147
social democracy / social democratic party, 270
   Germany, 56, 248
   Sweden, 56
   see also socialism; socialist governments
social democratic governments, 150–1, 245
social dialogue, 59, 63, 154–5, 157–8, 163, 164, 167–71, 172, 178, 181
   Val Duchesse talks, 164
social dimension, 34, 135, 141, 152, 155 n.4, 159, 165, 168, 169, 174, 177–8, 181, 245, 246
social dumping, 156, 169, 172–3, 180
social egalitarianism, 283
social inequality, 260
social movements, 258, 269, 273
social partners, *see* collective bargaining; Economic and Social Committee; employer organizations; industrial relations; social dialogue; trade unions
social policy, 2, 44, 63–4, 66, 74, 117, 122–3, 133, 138, 149, 151, 154–83, 200, 256, 258–9
   at intergovernmental conference 1985, 153, 156, 158, 161, 163
   politicization of, 152
   theoretical explanations for, 152–3, 160, 163, 171, 174, 179–83
social protection, 154–55, 178
Social Protocol, *see* Treaty on European Union
social regression, 180, 183
social rights, 172
   see also Social Charter of EC; Treaty on European Union, Social Protocol
social security, 156 n.7, 159, 178, 258
socialism / socialist party, 176, 270
   France, 42, 53, 56–7, 155 n.4
   Greece (PASOK), 130
   see also Labour Party; social democracy
socialist governments, 173, 245
societal consensus, 122

Index

societal model, 8, 31, 36, 94, 122
 class-polarized, 272
 Keynesian/neocorporatist, 4, 14–17, 21, 31–2, 41, 71, 261, 273, 274, 280
 liberal, 14
 Western, 31, 34
 see also European societal model
Société Générale de Belgique, 82, 83, 189, 196–7, 199, 202–3, 205–7, 208–9, 247
socio-institutional subsystem, 16, 277
Sofina, 196, 203, 205–7
Solemn Declaration (Stuttgart 1983), 45–6, 62, 79, 80–1
Solvay, 196, 202, 204–7, 232
South Korea, 279
 transnational corporations, 23
sovereignty, 9, 27, 68 n.37, 72, 143, 166, 183, 250–1, 264–7, 278
 see also integration theory, neorealist; state
Soviet Union, dissolution, 3, 262
Spain
 and agricultural policy, 140
 big business, 204
 and industrial decline, 144
 liberalism, 270
 public opinion, 176, 241
 and regional policy, 132, 140, 143, 144, 146
 and social policy, 172
 trade balance, 150 n.40
 transnational corporations, 23
 and underdevelopment, 144
 see also enlargement of EC, second round; Mediterranean countries
Spethmann, Dieter, 189 n.5, 203
spillover, 27, 44, 149 n.37, 182
Spinelli, Altiero, 46
standardization, 6, 162 n.16
Standard Oil, 190
state
 and capital, 26, 93, 96
 competing forms of, 280
 control over economy, 165
 federal, 13, 264
 legitimizing function, 93, 258
 modern, 6–8, 13
 nation-state, 284
  establishment of, 265, 276
  regulatory capacity, 70, 72, 183, 252
  welfare functions, 259
  see also nationalism
 resource bases, 26
 supranational, 278, 283
 theory, 270–1

world, 7
 see also confederation; multi-level governance; parastatist organization; regions; sovereignty
state-building, 8, 268–72, 284
 in EC/EU, 6, 166, 186
 United Kingdom, 268, 272, 280
 United States of America, 268, 280
 see also United Provinces of North Holland
statehood, 9–10, 245, 263
 European, 6
steel industry, 156 n.7
STET, 107
Stora Kopperberg, 197
Strategic Defense Initiative (SDI), 98
Streeck, Wolfgang, 180, 194–5, 259 n.9, 268
Strenger, Herrmann, 206
structural adjustment, 136, 245
Structural Biology Industrial Platform, 240
structural funds, 133–7, 139, 141, 142–4, 148, 149 n.37, 150, 258–9
 see also European Agricultural Guidance and Guarantee Fund; European Regional Development Fund; European Social Fund
structural policy, 74, 129, 133, 138, 144, 147
 see also regional policy
subnational state bodies, *see* regions
subsidiarity principle, 138, 179, 259 n.9
subsidization, *see* agricultural subsidies; biotechnology; European Regional Development Fund; information technology; structural funds
Suez (company), 196–8, 203, 206–7, 208–9
summit meetings, *see* European Council
supply-side economics, 31
supranationality, 9, 27, 35, 65, 123, 250, 251, 253, 265–6, 278, 283
 regional policy, 127, 128, 132, 146, 151
 social policy, 122
 see also integration project; integration relaunch
Sutherland, Peter D., 190, 209
Svanholm, Poul, 190
Sweden, 14
 big business, 189 n.5, 195, 203–4
 and biotechnology, 223, 225
 model of wage-earner funds, 55
 neocorporatism, 55
 science and technology policy, 102
 transnational corporations, 23

Switzerland, 14, 223, 224
  big business, 189 n.5, 195–6
  chemical industry, 226
  transnational corporations, 25

Tabaksblat, Morris, 190
Taiwan, transnational corporations, 23
Tarifautonomie, 157
tariffs, elimination, 12
Task Group on Public Perceptions of Biotechnology, 232–3
taxes, 180
  upon business, 200
  harmonization, 44, 64
Taylorism, 17
techno-economic subsystem, 16, 277
technological innovation, 98
  resistance to, 49, 215
technological revolution in 1970s, 98
technological style, 4, 14, 15–17, 31, 277–8, 281
technology, 189
  corporatism, 18–19, 73, 93–7, 102, 112, 114, 119–20, 121, 185, 210–11, 225, 243, 250
  definition, 94–5
  and institutions, 17
  policy, 5, 65, 66, 68, 70–1, 93–121, 122, 134, 216, 254, 256
  politicization of, 116–17
  see also biotechnology; Esprit; information technology
telecommunications industry, 199, 277, 282
  see also information technology
Telefónica de España, 204–5
textile industry, 156 n.7
Thatcher, Margaret, 48, 51, 53 n.24, 69 n.38, 82, 85, 87, 111, 130 n.10, 143, 161, 168 n.25, 176
  speech in Bruges 1988, 172 n.30
Thatcherism, 42
Thirty Years War, 280
Thomson CSF, 103, 107, 116
Thorn, Gaston, 52–3, 212
  see also European Commission, presidency
Thyssen AG, 189 n.5, 196, 197, 203–7, 209
Tiedemann, W.A., 170
Titan, 204
Total SA, 196, 203, 205, 207, 247
trade unions, 17, 153, 165, 167, 171, 174, 176, 180, 181, 193, 194–5, 208, 237, 254, 257, 261
  chemical workers, 226
  see also European Federation of the Chemical Unions
  France, 55
  Germany, 169
  United Kingdom, 172, 182
  see also European Trade Union Confederation
Trades Union Congress (TUC, United Kingdom), 172
Transatlantic Business Dialogue, 209
Transgene, 232 n.5
transnational corporations (TNC), 1, 20–5, 28, 88, 89, 93–4, 106, 109, 254–6, 260, 262, 274, 279
  world's 100 largest, 24–5
  see also European Roundtable of Industrialists
transportation industry, 199
Treaties on the European Communities
  Art. 8 a, 66, 75
  Art. 8 b–c, 66
  Art. 17, 158
  Art. 57, 66
  Art. 59, 66
  Art. 70, 66
  Art. 84, 66
  Art. 99, 66
  Art. 100a, 63, 66, 156
  Art. 102a, 66
  Art. 117, 157
  Art. 118 a–b, 66, 152, 157–63, 170
  Art. 130
    a–e, 66, 104–5, 135
    a, 135
    c, 136
    d, 137
  Art. 130
    f–q, 66, 116, 217
    k, l, n, 237–8
  Art. 130 r–t, 67
  Art. 145, 67
  cohesion target, 122
  and regional policy, 124, 147
  and social policy, 158, 168
Treaty on European Union, 3, 4, 9, 10, 35, 46 n.12, 154, 182, 244, 247, 264, 274, 279
  Art. 46, 266 n.1
  cohesion fund, 33, 148
  German Constitutional Court ruling, 179
  referenda in Denmark and France, 179
  Social Protocol, 178, 182
triad competition, 4, 19, 49, 83, 86, 96, 100, 106, 118, 186, 210, 213, 240, 243, 274, 279, 280, 282
  see also Japan; United States of America

Index

Trilateral Commission, 190, 201
Triumph-Adler, 197
Turkey, big business, 199, 202
Tyszkiewicz, Zygmunt, 170

unanimity principle, *see* Council of Ministers
underdevelopment, 135, 144
  Italy, 125
  Mediterranean region, 130
unemployment, 35, 99, 125 n.2, 144, 156, 158, 173, 179, 279, 281
  of youth, 144
  see also employment policy; social policy
UNIDATA project, 105–6
Unilever, 189, 190, 196, 201, 203–5, 207, 209 n.14, 228, 232
Union of Industrial and Employers' Confederations of Europe (UNICE), 81–2, 85, 91, 92, 141, 142, 155, 161, 163, 164, 169–70, 174, 175, 189, 192, 194–5, 198, 207
  see also employer organizations
United Kingdom, 14, 35, 45, 75
  and agricultural policy, 140
  agricultural sector, 126
  big business, 195–6, 208
  and biotechnology, 216, 217, 223
  conservative government, 48, 149 n.37, 151
  see also Conservative Party; Thatcherism
  corporate law, 202
  Council presidency, 139
  desire for budgetary correctives, 50, 111, 126, 130, 140, 143, 151
  economy, 100 n.2
  elite clubs, 193–4
  and Esprit, 111
  Foreign Affairs Committee, 249
  integration project, 60, 250
  and intergovernmental conference 1985, 60, 63, 66–7, 68–9, 132, 156–8
  Labour government, 126
  see also Labour Party
  as net payer, 43 n.7, 145
  and regional policy, 126, 128, 142–3, 145, 150
  revolution, 269
  science and technology policy, 102–3, 104
  and Single European Act, 249
  and social dimension, 34
  and social policy, 156–8, 161–3, 175–6, 182
  and sovereignty, 250

state-building, 268, 272, 280
trade unions, 172, 182
transnational corporations, 189 n.5
United Nations Charter, 271
United Nations Educational, Scientific and Cultural Organization (UNESCO), International Bioethics Committee, 237
United Provinces of North Holland, 7, 13, 268, 271, 280, 284
United States of America, 4, 14, 78, 86, 101, 190, 209, 212, 261, 265, 273, 279, 280–2, 283
  biotechnology, 210, 213–16, 219, 224, 225, 229, 230, 232, 240–1, 243, 281
  decline of hegemony, 1, 21, 30–2
  information technology, 96–7, 106, 281
  market size, 88
  passion for deregulation, 282
  revolution, 269
  state-building, 268, 280
  transnational corporations, 23–5
  see also North Atlantic Treaty Organisation
Universal Exposition, Seville 1992, 3

Vallance, Iain, 199
Varfis, Georgis, 129, 139
variable geometry, 51
VEBA, 197, 199, 202–7, 209 n.14
Védrine, Hubert, 41 n.5, 42–3
Venice, Republic, 7, 268, 272
Venturini, Patrick, 172 n.33
  see also European Commission, Venturini report
veto
  culture of, 65, 244, 249, 251
  European Parliament's power of, 194
  national power of, 45, 251
  see also Council of Ministers, unanimity principle
Vogel, Dieter, 197
Volvo AB, 188–9, 197, 198, 201, 203–4

Wallenberg, Peter, 189, 197, 204
Weber, Max, 7, 25
welfare state, 6, 8, 17, 122, 125, 259
  see also social policy
White Papers, *see* European Commission
workers' rights, 156
  association, 178
  information, consultation and participation, 177, 178
  strike, 178
  see also Social Charter of EC; social protection
working environment, 158–60, 162, 178

working hours, reduction, 155
World Bank, 281
World Business Council for Sustainable Development, 201
world economic crisis, 14, 21
World Economic Forum (WEF), 201
world market, 278
  information technology, 100
  for protection, 36
world society, 283

world system, 7, 274, 280
world trade, 21, 199, 280
World Trade Organization (WTO), 265, 282
World War (First and Second), 30, 272
Worldwide Fund for Nature (WWF), 233, 238
Worms, Gérard, 206

Zeneca, 228, 232 n.5

For EU product safety concerns, contact us at Calle de José Abascal, 56-1°, 28003 Madrid, Spain or eugpsr@cambridge.org.

www.ingramcontent.com/pod-product-compliance
Ingram Content Group UK Ltd.
Pitfield, Milton Keynes, MK11 3LW, UK
UKHW020352060825
461487UK00008B/631